Table of Contents

The **Handling Air Passengers Unit** will be available to download from our resources website **www.tandtonline.co.uk** in early 2011 when the unit is released by Edexcel. You will need to register for tandt*ONLine* using the unique code printed on the inside rear cover of this book to be able to access the unit.

Travel & Tourism

for BTEC National Level 3

BOOK TWO
3rd edition

Published by Travel and Tourism Publishing Limited.

www.tandtpublishing.co.uk
info@tandtpublishing.co.uk

First published 2010

British Library Cataloguing in Publication Data is available from the British Library on request.
ISBN 9780956268068

Acknowledgements

This one's for Kath.

The publishers extend thanks to the following for granting permission to reproduce images throughout this book – Accor Hotels, Arabella Stewart, Association of Train Operating Companies (ATOC), At Bristol, Barbados Tourism Authority, Best Western Hotels, Birmingham Convention Bureau, Birmingham International Airport, Brecon Beacons National Park Authority, British Museum, Brittany Ferries, Canvas Holidays, Cardiff Tourism, Chessington World of Adventures, Cosmos, Costa Cruises, Cunard, Delta Airlines, Dartmoor Tourist Association, Dragoman Overland Travel, easyJet, Eden Project, English Heritage, Exodus Travel, First Choice Holidays, First Group, flybe, Glasgow Airport/BAA, Headwater Holidays, High & Wild Adventure Travel, Hilton London Metropole, Mountain Kingdoms (formerly Himalayan Kingdoms), Inghams Travel, InterContinental Hotels Group, Ironbridge Gorge Museum, Jorvik Viking Centre York, Keycamp Holidays, Kuoni Travel, Legoland Windsor, London & Continental Railways, Longleat, M6 Toll, Manchester United plc, Monarch Airlines, MORI, National Space Centre, Neilson Holidays, Ocean Village, Old Course Hotel St Andrews, Outward Bound Trust, P&O Cruises, Ray Youell, Royal Caribbean International, Science Museum, Ski Club of Great Britain, Stagecoach, St David's Hotel and Spa, Cardiff, Sustrans, Swissport International Ltd., Thomas Cook, Transport for London, Travmedia, TUI UK/Thomson Holidays, Virgin Atlantic Airways, Virgin Group, Visit Cardiff, Warwick Castle, Wedgewood Museum, World Travel Market.

Designed and typeset by Saxon Graphics Ltd, Derby
Printed in the UK by Butler Tanner & Dennis Ltd

Introduction

Exactly matched to the 2010 Edexcel BTEC National Level 3 Travel and Tourism specifications, this third edition of our popular textbook provides comprehensive coverage of eight optional units for the qualification, which contribute to the Level 3 Certificate, Subsidiary Diploma, Diploma and Extended Diploma. The book builds on the 13 units contained in *Travel and Tourism for BTEC National Book 1 3rd edition* (ISBN 9780956268044). Details of Tutor's CD-ROMs for Book 1 and Book 2 can be found at **www.tandtpublishing.co.uk**.

How to use this book

Each unit includes:

1. **An introductory page** – giving details of the content and assessment for the unit;
2. **Clearly-labelled sections** – exactly covering the specification content for the unit;
3. **Activities** – based on the assessment criteria to help you learn more;
4. **Focus on industry** – short practical examples of how industries in the travel and tourism sector carry out the key topics in the unit;
5. **Weblinks** – internet links to organisations and topics in the unit;
6. **Case studies** – longer examples of organisations and topics included in the unit, with questions and activities to expand your knowledge;
7. **Unit summary** – concise overview of key topics covered in the unit;
8. **Test questions at the end** – to build your knowledge of what's been covered in the unit;
9. **Sample assignment** – covering all the grading criteria for the unit.

About tandtONLine

Everybody who buys this book can register for free access to extra teaching and learning resources at tandt*ONLine* – our unique web resource for travel and tourism students and staff. It gives you a host of extra features that are regularly updated by academic staff and industry experts, including:

- Latest news from the travel and tourism industry;
- Key statistics on UK, European and global tourism;
- Glossary of common terms and key definitions;
- Links to all the websites featured in the textbook;
- Extra staff teaching resources linked to textbooks, including blank maps and forms, assignments and suggestions for extra information sources and reading.

Register by going to **www.tandtonline.co.uk** and completing the online registration form using the unique book code found on the inside back cover of this book.

I hope you find this book a useful companion for your BTEC course and wish you well in your studies.

Ray Youell
Aberystwyth
September 2010

UNIT 11

Investigating the Cruise Industry

INTRODUCTION TO THE UNIT

Cruising is one of the fastest-growing industries in the travel and tourism sector, offering a wide variety of job opportunities to people from all backgrounds who want to see the world while they work. Cruising has a very glamorous image and has long been considered an expensive way to travel and explore destinations. However, the cruise industry is changing rapidly – new companies have entered the market and offer cruises at package holiday prices. Also, cruising is no longer just for the rich and famous! People from all walks of life go on cruises, tempted by the lower prices and the informality offered by some of the new cruise companies.

In this unit you will learn about the development of cruising and the structure of the cruise industry. You will look in detail at the many employment opportunities in cruising, both on board ship and ashore, and consider the advantages and disadvantages of taking a job in the industry. The unit also examines the cruise market – cruise areas, types of cruises, ships, design features and products. You will learn how to select cruises that appeal to cruise customers and meet specific needs. You will also have the opportunity to investigate potential future developments in cruising and explore the positive and negative effects of an expanding cruise industry.

WHAT YOU WILL STUDY

When you have completed this unit you should:

1. Know about the cruise industry;
2. Understand the cruise market;
3. Be able to select cruises that appeal to cruise customers and meet specific needs;
4. Understand the effects of an expanding cruise industry.

You will be guided through the main topics in this unit with the help of the latest developments, statistics, industry examples and case studies. You should also check out the weblinks throughout the unit for extra information on particular organisations or topic areas and use the activities throughout the unit to help you learn more.

ASSESSMENT FOR THIS UNIT

This unit is internally assessed, meaning that you will be given an assignment (or series of assignments) to complete by your tutor(s) to show that you have fully understood the content of the unit. A grading scale of pass, merit or distinction is used when staff mark your assignment(s), with higher grades awarded to students who show greater depth in analysis, evaluation and justification in their assignments. An assignment for this unit, which covers all the grading criteria, can be found on page 33. Don't forget to visit **www.tandtonline.co.uk** for all the latest industry news, developments, statistics and links to websites in this unit to help you with your assignments.

SECTION 1 Know about the cruise industry

Icebreaker

This unit examines many aspects of the cruise industry – one of the most vibrant areas of worldwide travel and tourism. Working by yourself, or in small groups under the direction of your tutor, see how you get on with the following tasks to help you make a start on this unit:

- Make a list of five different companies that offer cruises;
- Name three popular cruise areas of the world;
- Name three UK ports that cruise ships use to start and/or finish cruises;
- Make a list of the reasons why you think cruising has grown in popularity in recent years;
- Think about the sort of impacts (good and bad) that cruising can have on an island destination in the Caribbean;
- Name three specific on-board jobs that cruise companies offer;
- Make a list of the different types of people attracted to cruising and the specific facilities that each looks for when booking a cruise holiday.

When you've finished, show your answers to your tutor and compare your answers with what other students in your class have written.

The cruise industry is currently going through a period of rapid growth and change. In the past, cruising was seen as the preserve of the elderly, rich and famous. Today the number of cruise passengers is growing steadily and the industry has introduced products aimed at a wide range of customers, including families, young people and groups. Prices for many cruise products have fallen as the major tour operators have entered the market. Latest figures from the Passenger Shipping Association (PSA), the trade body representing passenger shipping interests in the UK (see case study on page 10), show that 1.65 million British people are expected to take a cruise in 2010 – more than double the figure recorded in 2000. Before looking in more detail at the structure of the present-day cruise industry, we begin this section with an overview of the history and development of cruising.

Cruising is growing in popularity

History, development and growth of the cruise industry

Although several theories have been put forward to explain the origins of the concept of cruising, the most widely-accepted story concerns a fantasy article in the *Shetland Journal* in 1835, in which Arthur Anderson proposed the idea of sailing for pleasure as a passenger on an ocean-going vessel. He suggested trips between Scotland and Iceland in the summer and as far as the Mediterranean in the winter. Two years later his dream moved closer to reality when he co-founded the Peninsular and Oriental Steam Navigation Company, later shortened to P&O.

The early days of cruising

Long-distance international travel by sea dates back to the mid-19th century, when Cunard Line's RMS Britannia (RMS stands for Royal Mail Ship) became the first ship to take passengers on regularly-scheduled, trans-Atlantic crossings aboard the vessel Britannia. This came about because of the need to introduce a dependable mail service between Britain and America, which prompted Queen Victoria's government to invite interested parties to bid for the contract. Samuel Cunard of Halifax, Nova Scotia in Canada was the successful bidder and his contract to deliver the mail across the Atlantic from Britain to North America was signed on 4th May 1839. Cunard was a highly successful and enterprising Canadian businessman and one of a group of 12 individuals who directed the affairs of Nova Scotia. In order to carry out the trans-Atlantic contract successfully, he worked with the engineer Robert Napier and three other businessmen who provided financial backing for the project. These five men founded the British and North American Royal Mail Steam Packet Company – later to become known as the Cunard Line.

In the 1880s, the Orient Line and North of Scotland Company, both later to be taken over by P&O, pioneered modern-style cruises and in 1904 P&O offered its first cruise holiday programme, arranged by Thomas Cook. The tour used the liner Rome, renaming her Vectis in her new role as a 'cruising yacht'.

Cruising in the 20th century

The first half of the 20th century was the heyday for large cruise liners, which were built to serve the increasing numbers of passengers travelling between Europe and North America. The largest passenger steamship of the time, the Titanic, was launched in 1912, but tragically sank on its maiden voyage on the night of 14th April, with the loss of nearly 1,500 lives. The sinking of the Titanic led to safety and communications improvements on board passenger ships to reduce the likelihood of such an event ever happening again. By the end of the 1930s, Cunard operated trans-Atlantic crossings every 10 weeks. Bigger and better ships were introduced and they competed to make the fastest crossing of the Atlantic. Many raced for the 'Blue Riband' trophy awarded to the ship making the fastest trans-Atlantic crossing, most notably the Queen Mary and Queen Elizabeth, launched in 1934 and 1938 respectively. Other important ships of the time included the Mauretania, the Aquitania and the Windsor Castle. Cruising in these ships was a luxurious experience, only available to the rich and famous.

By the 1930s, cruise-orientated amenities and facilities began to feature more prominently in passenger ship design. American ocean liners introduced air conditioning, a majority of cabins with private facilities and some with private verandas. Grace Line's Santa liners even had retractable roofs over their dining rooms to allow passengers to dine under the tropical stars.

The majority of ships in cruise service after World War Two (1939-1945) were liners whose sources of income gradually began to diminish. The number of people emigrating began to decrease (emigrants were an important market for many ship companies). Also, the development of the jet engine and long-haul passenger aircraft, such as the Boeing 707 in 1958, led to a dramatic reduction in the number of passengers using cruise ships from the mid-20th century onwards. The decline began in the late 1950s and resulted in ships like the Queen Elizabeth becoming redundant. By the 1970s, the advent of the Boeing 747 jumbo jet really saw the end of the golden period of trans-Atlantic cruise liners. With no regular mail contracts for the shipping companies after 1945, cruising became even more important to the shipping industry. P&O's

last ship built for scheduled voyages, the Canberra, was launched in 1961, but in little more than a decade jet aircraft had taken many of the company's regular passengers and freight was transferred onto purpose-built cargo ships.

In the late 20th century the true ocean liners declined and diminished in number, being succeeded by cruise liners such as the Oriana, Aurora, Royal Princess, Royal Princess, Voyager of the Seas, Monarch of the Seas and many others. Between 1964 and 1972, four companies that came to be known as the 'big four' were founded – Carnival Cruises, Royal Caribbean Cruise Line, Princess Cruises and the Norwegian Caribbean Line.

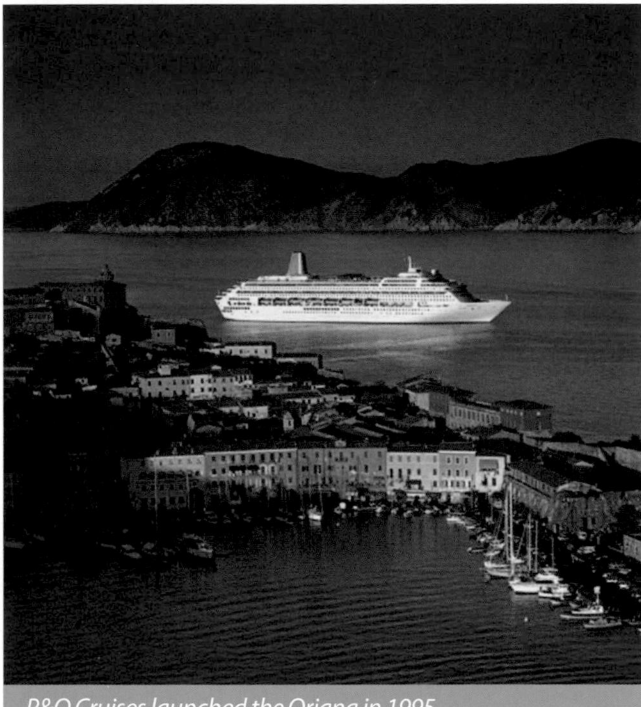

P&O Cruises launched the Oriana in 1995

21st century cruising

The cruise boom of the 1980s continued into the 21st century despite a brief blip in the early 1990s when fewer cruise ships were built due to concerns about a possible slowdown in the cruise industry. Today, bigger and brasher cruise ships are being built to service a growing demand from travellers. Despite there being considerable integration and standardisation in the industry, with just three big players – Carnival, Royal Caribbean International and Star/Norwegian Cruise Line – plus other independent operators, there is still a great deal of variety in terms of ships and the products they offer their passengers, whether it be mass-market, small-ship, luxury, family-orientated, adventure or luxury cruising. The cruise ships of the early 21st century tend to be floating hotels or resorts and destinations in their own right.

In 2000 P&O Cruises introduced the Aurora as the UK's second superliner to follow the Oriana. In the same year a notable development took place in the cruising world, with the introduction of the world's first timeshare residential cruise ship called The World, which is the first step at turning the cruise ship into a floating city. In 2004 Cunard launched the Queen Mary 2, the first trans-Atlantic liner to be built for a generation and a year later P&O Cruises introduced the Arcadia. Based on the Vista class ships of the Holland America Line, Arcadia shows how cruise ships have become more standardised in terms of design, but can still show their individualism by brand and company heritage. The world's biggest cruise ship, and flagship of Royal Caribbean International, the Freedom of the Seas, was launched in 2006, boasting the world's first on-board surfing pool, a skating rink and a rock-climbing wall! The vessel can accommodate 4,375 passengers at a time and is used for Caribbean cruises.

The Queen Victoria was launched in 2007 (courtesy of Cunard)

Activity 11.1

Design and make an illustrated wall chart or display that explains the key milestones in the development of the cruise industry.

This activity is designed to provide evidence for P1.

Changing consumer demands and needs in cruising

The changing demands and expectations of passengers are a constant challenge for cruise companies, which must offer new products and services to a wide variety of customers in order to remain competitive. This has resulted in a number of recent developments in the cruise industry, including:

1. The changing popularity of cruise areas;
2. Changes in customer demographics;
3. More informal cruising;
4. The growth in ex-UK cruises;
5. More demand for ultra-luxury cruising.

The changing popularity of cruise areas

Data from the PSA's *Annual Cruise Review* indicates that the Mediterranean remained the most popular cruise destination with the British in 2009. However, cruising in Northern Europe is now more popular with British people than cruising in the Caribbean. Cruise destinations showing the biggest rise in popularity in recent years with British cruise passengers include Norway, the Baltic, Greenland, the USA, the Black Sea and the UK itself.

Changes in customer demographics

Although the UK population is ageing, with an increasing proportion of over-50s compared to under-30s, the average age of cruise passengers continues to fall. This is partly due to the increased numbers of families with children now going on cruises. It is also a reflection of the younger people being attracted to cruising by the new, informal and activity-orientated brands, such as Ocean Village, Island Cruises and easyCruise. All of these factors combine to paint a picture of a changing profile of customers that are attracted to cruising. In short, cruise passengers are:

- Younger than in the past;
- Interested in activities while on board ship and on shore;
- Looking for short cruises as well as extended journeys;
- Interested in travelling with families and friends;
- Looking for adventure.

Cruise companies are increasingly segmenting the market, i.e. developing cruise products and services to meet the needs of individual segments of the market, for example families, singles, groups and younger passengers.

More informal cruising

A success story in recent years has been the introduction of more informal cruises, led by companies like Ocean Village, Island Cruises and easyCruise. These fashionable cruises are aimed at younger, and particularly first-time, cruisers. Formality is at a minimum, with no formal dress code, no fixed meal times or seating places, lots of activities on board and ashore, plus coffee shops and alternative entertainment.

The growth in ex-UK cruises

More people than ever are choosing to start their cruise holiday from a UK port, thereby saving the time and inconvenience of travelling abroad to a departure port. Between 2003 and 2009, the number of passengers starting their cruises from a UK port rose from 375,000 to 733,000 – an increase of more than 90 per cent. The number of UK ports attracting cruise ships fluctuates year-on-year, but is within the range of 40-45, thereby spreading the economic benefits of the cruise industry even further. Popular UK cruise ports include Southampton, Belfast, Newcastle and Liverpool.

More demand for ultra-luxury cruising

The growth in the popularity of mass-market cruising, aimed at a wide variety of passengers travelling on a budget, has led some wealthy customers to seek out small, exclusive cruises that offer exceptional personal service and attention to detail.

FOCUS ON INDUSTRY

ULTRA-LUXURY CRUISING

Figures from the Passenger Shipping Association indicate that the demand for ultra-luxury cruising has grown rapidly in recent years. Brands such as Crystal Cruises, Ponant Cruises, Regent Seven Seas, SeaDream Yacht Club, Silversea Cruises and Yachts of Seabourn saw their 2009 sales grow by more than 50 per cent over 2008. This increased the ultra-luxury share of the overall cruise market by a similar amount. In fact, with UK passengers also booking more top suites on other cruise brands, it meant that 31,000 passengers paid more than £5,000 per person for their cruise with another 200,000 paying between £2,500 and £5,000.

Weblink Check out this website for more information on the market for ultra-luxury cruising.
www.the-psa.co.uk

Current position of the cruise industry

According to statistics from the Passenger Shipping Association, the UK cruise industry defied the economic recession in 2009 and British people:

- Booked more cruises than ever before;
- Took more cruises in a single year than ever before;
- Booked more cruises instead of package and other holidays than ever before;
- Bought more of the most expensive, most luxurious cruises than ever before.

As a result, the number of UK cruise passengers grew 4 per cent in 2009 to top 1.5 million for the first time and is on course to reach 1.75 million in 2011 and 2 million by 2014. In 2010 alone, there is forecast to be an 8 per cent increase in passenger numbers to 1.65 million due mainly to the arrival of four ships dedicated primarily to the UK market – P&O Cruises' Azura, the Celebrity Eclipse, Cunard Line's Queen Elizabeth and the Thomson Dream. Fourteen cruise ships are being introduced in 2010 adding more than 32,000 berths to the global cruise fleet. Royal Caribbean International's Independence of the Seas will also be making its inaugural winter series of cruises out of Southampton. Other brands such as Holland America Line, Disney Cruise Line, MSC Cruises and Cruise & Maritime Voyages are also increasing their ex-UK capacity. In 2009, the British were also booking longer cruises so the increase in the number of cruise days was even greater at 10 per cent.

Activity 11.2

Carry out some research to discover the latest statistics on the cruise industry, to include names of cruise lines and employment.

This activity is designed to provide evidence for M1.

Stakeholders in the cruise industry

Cruising is a global industry, not just in terms of the worldwide destinations visited, but also from an ownership perspective, with just three companies dominating world cruising – Carnival, Royal Caribbean International and Star/Norwegian Cruise Line. In the following sections of this unit we will examine the range of cruise operators in more detail and explore how cruising links with other industries in travel and tourism.

Cruise operators

There are many well-established cruise operators across the world, with three companies dominating the industry and accounting for over 80 per cent of all cruise bookings worldwide (see Figure 11.1).

As Figure 11.1 demonstrates, Carnival is by far the biggest cruise company in the world, followed by Royal Caribbean International (RCI) and Star Cruises. Together, these three operators control approximately 83 per cent of the global cruise market, according to

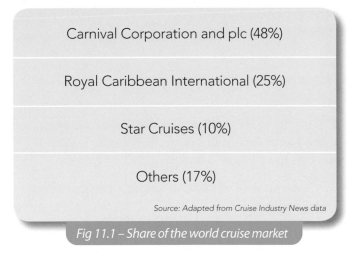

Carnival Corporation and plc (48%)
Royal Caribbean International (25%)
Star Cruises (10%)
Others (17%)

Source: Adapted from Cruise Industry News data

Fig 11.1 – Share of the world cruise market

data in the *Cruise Industry News Annual Report*, leaving a variety of smaller, independent cruise companies to make up the remainder. There is a detailed case study on Carnival below.

Founded in 1969, RCI currently has a fleet of 20 ships, branded as Royal Caribbean and Celebrity Cruises. Royal Caribbean has ten ships and appeals particularly to families and middle-market customers with its combination of value for money and quality. Celebrity Cruises operates at the top end of the mainstream, large cruise ship market. Renowned for good service, high-quality catering and on-board facilities, Celebrity has a fleet of ten ships – ranging from the 13,000-15,000 passenger bracket to those carrying around 1,800.

Star Cruises was founded in 1995 and is already the world's third largest cruise operator. It tapped into the cruise potential of the Asia Pacific region and has since acquired Norwegian Cruise Line (NCL) and Orient Lines. Star currently owns a combined fleet of 18 ships cruising to over 200 destinations and offering approximately 35,000 lower berths. Star Cruises is part of Genting Hong Kong, a leading global leisure, entertainment and hospitality corporation.

CASE STUDY

Carnival Corporation and plc

Introduction

Carnival Corporation and plc is the world's biggest cruise operator, accounting for nearly half of all cruises booked across the globe. Many of the best-known names in the cruising industry are wholly or partly-owned by Carnival, including Cunard, Princess Cruises and Ocean Village. In 2003, Carnival Corporation and P&O Princess Cruises plc formally merged, the latter now adopting the Carnival name. Carnival's mission is:

'To deliver exceptional vacation experiences through the world's best-known cruise brands that cater to a variety of different lifestyles and budgets, all at an outstanding value unrivalled on land or at sea'.

With its headquarters in Miami, Florida and London, England, Carnival has more than 85,000 employees worldwide and operates a fleet of 97 ships, with a further 10 new ships on order (as of 2010). With 144,000 berths and almost 55,000 crew members, there are roughly 175,000 people at sea with Carnival at any given time. The company also owns two tour businesses that complement its cruise operations – Holland America Tours, and Princess Tours in Alaska and the Canadian Yukon. Carnival's combined holiday companies cater for around 8.5 million customers every year.

Carnival brands

Carnival has 11 distinct cruising brands aimed at particular market segments, made up of the leading cruise operators in North America, Europe and Australia:

1. Carnival Cruise Lines (**www.carnival.com**) – reputed to be the most profitable cruise line in the world, this brand operates 22 'fun ships', aimed primarily at the North American market. Destinations include the Bahamas, Canada, the Mexican Riviera and Alaska, with most cruises ranging from 3 to 7 days;

2. Holland America Line (**www.hollandamerica.com**) – a 15-strong fleet of five-star, premium ships sailing from 15 North American home ports, including Baltimore and Boston;

3. Princess Cruises (**www.princess.com**) – there are 17 ships in the Princess fleet aimed mostly at the mid to upper market. The ships are deployed all around the globe, calling at more than 200 ports worldwide;

4. Seabourn Cruise Line (**www.seabourn.com**) – a 5-ship fleet of luxury all-suite ships carrying just over 200 passengers each (Seabourn Legend, Seabourn Pride and Seabourn Spirit). Seabourn operates a passenger/crew ratio of close to 1/1;

5. AIDA Cruises (**www.aida.de**) – this is the best-known cruise brand in the fast-growing German cruise industry. The company's 7 ships cruise to the Mediterranean, Baltic, Norwegian fjords, Canary Islands and the Caribbean;

6. Costa Cruises (**www.costacruise.com**) – a 14-ship fleet ranging from the 800-passenger Costa Allegra to their latest three 2,200-passenger ships – Costa Atlantica, Costa Mediterranea and Costa Fortuna;

7. Cunard Line (**www.cunard.com**) – a fleet of three ships comprising the Queen Mary 2, Queen Victoria, which joined the Cunard fleet in summer 2007, and the new 92,000-ton liner, Queen Elizabeth, which is scheduled to enter service in October 2010;

8. P&O Cruises (**www.pocruises.com**) – is the largest cruise operator in the UK, with 8 ships around the 2,000-passenger mark – the Adonia (due in 2011), Arcadia, Artemis, Aurora, Azura, Oceana, Oriana and Ventura;

9. Ocean Village (**www.oceanvillageholidays.co.uk**) – a cruise brand in the UK, which has been established to provide informal, contemporary and affordable holidays at sea for younger people;

10. P&O Cruises Australia (**www.pocruises.com.au**) – as its name implies, this company caters for the Australian market with two ships, Pacific Sky and Pacific Sun, offering 7 to 14-night cruises to New Caledonia, Vanuatu and Fiji from the home ports of Sydney, Brisbane and Auckland;

11. Iberocruceros (**www.iberocruceros.com**) – a British-American and Spanish-owned cruise line based in Madrid. The company currently operates 4 ships aimed at the Spanish and Portuguese market.

Carnival cruise destinations

With such a large range of cruise companies under its wing, Carnival operates in a wide variety of cruise destinations around the world, including Alaska, the Caribbean, Canada, Eastern USA, the Mediterranean, the Pacific, Western USA and Mexico, plus trans-Atlantic and round-the-world cruises.

Case Study Questions and Activities

1. Explain how Carnival Corporation and plc is an 'integrated' company.
2. Why has Carnival chosen to enter into mergers and takeovers with other cruise lines?
3. Choose one of the Carnival brands and carry out some further research on the company, so that you could advise a customer who wants to take a cruise with that operator.
4. Which other industries in the travel and tourism sector do Carnival's cruise companies work with on a regular basis?

This case study is designed to provide evidence for P1 and P2.

Weblink

Check out this website to help answer the questions in this case study and for more information on cruising with Carnival.

www.carnival.com

Integration in the cruise industry

You have learned in other units on your course that there are many links between different companies and industries in the travel and tourism sector – this is sometimes referred to as integration. Horizontal integration occurs when a company owns or controls other businesses at the same level of the distribution chain or in the same industry, e.g. Thomas Cook owns a wide range of tour operating companies, including Club 18-30, Bridge, Cresta, Thomas Cook Signature and Tradewinds. Vertical integration is when a company owns or controls more then one level of the distribution chain, e.g. Thomas Cook not only owns tour operating companies, but also the chain of Thomas Cook and Going Places travel agencies and its own airline Thomas Cook Airlines. Companies get involved in integration via mergers and takeovers as a way of increasing their sales and gaining an advantage over their competitors.

Integration also occurs in the cruise industry. The three major cruise lines – Carnival, Royal Caribbean International (RCI) and Star Cruises – are all integrated companies, i.e. they own other shipping lines that operate under different names. For example, we saw earlier in the case study on Carnival (see page 7) that it owns 11 different cruise companies under different brand names, including Cunard, Ocean Village and P&O Cruises. RCI owns Celebrity Cruises, while Star Cruises own Norwegian Cruise Line and Orient Lines.

Links with other industries in travel and tourism

Like most industries in the travel and tourism sector, cruise operators work in partnership with many companies and organisations in the course of their work. These partners include:

- Travel agents – these are the retail arm of the industry, advising and selling cruise holidays to customers. British holidaymakers continue to use the internet to research their cruise holidays, but 80 per cent of cruise bookings are made through a travel agent. A cruise is often an expensive purchase, so many customers prefer the personal contact and reassurance of dealing with an agent. Agents benefit as well, since cruise companies pay good commission on sales;
- Hotels and other accommodation – cruise lines use a variety of accommodation for 'cruise and stay' holiday passengers;

- Visitor attractions – cruise passengers often visit natural and built attractions as part of an excursion on shore;
- Transport operators – coach companies and taxi firms provide transfers to and from destination ports, as well as excursions on shore. Some up-market cruise lines even offer chauffeur-drive and helicopter transfers as options for passengers;
- Airlines – cruise lines contract with either scheduled or charter airlines when arranging fly/cruise holidays for passengers;
- Web-based cruise agents – companies such as 1st4Cruising.com, ROL Cruise and Oceanworld travel.com sell cruise holidays at discounted prices via the internet and call centres.

Regulatory and trade bodies in cruising

Travel and tourism regulatory bodies exist to make sure that organisations serve the travelling public safely, fairly and efficiently. The International Maritime Organisation (IMO) is a specialised agency of the United Nations with 169 member states and its headquarters in London. It is responsible for measures to improve the safety and security of international shipping, including cruising, and to prevent marine pollution from ships. It is also involved in legal matters, including liability and compensation issues and the facilitation of international maritime traffic.

Trade bodies are set up to represent the interests of companies operating in a particular industry sector. In the UK, the Passenger Shipping Association (PSA) is the principal trade body representing the cruise industry (see case study below). In the USA, there are a number of trade organisations that claim to represent the interests of the cruise industry, e.g. the International Council of Cruise Lines (ICCL) and the Cruise Line International Association (CLIA). Both organisations include the majority of cruise lines in their membership and are actively involved in training, marketing, research, safety and security in the cruising industry. The European Cruise Council (ECC), formed in 2004, promotes and defends the interests of the cruise industry within European Union institutions, collates industry statistics to demonstrate the scale and breadth of the cruise industry, and provides a resource for the promotion of cruises in Europe. The 24 members of the ECC include Fred. Olsen Cruise Line, RCI, Saga Shipping, Thomson Cruises and Costa Cruises.

CASE STUDY

The Passenger Shipping Association (PSA)

Introduction

The Passenger Shipping Association (PSA) is a trade organisation that represents the interests of the leading UK-based cruise and ferry operators. The PSA was originally set up as Ocean Travel Development (OTD) in 1958 by a group of passenger ship owners. They had seen, for the first time in 1957, the number of passengers travelling across the Atlantic by air exceeding those travelling by sea on the great liners. OTD's main objective was to focus public attention, and that of the travel trade, on sea travel as a holiday and leisure pursuit, and as a modern alternative to transportation from A to B. The shipping lines conceded that they could no longer compete with the developing airlines, both on travel times and cost, and recognised that their future lay in full-time cruising. In 1976, it was agreed by the shipping lines that OTD's name should be changed to the Passenger Shipping Association, to reflect more accurately the aims of the association.

Mission statement and objectives

PSA's mission statement is:

'To provide a service of excellence to the Members and Associate Members of the PSA. To ensure that the PSA is the recognised industry body for the cruise and ferry sectors. To act as a forum for discussion on areas of mutual interest'.

Its objectives are:

1. The promotion of travel by sea by the public;
2. To encourage expansion in the volume of passenger travel by sea and river;
3. To work towards the removal or prevention of the imposition of restrictions or taxes on passenger travel by sea;
4. To advise member lines to ensure that passengers travel in a safe, healthy and secure environment.

What does the PSA do?

In order to meet its mission and objectives, the PSA has a very wide-ranging work programme, which includes:

- Lobbying the government and officials in the European Union;
- Working with and through other bodies, notably ABTA, the Chamber of Shipping and the European Community Shipowners' Association (ECSA);
- Providing a forum for the training and education of travel agents through its subsidiary company ACE (see below);
- Acting as a spokesperson for the industry;
- Co-ordinating activities of its member shipping lines;
- Acting as an information centre for member lines and associate members;
- Acting as a statutory bonding authority for member lines as required;
- Promoting market growth in the passenger shipping industry through public relations campaigns;
- Ensuring that member companies are aware of the best practice and the statutory regulations on safety, the protection of the environment, health, hygiene and security.

Membership of the PSA

Currently, the PSA has 38 cruise line members, including Cunard, Carnival UK, Thomson and Royal Caribbean Cruise Lines. Its 12 ferry company members include Brittany Ferries, Stena Line, Sea France and Condor

Ferries. Associate members of the PSA, who work closely with the cruise and ferry sectors, include the Port of Tyne Authority, Eurolines, VisitBritain and the Port of Dover.

ACE

The Association of Cruise Experts (ACE) was formed in 1987 as the Passenger Shipping Association Retail Agents' Scheme (PSARA) – which was entrusted with fulfilling the Association's travel agency educational role. PSA's new subsidiary company ACE provides a means of educating and supporting travel agents in the detail and dynamics of the cruise industry, recognising that for most holidaymakers, cruising is a very different concept to mainstream land-based holidays. ACE has worked with more than 36 cruise line members, over 3,000 travel agencies and has won industry awards that recognise the quality and depth of the learning that the Association offers. Online training, newsletters, product information, visits to ships and an extensive programme of regional meetings, are the basis of the benefits to ACE members.

Case Study Questions and Activities

1. What is the role of the PSA and what are the benefits of being a member to an individual cruise company?
2. Over what sort of matters and concerns do you think that the PSA lobbies members of the government and the European Union?
3. Carry out some further research on the Association of Cruise Executives (ACE) and make a list of the benefits of membership for travel agents;
4. Log on to the PSA's website and write a summary of two recent press releases concerned with cruising issues.

This case study is designed to provide evidence for P2.

Weblink

Check out this website to help answer the questions in this case study and for more information on the Passenger Shipping Association.

www.the-psa.co.uk

Employment in the cruise industry

The rise in popularity of cruising worldwide means that there are many job opportunities in the industry for people with the right qualifications, skills and personal qualities. In this section we investigate key facts about working in cruising and examine the many job opportunities available on board and on shore.

On-board job opportunities

There are literally hundreds of different on-board jobs on offer with cruise lines. Jobs are offered in different departments on board ship, for example:

- Galley (kitchen);
- Engineering;
- Beauty and hairdressing;

- Hotel (reception);
- Housekeeping;
- Casino;
- Deck;
- Entertainment;
- Medical;
- Food and beverage;
- Tours and excursions;
- Photography;
- Sports, pool and gym.

Some jobs are more technical than others and require specialist qualifications, for example posts in medical, deck, engineering and gym work.

Staff working for Cunard on board the Queen Mary 2

On-shore job opportunities

Job opportunities with cruise lines on shore include:

- Marketing;
- Reservations and sales (including call centre work);
- Finance;
- Administration;
- Human resources;
- IT;
- Check-in and operations;
- Customer service;
- Baggage handling;
- Catering.

There are many websites that offer advice on getting a job in the cruise industry and some have lists of posts available, for example **www.cruiseworking.com** and **www.cruiseplacement.com**.

Activity 11.3

Log on to either of these cruise employment websites **www.cruiseworking.com** or **www.cruiseplacement.com** and find details of three jobs in cruising that interest you. Make a note of job roles and responsibilities, salary, contract period, location, etc.

This activity is designed to provide evidence for P3.

Figures 11.2 and 11.3 give details of two jobs on board cruise ships – an Entertainments Officer and an Assistant Bartender.

Summer Cruises plc

Job description

Title of post: **Entertainments Officer**
Post no: SC/08/08
Location: On board
Responsible to: Cruise Director

Job summary

The Entertainments Officer is responsible for assisting the Cruise Director and his/her Deputy in the smooth running of all aspects of the Entertainments Division of the Hotel Services and Entertainments Department. The Entertainments Division is responsible for providing a diverse range of entertainment and leisure opportunities during both the day and evening for passengers in order to enhance their cruise experience. This includes production shows, guest lecturers' activities, quizzes, bingo, cabaret, musical programmes, karaoke and deck activities such as quoits, golf, tennis, cricket, football, etc.

Requirements

1. You must possess a warm, outgoing personality to ensure that passengers always have a friendly and understanding person to talk to;
2. Experience in hosting/introducing professional cabaret entertainment;
3. Effective communication skills, both written and oral;
4. You need to be available and visible to passengers at all times and to be easily identifiable as one of the public faces of the on board entertainment product;
5. You will undertake a pro-active role in the various activities delivered by the Entertainments Division.

Salary and benefits

- Competitive salary and benefits package is offered;
- Training and development is delivered mainly through in-house workshops, courses and programmes;
- Contract period of a minimum of 4 months to a maximum of 6 months with a 6-8 week unpaid leave period;
- Concessionary travel after a qualifying period of service.

Application procedure

To apply in the first instance, send a photo and CV to HR Division, Summer Cruises plc, Southampton.

Dated: 1st November 2010

Figure 11.2 – Job description for the post of Entertainments Officer

Summer Cruises plc

Job description

Title of post: **Assistant Bartender**
Post no: SC/09/08
Location: Fleet
Responsible to: Bartender

Job summary

- To ensure the smooth and efficient operation of the bar, under the direction of the bartender, in order to achieve passenger satisfaction;
- To generate and maximise revenue opportunities both individually and as a team;
- To portray a positive and professional image to all outside consultants, agencies, suppliers, passengers, officers and crew;
- To contribute to the creation and maintenance of an enthusiastic, motivated working environment;
- To maintain prescribed systems for the monitoring and control of stock and relevant costs in accordance with company procedures;
- To ensure all revenue is correctly posted to on board accounts;
- To assist with stock takes as required by the Finance Manager.

Requirements

1. Applicants should have attended catering college and obtained a City & Guilds pass in Food and Beverage Service 707;
2. Alternatively, applicants should have had experience in a superior class hotel, club or restaurant;
3. Applicants should have experience of mixing and serving cocktails, and have a thorough knowledge of wines and liquors.

Salary and benefits

- Competitive salary and benefits package is offered;
- Training and development is delivered mainly through in-house workshops, courses and programmes;
- Contract period of a minimum of 4 months to a maximum of 6 months with a 6-8 week unpaid leave period;
- Concessionary travel after a qualifying period of service.

Application procedure

To apply in the first instance, send a photo and CV to HR Division, Summer Cruises plc, Southampton.

Dated: 1st November 2010

Figure 11.3 – Job description for the post of Assistant Bartender

Qualifications, experience and skills required

Not all jobs in the cruise industry require formal qualifications. However, ambitious people who wish to develop their careers in cruising will generally find that their progression will be quicker if they have qualifications that are relevant to their job. Experience counts for a lot in the cruise industry – people who have on-shore experience of, for example retail, entertainment, hospitality and catering, will be more attractive to the cruise lines than applicants with no experience at all.

Personal skills and qualities, such as good appearance and grooming, a positive attitude, enthusiasm and reliability, are of paramount importance in the cruise industry, which is all about meeting and even exceeding passengers' expectations. In general, cruise lines look for people who:

- Are highly-motivated and enthusiastic;
- Are keen to take on a challenge;
- Have a strong desire to work on a cruise ship;
- Get on well with other people;
- Are happy to be away from home for long periods;
- Have a helpful and patient customer service manner;
- Are well-presented.

The working environment in cruising

Working on board a cruise ship can be an exciting and rewarding experience, visiting exotic ports of call, working with people from all parts of the world, earning a good living, and having your room and board provided for free. However, as in other industries in the travel and tourism sector, life on board ship is also demanding and challenging, working long hours (often 7 days a week), sharing accommodation with work colleagues and following the ship's rules and regulations.

Most cruise lines offer an average contract of six months, but depending on the position and the company it could be as short as four months or as long as ten. Staff are paid only while on contract – holidays are unpaid and usually last two months. Once you've completed a contract you are not obliged to return to the same ship or company, but if you have enjoyed your work and have received a good reference, you are likely to be offered another period of work.

Details of jobs in cruising are available direct from individual cruise lines or through agencies, some of which charge applicants a fee for their services. The cruise industry has a relatively high staff turnover, so companies need to fill vacancies all year round with suitable people. Staff leave for new jobs on different ships, companies or countries. Others leave mid-journey for various reasons, including personal or family circumstances.

Crew entertaining guests on an Island Cruises' holiday

SECTION 2 Understand the cruise market

We saw earlier in this unit that cruising now caters for many different types of customers, with the industry offering a wider-than-ever range of products to suit all tastes and budgets. As a consequence, there are many different types of cruises on offer, geared to different segments of the market, using a wide range of ships with an array of on-board facilities and design features.

Cruise areas of the world

The following is a selection of cruise areas that are popular with the British:

1. The Caribbean and Panama Canal;
2. The Mediterranean;
3. Scandinavia and the Baltic;
4. Alaska;
5. Antarctica/South America;
6. Far East/Australia;
7. UK;
8. The Canary Islands and Madeira;
9. The Nile;
10. Black Sea.

The Caribbean and Panama Canal

There are 7,000 islands in the Caribbean Sea, lying between the southern tip of the eastern USA and the north coast of South America. The area stretches for more than 2,500 miles, so cruising is an excellent way to experience as much as possible of this part of the world. The area has a rich culture and heritage, with many languages spoken and varied geographical features. Nearly all UK passengers opt for a fly/cruise arrangement when buying their Caribbean cruise, allowing them to fit a cruise to a long-haul destination into a normal holiday period. All of the major shipping lines offer Caribbean cruises, including Royal Caribbean International, Carnival, Costa Cruises, Cunard, P&O Cruises, Celebrity Cruises, Orient Lines and Ocean Village.

Caribbean cruises can last anything from three days for a short holiday between Florida and the Bahamas to holidays lasting a month and covering the whole area. Examples of countries that could be visited on a Caribbean cruise include:

- Western Caribbean – Cozumel or Playa del Carmen in Mexico, the Cayman Islands and Jamaica;
- Eastern Caribbean – Puerto Rico, the US Virgin Islands (St Thomas and St Croix), St Martin, Dominica, Barbados, St Kitts and Martinique;
- Southern Caribbean – Puerto Rico, US Virgin Islands, Guadeloupe, Grenada, Barbados, Antigua, St Lucia, Martinique, Venezuela and Aruba.

Activity 11.4

Using an atlas for reference, draw a map of the Caribbean region and locate the above list of cruise ports found in the area.

This activity is designed to provide evidence for P4.

The Panama Canal can also be combined with a Caribbean cruise. Passengers can choose to take a one-way or 'line journey' from Fort Lauderdale, Miami or Puerto Rico through to Acapulco or Los Angeles. Alternatively they can take a cruise that travels half way along the canal before returning.

Figure 11.4 shows an example of a 7-night Caribbean fly/cruise offered by Norwegian Cruise Line (NCL) starting and finishing in Charleston, South Carolina. Highlights of the cruise include time to visit historic Charleston, the Mayan ruins in the Yucatan, Ernest Hemingway's home in Key West and the fashionable resort of Cozumel.

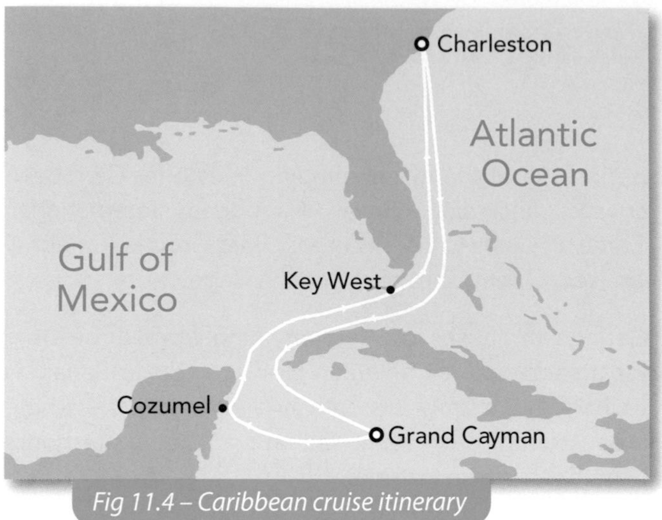

Fig 11.4 – Caribbean cruise itinerary

The Mediterranean

The Mediterranean Sea stretches for more than 2,200 miles, from the 22-mile wide straits of Gibraltar to the Black Sea in the east and the Suez Canal in the south-east. It offers cruise passengers a mixture of ancient and modern, with many different cultures, geography and history all set in a beautiful climate. The Greeks, Romans and Egyptians all built their empires around the Mediterranean and have left behind some of the world's best-known tourist attractions, including the Pyramids, the Acropolis and the Coliseum. Most Mediterranean cruise itineraries include a short flight from the UK to Genoa, Palma or Athens, thereby avoiding the sometimes rough waters of the Bay of Biscay and offering instant sunshine. Alternatively passengers can take a coach, train or drive to their Mediterranean departure port. Others may opt for a cruise that starts and finishes in a UK port. All of the major shipping lines offer Mediterranean cruises, including Thomson, Costa Cruises, Cunard, P&O Cruises, Celebrity Cruises, Swan Hellenic, Island Cruises and Ocean Village.

Ports of call that might be visited on a Mediterranean cruise include:

- Spanish mainland ports such as Barcelona, Cadiz, Malaga and Valencia;
- The Balearic Islands of Ibiza, Majorca and Minorca;
- Canary Islands such as Tenerife, Gran Canaria, La Palma, La Gomera and El Hierro;
- French ports of Cannes, Monte Carlo, St Tropez and Ajaccio (Corsica);
- Italian ports such as Genoa, Civitavecchia, Livorno, Venice, Sardinia, Amalfi and Catania;
- Valetta (Malta's main port);
- Cyprus ports of Limassol, Paphos and Larnaca;
- Piraeus, Corfu, Rhodes, Heraklion, Mykonos and Skiathos in Greece;
- Turkish ports of Izmir, Kusadasi, Bodrum and Antalya;
- Israeli ports of Haifa, Tel Aviv and Ashdod;
- Ports in Egypt, including Alexandria, Port Said and Safaga;
- North African ports of Sidi Bou Said in Tunisia and Tangier, Agadir and Casablanca in Morocco.

Activity 11.5

Plot the above list of Mediterranean cruise ports on a blank map of Europe, which registered tandtonline users can download from www.tandtonline.co.uk

This activity is designed to provide evidence for P4.

Figure 11.5 shows an example of a 14-night Mediterranean cruise offered by P&O Cruises, starting and ending in Southampton. Highlights of the cruise include time to explore the history and culture of a variety of Mediterranean cities, including Barcelona, Valencia, Rome and Naples.

Activity 11.6

Study the itinerary shown in Figure 11.5 and make notes on the type of passengers that you think the cruise would appeal to. Research three of the ports of call and make notes on the tourist attractions that cruise passengers could visit.

This activity is designed to provide evidence for P4.

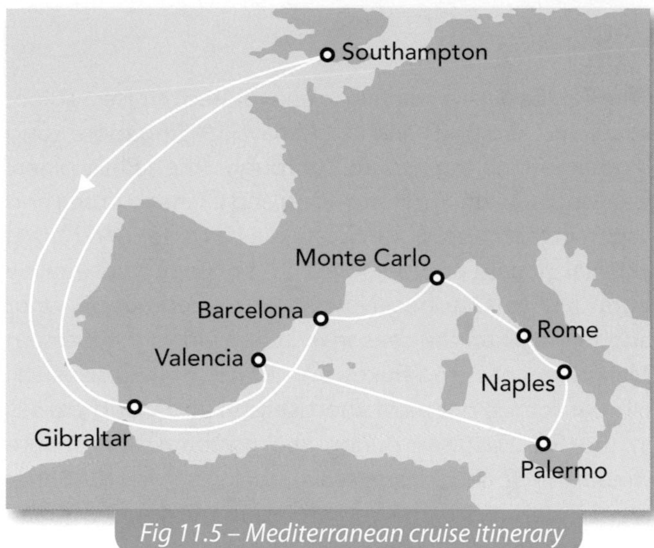

Fig 11.5 – Mediterranean cruise itinerary

Scandinavia and the Baltic

Cruises in Scandinavia and the Baltic appeal to people with an interest in history, culture and nature, rather than beaches and hot weather. Baltic cruise itineraries include the great cities of Northern Europe, and the majority of cruises include a visit to the historic port of St Petersburg. Scandinavia offers cruise visitors tranquil fjords and breathtaking scenery.

Cruises that take in the Norwegian fjords and coastline often include the following ports of call:

- Bergen;
- Trondheim;
- Alesund;
- Tromso;
- Hammerfest;
- The North Cape.

Cities that often feature in Baltic cruise itineraries include:

- Amsterdam;
- Copenhagen;
- Helsinki;
- Stockholm;
- Oslo;
- Tallinn;
- Riga;
- St Petersburg.

Activity 11.7

Plot the above list of Norwegian and Baltic cruise ports on a blank map of Europe, which registered tandtonline users can download from **www.tandtonline.co.uk**

This activity is designed to provide evidence for P4

Alaska

Alaska attracts cruise passengers, from May to October, to see its vast and unspoilt landscape of mountains, forests, glaciers and fjords. Its scenery and wildlife are the main attractions of the area, which covers more than 580,000 square miles. There are two basic Alaska cruise itineraries:

1. The classic 'inside passage' – this is a round-trip, one-week cruise, beginning and ending in Vancouver, named because it lies within a long chain of coastal islands that act as a buffer to the open waters of the North Pacific. This type of cruise usually includes visits to tidewater glaciers, such as those at the head of narrow, cliff-sided Tracy Arm, or those found in the many inlets of Glacier Bay;
2. The 'glacier route' itinerary – this includes the Gulf of Alaska in a one-way route between Vancouver and Anchorage. These cruises include some of Alaska's most impressive tidewater glaciers, such as Hubbard Glacier in Yakutat Bay and Columbia Glacier in Prince William Sound.

Cruise companies that feature Alaska include Norwegian Cruise Line, Royal Caribbean International, Crystal Cruises, Holland America Line and Celebrity Cruises.

Figure 11.6 shows an example of a 7-night Alaska fly/cruise offered by Norwegian Cruise Lines, starting and ending in Vancouver. Highlights of the cruise include time to explore Vancouver's historic Gastown and cosmopolitan Yaletown, plus cruising by the Sawyer Glacier and viewing a wide variety of wildlife.

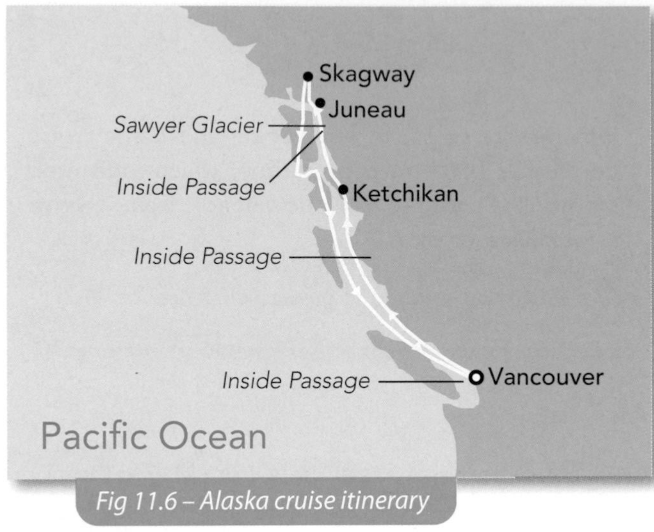

Fig 11.6 – Alaska cruise itinerary

Activity 11.8

Study the itinerary shown in Figure 11.6 and make notes on the type of passengers that you think the cruise would appeal to. You may like to do some further research in brochures and on websites to help you with this task.

This activity is designed to provide evidence for P4 and P5.

Antarctica

Cruising the cold waters of the Antarctic appeals to travellers who are looking for the ultimate in natural, wildlife experiences. Cruises are carefully controlled to maintain environmental standards, but passengers can still expect to see penguins, seals, whales and numerous seabirds in a landscape that is dominated by massive ice cliffs and floating icebergs. Companies that offer cruises in Antarctic waters include Hurtigruten, Abercrombie & Kent and Quark Expeditions. Cruising is only possible during the southern hemisphere summer from November to March, when temperatures can still be minus 5°C to minus 8°C and wind chill can be a significant factor. Proper protective clothing is essential for Antarctic cruises, although higher temperatures are found in the northerly islands.

Far East

The Far East is a relatively unexplored cruise region, stretching from Thailand, Malaysia, Singapore and Indonesia in the south, through the Philippines, Cambodia, Vietnam, Hong Kong and China to Korea and Japan in the north. South East Asia has a hot and humid tropical climate and is subject to monsoon rains mainly from July to October. November to February is drier and this is when the seasonal cruises along the western Malaysian coast to Phuket take place. Star Cruises sail all year round, but most short season and world cruises in the Far East sail during the northern hemisphere winter or spring, from November to March. Other cruise operators in this region include Royal Caribbean International, P&O, Cunard and Costa Cruises.

The UK

There are a growing number of cruises starting and finishing in UK ports, offering passengers the convenience of beginning their holiday closer to home. Some ex-UK cruises follow the coast line of Western Europe calling at Dutch, UK, French and Spanish ports going as far south as Lisbon in Portugal. Others may circumnavigate the coast of England, Wales, Ireland and Scotland, calling at major cities like Dublin, Liverpool, Glasgow, Belfast and Edinburgh, as well as visiting outlying islands like the Channel Islands and the Isles of Scilly. Hebridian Island Cruises specialise in cruising around the Scottish islands. Longer cruises go as far as the Greenland east coast or volcanic Iceland visiting Reykjavik and calling at the rugged Faroe Islands and the Irish coast en route.

The Canary Islands

The seven Canary Islands are scattered some 70 miles off the coast of Morocco. Gran Canaria offers busy resorts, impressive architecture and a mini Sahara desert, while Tenerife has mountainous rainforests and impressive beaches. Lanzarote features moon-like landscapes in its Fire Mountain Volcanic Park and is close to the semi-desert island of Fuertaventura, with its extensive sandy beaches. Further out into the Atlantic are the unspoilt mountainous volcanic islands of La Palma, La Gomera and El Hierro. The climate of the Canaries offers an all-year-round destination for tourism, with the majority of cruises taking place between autumn and spring. Cruises to the Canaries can be taken from the UK or Mediterranean ports such as Genoa either as return voyages of 7 to 14 days or as a sector of a trans-Atlantic voyage. There are also cruises around the islands leaving from Tenerife or Gran Canaria.

The Nile

The River Nile and the Rhine/Moselle are the most popular river cruise destinations with British people. Nile cruisers are attracted by the thousands of years of history in the region, inspiring monuments such as the Pyramids and Sphinx at Gizeh, the temples at Karnak, Philea and the Valley of the Kings. The majority of British visitors to Egypt include a short cruise on the Nile between Luxor and Aswan during their stay. Cruises of the 140-mile stretch of the Upper Nile typically last for four or five days. A number of Nile cruise operators combine a stay in Cairo with their cruises, giving passengers the chance to visit the Tutankhamun treasures in the Museum of the Antiquities. Companies that feature Nile cruises include Abercrombie & Kent, Discover Egypt and Somak. River cruises on the Rhine/Moselle are available from a number of cruise companies including Noble Caledonia, Sea Cloud and Phoenix Holidays.

The Black Sea

Cruises in the Black Sea are for people who wish to experience the different cultures of eastern bloc countries, like Bulgaria, Ukraine and Romania, or visit the northern coast of Turkey. Although there are Mediterranean cruises from the UK that include the Black Sea in their itineraries, most are fly/cruises sailing from Athens or Istanbul and many will also include some Greek Islands in the itinerary. Popular cruise ports on the Black Sea include Varna and Nesebur in Bulgaria, Yalta and Odessa in the Ukraine, and Constanta in Romania.

Activity 11.9

Analyse the range of cruises and ships currently operating in one named cruise area, including their appeal to different types of customer.

This activity is designed to provide evidence for M2.

Types of cruises

The cruise industry has responded to the changing demands and expectations of travellers by developing different types of cruises to suit all tastes, including:

- Fly/cruise;
- Round-the-world;
- Mini-cruise;
- River cruise;
- Luxury cruise;
- Special interest cruise;
- Trans-Atlantic cruise;
- Sail ship;
- All-inclusive;
- easyCruise.

Fly/cruise

Fly/cruise is a popular travel arrangement that allows cruise passengers to combine their time at sea with a flight to or from the home port of their cruise, thereby beginning their cruise as soon as possible. All major cruise operators offer fly/cruise holidays for an all-inclusive package price. Cruise companies use charter airlines and scheduled services, depending on the destination and type of cruise. Scheduled services with major airlines tend to be offered on the more expensive cruises. Cunard, for example, has an arrangement with British Airways to transport its cruise passengers, offering flight upgrades on payment of a supplement. Wherever possible, passengers on Thomson cruises fly to their cruise home port with Thomson Airways, which is part of the same company. This is an example of vertical integration that we discussed in the first section of this unit.

Round-the-world cruise

A round-the-world trip is most people's idea of the ultimate cruising experience – but you need the money and time to do it! For example, Cunard's 2011 maiden world cruise on the Queen Elizabeth lasts for 103 nights and the full brochure prices start at £9,561 per passenger. Not surprisingly, therefore, these types of cruises tend to appeal to people with time to spare and a good income or savings. UK passengers wanting a round-the-world cruise can leave from Southampton or fly straight to the sun and start their circumnavigation at a port such as Miami or Los Angeles. Another option is to start the cruise from New York. Passengers who can't spare the time for a full world cruise can sample part of the experience – all world cruises are broken down into fly/cruise segments to allow passengers to select the time periods and destinations that are most convenient for them. One of the most popular options is a semi-circumnavigation sailing between the UK and Australia.

A world cruise aboard Cunard's Queen Mary 2 lasts for 103 nights

Activity 11.10

Plot the route of a Cunard round-the-world cruise on an outline map of the world, marking the embarkation port and all ports of call on the journey. Registered tandtonline users can download a free blank world map from **www.tandtonline.co.uk**

This activity is designed to provide evidence for P5.

Mini-cruise

Busy, modern lifestyles have created a growing demand for short trips or mini-cruises on board ship, giving passengers the chance to relax and unwind. Nearly one in five cruises booked by British people is of five days' duration or less. Typically, a mini-cruise (a trip of less than seven nights at sea) gives passengers the chance to visit two or three destinations in a short period of time. Short cruises starting and ending in UK ports are growing in popularity, although short trips from Mediterranean ports continue to be in greatest demand.

River cruise

River cruising offers passengers the opportunity of exploring an area at close quarters in a cosy, intimate environment. River ships typically carry up to 200 passengers and can make up to three stops a day, allowing plenty of time for sightseeing and shopping. The ships travel by day and moor up at night, the opposite of a typical ocean cruise. The Rivers Rhine and Nile are the most popular river cruise destination for British people.

Activity 11.11

Carry out some research into three river cruise operators – one operating in the UK, one in Europe and one in the USA. Produce three fact sheets that include information about each operator for use by prospective river cruise passengers, e.g. company history, products on offer, prices, duration of trips, destinations visited, etc. The website **www.choosingcruising.co.uk** is a good place to start this activity.

This activity is designed to provide evidence for P5.

Luxury cruise

Most cruise liners offer an element of luxury – indeed the very concept of cruising is closely tied up with luxury and opulence. However, there are only a handful of cruise operators that offer the ultimate luxury cruise experience. Passengers who book a luxury cruise can expect to be greeted on arrival with a complimentary bottle of champagne, to have a spacious cabin with walk-in wardrobe, an elegant bathroom, a well-stocked mini bar and 24-hour room service, with full in-suite dining available during restaurant hours. Passengers never have to queue for food and drink, and never have to wait to use equipment in the gym or to be seated in the dining room, because true luxury ships have more than enough space to accommodate everybody on board in comfort. The small, luxury ships owned by Yachts of Seabourn and Regent Seven Seas Cruises are amongst the most exclusive in the world for cruise passengers.

Special interest cruising

Realising that the interests of potential cruise passengers are very varied, cruise operators try to offer as wide a variety of special interests or themes as possible in their programmes. These cruises give passengers the chance to enjoy a favourite hobby in a different setting, learn new skills or just increase their knowledge. They can choose from a wide variety of subjects – from gourmet cuisine, gardening and music to culture, art appreciation and sculpture. Many special interest cruise operators feature well-known guest speakers, performances by noted entertainers or related shore excursions and the chance to mingle with leading figures in a particular field. Orient Lines is an award-winning ship line operating the Marco Polo 2, which offers special interest, destination-focused cruises. Celebrity Xpedition, part of the Celebrity Cruises' fleet, carries just 92 passengers and is designed for exclusive, expeditionary cruises to the Galapagos Islands.

FOCUS ON INDUSTRY

SWAN HELLENIC CRUISES

Swan Hellenic has been offering discovery cruises for more than 50 years to a variety of lesser-known locations throughout the world. The itineraries on board its ship Minerva include diverse landscapes, cultures and historical settings – from the mysterious temples and pyramids of the Maya at Chichen Itza, the glacial landscapes of Arctic Norway to the tropical environment of the Amazon interior. The Swan Hellenic brand was purchased in April 2007 by Lord Sterling to secure its future.

Weblink @ Check out this website for more information on Swan Hellenic. www.swanhellenic.com

'Soft adventure' is the name given to any type of tourist activity that gives people the chance to try out a new experience – but nothing too dangerous! Cruise lines now offer more adventurous shore excursions and have been developing new products geared specifically at those who like to get active on holiday. A prime adventure destination is Alaska, where a number of cruise operators, including Princess Cruises, Norwegian Cruise Line and Holland America Line, have been updating shore tour programmes to include more unusual options like dog sledding, whale watching, hiking in the forest, go-karting, mountain biking and rock climbing. Passengers on Caribbean cruises can try their hand at diving or snorkelling, while Mediterranean cruise activities include abseiling, roller-blading, water rafting and cycling expeditions. Ocean Village is a good example of a cruise brand that appeals to younger, first-time cruisers who are keen to take part in activities while on holiday.

Ocean Village offers a variety of activities for passengers

Trans-Atlantic cruises

Cruising across the Atlantic appeals to people who like to spend lots of days at sea. Trans-Atlantic cruises may go direct to their destination port or cruise the destination region for a few days before arrival. The majority of trans-Atlantic cruises are repositioning cruises, i.e. journeys that allow ships to get to a particular area to begin a new cruise season. As such, they can offer very good value for money. These cruises can take place all year, but most take place from April to October. Weather conditions and the time of year will dictate the route taken.

The classic Southampton to New York (or reverse) 6-night trans-Atlantic voyages offered by Cunard are still available, but there are other cruises from northern Europe to east coast USA or Canada on offer. Many cruise ships are repositioned from Europe to the Caribbean for the winter season. Cruises depart from the major European ports and call at the Canaries, Madeira and/or the Azores before arriving in the Caribbean. A similar repositioning takes place to South America for the northern winter, although there are only a few cruises on offer.

Sail ship

Cruising in a sailing ship is a niche product that appeals to a small number of people who are looking for a more authentic and traditional cruising experience. There are many companies that offer sail cruising, including Monaco-based Star Clippers and Windstar Cruises. Sailing ships are small by cruise standards so the facilities on board are limited, but they do offer the combination of sailing tradition with cruise ship comforts.

All-inclusive

Passengers who choose an all-inclusive cruise have the certainty of knowing that everything is provided for them in the price they pay for their holiday. There are no hidden costs for on-shore excursions, tips for staff, port/airport taxes, on-board activity sessions, drinks, etc. Some cruise operators offer an all-inclusive arrangement as an upgrade for customers, for example Island Cruises.

'Cruise and stay' is an arrangement that allows passengers to combine a fly/cruise holiday with a period of time in a hotel or other type of accommodation, which can be on an all-inclusive basis. For example, a passenger could fly to Florida and spend a week visiting the area and its many attractions, then join a cruise from Miami to the Caribbean for a second week. Cruise and stay is popular with people who are new to cruising and want to try it out before committing to a longer holiday.

Informal cruising

easyCruise is one of a new breed of cruise companies offering a more informal cruising experience. Part of the easy Group of Companies, whose brands include easyJet and easyCar, easyCruise operates the easyCruise Life ship, offering cruise holidays in the Greek islands and Turkey. Unlike traditional cruising, easyCruise sails for just a few hours each morning, arriving at each port around lunchtime, allowing passengers time to explore each destination in the afternoon and evening. easyCruise Life features restaurants and bars, with à la carte dining offering fusion cuisine, as well as a spa. Designed to appeal to younger customers, easyCruise offers cabins that are minimalist in design. Like easyJet, cruise prices vary according to demand and they generally rise as the ship fills up, so early bookers secure the best prices. Online prices are for cruises on a room-only basis, with all meals, drinks, spa treatments, tours and housekeeping services paid for on board. Cruise passengers must make their own travel arrangements to get to and from their easyCruise ship.

Cruise ships

The *Annual Cruise Review* estimates that there are currently 25 new cruise ships on order through to spring 2014. Almost all are large 'mega-ships', with a much wider range of dining and entertainment facilities to appeal to families and a much broader age group generally. The average maximum capacity of the world's cruise ships has already doubled over the past 10 years, while the average capacity of ships built in the 1990s was just over 1,600 passengers, this decade the average will be more than 2,600.

This trend towards building larger ships not only makes good financial sense for the cruise operators because of the economies of scale, but it also allows the companies to offer ever more elaborate facilities for guests on board ship, e.g. large show rooms with state-of-the-art lighting and sound equipment, shopping malls, ice skating rinks, fitness suites and even rock climbing walls! More restaurants on board have led to the introduction

Many cruise ships now have excellent fitness suites on board (courtesy of Island Cruises)

of new dining concepts where passengers are free to choose where and with whom they want to dine. Entertainment on board has developed from shows performed by talented crew members in the 1970s to full scale Hollywood and Las Vegas production shows on today's mega-liners. Last but not least, cabins (often referred to now as staterooms) with balconies, internet access, the latest movies on television and even butler service or 24-hour room service, have been introduced on the new breed of cruise ships.

It is not just new ships that are being designed to appeal to first-time cruisers, families and younger passengers. Cruise lines are now starting to revitalise their existing ships, adding more cabins with balconies, internet cafés and family entertainment areas. Some, like RCI with the Enchantment of the Seas, are even 'stretching' ships by having them cut in half and adding a new central section with more cabins, restaurants, bars and entertainment venues.

Design features and on-board facilities

Spending so much time at sea makes the design, quality, availability and type of facilities on board ship very important to passengers. Cruises vary from very small, intimate experiences with a small number of fellow passengers to mega-cruises with thousands of passengers on board and a variety of facilities such as shops, bars, restaurants, entertainment venues, internet cafés, currency exchange facilities and children's play areas. The facilities on offer must reflect the number of passengers, type of cruise, target market and the price paid by the passengers.

Perhaps the most important facility on board is the cabin (often referred to as the stateroom). Cabins vary in size and price according to where they are located on the ship. Inside cabins on lower decks tend to be the cheapest, while upper deck cabins and suites with sea views command the highest prices. Cruise brochures and websites include colour-coded deck plans indicating the location and prices of cabins with different facilities (see Figure 11.7).

Activity 11.12

Research and compile two fact sheets that compare and contrast the routes and ship facilities offered by Cunard's Queen Mary 2 and Island Cruises' Island Star.

This activity is designed to provide evidence for P5.

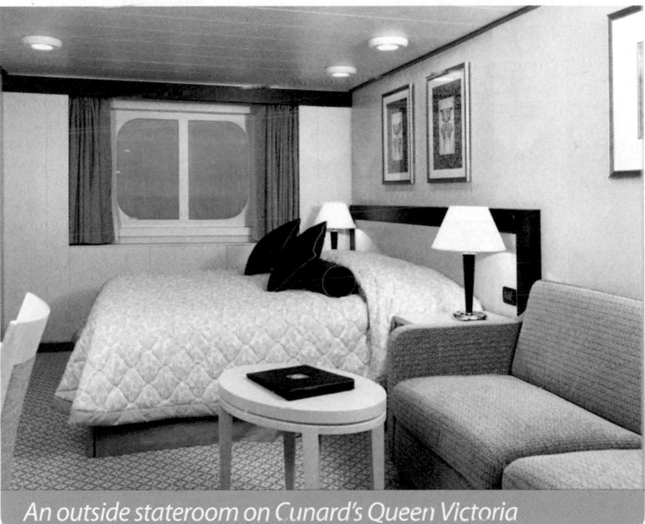

An outside stateroom on Cunard's Queen Victoria

Products developed to expand the market

The number of cruise passengers worldwide has grown dramatically over the last 10 years due in no small part to the development of new and innovative products and on-board facilities. Cruise companies have segmented the market and introduced products such as freestyle

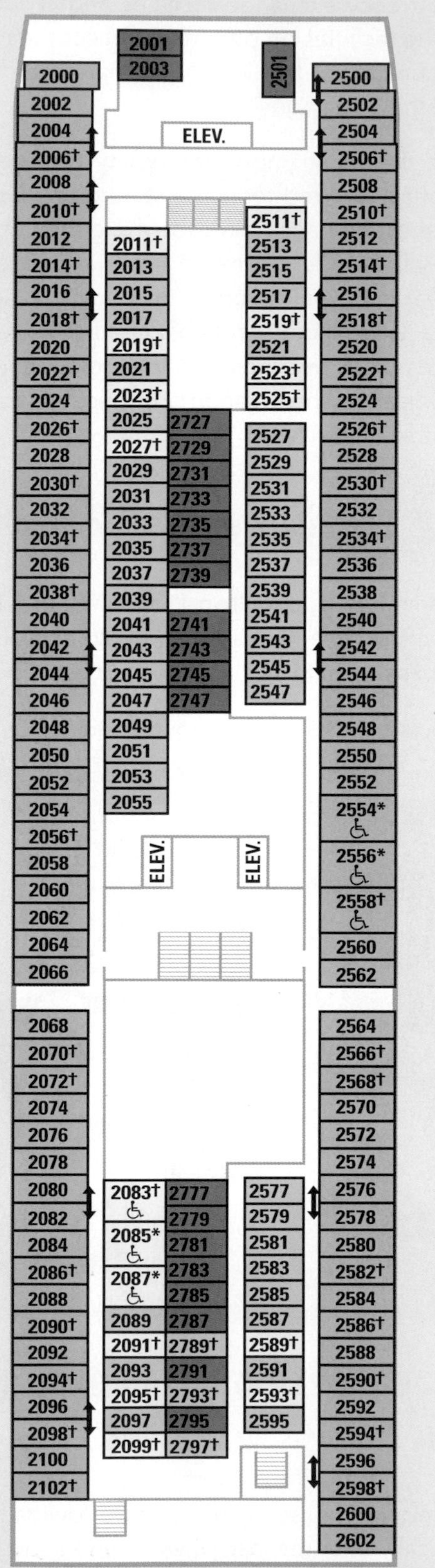

Fig 11.7 – Section from a typical deck plan (courtesy of Royal Caribbean International)

cruising, 'cruise and stay' itineraries and mini-cruises. We have also seen the growth of 'fun ships', adult-only cruises and more facilities for families and children, including children's clubs and computer games.

Atrium on a Costa Cruises ship

Activity 11.13

Compare and contrast the product and facilities offered by one named mass-market cruise operator and one named ultra-luxury cruise company.

This activity is designed to provide evidence for P6.

SECTION 3 Be able to select cruises that appeal to cruise customers and meet specific customer needs

Types of customers

No one cruise company can hope to meet the very different needs of every cruise passenger. Cruise operators target particular customers, providing services and facilities to meet their needs. Customers can be categorised as families, couples, groups and individuals and can be segmented by:

- Age – a cruise company may target older customers or young, first-time cruisers;
- Lifestyle – cruise operators can cater for adventurous travellers or people seeking a cultural experience, etc;
- Income – some cruises are aimed at affluent, up-market clientele, while others appeal to people on a tight budget;
- Special interest – everything from wine tasting, art appreciation and history to sports, cooking and gardening are offered by cruise specialists.

Cruise operators develop products and itineraries to appeal to one of more of these markets and use a variety of marketing techniques to persuade them to book with their company, e.g. advertising, direct mail, sales promotions and public relations activities.

Activity 11.14

Gather information on three companies that offer cruises for (1) an elderly couple wanting to explore Antarctica; (2) a family with young children looking for a 7-night Mediterranean cruise. Explain how the selected cruises would appeal to the customers.

This activity is designed to provide evidence for P7 and P8.

Cruise weddings are growing in popularity (courtesy of Island Cruises)

Appeal of cruising

The growth in popularity of cruising clearly shows that it has great appeal to many different types of people from all backgrounds and regions of the world. Cruising still appeals to the traditional market that has always enjoyed the experience, but there are now many new types of customers attracted to cruising, including younger, first-time cruisers, groups and families. Whatever their characteristics, cruise passengers choose their cruise based on the itineraries on offer, the ship and cruise line, the type of on-board facilities and the social aspects of cruising.

Cruises appeal to customers for a variety of reasons, for example:

1. Appeal in relation to itinerary – factors such as the embarkation point (where the cruise begins), number and type of on-shore excursions, climate at ports, special themes, ports of call, cruise areas visited and variety of sights, influence a passenger's choice of cruise line and itinerary;

2. Appeal in relation to the ship – the cruise operator and type of ship, for example a small, intimate vessel or a large cruise liner, will have a bearing on a passenger's choice of cruise. Also, the passenger/crew ratio (PCR) will be important to many cruisers – the lower the PCR, i.e. the more crew available per passenger, the better the level of service provided and the overall passenger experience. The passenger/space ratio (PSR) is another important factor – the lower the PSR, i.e. the more space available per passenger, the greater the feeling of space on board and less queuing for facilities;

3. Appeal in relation to on-board facilities – shipping companies are actively developing their on-board facilities in order to capitalise on the overall growth in the cruise industry and to satisfy the new customers that have been attracted to cruising. The quality and availability of accommodation and entertainment facilities, plus sporting, children's clubs and health and beauty, are important factors when deciding which cruise ship and company to choose;

4. Appeal in relation to social aspects – issues such as dress code and tipping policy can influence passenger choice, e.g. a person may prefer a more informal type of cruise with few formalities to a traditional cruising experience with a more formal dress code. Also, whether to choose an all-inclusive arrangement of pay for extras on board will feature in a passenger's choice, as will the total cost of the cruise in relation to their overall budget. A cruise that gives passengers the opportunity to meet and make friends with fellow passengers from a wide variety of social backgrounds and countries around the world may also be an important consideration.

Activity 11.15

Gather information on three companies that offer cruises for (1) a group of students wanting a short cruise in the Mediterranean as part of an overseas study visit; (2) a couple wanting to spend their honeymoon on a Nile cruise. Explain how the selected cruises would appeal to the customers.

This activity is designed to provide evidence for P7 and P8.

SECTION 4

Understand the effects of an expanding cruise industry

We have seen that cruising is a global industry that is growing rapidly. In this section we investigate potential future developments in cruising and explore the positive and negative impacts of the industry on cruise areas of the world.

Weblink

Check out this website for more information on CruiseBritain.

http://www2.visitbritain.com/en/travel-trade/cruise-britain/index.aspx

Future developments in cruising

The Passenger Shipping Association (PSA) has forecast that UK cruise passenger numbers will grow to 2 million per year by 2014, from the 2009 figure of 1.5 million per annum. Cruise operators are responding to this demand by building ever-bigger ships that offer more on-board facilities for guests and greater cost savings for the companies. Cruise operators are competing for traditional package holiday customers by cutting prices and designing ships that appeal to a wider market.

Potential future developments in the cruise industry include:

1. More demand for ultra-luxury cruising;
2. Larger, more fuel-efficient ships;
3. Environmental considerations – e.g. better waste management systems, more use of solar panels on ships, sponsoring marine conservation projects, etc.
4. New cruise areas – as the market for cruising grows, cruise operators will explore new areas for cruises, for example more Northern European cruises offering wildlife watching;
5. UK port developments – more UK ports will develop facilities for welcoming cruise ships. The CruiseBritain initiative between the PSA, VisitBritain and the cruise industry has been established to promote cruise tourism in the UK and encourage more ports to get involved in cruising.

Activity 11.16

Outline one potential future development in the cruise industry based on current trends. Evaluate how your chosen development could increase or decrease the negative and positive impacts of cruising.

This activity is designed to provide evidence for P9 and D2.

Impacts on cruise areas

Travel by sea has opened up many opportunities that didn't exist before, but by its very nature it has an impact on the environment. Many people want to go on holiday, so the challenge to cruise lines is to protect the environment, minimise negative impacts, improve positive impacts and support sustainable tourism while meeting the increasing demand for travel. Cruising has both negative and positive impacts, particularly in the ports and cruise destinations visited by passengers. This can have serious implications for ports of call that have to accommodate increased numbers of tourists and provide them with facilities and services.

Positive economic impacts on cruise ports and destinations include:

- Increased revenue – cruise passengers tend to visit ports in groups on organised excursions. While in port they spend money in shops, restaurants, attractions and on entertainment, thereby adding to the local economy. Taxi firms and coach companies also benefit financially from cruise passengers. The

PSA estimates that cruising contributed 2.3 billion Euros to the UK economy in 2008;

- Employment – cruising not only provides jobs for people working for the cruise lines, but also for travel and tourism businesses in ports, e.g. in hotels, restaurants, tourist attractions, tour operators and travel guides. The PSA estimates that cruising created 49,000 UK jobs in 2008. Additionally, cruising contributes towards indirect employment, i.e. jobs in non-tourism sectors that nonetheless benefit from influxes of cruise passengers, including construction, banking, retail and craft industries.

The sheer scale of the cruise industry, as well as the numbers of passengers carried on each ship, can cause environmental, social and cultural problems, as the following case study on the impact of cruise tourism in Belize explains.

CASE STUDY

The impact of cruise tourism in Belize

Introduction

Belize is a small country situated at the base of the Yucatan in Central America. It borders Mexico and Guatemala, with the Caribbean Sea to the east. The country's area includes many small islands, known as cayes, which straddle a coral reef second only in size to the Great Barrier Reef in Australia. Belize has been developing its tourist industry in recent years based on its natural beauty and the ruins associated with the ancient Mayan civilisation. Belize is included in the itineraries of cruise operators in the Western Caribbean, including Carnival Cruises.

The Belize Ecotourism Association (BEA)

The potential harmful impacts of cruise tourism on Belize have been brought to light by the Belize Ecotourism Association (BEA), a body set up in 1993 to:

'Promote environmentally responsible tourism, to be sensitive to the impact of tourism, to promote pollution prevention and environmental concerns, to continually observe the effects of all the above and to promote education for locals and visitors'.

The organisation is particularly concerned about the way that the type of mass tourism associated with cruises may harm the country's economy in the long term, by alienating visitors to the country's small-sale tourism developments that have been nurtured over the last 20 years, based on ecotourism principles. The BEA wants to see a long-term plan for the sustainable development of all forms of tourism to Belize, including cruises.

Environmental concerns

BEA highlights a number of issues concerned with the environmental impacts of cruise tourism, including:

- Ancient Mayan ruins are under pressure from the large, and growing, number of cruise passengers;
- There is evidence of environmental deterioration on the cayes and coral reefs;

- Riverside erosion is increasing due to wash from the high-speed launches taking cruise passengers on adventure trips;
- Road systems are under pressure from the extra volume of traffic generated by cruise tourism;
- Solid waste from cruise passengers is increasing the burden on the area's sanitary infrastructure.

Cultural impacts

BEA believes that tourism should always contribute to cultural exchanges between visitors and the people of Belize. Visitors attracted to Belize by the small-scale tourism developments, with the opportunity to learn about the local people and their traditions, are rewarded with warmth and kindness. With mass tourism associated with cruising there is a danger that these experiences may well be reversed. Expectations by street sellers of big sales are often disappointed. Passengers are hustled and their reactions may be seen to be hostile. The interaction, instead of being one of pleasure, can become one of distaste and an unwillingness to return to the country or recommend it to others.

The future

Tourism in Belize is estimated to be worth BZ$270 million to the country's economy, with cruise tourism accounting for some BZ$40 million. The Belize Ecotourism Association would like to see the burden of tourist taxes being spread more evenly amongst all visitors to the country – at present, tourists who stay overnight pay a higher tax than those just visiting for the day, including cruise passengers. They believe this is unfair, since the environmental impacts caused by cruise tourists are greater than long-stay visitors. A rise in the tourist tax for day visitors would give the government extra funds to allow proper monitoring of the impacts of cruise ship tourism. Also, it may attract higher-spending tourists to Belize, thereby benefiting the economy even more. The BEA would also like to see improvements in the country's infrastructure before any future plans for cruise tourism developments are considered and measures are in place to monitor developments for their environmental and cultural impacts.

Case Study Questions and Activities

1. Why is it important for the government of Belize to monitor cruise tourism?
2. What measures could be introduced to reduce the pressure from tourists at the ancient Mayan ruins?
3. How can the government of Belize maximise the benefits from cruise tourism while at the same time minimising its negative impacts?
4. Carry out some further research to find examples of how cruise lines try to reduce their harmful environmental and cultural impacts.

This case study is designed to provide evidence for P10 and M3.

Weblink

Check out this website to help answer the questions in this case study and for more information on the Belize Ecotourism Association.

www.bzecotourism.org

Carry out some research on cruises in Antarctica and make notes on the impacts of cruising in the area, its gateway ports and ports of call. Make realistic recommendations about how to maximise the positive and minimise the negative impacts of cruising in Antarctica. The website **www.choosingcruising.co.uk** is a good place to start this activity.

This activity is designed to provide evidence for P9 and D2.

UNIT SUMMARY

This unit has explored the cruise industry, from the early beginnings in the mid-19th century to the present day global industry. You have seen that cruising has undergone a period of rapid growth and change in recent years, with new ships and on-board facilities being developed to cater for new markets around the world. The links between cruising and other industries in travel and tourism have been fully examined. The unit has also looked at the many employment opportunities on offer with cruise lines and the qualifications, experience and personal qualities needed to succeed in the industry. You have investigated the main cruise areas of the world, including the Mediterranean, Caribbean and Alaska. The unit has also explored different types of cruises, ships and the facilities they offer, before examining how cruises are tailored to meet specific customer needs. Finally, you have looked at potential future developments in cruising, plus the positive and negative impacts of the industry on cruise destinations. Throughout the unit you have been shown many industry examples, while the case studies on Carnival Corporation and plc, the PSA and the impact of cruise tourism in Belize, highlight key issues in the operation and development of the cruise industry.

If you have worked methodically, by the end of this unit you should:

- Know about the cruise industry;
- Understand the cruise market;
- Be able to select cruises that appeal to cruise customers and meet specific needs;
- Understand the effects of an expanding cruise industry.

You are now in a position to complete the assignment for the unit, under the direction of your tutor. Before you tackle the assignment you may like to have a go at the following questions to help build your knowledge of the cruise industry.

TEST YOUR KNOWLEDGE

1. Why do you think that cruising has grown in popularity in recent years?
2. Which cruise destination is the most popular with British cruisers?
3. In what ways is the customer profile of cruise passengers changing?
4. Name three companies that offer informal cruising.
5. Which three companies have the biggest share of the global cruise market?
6. Name five cruise brands that are owned by Carnival Corporation and plc.
7. Describe the links that cruising has with other industries in the travel and tourism sector.
8. What role does the PSA play in the cruise industry?
9. Give two examples of vertical and horizontal integration in the cruise industry.
10. List ten ports of call used in Mediterranean cruise itineraries.
11. What type of cruise passengers are attracted to cruises in Alaska?
12. Describe some of the environmental impacts of cruise tourism.
13. Describe the features and benefits of five different types of cruises.
14. Describe a variety of external factors that affect the global cruise industry.
15. What personal qualities do the cruise lines look for in new recruits?

Answers to these questions can be found in the Book 2 Tutor's CD-ROM that accompanies this book (ISBN 9780956268075). Full details can be found at **www.tandtpublishing.co.uk**

UNIT 11 ASSIGNMENT

Investigating the Cruise Industry

Introduction

This assignment is made up of a number of tasks which, when successfully completed, are designed to give you sufficient evidence to meet the Pass (P), Merit (M) and Distinction (D) grading criteria for the unit. If you have carried out the activities and read the case studies throughout this unit, you will already have done a lot of work towards completing the tasks for this assignment.

Scenario

As part of a forthcoming open day for prospective students at your college/school, your group has been asked to prepare some presentations and displays on different industries in the travel and tourism sector, to give the students and their parents an idea of the type of work you do on your course. You have been chosen to work on the cruise industry and must complete the following tasks.

Task 1

Research, prepare and deliver a presentation in which you should:

a. Describe key stages in the development of the cruise industry (P1). This should focus on the last 50 years and in particular the last ten years.

b. Describe the roles of stakeholders involved in the cruise industry (P2). This must cover cruise operators, regulatory bodies and their links with other travel and tourism industries. You should identify the cruise operators that are independent and those that are part of larger organisations.

c. Describe employment opportunities available within the cruise industry (P3). You should identify employment opportunities both on board and on shore with different types of cruise operators, and then research at least two different types of on-board jobs, e.g. purser, entertainer, shore excursion staff, social host, etc. plus one job on shore, e.g. check-in clerk, call centre operator, sales executive, etc. The jobs described could be with two or more cruise operators. These jobs should be described in terms of roles, responsibilities, entry requirements, working environment, terms and conditions.

d. Statistically assess the cruise industry today, including stakeholders and employment (M1). You should present a brief profile of the main cruise operators identifying those that are owned by the same parent company and those that are independent. Your presentation should include statistical information about the number of passengers they carry, the number of ships in operation and the number and nationality of the crews. You should also assess how the cruise operators link with other industries, e.g. transport, tour operators, retail agents, specialist web-based cruise agents, etc.

This task is designed to produce evidence for P1, P2, P3 and M1.

Task 2

You are to create a display in which you must:

a. Identify major cruise areas available to the UK market (P4). This can be presented using a large world map or a variety of smaller maps.

b. Describe the different types of cruises available to customers (P5). You must provide evidence that describes at least three different types of cruises available to customers. It is important to start with a description of the different types of ship and their design features, and then link these to the different types of cruises on offer, e.g. fly/cruise, mini-cruise, special interest cruise, etc.

c. Explain how cruise lines have developed products for a growing cruise market (P6). You should identify a range of products and then select a minimum of two and explain how and why each product has been developed over recent years to meet the needs of a growing cruise market.

This task is designed to produce evidence for P4, P5 and P6.

Task 3

This task is about selecting cruises that appeal to different types of customers.

a. Use brochure information to select cruises that appeal to cruise customers and meet their specific needs (P7). The first customer is a young, single male looking for a short fly/cruise in the Mediterranean in September. He has a limited budget and is looking for a lively nightlife scene. The second customers are a couple celebrating their golden wedding anniversary and looking for a 14-night cruise in the Caribbean in November, with the chance to visit some interesting heritage and cultural attractions during their holiday. They are looking for a fly/cruise departing from Gatwick Airport. Once you have selected the cruises you should provide the details in a written format and identify the elements that meet the needs of the customers within the customer briefs.

b. Explain how the selected cruises will meet the needs of the different types of customers (P8). You should support your explanations with details of the cruises taken from brochures and websites.

c. Analyse the range of cruises and ships operating currently in a named cruise area, including their appeal to different types of customer (M2). You could select, for example, the Western Mediterranean or the Eastern Caribbean, and analyse the range of cruises and ships operating currently in that area. You should describe the cruises and the ships, and explain how these appeal to different types of customer. Your evidence can be presented in written or oral format.

d. Evaluate how operator, product and ship developments have increased the appeal and growth of cruising over the last ten years and increased cruise operator employment (D1). You must demonstrate your understanding of the following aspects – how operators have developed through mergers and takeovers or by remaining independent and exclusive; how products have been developed to meet specific trends and demands; how ships have been developed to accommodate trends and demands; how cruise operator employment has increased; how all these aspects have increased the appeal and the growth of cruising over the last ten years. Your evidence should be presented as a written report.

This task is designed to produce evidence for P7, P8, M2 and D1.

Task 4

Research, prepare and deliver a presentation in which you should:

a. Outline potential future developments in the cruise industry based on current trends (P9). You must outline at least two potential future developments in the cruise industry based on current industry trends. Your evidence must be supported with articles, research papers, reports, etc. to substantiate each development.

b. Explain how cruises impact on a cruise area, the gateway ports and ports of call (P10). You should explain how one cruise itinerary impacts on one cruise area, its gateway ports and ports of call. You should select one cruise area, e.g. the Western Mediterranean, and describe the impact of one cruise itinerary on the gateway ports and ports of call, e.g. Ibiza Town, Messina, Naples, Toulon, Barcelona, etc. The impacts should be both positive and negative and can include economic, social and environmental impacts.

c. Compare the negative and positive impacts of cruising on two different ports within one cruise area (M3). You can use the same cruise area and itinerary as in Task 4b or use a different area and itinerary to generate your evidence. You must compare the negative and positive impacts of cruising on two different ports within the one cruise area. The comparison should be detailed and supported with other material such as pictorial, newspaper or web-based articles and statistics.

d. Evaluate how potential future developments could increase or decrease the negative and positive impacts of cruising (D2). For example, if cruising continues to grow, with more and more ships using particular ports of call and many more passengers travelling on excursions, the impacts around the ports could be very negative due to congestion and pollution. At the same time, however, there could be positive economic benefits for coach operators, tour guides, tourist attractions and the retail and hospitality facilities within them. The new ships being built are more fuel-efficient and have advanced waste management systems, so these have the potential to decrease negative environmental aspects of cruising.

This task is designed to produce evidence for P9, P10, M3 and D2.

UNIT 13

Tour Operations

INTRODUCTION TO THE UNIT

Tour operators play a very important role in travel and tourism, by arranging the package holidays that are such an important feature of life in the 21st century. Tour operators are at the forefront of today's travel and tourism sector, seeking out new destinations and holiday experiences to satisfy the ever-changing needs and expectations of travellers. They work in partnership with airlines, hoteliers, car hire companies and a variety of other travel service suppliers to package their holiday products. Tour operators sell holidays through travel agents and direct to the public, with internet bookings showing dramatic rises in recent years.

In this unit you will examine the UK tour operations environment, including links with other travel and tourism component industries. You will investigate the many challenges facing tour operators, such as integration and the growth in online sales. Different types of tour operators will be identified and you will learn how products and services are developed to meet a variety of customer needs. You will explore how tour operators plan, sell, administer and operate a package holiday programme. Finally, you will have the chance to develop your practical skills by planning and costing a typical package holiday, allowing you to appreciate some of the commercial decisions necessary to be profitable in this industry.

WHAT YOU WILL STUDY

When you have completed this unit you should:

1. Understand the tour operations environment;
2. Know the range of products and services offered by tour operators for different target markets;
3. Know how tour operators plan, sell, administer and operate a package holiday programme;
4. Be able to plan and cost a package holiday.

You will be guided through the main topics in this unit with the help of the latest developments, statistics, industry examples and case studies. You should also check out the weblinks throughout the unit for extra information on particular organisations or topic areas and use the activities throughout the unit to help you learn more.

ASSESSMENT FOR THIS UNIT

This unit is internally assessed, meaning that you will be given an assignment (or series of assignments) to complete by your tutor(s) to show that you have fully understood the content of the unit. A grading scale of pass, merit or distinction is used when staff mark your assignment(s), with higher grades awarded to students who show greater depth in analysis, evaluation and justification in their assignments. An assignment for this unit, which covers all the grading criteria, can be found on page 71. Don't forget to visit **www.tandtonline.co.uk** for all the latest industry news, developments, statistics and links to websites in this unit to help you with your assignments.

SECTION 1 Understand the tour operations environment

Icebreaker

This unit examines the world of tour operations – the industry concerned with arranging and selling package holidays. Working by yourself, or in small groups under the direction of your tutor, see how you get on with the following tasks to help you make a start on this unit:

- Name five different tour operating companies that you are familiar with;
- Try and come up with a definition of a 'tour operator';
- Make a list of what you think a new tour operator would have to do to organise, plan and sell its holidays;
- Make notes on the range of internal and external influences on a tour operating company that could affect its profits;
- Think about the laws and regulations that tour operators must comply with in the course of their work;
- Name three specific jobs that are offered by the major holiday companies;
- Make a list of the costs that a tour operating company will incur in the course of its work.

When you've finished, show your answers to your tutor and compare your answers with what other students in your class have written.

Tour operations is a dynamic and complex business environment, where companies must work with many different travel and tourism component industries, comply with laws and regulations, and deal with a variety of external influences and challenges.

Links with other component industries

Unlike travel agents, who sell holidays and a range of other travel products, tour operators actually assemble the different parts of a holiday, i.e. the type of travel, accommodation, facilities, transfers, excursions and other services. If we consider that travel agents are the retail arm of the travel business, then tour operators are the wholesalers, since they buy in bulk from the providers of travel services, such as the hoteliers and airlines, break the bulk into manageable packages and offer the finished product – the package holiday (or inclusive tour) – for sale via a travel agent or direct to the public. The package is sold for an all-inclusive price, which is generally lower than if the different parts of the holiday had been booked individually by the holidaymaker. Figure 13.1 shows the position of tour operators as intermediaries between the suppliers of travel products and travel agents. There is a growing trend for people to book direct with tour operators rather than booking through a travel agent. This trend is set to continue and gather pace as the popularity of the internet, mobile technology and interactive TV grows.

In working with other travel and tourism industries, tour operators develop links with a wide range of organisations, including:

- Travel agents – using agents as a sales outlet for the tour operator's holidays and agreeing commission payments and booking procedures;

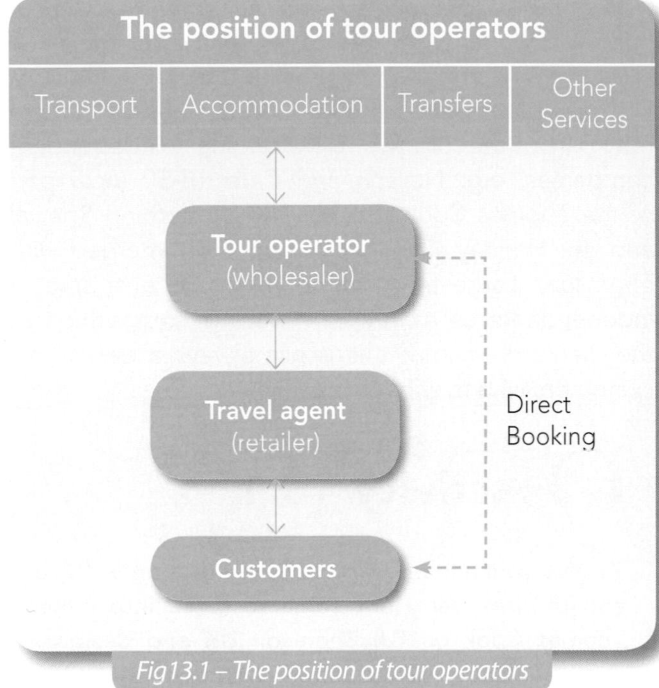

Fig 13.1 – The position of tour operators

- Transport providers – negotiating and agreeing contracts with airlines (charter and scheduled), rail operators, coach companies, taxi operators, etc. to supply transport services for holidaymakers;
- Hotels and other accommodation providers – negotiating allocations of bed spaces that form the accommodation element of the package holiday;
- Ancillary service providers – contracting with companies to supply representative services, transfers, 'meet and greet' arrangements, insurance, car hire, activities, excursions, etc.

Even the large, vertically-integrated travel groups (see next section) have to liaise on different functions within their own organisations, since individual parts of the group are usually separate companies in their own right, e.g. staff from Neilson Holidays, part of the Thomas Cook Group, would negotiate with staff at Thomas Cook Airlines to agree seat allocations for a season.

Horizontal and vertical integration

As competition in the travel and tourism sector has intensified, tour operators have taken over or merged with other travel and tourism businesses as a way of maintaining or increasing their market share and maximising their profits. This is most noticeable in the tour operator/travel agent relationship, where:

- TUI Travel UK owns Thomson and First Choice tour operating businesses, and the Thomson travel agency chains (TUI UK is itself controlled by the German company TUI AG);
- Thomas Cook AG (a German group) owns a number of Thomas Cook tour operating brands/companies, plus the Thomas Cook and Going Places chains of travel agencies.

These 'big two' travel groups were formed in 2007 from the mergers of Thomson and First Choice Holidays, and Thomas Cook with MyTravel. They dominate the sale of package holidays in the UK, accounting for just under 50 per cent of all sales. These are examples of vertical integration in the travel and tourism industry, which is when a company has control over other companies that are at different levels in the chain of distribution or in different industries. Some of the largest tour operators also own their own airlines, giving even greater control over the component parts of package holidays. Figure 13.2 shows how TUI UK is a vertically-integrated travel company, with ownership of tour operators (wholesalers), travel agencies (retailers) and an airline.

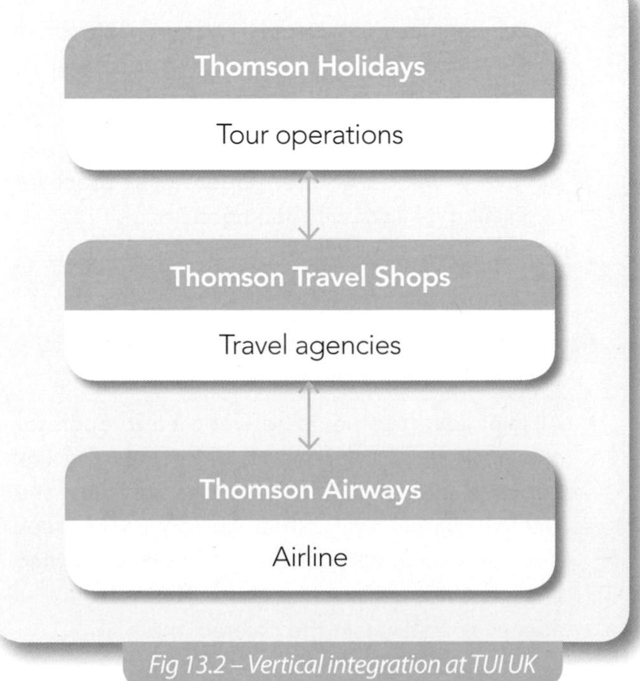

Fig 13.2 – Vertical integration at TUI UK

Weblink  Check out these websites for more information on each of the 'big two' vertically-integrated travel companies.

www.thomson.co.uk;
www.thomascook.com

Vertical integration makes sense for the travel companies since they benefit from bulk discounts and make savings by using their own companies as suppliers. However, there is concern that vertical integration of this sort may not always be in the public's interest, since it can reduce the number of companies and give customers less choice when buying holidays. Also, customers may not know that a tour operator is owned by the travel agency that is selling their holiday. Since 2000, all vertically-integrated travel companies have been obliged to make their links to other travel companies clear by, for example, having notices in their travel agencies and printed in brochures.

FOCUS ON INDUSTRY

DISCLOSURE OF INDUSTRY LINKS

Travel businesses must comply with the following regulations concerning their links with other companies:

- Travel agents must display a prominent notice in the front window of each shop outlining its ownership links;
- A notice must be displayed on the front cover of every in-house tour operator's brochure explaining its links with the agency;
- The name of every tour operator that is part of the same group must be listed inside the shop;
- All company stationery must outline the ownership links of the agent;
- All joint advertisements between a tour operator and an in-house agent must spell out the link between the two. This includes internet and Teletext pages that direct customers to book through a sister company, e.g. a Thomson-owned site that refers people to a Thomson travel agency must explain the connection.

Horizontal integration is when a company owns or has control over a number of companies at the same level in the distribution chain or in the same industry. For example, many tour operating businesses that are now part of the 'big two' were originally independent companies, e.g. Neilson and Club 18-30 (now part of the Thomas Cook Group), and Something Special and the Holiday Cottages Group (now merged with Thomson). Large travel companies take over smaller independents as a way or reducing competition in the marketplace, but this is not always a benefit for customers who may have less choice.

Activity 13.1

To give yourself an example of integration in travel and tourism, carry out some research into either Thomas Cook or TUI Thomson UK and design a chart that shows all the different companies it owns across tour operations, travel agencies and transport operations.

This activity is designed to provide evidence for P1.

Links with trade and regulatory bodies

Trade bodies and associations are established to represent the interests of companies in a particular industry sector.

Trade bodies

ABTA – The Travel Association, is the main trade body for both travel agents and tour operators in the UK. Its members are responsible for the sale of over 90 per cent of package holidays and 45 per cent of independent travel arrangements in the UK. ABTA's role is to ensure that customers benefit from high standards of trading practice in the travel industry and that the standards of service and business throughout its membership are of the highest calibre. All ABTA members – travel agents and tour operators – adhere to a strict code of conduct (there is a full case study on ABTA in *Travel and Tourism for BTEC National Book 1 3rd edition*).

Weblink Check out this website for more information on ABTA – The Travel Association.
www.abta.com

AITO (the Association of Independent Tour Operators) is a trade organisation representing more than 150 of Britain's specialist tour operators. Its members are independent companies, most of them owner-managed, specialising in particular destinations or types of holiday (there is a full case study on AITO in *Travel and Tourism for BTEC National Book 1 3rd edition*).

Weblink Check out this website for more information on AITO.

www.aito.co.uk

UKinbound (formerly BITOA – the British Incoming Tour Operators' Association) is a trade association representing the interests of companies specialising in inbound tourism to the UK.

Weblink  Check out this website for more information on the work of UKinbound.
www.ukinbound.org

The European Tour Operators' Association (ETOA) was founded in 1989 as a direct result of the introduction of the EU Package Travel Directive, which made tour operators aware of the power the European institutions had to influence policy and legislation affecting tour operators. ETOA now has 400 members and has established a track record of influencing travel and tourism legislation at both national and European levels. It promotes greater awareness of the benefits provided by the travel industry in Europe, particularly the increased income and employment.

Weblink Check out this website for more information on the European Tour Operators' Association.
www.etoa.org

The International Federation of Tour Operators (IFTO) is a grouping of trade associations representing tour operators' interests in the various regions of the world. Its vision is to *'ensure the continued long-term success of the organised holiday by influencing legislators and civil servants in the EU, originating and destination countries, as well as other opinion formers, on the benefits to consumers and other public and private stakeholders of organised holidays'*. The secretariat for IFTO is provided by the UK-based Federation of Tour Operators (FTO), one of the most influential of all trade associations in the UK tour operations industry and the subject of the following case study.

CASE STUDY

The Federation of Tour Operators (FTO)

Introduction

The Federation of Tour Operators (FTO) works on behalf of its members to ensure the continued, long-term success of the air-inclusive holiday business. It does this by influencing governments and opinion formers on the benefits to consumers and other stakeholders of air-inclusive holidays compared to other forms of holiday arrangements.

FTO's activities

The following is a brief overview of the activities FTO undertakes:

- Bring about change and improvement in all areas affecting overseas holidays;
- The point of contact for government (UK, EU and destinations) on all UK-outbound tour operating issues;
- Co-ordinate members' activities in key areas of operational delivery – crisis handling, health and safety, sustainable tourism, operational issues, and establishing best practice;
- Co-operation and co-ordination with other trade associations and interested parties;
- Lobby to ensure that the tax burden on holidaymakers is as low as possible;
- Promote the professional and positive image of the industry;
- Provide public relations support;
- Currently acts as a regulator of financial protection on behalf of its members in relation to their non-ATOL business;
- Represent its members at meetings of the International Federation of Tour Operators (IFTO), the European trade association for tour operators.

FTO membership

Full membership is by invitation and subject to the agreement of all existing FTO members. Prospective members must sign up to a set of core values:

1. Able to recognise the benefit of working with others in the industry to achieve common objectives, which are of a non-competitive nature, and willing to give appropriate attention and resource to achieving those objectives;
2. Customer-focused – will aim to prioritise product quality and service delivery;
3. A responsible business with effective implemented standards of health and safety, and a balanced approach to environmental issues;
4. Trades in a way that attempts to ensure long-term financial stability.

FTO member companies account for over 70 per cent of all package holidays sold in the UK. Current members include some of the best-known names in the travel and tourism industry, including:

- Cosmos – an independent UK tour operator;
- Inghams – tour operator offering skiing, lakes and mountains, and city holidays and short breaks;
- Kuoni – a market leader in long-haul travel;
- Shearings Holidays – one of the UK's largest tour operators;

- Group RCI – serving the timeshare vacation market;
- Thomas Cook – tour operator and high street travel retailer;
- Thomas Cook Signature – tailor-made holiday solutions' company;
- TUI UK – the UK's largest holiday company;
- Virgin Holidays – long-haul and ski tour operator.

FTO and responsible tourism

Responsible tourism is about making a positive difference when we travel, by:

- Enjoying ourselves and taking responsibility for our actions, respecting local cultures and the natural environment;
- Giving fair economic returns to local people, helping to spread the benefit of our visit to those who need it most;
- Recognising that water and energy are precious resources that we need to use carefully;
- Protecting endangered wildlife and preserving the natural and cultural heritage of the places we visit for the future enjoyment of visitors and the people who live there.

Members of the FTO are becoming increasingly aware of the socio-cultural, environmental and economic impacts of their products and services. In 2003, they formed a Responsible Tourism Committee and are developing a series of initiatives to assist tour operators to integrate responsible tourism practices into their core business.

Case Study Questions and Activities

1. What are the core values that prospective FTO members must agree to adhere to?
2. Outline the work that the FTO does in the area of health and safety in the air-inclusive tour operating industry;
3. How is the FTO structured and funded?
4. What is responsible tourism and what activities do the FTO and its members undertake to promote this type of approach to tourism?

This case study is designed to provide evidence for P1.

Weblink @ Check out this website to help answer these questions and for more information on the FTO.
www.fto.co.uk

Regulatory bodies

Regulatory bodies exist to make sure that tour operating companies operate in a fair, honest, efficient, safe and secure manner, for the good of the companies, their customers, suppliers and society at large. There are many regulatory bodies whose rules and regulations must be followed by all companies, including tour operators, e.g. Companies House and HM Revenue and Customs. Specific regulatory authorities concerned with tour operating include:

- The Civil Aviation Authority (CAA) – the UK's independent aviation regulator and controller of air traffic services. It manages the UK's largest system of consumer protection for travellers, the Air Travel Organisers' Licence (ATOL) used by tour operators;
- The Health and Safety Executive (HSE) – responsible for many aspects of the safe operation of tour operators' products and services;
- Trading Standards Officers – enforce the Package Travel Regulations (see below);
- The Foreign and Commonwealth Office (FCO) – advises on travel to and from all parts of the world, including those seen as a risk to UK travellers.

Weblink @ Check out these websites for more information on the work of the CAA, HSE and FCO

www.caa.co.uk; www.hse.gov.uk; www.fco.gov.uk

Legal framework

Tour operators must follow a variety of consumer protection and contract laws and regulations when carrying out their business activities, as the following sections of this unit explain.

Package Travel Regulations

The Package Travel, Package Holidays and Package Tours Directive was adopted in June 1990 and came into operation on 1 January 1993 in the then 12 Member States of the European Union as the Package Travel, Package Holidays and Package Tour Regulations. The main aim of the Regulations is to give people buying package holidays more protection and access to compensation when things go wrong, while at the same time harmonising the rules covering packages operated throughout European Union countries. The provisions of the Directive did not replace national laws and, in the case of the UK, simply consolidated existing legislation and industry codes of conduct. The Package Travel Directive has, nonetheless, caused something of a stir in the UK travel and tourism industry, given its wide-ranging powers and scope. Up to the introduction of the Regulations, tour operators had been able to disclaim responsibility when holiday arrangements went wrong, for example overbooking at a hotel or the failure of a coach transfer to arrive, on the grounds that they had no control over these unfortunate events. Under the terms of the Package Travel Regulations, tour organisers must accept legal responsibility for all the services they offer to travellers. Exceptions would be made in circumstances which could neither have been foreseen nor overcome, although in such circumstances, organisers must give all necessary assistance to consumers.

The Package Travel Regulations place a number of duties and responsibilities on the organisers of packages, namely:

- Providing information to customers on who is responsible for the package they have booked. That person or organisation is then liable in the event of failure to deliver any elements of the package;
- Providing clear contract terms;
- Giving emergency telephone numbers;
- Providing proof of the organiser's security against insolvency and information on any available insurance policies;
- Giving immediate notification with explanation of any increase in prices permitted within the terms of the contract;
- Providing a variety of compensation options if agreed services are not supplied;
- Producing accurate promotional material including brochures.

The Regulations apply to packages sold or offered for sale in the UK, regardless of the operator's place of establishment. They do not apply to packages sold in other countries by operators established in the UK, although similar provisions apply in other member states of the European Union and in those countries that are part of the European Economic Area (EEA). The Regulations do not apply to packages sold in the Channel Islands or the Isle of Man, although the regulations do apply to organisers based in these areas, or anywhere else in the world, who sell their packages within the UK.

The Package Travel Regulations are designed to protect holidaymakers

Trade Descriptions Act

This Act protects consumers against false descriptions made knowingly or recklessly by anybody selling products and services, including holidays and other travel products. Any description of, for example, a hotel or resort must be truthful at the time it was written (if circumstances change, then the company must inform the customer of the nature of the changes). The Act places a duty on owners and operators of travel and tourism facilities to produce brochures, websites and other promotional materials that are not intended to deceive customers.

Supply of Goods and Services Act 1982 (as amended by the Sale and Supply of Goods Act 1994)

This legislation states that any contract for a holiday should be carried out using 'reasonable care and skill'. The tour operator and travel agent should ensure that the booking is carried out correctly and that the holiday itself should be of a generally satisfactory standard, complying with any descriptions made. Tour operators must take great care when selecting accommodation, transport and any services they provide as part of their package holidays.

Consumer Protection Act

The Consumer Protection Act makes it a criminal offence for an organisation or individual to give misleading price information about goods, services, accommodation or facilities they are offering for sale. The Act defines a misleading price as one which:

- Is greater than the price given in any promotional material;
- Is described as being generally available, but in reality is only available in certain circumstances;
- Does not fully state what facilities are included in the price and the fact that surcharges will be payable after booking.

The Act has special significance for tour operators, which must ensure the accuracy of any price information in their brochures and other online publicity material. This is because it is an offence to include incorrect price information even if the inclusion was innocently undertaken, but is later shown to be misleading.

Unfair Contract Terms Act 1977 and Unfair Contract Terms in Consumer Contracts Regulations 1999

These laws allow customers to challenge any terms in a contract that they consider to be unfair or unreasonable, unfairly weighted against them, or that are ambiguous.

Standard contract terms should be written in clear, understandable language. It is illegal to have a contract term that attempts to restrict the customers' statutory rights or avoids responsibility for death or personal injury. In certain cases, the Office of Fair Trading (OFT) may be able to prevent a company from using an unfair contract term in the future.

Contract law

Contrary to popular belief, most contracts do not need to be in writing. From a lawyer's standpoint, a contract is any agreement that the law will enforce, whether in writing, verbal or implied, i.e. assumed from the conduct of the parties. Contracts range from the very simple, e.g. buying a drink at a resort complex, to the very complex, e.g. building a cruise ship. The law of contract is principally concerned with promises that constitute part of an agreed exchange. It governs such questions as which agreements the law will enforce, what obligations are imposed by the agreement and what will happen if the obligations are not carried out.

The following conditions must be satisfied if a contract is to be legally enforceable:

1. There must have been agreement between the parties on all material aspects of the contract;
2. The parties must have intended to create a legally binding contract;
3. There must be at least two parties to the contract.

It is an essential requirement of English law that, for a contract to be legally binding, each party must have agreed to provide something of value to the other. For example, when a customer books a package holiday, but the booking has yet to be confirmed, the contract between the customer and the tour operator may still be legally binding even where he or she has not yet paid for it. The important point is that the customer has promised to pay the price for the holiday when required to do so. The tour operator, by the same token, promises that the holiday is available.

It is important to remember that when a holidaymaker books a package holiday through a travel agent, the contract is between the customer and the tour operator, with the travel agent merely acting as an intermediary. It is against the tour operator that the customer must seek legal redress in the event of a breach of contract, although the travel agent may be liable to the customer for any other extras that are not part of the brochure holiday, such as currency exchange, airport car parking, travel insurance, etc.

Licensing and bonding

All tour operator members of ABTA must provide a bond securing their liability in respect of all forms of transportation, accommodation, travel and holiday arrangements, whether outside or within the UK. The bond is a formal undertaking from an approved bank or insurance company to pay a sum of money to ABTA or the Civil Aviation Authority (CAA) in the event of the company's financial failure. The bond monies are used primarily for the purpose of reimbursing customers who would otherwise lose money that they had already paid, so that:

- Clients whose holidays are actually taking place when a tour operator ceases trading can continue with their holiday as planned or be brought back to the UK;
- Clients who have yet to travel on holidays already paid for can get their money back when an operator fails;
- Alternative holiday arrangements can be made for clients, who have paid for trips that have yet to take place, when a tour operator ceases trading.

For bonding purposes, tour operators are classed as either licensable or non-licensable. Licensable activities are those that require the operator to hold an Air Travel Organisers' Licence (ATOL); all other tour operations are classed as non-licensable. The CAA bonds provided by ATOL holders provide the first line of defence for licensable activities when things go wrong, whereas ABTA bonds provided by members fulfil the same function in respect of non-licensable activities.

FOCUS ON INDUSTRY

AIR TRAVEL ORGANISERS' LICENCE (ATOL)

An ATOL is a licence issued by the Civil Aviation Authority (CAA) and is required by all individuals and companies selling holidays and seats on charter flights. Applicants must show that they are fit to hold an ATOL, have adequate financial arrangements and must lodge a bond with the CAA. In the event of company failure, the bond money is used to repatriate clients who might otherwise be stranded overseas and to refund, as far as possible, passengers who have paid in advance but have yet to travel. Where the bond is insufficient to meet all claims, the Air Travel Reserve Fund, managed by the CAA, meets the shortfall.

Weblink Check out this website for more information on ATOLs.
www.caa.co.uk

External influences on tour operators

The tragic natural and human events that have occurred around the world since the start of the new millennium serve to illustrate the uncertain conditions that all tour operators face in the course of their work. They have to take into account a range of external influences as shown in Figure 13.3 and described in the following sections of this unit.

Fig 13.3 – External influences on tour operators

Environmental factors

Natural disasters, such as hurricanes, volcanic eruptions, floods and avalanches, can have serious consequences on an area's travel and tourism sector. The Asian tsunami that affected Indian Ocean countries in late 2004 and Hurricane Katrina's devastation of New Orleans in 2005 are examples that are all too familiar, as is the hurricane that devastated much of Haiti in January 2010. The 2010 eruptions of the Icelandic volcano and subsequent ash cloud over Europe is another case in point. Air travel was halted at an instant, with serious consequences for airlines, tour operators and other travel and tourism industries. Although tourism can be badly affected very quickly when natural disasters occur, the sector has proved itself to be very resilient in the face of adversity. Tourism in areas affected by natural disasters usually returns to its former state, on the back of investment in new hotels, infrastructure and other tourist facilities.

Accidents or deliberate acts of vandalism that lead to oil spillages and chemical leaks can have localised impacts on tourism. The Sea Empress oil spill off the coast of Pembrokeshire in February 1996 had a devastating impact on the county's tourism industry in that year and in subsequent summer seasons. The outbreak of foot and mouth disease (FMD) in 2001 had a severe impact on tourism in many rural parts of Britain. Research carried out for the Countryside Agency estimated a loss of £2-3 billion in tourism revenue in 2001.

Although it is impossible to predict when disasters of the type described above will occur, tour operators must have contingency plans in place should they be needed.

> **Weblink**
> 
> Check out this page of the Federation of Tour Operators' website for advice on crisis management for tour operators.
> **www.fto.co.uk/operators_factfile/uk_operational_support/**

Political factors

Political acts such as war and terrorism can have devastating impacts on a destination and its travel and tourism sector. This is particularly true when the destination is heavily reliant on tourism and has few other economic activities. The effects of the 9/11 disaster on world travel still persist today, while recent bombings in Bali, Nairobi, Madrid and Cairo, have immediate impacts on tourism, although most destinations eventually recover lost trade. Strikes and industrial disputes, for example at airports and railway stations, can also disrupt travel and tourism, thereby affecting tour operations.

Economic factors

Tour operations can be a risky business! A sudden change in world currency exchange rates can wipe out a company's profit margins overnight. Similarly, rises in the cost of oil and other natural resources can push up a tour operator's costs and affect its profitability. Holiday companies use a number of mechanisms to try and reduce the impacts of these situations. They can pay for foreign currency and commodities in advance when rates are favourable and sometimes pass the extra costs on to travellers in the form of extra taxes and duties, e.g. in the form of an aircraft fuel surcharge or holiday supplement.

Social factors

Tour operating companies have to keep abreast of social changes and adapt their products to reflect a changing society. The fact that people are generally living longer, are choosing to have children later in life (or not have children at all), changes in the composition of families, working methods and the home/life balance, all impact on the products and services that tour operators offer their customers. For example, Ocean Village have introduced a greater number of 3-person berths on their cruise ships in response to the growing numbers of lone-parent families buying their holidays.

Tour operators are becoming increasingly aware of the impacts (good and bad) that their activities have on the destinations they use in their tour programmes, in particular how tourism can have harmful effects in areas such as exploitation, poverty, corruption and unemployment. A number of initiatives have been established to try to make tourism in developing countries a force for good, by attempting to alleviate poverty and by promoting sustainable principles and practices. These include the work of the Travel Foundation, Tourism Concern and the Tearfund charity.

Activity 13.2

Log on to the Travel Foundation's website (www.thetravelfoundation.org.uk) and produce an information sheet on the Foundation's aims, work, structure, partners, etc.

This activity is designed to provide evidence for P1.

Technological factors

The travel and tourism sector has always been at the forefront of new technological developments. The dramatic growth in the use of the internet for researching and booking holidays is having a major impact on the way that tour operators sell their holidays. Trends such as the rise in dynamic packaging (see page 49) and the computerised reservation systems (CRS) used by travel agents are changing the way that tour operators work.

Challenges to tour operators

We have seen that tour operators work in a very challenging and fast-moving business environment, sometimes having to react to changing circumstances at very short notice. Tour operators also face a range of business challenges, as the next sections of this unit describe.

Dynamic packaging

Dynamic packaging is when travellers use the internet to research their holidays and make their own travel arrangements direct with airlines, hotels, car hire companies, etc. It offers people greater flexibility than buying standard holidays from a travel agency and can sometimes work out cheaper as well. Dynamic packaging is a serious threat to tour operators and travel agencies, since they stand to lose business to these 'DIY travellers'. Many tour operators, traditional and online, are fighting back by offering customers a more tailor-made experience, using new web-based technologies. In effect, tour operators are themselves getting involved in dynamic packaging to maintain their market share.

Distribution channels and integration

New technologies, especially the internet, are having major impacts on the way that holidays are distributed to customers. Traditionally, a person would visit their local travel agency to get advice and book their holiday. This, of course, still happens up and down the country, but travellers are increasingly using the internet to research their holidays and make their own travel arrangements direct with airlines, hotels, car hire companies, etc., the process known as dynamic packaging that we discussed earlier in this unit. The major integrated travel companies are changing the way that they sell their holidays, with fewer high street travel agencies and more investment in internet technologies.

We saw earlier in this unit when discussing integration that many tour operators are part of much bigger travel groups, which own their own their own travel agencies and even airlines. Travel companies become integrated to improve their competitive position in the marketplace and increase their market share by having more control and benefiting from economies of scale, e.g. when a travel agency and tour operator are owned by the same organisation, company functions such as purchasing, finance and human resource management can be carried out by fewer staff, thereby reducing costs.

Budget airlines

One of the most important developments in the transport industry in recent years has been the introduction of budget or low-cost airlines, helped by the growth in internet use. The budget airlines, including easyJet, Ryanair, flybe and bmibaby, offer a cheap, 'no frills' service to people looking to travel on a budget. They are able to offer cheap fares by keeping support services to a minimum and selling direct to travellers via the internet and telephone, thereby saving travel agents' commission charges. They also use smaller regional airports that charge lower landing fees and the airlines sell ranges of add-on products, such as travel insurance, phone cards, car hire, rail tickets and accommodation on a commission basis. The low-cost carriers are having important impacts on the work of tour operators, some positive and some negative. On the positive side, tour operators are able to use the network of routes offered by the budget airlines when developing their holidays, thereby offering a greater variety of destinations at reduced prices. The negative impact is to do with the fact that travellers are using the low-cost airlines to put together their own holidays – dynamic packaging – often by-passing the need for a tour operator's services altogether.

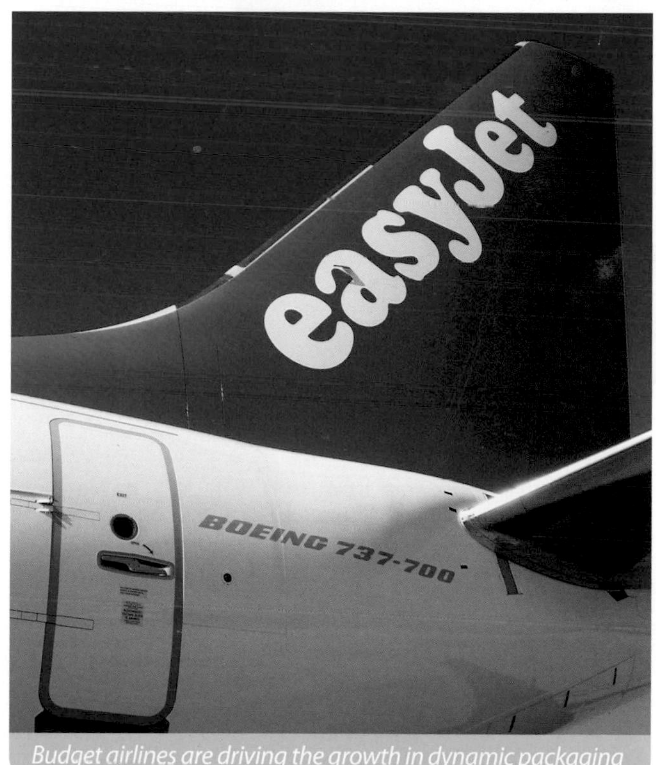

Budget airlines are driving the growth in dynamic packaging

Maintaining market share

Market share in tour operations refers to the percentage sales of holidays that a single company achieves. For example, if a tour operator specialising in safari holidays to an African country sells £10 million pounds worth of holidays per year and the total sales of safari holidays to that country is £100 million, the company is said to have a market share of 10 per cent. Maintaining market share is difficult in the competitive travel and tourism sector since competitor companies offering similar holidays will be constantly looking for ways to increase their market share. Tour operators try to maintain or even increase their market share in a number of ways:

- Through mergers and takeovers – buying a competitor company that offers similar holidays will immediately increase market share and reduce competition;
- By reducing prices – this can increase business and is often used when new companies start up;
- Increasing promotion – can raise awareness of a tour operator and lead to increased sales;
- Improving quality – this can improve customer satisfaction and increase repeat business and recommendations to friends and family members;
- Training staff – allows tour operators to improve customer service and selling skills.

Trend towards independent travel

In recent years there has been a gradual increase in independent travel at the expense of traditional package holidays taken by the British. Many people prefer to research their own holidays using guide books and the internet rather than visiting a travel agent or tour operator to book a package holiday. The following figures from the Office for National Statistics demonstrate this trend, showing a growth in independent travel overseas from 53.9 per cent of all holidays in 2004 to 60.7 per cent in 2008:

Year	Total no. of holidays	% independent	% packaged
2004	42.9m	53.9	46.1
2006	45.2m	58.2	41.8
2008	45.5m	60.7	39.3

Responsible tourism

Responsible tourism is all about developing tourism that does the least harm and provides the greatest benefit for destinations, tourists and the travel and tourism sector in the long-term. There are many different terms used to describe responsible tourism – sustainable tourism, green tourism, alternative tourism, ethical tourism, ecotourism, fair-trade tourism, slow tourism, soft tourism – but they all refer to the same type of tourism that is respectful of the environment and cultures of destinations and the people who live there (the host community). As companies who send millions of tourists to destinations across the world, tour operators have an important role to play in achieving responsible tourism, through education, sympathetic management and getting involved in projects that protect the environment and local communities.

Weblink

Check out this website for more information on how tour operators are helping to achieve responsible tourism in destinations.

www.toinitiative.org

Activity 13.3

Write a 500-word newspaper article that discusses the impact of challenges facing tour operators and evaluate the effectiveness of two named tour operators that are responding to the challenges.

This activity is designed to provide evidence for M1 and D1.

SECTION 2 Know the range of products and services offered by tour operators for different target markets

This section investigates the different categories of tour operators found in the UK, the products they offer and the different types of customers (target markets) they cater for.

Categories of tour operator

Tour operators come in all shapes and sizes! Most people are familiar with the big, well-known holiday companies that sell millions of holidays abroad every year, e.g. Thomas Cook and Thomson Holidays. Not so well-known are the many specialist operators that provide packaged and tailor-made holidays to meet particular customer needs, and the domestic operators that sell holidays and short breaks in this country. To complete the picture, inbound/incoming tour operators service the needs of overseas visitors to Britain.

We will look in detail at types of tour operators in the following categories:

1. Outbound – companies that offer holidays for British people travelling abroad;
2. Inbound – tour operators that service the needs of overseas visitors to the UK;
3. Domestic – companies that develop and sell holidays in Britain;
4. Specialist – holiday companies that specialise in a particular type of holiday or destination, for example golfing trips or expeditions to the Himalayas;
5. Mass-market – the large, well-known holiday companies that sell millions of package holidays every year.

Activity 13.4

Find out some detailed information on one tour operating company in each of the following categories:

1. Outbound;
2. Inbound;
3. Domestic;
4. Specialist;
5. Mass-market.

Produce a fact sheet on each company that describes the products and services it provides for its target market(s).

This activity is designed to provide evidence for P2.

Outbound tour operators

Outbound tour operators develop and sell holidays for British people wanting to travel abroad. Some are very big companies that sell millions of holidays every year – the so-called mass-market tour operators (see page 54) – while others are small and medium-sized enterprises (SMEs) employing just a few people.

As well as offering popular Mediterranean holiday destinations, tour operators are selling more packages to long-haul destinations, such as Florida, the Caribbean, Australia, New Zealand and the Far East, as travellers seek out new destinations and travel experiences. In recent years, there has also been a gradual move away from traditional package holidays and an increase in demand for more individualised, tailor-made holidays as people become more sophisticated and discerning. This is reflected in the numbers of passengers carried by the mass-market operators, which have fallen in recent years.

Another trend is the rise in popularity of internet-based tour operators (e-operators), which offer 24/7 access for customers and the chance for people to put together their own holidays. Leading operators in this field are lastminute.com, Expedia and ebookers. Tour operators are also developing new sales outlets for their products, such as interactive TV and telephone call centres. These trends are making the distinction between tour operators and travel agents less clear.

Inbound tour operators

Inbound, or incoming, UK tourism is concerned with meeting the needs of the increasing numbers of overseas visitors who choose to visit Britain – outbound tourism, on the other hand, deals with UK people taking holidays abroad. Just as we might visit a travel agency to book our annual overseas holiday or business trip abroad, many overseas visitors do the same in their own country when they want to come to Britain. A travel agent in the USA, for example, who has a client wanting to spend a week in Scotland, has to contact a tour operator to make all the arrangements. This operator, who may be based in the USA or in Scotland, is known as an incoming tour operator, since it is providing a service for incoming visitors to Britain. Many incoming tour operators in the UK are members of UKinbound, formerly BITOA – the British Incoming Tour Operators' Association.

Domestic tour operators

Domestic tour operators are companies that specialise in holidays in the UK for British people. They offer a very wide range of holiday products, from packages in holiday centres such as Center Parcs and Butlins, to coach holidays in all parts of Britain. Many domestic tour operators deal directly with their customers rather than selling through travel agents. This is partly to do with the fact that small, domestic operators are sometimes reluctant to pay commission to agents and also because many British people see travel agents as a place to go to book a holiday abroad. However, there are some domestic tour operators that sell packages through travel agents and pay commission, for example Superbreak, Hoseasons Holidays and Shearings.

FOCUS ON INDUSTRY

UKINBOUND

UKinbound was founded in 1977 as BITOA (the British Incoming Tour Operators' Association) and was renamed UKinbound in November 2004. Its main aim is to represent the interests of companies deriving a substantial part of their income from the provision of tours and tourism services for overseas visitors within Britain. UKinbound is concerned with helping its members to manage successful, profitable businesses that are part of a vibrant and sustainable inbound tourism industry. It does this by focusing on three key areas:

- Advocacy – to champion the interests of UKinbound members with government;
- Professionalism – to promote best practice and encourage lifelong learning through training and staff development;
- Networking – to provide opportunities for its members to develop relationships with suppliers, buyers and partners in the UK and overseas.

UKinbound members include Gullivers Sports Travel, Evan Evans Tours and Pathfinders.

Weblink

Check out this website for more information on the work of UKinbound.
www.ukinbound.org

Specialist tour operators

There is a growing demand for specialist tour operators from a travelling public that is looking for something more than the mass-market companies offer. There are literally hundreds of specialist tour operators in the UK travel and tourism sector, including:

- Companies offering holidays and other travel arrangements to a particular geographical region or destination, e.g. Pure Crete and Journey Latin America;

FOCUS ON INDUSTRY

SHEARINGS HOLIDAYS

Shearings Holidays is a major UK domestic tour operator specialising in coach holidays, aimed primarily at older people – the so called 'grey market'. Shearings is a diversified business providing cruise and air travel holidays as well as coach-based trips. In addition to its 300 coaches, the company's assets include a chain of 44 hotels and 8 high street travel agency shops. Shearings Holidays' core business is in operating coach tours, in the UK, the Irish Republic and continental Europe. In the British Isles, their destinations include London, traditional seaside resorts such as Newquay and Great Yarmouth, countryside areas such as Galway in Ireland and heritage destinations like Stratford-upon-Avon. Shearings also operates coach holidays to 17 different countries on the continent. The company employs approximately 3,000 people and serves a customer base of around three million, mostly in the over-50 age group. About a million passengers travel with the company every year.

Weblink Check out this website for more information on Shearings Holidays.
www.shearings.com

- Those that cater for a particular segment of the market, e.g. PGL Adventure Holidays for young children and Saga Holidays which specialises in the senior market;
- Operators that specialise in a particular type of activity, e.g. walking holidays offered by HF Holidays and Susi Madron's Cycling for Softies, which offers all-inclusive cycling packages to rural France;
- Tour operators that cater for the special interests of their clients, e.g. wine tasting holidays in the Loire and art history tours to Italy;
- Those that specialise in sporting holidays and breaks, e.g. Longshot Golfing Holidays and tours to see the Formula One Grand Prix around the world;
- Companies that use a specific type of accommodation or form of transport, e.g. Eurocamp, which organises self-drive camping holidays in the UK and on the Continent, and operators that offer tours on steam railways, e.g. Ffestiniog Travel.

Many specialist operators join the Association of Independent Tour Operators (AITO) to help their businesses grow and to develop the interests of the sector (there is a case study on AITO in *Travel and Tourism for BTEC National Book 1 3rd edition*).

Activity holidays are growing in popularity

Activity 13.5

Visit the AITO website (**www.aito.co.uk**) and choose one tour operator that offers holidays to Europe. Compile a fact sheet that describes the products and services offered by the tour operator, analysing how these meet the needs of its target market(s). Recommend, with justification, how the tour operator could expand its range of products and services for its current target market(s) or adapt its range of products and services to appeal to a new market.

This activity is designed to provide evidence for P2, M2 and D2.

Special interest groups are well catered for by domestic operators. Activity holidays are growing in popularity and tour operators, large and small, are emerging to cater for the demand, for example YHA Holidays, Acorn Adventures, PGL, HF Holidays and Cycleactive. Companies offering specialist services and facilities, ranging from sketching holidays to ballooning breaks, are being increasingly sought by people looking for something unusual to do in their leisure time.

Mass-market tour operators

The mass-market tour operators are amongst the best-known names in the travel and tourism sector, courtesy of their big advertising budgets! They include companies such as Thomson Holidays, Thomas Cook, Virgin Holidays and Cosmos. In many respects they are the supermarkets of the travel industry, since they sell large volumes of value-for-money holidays to millions of customers every year. Figures from the Civil Aviation Authority (CAA) for the year ending September 2010 give the top 10 tour operators in terms of passenger numbers carried as follows:

Tour operator	Passengers carried
TUI Travel	5,595,000
Thomas Cook Group	5,431,000
Monarch and Cosmos	660,000
Expedia	582,000
Virgin Atlantic	451,000
Travelworld Vacations	400,000
Co-operative Group	384,000
Trailfinders	347,816
Carnival Corporation	265,000
Kuoni Travel	173,000

Between them, TUI/Thomson and Thomas Cook arrange package holidays and flights for around 11 million UK travellers every year, accounting for just under 50 per cent of all such products sold.

CASE STUDY

Thomson Holidays

Introduction

Thomson Holidays is Britain's biggest tour operator, selling more package holidays and flights than any other travel company – a position it has held since 1974. It is part of TUI Travel plc, which was formed in 2007 from the merger of TUI UK Ltd, which included Thomson, with another mass-market, UK-based tour operator, First Choice Holidays. TUI UK is the UK's largest holiday company and part of the German-based TUI AG Group, the largest tourism and services group in the world, employing 80,000 people in 500 companies. TUI AG owns many of Europe's best-known holiday brands, including Thomson Holidays in the UK. It has leadership positions in airline, inclusive tour operations and travel agency sectors. The group employs 17,500 people in the UK, Ireland, Sweden, Norway, Denmark and Finland. TUI UK employs around 9,000 people, 7,000 of whom work overseas in some 40 holiday destinations.

History

In 1965, at the height of the boom in demand for package holidays to the sun, entrepreneur Lord Thomson bought three travel and tourism companies – the charter airline Britannia Airways and the tour operators Riviera Holidays and Universal Skytours. His companies continued to trade successfully, as demand for package holidays continued to rise. By the late 1960s, Thomson had introduced winter sun, cruise, and lakes and mountains package holidays to the UK mass market.

It was not, however, until 1972 that the brand name Thomson Holidays was created, when Lord Thomson combined his tour operating brands into one company. The package holidays market was continuing to grow rapidly and Thomson Holidays grew with it. By 1974, two more companies, Sunair and the high street travel agency Lunn Poly, had been brought into the Thomson fold. Thomson Holidays had now become the UK's largest vertically-integrated travel company, carrying out tour operator, transport principal and travel agent functions

Today, Thomson Holidays sells more package holidays than any other UK-based tour operator, making it the market leader in the air-inclusive holiday sector. Its head office is in London, but the majority of its 3,000 employees work overseas.

Distribution and branding

Thomson's UK retail distribution channels include:

- Thomson travel agencies – more than 650 retail stores;
- Thomson UK's call centre operation;
- Thomson's website **www.thomson.co.uk**, where customers can research, book and pay for holidays online.
- Through these channels, Thomson sells around 5 million holidays and flights per year.

As well as the main Thomson tour operating brand, Thomson's portfolio also includes several specialist and niche holiday brands, including Jetsave, Jersey Travel, Simply Travel, Headwater Holidays, the Magic Travel Group, Crystal Holidays, Thomson Ski and Snowboarding, and Thomson Lakes and Mountains.

Airline operations

For more than 40 years, Britannia Airways was Thomson's charter airline and the world's leading holiday airline. This changed on May 1st 2005 when TUI UK's aircraft fleet was renamed and re-branded as Thomsonfly, to reflect the single Thomson name that now applies to all parts of the group's operations. The airline was renamed Thomson Airways in 2008 and has a fleet of 77 planes flying to more than 80 destinations around the world. Based at London Luton Airport, the airline carries more than 5.5 million passengers abroad every year and employs over 5,000 people in the UK.

Case Study Questions and Activities

1. What are the advantages to TUI UK of owning its own tour operations, travel agency and airline companies?
2. Log on to the Thomson website (www.thomson.co.uk) and make a list of the different tour operating brands that it offers in the UK. Why do you think it has so many brands available to customers?
3. Analyse how TUI/Thomson's portfolio of products and services meets the needs of its target markets.
4. Recommend how TUI/Thomson could expand its range of products and services for its current target markets or adapt its range of products and services to appeal to a new market.

This activity is designed to provide evidence for P2, M2 and D2.

Some material in this case study is reproduced with permission from Travel & Tourism Case Studies by Stephen Rickerby (ISBN 9780955019067).

Weblink

Check out this website to help answer these questions and for more information on Thomson Holidays/TUI Travel.

www.thomson.co.uk

Products

Figure 13.4 shows a breakdown of the main products sold by the four main categories of UK-based tour operators. They all sell package holidays of one type or another, although the mass-market operators we discussed earlier in this unit offer the standard packages that are so familiar today.

Package holidays

At its simplest, a package holiday is an arrangement that includes transport to a destination, accommodation, transfer arrangements and the services of a representative for an all-inclusive price. Tour operators assemble these different components into a saleable product that meets the needs and expectations of the customer. They are sold though travel agents and via less traditional distribution channels, such as the internet, TV and call centres.

The introduction of the package holiday has been one of the great success stories of the travel and tourism sector in the last 50 years. Sales of package holidays really took off in the early 1970s and have continued to grow ever since, with a slight tailing off in recent years due to the growth in independent travel and the global economic recession (see Figure 13.5). Low prices have given millions of British people the chance to travel abroad for the first time.

Today, however, package holidays are under threat from the growth of low-cost airlines and the internet, which allow people to assemble their own holidays, bypassing travel agents and tour operators altogether. Increasing numbers of people are looking for an 'unpackaged holiday', individually tailored to their particular needs and desires.

Tailor-made holidays

Tailor-made travel arrangements involve designing all aspects of a customer's holiday on an individual

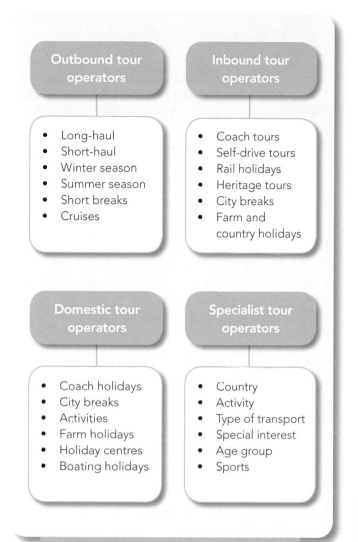

Outbound tour operators

- Long-haul
- Short-haul
- Winter season
- Summer season
- Short breaks
- Cruises

Inbound tour operators

- Coach tours
- Self-drive tours
- Rail holidays
- Heritage tours
- City breaks
- Farm and country holidays

Domestic tour operators

- Coach holidays
- City breaks
- Activities
- Farm holidays
- Holiday centres
- Boating holidays

Specialist tour operators

- Country
- Activity
- Type of transport
- Special interest
- Age group
- Sports

Fig13.4 – The range of tour operators' products

basis rather than selling a ready-assembled package holiday. The customer benefits by getting a holiday that is individually tailored to their needs, but it does mean more work for the tour operator. This type of arrangement is growing in popularity as more people seek out holidays and destinations that offer something different.

FOCUS ON INDUSTRY

TAILOR-MADE ARRANGEMENTS AT NATIONAL HOLIDAYS

National Holidays specialises in coach-based holidays and short breaks in the UK and Continental Europe. For groups of 30 or more, the company offers tailor-made travel and accommodation arrangements. Members of the group choose the resort, hotel, meal arrangements and excursions, and the company designs the holiday to meet the needs of the group. The group organiser can either discuss arrangements with a member of National Holidays' staff or complete an online form for a quotation.

Weblink @ Check out this website for more information on National Holidays.
www.nationalholidays.com

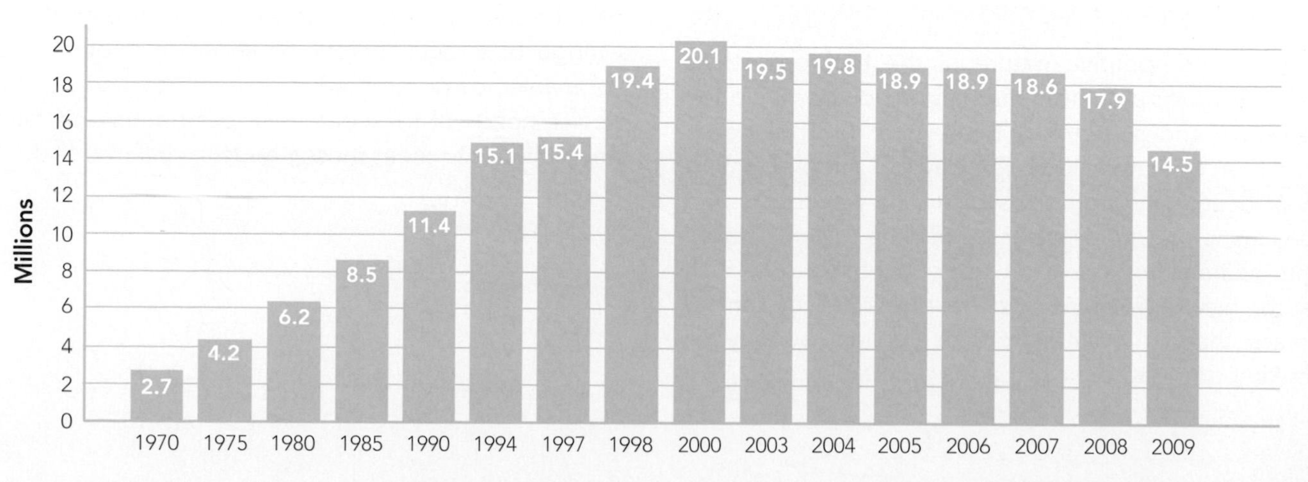

Fig 13.5 – Overseas package holidays taken by British people 1970-2009

More tour operators are using internet-based systems to help them assemble tailor-made travel solutions for customers. This is known as dynamic packaging, since it is totally driven by the needs of the customer. This is a trend that will grow as travellers look for a more personal service from tour operators and the companies themselves react to developments in new technology.

Destination, accommodation and transport options

Tour operations has developed a great deal since the introduction of the first package holiday more than 50 years ago. Developments in aircraft technology and reductions in prices have opened up new, long-haul destinations, including Florida, the Caribbean, Brazil, Mexico, Dubai, the Far East, Australia and New Zealand. At the same time, tourist boards have helped businesses to improve accommodation standards by introducing quality grading schemes in destinations. New board arrangements, such as the introduction of all-inclusive hotels and resorts have given visitors greater holiday choices. In addition to aircraft developments, high-speed rail services that cut travel times between major cities continue to be developed across the world. The growth of low-cost airlines, firstly in the USA and Europe but now spreading to India and Asia, is having a major impact on travel patterns and the development of new holiday destinations.

Ancillary products and services

The very competitive nature of the tour operations industry means that profit margins on holidays are often very low (and sometimes non-existent!). This means that tour operators look for ways of supplementing their income through sales of ancillary products and services, either in-resort or before their clients travel. The income they make on the sale of add-ons, such as car hire, excursions and travel insurance, can be greater than the profit margin on a holiday, so they are very important to the company's profitability.

Activity 13.6

Look through a variety of tour operators' brochures (outbound and domestic) and draw up a list of the different types of ancillary products and services they offer. Make a note of the similarities and differences you find between operators.

This activity is designed to provide evidence for P2.

Target markets

A 'target market' refers to the customers that a tour operator is trying to attract to buy its holidays. Typical target markets for which tour operators develop holidays include:

- Singles;
- Families;
- Couples without children;
- Groups;
- Special interest market;
- Business travellers;
- Youth market;
- Activity market;
- Senior market;
- People with specific needs.

A tour operator may concentrate on a single target market or develop holidays that appeal to a variety of customers. Himalayan Kingdoms, for example, has a very clearly-defined target market – people wanting a trekking holiday in the Himalayas. Thomas Cook, on the other hand, offers a wide variety of holidays to suit a range of target markets, as shown in Figure 13.6. Companies carry out market research to find out the precise needs of their particular customers and tailor their holidays to meet these needs.

Activity 13.7

Using the information in Figure 13.6 as a guide draw up a similar chart that shows Thomson Holidays' portfolio of holiday products/brands.

This activity is designed to provide evidence for P2.

Product	Brand
Package holidays (upper market range)	Thomas Cook
Package Holidays (lower market range)	Airtours
Direct sell packages	Direct Holidays
Scheduled flight packages	Thomas Cook Signature
Specialist products	Club 18-30/ Neilson/ Tradewinds
City breaks	Bridge/Signature/Cresta
Self-catering	Style Villas
Family market	Holiday Resorts/Disneyland Paris
Special occasions	Thomas Cook weddings

Fig 13.6 – Thomas Cook holiday products

SECTION 3

Know how tour operators plan, sell, administer and operate a package holiday programme

All tour operators have to carry out a variety of inter-related functions in order to plan, sell, administer and operate their package holiday programmes successfully. The same basic functions are carried out whether the company is a large, mass-market operator or a small, specialist firm employing just a few people.

Planning a package holiday programme

There are three key elements to planning a package holiday programme:

1. Research, forecasting and product development;
2. Contracting;
3. Costing the package.

The planning process involves a great deal of data input from a variety of staff members, all working to agreed timescales. The next sections of this unit look at each of these in turn, based on how the functions are carried out in a typical mass-market tour operator.

Research, forecasting and product development

A great deal of background research is carried out to make sure that tour operators develop products that have the best chance of meeting their sales potential. Sources of market research data available to help tour operators with this process include:

- The company's own internal sales data – gives a tour operator a clear idea of which products and destinations are in demand and which may need to be deleted or revised;
- External sales data – available from commercial sources, this information gives a tour operator a benchmark against which to measure its own performance;
- Analysis of competitors' programmes – can be very helpful in identifying new themes, destinations or product development opportunities;
- Market research reports – from companies such as Deloitte & Touche, Mintel and Nielsen give useful information on future trends and forecasting in the tour operating industry;
- Government data – is a useful tool for analysing past visitor numbers to particular destinations overseas, for example using the International Passenger Survey (IPS);
- Analysis of customer satisfaction questionnaires – provides a tour operator with valuable feedback on a range of issues, such as quality of accommodation, customer service standards, price, etc.
- Financial analysis – essential for forecasting future revenue streams and profitability.

Tour operators' research staff work with marketing department colleagues to identify potential new market opportunities, as well as assessing the changing needs, expectations and tastes of past customers. This is achieved by studying sales statistics and market research surveys. They particularly look at the feedback collected from existing customers via CSQs (customer satisfaction questionnaires). Staff try to predict what holidaymakers will want, in terms of which resorts, what type and length of holiday, what standard of accommodation, which departure airports and what price they are prepared to pay.

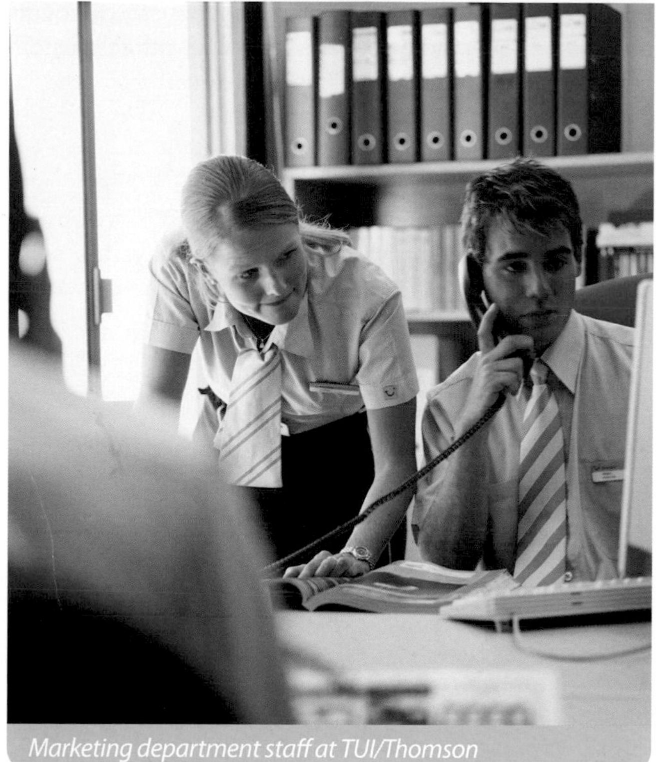
Marketing department staff at TUI/Thomson

In large tour operating companies, it is the staff employed in the marketing department who are responsible for product development, i.e. planning and designing new holidays based on market research findings. They focus on the selection of resorts, choice of accommodation and selection of regional UK departure airports. Planning and organising a holiday programme does not happen overnight. Staff in the marketing department often start making plans for a season 12-18 months before the holidays go on sale. The first task is to assess the total number of holidays that will be taken during a season by all UK holidaymakers. Having calculated this total market figure, individual Brand Managers or Product Managers decide what share of the market it is realistic to sell – the programme capacity. Having decided on the capacity of the programme, detailed planning on how many holidays should be arranged in each resort and what accommodation and flights are needed can begin. Marketing staff are also responsible for the key activity of pricing the holidays, which can be very risky given the advance planning necessary before the launch of a programme and the potential for fluctuations in currency exchange rates and aviation fuel prices.

Activity 13.8

Draw a flow chart of the main tasks involved in developing a package holiday programme to a new long-haul destination in South America. Include timescales and staff/departmental responsibilities in your chart.

This activity is designed to provide evidence for P3.

Methods of contracting

Once the structure of a tour operator's programme is finalised, staff in the contracts department negotiate with accommodation providers over the number of beds and type of accommodation required. This function is often the responsibility of senior management, under the direction of the Overseas Regional Manager, who may be assisted by specific Product Managers. The staff involved in contracting the accommodation and related services have to negotiate on price, quantity and quality, within a very competitive environment. It is likely that other mass-market operators will be using the same hotels in their programmes. An operator may try to negotiate exclusive use of particular accommodation, but this will involve a financial commitment on behalf of the operator that it may not be willing to risk.

There are three main types of contracts used in tour operating:

- Commitment/guarantee – where the tour operator guarantees to pay for a certain number of bed spaces;
- Allocation and release back – where the tour operator agrees an allocation of a certain number of bed spaces with the hotel and agrees to give back any that it has not sold by a certain date;
- Ad hoc – this is the most flexible arrangement, when a tour operator agrees a contract (discounted) rate with a hotelier and makes bookings as and when required.

Negotiations on contract terms usually start a year before the holidays are sold.

Tour operators negotiate contract rates with hoteliers

At the same time as accommodation contracting is under way the flight programmes have to be negotiated, either with their own in-house airline in the case of the large tour operators, or with charter or scheduled airlines in the case of smaller tour operators. In large tour operating companies, teams working on different programmes and products liaise with the flight or aviation department over how many seats they will need, which regional airports are to be used and whether day or night flights are required. The flight department must make optimum use of its resources, which includes selling spare capacity in the flight-only market. Contracts are generally agreed more than 12 months in advance of holidays going on sale.

Costing the package

Section 4 of this unit looks in detail at the process of costing a package holiday (see page 67). Pricing holidays has to be based on the best available knowledge and experience. A mass-market tour operator that sets the prices of its main summer programme holidays too high in relation to its competitors will not achieve optimum levels of sales. Too low, on the other hand, and it will find it difficult to produce an adequate profit.

We have seen that tour operators rely on obtaining the elements of their tour programmes at discounted rates, from suppliers such as hoteliers and airlines, which are happy to negotiate a discount in return for releasing an agreed amount of stock. Discounting is also prevalent at the other end of the distribution chain, namely discounted holidays offered for sale in travel agencies, via the internet and on TV channels. In the past, tour operators often frowned on travel agents that offered cut-price holidays, but in today's very competitive holiday industry discounts are a common way for a travel agent to attract custom and for tour operators to sell unsold stock.

Selling package holidays

This section looks at how package holidays are sold, starting with brochure production.

Brochure production

Even in this digital age, brochures are amongst the tour operator's most important sales tools, although they often cause storage problems for travel agents! Brochures provide clients with detailed information, images and prices designed to persuade them to make a booking. In particular, brochures aim to:

- Accurately present products and services to the reader;
- Supply product information to travel agents;
- Convey an image of the company;
- Offer a means of booking a holiday;
- Explain booking and contractual conditions;
- Present the information within the bounds of current UK and European Union legislation.

Above all, brochures should be designed in such a way that they have the best chance of converting enquiries into sales. Teams working in a tour operator's marketing department will liaise with brochure production staff to finalise design, copy (the words that are written) and images.

Figure 13.7 lists the main stages in the brochure production process for tour operators, starting with the design brief that is given to the in-house or agency designers and ending with the final product distributed to travel agents or direct to the public. It is common for new editions of brochures to be issued with revised prices, but this can cause confusion with travel agents and clients. Many companies now update their brochure prices via their websites to save time and re-printing costs. A lot of brochure printing takes place outside the UK to save on costs.

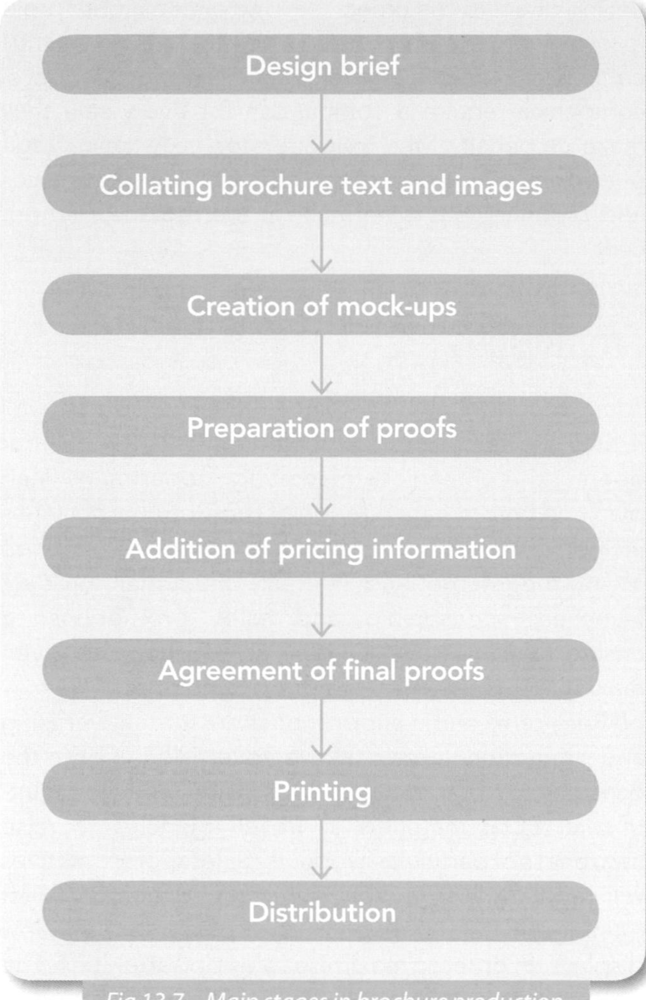

Fig 13.7 – Main stages in brochure production

The ABTA Tour Operators' Code of Conduct lays down the minimum standards for brochures, requiring that they contain clear, comprehensive and accurate descriptions of facilities and services offered. It details rules that govern booking conditions in brochures as they relate, for example, to the cancellation or alteration of tours, holidays or other travel arrangements by the tour operator. The Code also contains strict rules concerning the prompt handling of complaints and regulations relating to the business relationships between tour operators and travel agents.

Weblink Check out this website for more information on the ABTA Tour Operators' Code of Conduct.

www.abta.com

Activity 13.9

Carry out an analysis of six summer sun brochures from different tour operators and rate them on the following points:

1. Overall quality and content;
2. Use of images;
3. Style of copy;
4. Ease of use.

Make suggestions as to how the shortcomings you identified could be improved.

This activity is designed to provide evidence for P3.

Brochures are an important sales tool

Pricing strategies

There are two basic strategies that tour operators can use to arrive at the cost of a package holiday programme:

1. Cost-based pricing;
2. Market-based pricing.

Cost-based pricing involves calculating all the fixed and variable costs of a tour product, including any commission payments to agents, and setting the price at a level which covers all these costs and allows a profit margin. This is the method adopted by small, specialist operators who are unlikely to be operating in such a competitive environment as the mass-market holiday companies and whose products will have a degree of uniqueness. In large tour companies, it is not always easy to work out the exact proportion of fixed costs that should be levied on a tour programme.

Sometimes referred to as 'what the market will bear', market-based pricing sets pricing in a wider context by taking account of what competitors are charging when determining prices. Revising prices for package holidays is now commonplace among tour operators that are constantly checking competitor activity and making adjustments to maintain their market share. Following the market leader's pricing is a risky business, if a company has not fully taken into account its own costs of operation. The hope is that the economies of scale involved in tour operating will enable the larger operators to reduce their costs, but still allow a profit margin at the end of the day. In reality, pricing a typical package holiday programme is often a combination of both market-based and cost-based approaches.

Distribution

Tour operators sell their holidays through a variety of distribution channels, including:

- Travel agents;
- Online travel companies, e.g. Expedia, lastminute.com, etc.
- Direct to customers via the internet, telephone, television and brochures;
- In conjunction with newspapers and magazines.

Selling direct to customers tends to offer a higher profit margin for the tour operator, since there is no agents' commission to pay. Travel agents and online travel companies require a commission for every sale they make on behalf of the tour operator, i.e. a percentage of the total selling price. This varies between companies and products, but is normally in the region of 10 per cent.

Promotions

Tour operators must promote their products well if they are to reach their sales targets. In large tour operating companies, marketing department staff plan and co-ordinate a range of promotional activities including advertising in newspapers, magazines, on TV, on the internet and Teletext, direct mail, product launches, sponsorship and sales promotions to ensure that the travel company's products are given maximum exposure and sales opportunities. This may be long-term brand support or short-term advertising and promotion. It may involve advertising in both the consumer and trade press, or using special point-of-sale (POS) materials in travel agencies to raise awareness of particular products. Sales representatives will regularly visit travel agencies and offer product training and POS materials, such as posters and window displays, in order to maximise sales opportunities. The travel agencies that sell the most holidays will receive particular attention, including enhanced incentives for management and staff to encourage and reward high-volume sales.

Reservations

Tour operators employ reservations staff to handle bookings from travel agents and direct from the public. Most tour operators, whether large or small, use computerised reservation systems to process bookings, offer alternatives if a first choice of holiday is not available and generate the paperwork associated with a sale. With the growth in the use of the internet for online bookings, which are often confirmed electronically, many reservations staff are now found in call centres, handling high volumes of phone calls from agents and the public. Call centre staff are fully trained in the details of the products included in a tour operator's brochure or on its website. Large tour operators have separate reservations teams handling, for example, group bookings, winter ski holidays, cruises and last-minute sales.

Call centres are growing in popularity

Administration

The tour operator's administration department is responsible for producing invoices, receiving payments and issuing tickets and other documentation. Staff also produce passenger lists, known as manifests, for distribution to airlines, hoteliers, ground handling agents and resort representatives, plus carry out the full range of everyday administrative duties associated with the operation of a commercial concern.

Activity 13.10

Working as part of a small group, list the main tasks that would be undertaken by staff in the administration department of a major outbound tour operator. Use your list as the basis for drawing up a job description and person specification for the permanent post of Administrative Assistant for a mass-market operator based in Manchester.

This activity is designed to provide evidence for P3.

Operations

As well as being responsible for researching, planning, costing, promoting and selling package holidays as described earlier in this unit, UK-based tour operations staff have a number of important operational duties to perform to ensure that holidays run as smoothly as possible, including:

- Managing changes – to travel arrangements and bookings, e.g. overbooking, cancellations, errors, name changes, flight/coach transfers, consolidations (when a flight is cancelled and its passengers are transferred to another), etc.
- Duty office – this is the main link between resorts and UK operations, manned 24 hours a day in case of problems. In extreme cases of emergency, duty office staff can charter aircraft to repatriate customers as the need arises;
- Customer service – handles all aspects of the customer/tour operator interface before departure, in-resort and post-holiday.

In addition to these functions, the UK operations side of the tour operator handles personnel/human resource issues, including all recruitment for the UK and overseas operations, job evaluation, employee appraisal, training, payments to staff and pensions' management, plus all administrative matters related to employees and their welfare. Staff in the finance department handle the flow of revenue into the business and payments to suppliers in the UK and overseas. Senior staff will be responsible for meeting planned sales and revenue targets and managing budgets. The legal department advises on a range of matters, such as the content of contracts, health and safety matters, accuracy of brochure copy and statutory regulations concerning the company and its relationship with customers and suppliers.

Overseas operations

As well as having a general duty to provide a high standard of service to the tour operator's customers while abroad, staff in the overseas office of a major UK tour operator will have a number of specific responsibilities, including:

- Checking passenger manifests (lists of customers travelling);
- Organising transfers to and from the accommodation and airport;
- Selling and arranging excursions and other extras such as car hire;
- Finalising contracts with hoteliers and transport operators;
- The well-being, training and deployment of representatives;
- The handling of complaints and emergencies;
- Crisis management in the event of a major incident;
- Ensuring health and safety procedures are followed by staff and customers;
- Feeding back to the UK office any formal or informal research findings.

Smaller, specialist UK operators may have a small number of permanent employees based in overseas resorts, but will also use the services of seasonal and part-time UK staff. They also rely on the services of specialist individuals and companies in the resorts to provide a range of ground handling services, such as a 'meet and greet' service, coach transfers and welcome meetings for clients.

Activity 13.11

Design an illustrated chart that shows the different roles carried out in the UK and overseas by a major, mass-market tour operator.

This activity is designed to provide evidence for P3.

Commercial considerations

First and foremost tour operators are in business to make a profit. The secret of a profitable tour operating business is to keep costs to a minimum while at the same time maximising income – the bigger the difference between the two, the higher the profit! Senior managers must monitor all the costs associated with running the business and try to negotiate the lowest possible rates with suppliers, whether they be telephone companies, office equipment companies or banks. Also, they must negotiate the best rates when agreeing contracts with hotels and transport companies. Changes in currency exchange rates can have a serious impact of profitability. Some tour operators buy currency in advance when rates are favourable to offset this. Savings can also be made in the level of commission paid to travel agents. Lowering these commission rates will save the tour operator's costs, but will not be welcomed by the agents. Tour operators can use a variety of techniques to maximise income, for example selling extras such as car hire, airport parking, travel insurance, etc., and investing any surplus funds they may have to earn interest.

SECTION 4 Be able to plan and cost a package holiday

The final section of this unit gives you practice in planning and costing a typical package holiday, while gaining an appreciation of some of the factors that affect a tour operator's profitability.

Planning a package holiday

Section 3 of this unit has shown that a great deal of time and effort goes into planning a package holiday programme. Tour operators have to make decisions on:

- Destinations – how many and which to include in a tour programme;
- Transport – what types to offer, plus which departure and arrival points to use;
- Accommodation – location, type, quality and quantity needed;
- Excursions – whether included or optional, what type to meet customer needs;
- Additional services – for example, travel and accommodation upgrades, insurance, car hire, airport parking, etc.

Costing a package holiday

Calculating prices of package holiday programmes is one of the most difficult and risky aspects of the tour operating business. Tour operators have to consider a number of important factors when determining the final selling price of a holiday, including:

- The contracted rates that have been agreed with accommodation providers, airlines, car hire companies, transfer service providers, etc.
- Seasonal adjustments, e.g. low prices for the 'shoulder season' (either side of the peak) and higher prices for peak season demand;
- Load factor on the aircraft, i.e. the percentage of seats that need to be filled before the tour operator breaks even and begins to make a profit;
- Fixed costs, e.g. the cost of hiring a transfer coach is the same regardless of the number of passengers carried;
- Variable costs, e.g. credit card charges, which will increase as the number of holidays sold increases;
- Indirect costs, e.g. head office overheads;
- Direct operating costs, e.g. the cost of accommodation;
- Profit margins, i.e. the percentage added to the net selling price, covering all indirect costs and allowing for a profit.

Fixed costs are costs that do not alter with changes in the level of business activity, whereas variable costs alter in direct proportion to the volume of business generated by the tour operator. Examples of both types are given in Figure 13.8.

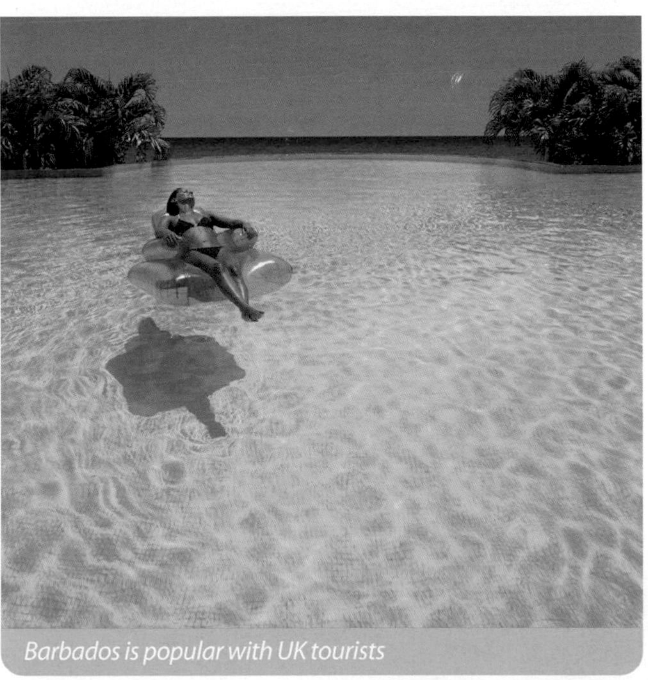

Barbados is popular with UK tourists

Fixed Costs	Variable costs
• Rates • Rent or mortgage • Interest on loans • Bonding monies • Maintenance • Cleaning • Insurance • Staff salaries • Lighting and heating • Market research	• Postage • Telephone, fax and internet • Computer and equipment hire • Printing and stationery • Advertising and publicity • Part-time staff • Professional fees and charges • Bank charges • Transaction charges, e.g. credit cards

Fig 13.8 – Fixed and variable costs in tour operations

Figure 13.9 shows a detailed costing for a package holiday to Corfu. The direct costs of the holiday are £324.37 per person. The tour operator uses this figure to determine a selling price that covers these costs plus an additional amount (mark up) to cover (1) a proportion of the fixed costs of the holiday; (2) any commission payments to travel agents and (3) a profit margin. The exact price charged will depend on a number of factors, including prices of similar holidays offered by competitors, the cost of the holiday last year and the season in which the holiday is taken.

If we assume a mark-up of 20 per cent, the final brochure price of the holiday to Corfu would be £324.37 + £64.87 = £389.24 per person.

Costing a package holiday to the Corfu – 14 nights half-board

Flight costs	£
26 return flights during the season @ £18,000 per flight	468,000
Empty leg at beginning and end of season	18,000
Total flight costs	486,000
Cost per occupied flight (£486,000 divided by 26)	18,692
Cost per seat based on 90% load factor on Boeing 737 with capacity of 168 passengers	123.62
Hotel costs per person for 14 nights	190.00
Transfers and handling fees per person	10.75
Total costs of package per person	£324.37
Final selling price (+20% mark-up)	£389.24

Fig 13.9 – Costing a package holiday to Corfu

Most holidaymakers travel by air

Activity 13.12

Your uncle has always wanted to set up a business offering walking holidays in the Pyrenees, after many years of enjoying similar holidays with HF Holidays, Headwater and Ramblers' Holidays. He has asked you to help him research the idea and put together a programme for six week-long tours in May and September. If these go well, he hopes to expand the number of weeks in future years. He will lead the tours himself and take no more than 12 walkers on each tour.

You will need to carry out some in-depth research to address the following points:

1. Which destination(s) to use in the Pyrenees;
2. What transport arrangements to get to the Pyrenees would suit best;
3. What type of accommodation is needed and on what accommodation basis;
4. What excursions and activities should be included in the package;
5. What precise dates and timescales should be agreed.

You can assume that all suppliers will give you discounted, inclusive tour (IT) rates for accommodation, travel, excursions, etc., but as this is a new venture you are only likely to be offered a discount of 25 per cent off their brochure rates, e.g. you will be charged £37.50 for a room that would appear in a hotel's tariff as £50.

Having designed and planned your package, you are now in a position to cost it. As with the example of the package holiday to Corfu on page xx, you will need to calculate all the direct costs of the holiday and add a mark-up of 20 per cent to cover fixed costs and a margin for profit. If you choose to fly your holidaymakers to the destination, you need not worry about load factors as you will be using a scheduled carrier (which could be one of the low-cost airlines).

Points to be bear in mind when costing include:

- Variations in accommodation and travel prices depending on the season;
- How your final prices compare with similar packages offered by other operators.

Present your planning and costing of the package as a short feasibility study, including all the information you have collected. Explain ways of maximising profitability during the different stages of planning, selling, administering and operating the package holidays.

This activity is designed to provide evidence for P4 and M3.

UNIT SUMMARY

This unit has examined the important role that tour operators play in the UK travel and tourism sector. You have examined the links between tour operators and other travel and tourism organisations, and considered the work of trade associations and regulatory bodies. The external influences on tour operations were discussed in detail, showing the impact of environmental, political, economic, social and technological factors on the work of tour operators. Different categories of tour operators and the products they offer to target markets have been explored in detail. You have seen that planning, selling, administering and operating a package holiday programme is a complex business, often giving only small profit margins. Finally, you were given the chance to plan and cost a package holiday of your own. Throughout the unit you have been shown examples of good industry practice in UK tour operations. The case studies on the FTO and Thomson Holidays gave an insight into the activities of a trade association and a mass-market, integrated tour operator.

If you have worked methodically, by the end of this unit you should:

- Understand the tour operations environment;
- Know the range of products and services offered by tour operators for different target markets;
- Know how tour operators plan, sell, administer and operate a package holiday programme;
- Be able to plan and cost a package holiday.

You are now in a position to complete the assignment for the unit, under the direction of your tutor. Before you tackle the assignment you may like to have a go at the following questions to help build your knowledge of tour operations.

TEST YOUR KNOWLEDGE

1. Why are tour operators sometimes thought of as wholesalers?
2. What is the difference between horizontal and vertical integration?
3. What is UKinbound and what activities does it undertake?
4. Name six members of the Federation of Tour Operators.
5. What is consolidation in tour operations?
6. What is an outbound tour operator?
7. Why are ancillary sales important to tour operators?
8. Why has the popularity of package holidays fallen in recent years?
9. What is an ATOL?
10. What sources of research are available to tour operators to help them plan their programmes?

11. What is the difference between a tour operator's fixed and variable costs?

12. List the main stages in the production of a tour operator's brochure.

13. Name three environmental and political events have affected tour operators in the last 5 years?

14. What impact is the internet having on the work of tour operators?

15. How do you think the tour operations industry will change in the next 10 years?

Answers to these questions can be found in the Book 2 Tutor's CD-ROM that accompanies this book (ISBN 9780956268075). Full details can be found at **www.tandtpublishing.co.uk**

UNIT 13 ASSIGNMENT

Tour Operations

Introduction

This assignment is made up of a number of tasks which, when successfully completed, are designed to give you sufficient evidence to meet the Pass (P), Merit (M) and Distinction (D) grading criteria for the unit. If you have carried out the activities and read the case studies throughout this unit, you will already have done a lot of work towards completing the tasks for this assignment.

Scenario

Your local Business Advisory Service has been in touch with your tutors to see if you can help out with a project they are just starting. Staff at the advice service are getting lots of requests for information on setting up travel and tourism businesses, and they would like some students to carry out research and produce some business advice materials. You have been selected to do the work on the tour operations industry.

Task 1

You are to produce an illustrated booklet on today's tour operations industry in which you must:

a. Explain the tour operations environment and the challenges it faces (P1). You must explain how tour operators work with other component industries of the travel and tourism sector. Links with travel agents, providers of transport, accommodation and ancillary products and services must be explained, together with the relationship tour operators have with trade and regulatory bodies. Horizontal and vertical integration has had a significant impact on the tour operations environment and you should demonstrate, with relevant examples, your understanding of these terms. Tour operators must work within a legal framework and the relevance of key regulations, laws and licensing should be described.

You should also demonstrate your awareness of the way in which environmental, political, economic, social and technological factors can influence the industry and highlight current challenges for the tour operations environment, for example the growth of budget airlines and the internet.

b. Discuss the impact of challenges facing tour operators (M1). A minimum of four challenges should be examined and analysed. Relevant examples showing how they impact on tour operators should be given to support your discussion.

c. Evaluate the effectiveness of tour operators in responding to challenges facing the sector (D1). At least two challenges should be addressed. This must be supported by recent examples and might include evidence of how tour operators have responded to the credit crunch or how specific tour operators are responding to challenges created by the internet or budget airlines. You must make some judgement on their effectiveness.

This task is designed to provide evidence for P1, M1 and D1.

Task 2

Staff at the Business Advisory Service would like you to design and deliver a presentation that:

a. Describes the products and services provided by different categories of tour operator for different target markets (P2). You should select one tour operator from each of the categories (five in total), identify their target market(s) and provide a review of the products and services they offer.

b. Analyses how a specific tour operator's portfolio of products and services meets the needs of its target market(s) (M2). You must demonstrate a sound understanding of what those needs are and how they are met by the current range of products and services.

c. Recommends, with justification, how a selected tour operator could expand its range of products and services for its current target market or adapt its range of products and services to appeal to a new market (D2). Your recommendations must be supported by a clear rationale and justification. Examples might be to add new destinations that would appeal to the current target market and complement existing destinations or to branch out to take advantage of recent trends and attract new target groups, for example extreme sports.

This task is designed to produce evidence for P2, M2 and D2.

Task 3

Produce a business advisory fact sheet that:

a. Outlines how tour operators plan, sell, administer and operate a package holiday programme, identifying commercial considerations (P3). Your evidence could relate to a visit to a tour operator, information gathered on an actual company or could describe the functions for a hypothetical tour operator.

Staff at the Business Advisory Service are particularly keen to alert potential new business start-ups to the processes involved in planning and costing a package holiday for inclusion in a tour operator's programme. They would like you to:

b. Plan and cost a package holiday for inclusion in a tour operator's programme (P4). You must plan a package holiday based on the following scenario, then calculate a selling price using load factors, mark-up or profit margin, currency conversions and fixed and variable costs. Evidence will be in the form of a description of the planned package, identification of all components, an accurate cost breakdown and a rationale for the decisions made on load factor and mark-up.

c. Explain ways of maximising profitability during the different stages of planning, selling, administering and operating the package holiday (M3). Aspects such as methods of contracting, consolidations, currency exchange, cancellation charge and commission must be explained to show how they could contribute to profitability.

Scenario: A family friend has always wanted to set up a business offering cycling holidays in the south of France based near Limoges. He has asked you to help him research the idea and put together a programme for six week-long tours in May and September. If these go well, he hopes to expand the number of weeks in future years. He will lead the tours himself and take no more than 12 cyclists on each tour.

You will need to carry out some in-depth research to address the following points:

1. Which destination(s) to use near Limoges;
2. What transport arrangements to get to Limoges would suit best;
3. What type of accommodation is needed and on what accommodation basis;
4. What excursions and activities should be included in the package;
5. What precise dates and timescales should be agreed.

You can assume that all suppliers will give you discounted, inclusive tour (IT) rates for accommodation, travel, excursions, etc., but as this is a new venture you are only likely to be offered a discount of 25 per cent off their brochure rates, e.g. you will be charged £37.50 for a room that would appear in a hotel's tariff as £50.

You will need to calculate all the direct costs of the holiday and add a mark-up of 20 per cent to cover fixed costs and a margin for profit. If you choose to fly your holidaymakers to the destination, you need not worry about load factors as you will be using a scheduled carrier (which could be one of the low-cost airlines).

Points to be bear in mind when costing include:

- Variations in accommodation and travel prices depending on the season;
- How your final prices compare with similar packages offered by other operators.

Present your planning and costing of the package as a short feasibility study, including all the information you have collected.

This task is designed to produce evidence for P3, M3 and P4.

UNIT 14

Specialist Tourism

INTRODUCTION TO THE UNIT

Specialist tourism is growing rapidly throughout the world, giving people the chance to enjoy their hobby, learn about new cultures or take part in an activity in a holiday setting. Specialist tourism is very wide-ranging and can include a number of different activities – everything from white-water rafting in New Zealand and trekking holidays in the Himalayas to cookery courses in France and art appreciation holidays to Italy. Changes in society, such as the ageing of the population, a greater desire for self-fulfilment, more use of technology, increased concern for the environment and a desire to learn more about different cultures, are fuelling an increased demand for specialist tourism products.

In this unit you will learn about the types and providers of specialist tourism. You will also explore how specialist tourism has developed and changes to market factors, such as increases in disposable income and leisure time. The unit also investigates the markets for particular types of specialist tourism. Finally, you will be given the chance to select specialist tourism holidays to meet specific customer profiles.

WHAT YOU WILL STUDY

When you have completed this unit you should:

1. Know the types and providers of specialist tourism;
2. Understand how specialist tourism has developed;
3. Know the market for a chosen type of specialist tourism;
4. Be able to select specialist tourism holidays to meet specific customer profiles.

You will be guided through the main topics in this unit with the help of the latest developments, statistics, industry examples and case studies. You should also check out the weblinks throughout the unit for extra information on particular organisations or topic areas and use the activities throughout the unit to help you learn more.

ASSESSMENT FOR THIS UNIT

This unit is internally assessed, meaning that you will be given an assignment (or series of assignments) to complete by your tutor(s) to show that you have fully understood the content of the unit. A grading scale of pass, merit or distinction is used when staff mark your assignment(s), with higher grades awarded to students who show greater depth in analysis, evaluation and justification in their assignments. An assignment for this unit, which covers all the grading criteria, can be found on page 104. Don't forget to visit **www.tandtonline.co.uk** for all the latest industry news, developments, statistics and links to websites in this unit to help you with your assignments.

SECTION 1

Know the types and providers of specialist tourism

Icebreaker

This unit examines specialist tourism, which combines hobbies and interests, social and cultural encounters, sport and adventure activities with tourism. Working by yourself, or in small groups under the direction of your tutor, see how you get on with the following tasks to help you make a start on this unit:

- Try and come up with your own definition of 'specialist tourism';
- List five different types of special interests that people can follow while on a holiday or short break;
- Name three different companies that offer specialist holidays in the UK;
- Make a list of why you think specialist tourism has grown in popularity in recent years;
- Name four regions that are popular for adventure holidays – two in the UK and two overseas;
- Think about the different reasons why people choose to go on a specialist holiday rather than a standard 'sun, sand and sea' package;
- Consider the role of the internet in the growth of specialist tourism;
- Name three different companies that offer specialist tourism holidays abroad.

When you've finished, show your answers to your tutor and compare your answers with what other students in your class have written.

Specialist tourism is one of the fastest-growing areas of the travel and tourism sector. People are becoming better educated, have more spending power and are seeking out new holiday experiences in their leisure time – cultural, educational, social and adventurous. At the same time, the travel and tourism sector is responding by offering an ever-wider choice of holidays and activities to meet this growing demand, both in the UK and overseas. In the opening sections of this unit we look at different types of specialist tourism, but we begin by asking just what we mean by 'specialist tourism'.

What is specialist tourism?

Given that there are so many different interests and activities that people can take part in while on holiday or a day visit, finding a suitable definition of specialist tourism is not an easy task! A simple definition is that specialist tourism is 'tourism with a purpose' – rather than just sitting on a beach or beside a pool, people taking specialist tourism holidays are looking to add something more to their experience. Taking this a little further, we can say that it is a type of tourism that appeals to people who have a particular interest that they want to pursue in a holiday setting – it is often the hub around which their total holiday experience is built.

Specialist tourism covers many different types of tourism, for example:

1. Sports tourism – e.g. travelling to the Algarve to play golf;
2. Adventure tourism – e.g. bungee jumping in South Africa;
3. Health tourism – e.g. staying at a spa hotel in Austria;

4. Nature and wildlife tourism – e.g. whale watching in the Antarctic;
5. Ecotourism – e.g. volunteering on a coral reef project in Belize;
6. Special interest tourism – e.g. a landscape painting holiday in Suffolk;
7. Educational tourism – e.g. students on a study visit to Barcelona;
8. Cultural tourism – e.g. visiting a cathedral;
9. Disaster tourism – e.g. visiting the site of the 9/11 tragedy in New York;
10. Rural tourism – e.g. staying on a farm in Devon;
11. Food tourism – e.g. visiting the Ludlow Food Festival.

It is important to remember that there is often overlap between these different categories of specialist tourism. For example, a family may visit the Scottish Borders for a mountain biking holiday – this will be both adventure tourism and rural tourism.

Activity 14.1

Using the list of different types of specialist tourism above, draw up a chart that includes the 11 categories and your own suggestions for three examples of each category.

This activity is designed to provide evidence for P1.

Adventure tourism in action (courtesy Outward Bound Trust)

Specialist tourism providers

The UK tour operating business has come a long way in the last 50 years, from offering just Mediterranean package holidays to the vast array of specialist holidays right across the world available today. New companies have entered the market to develop specialist products, while the long-established, mass-market tour operators have changed their holiday products to reflect the growing demand for special interests. It is not uncommon for mass-market tour operators such as Thomson Holidays and Thomas Cook to offer holidays that include cultural visits, activity tourism, wildlife tourism and other special interests, alongside their more traditional 'sun, sand and sea' package holidays.

Large, integrated tour operators often buy up smaller, independent businesses to increase their share of the holiday market. Most specialist tour operators are, however, small and medium-sized enterprises (SMEs), employing relatively small numbers of people. Many specialist tour operators are members of the Association of Independent Tour Operators (AITO), a trade organisation that represents their interests and helps to publicise their holidays through brochures, press work and its website.

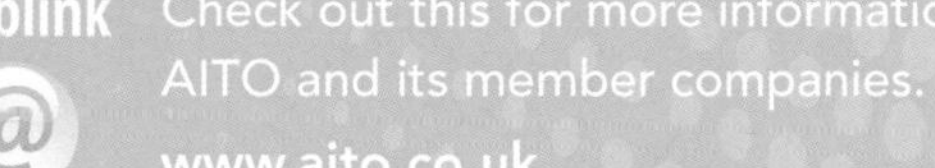

Weblink Check out this for more information on AITO and its member companies.
www.aito.co.uk

Most of today's specialist tour operators have an online presence, i.e. a website that allows customers to research holidays, sign up for e-mail newsletters, browse destinations and book holidays online. The power of the internet means that not having such a presence is a major disadvantage to a travel business, as people come to rely more and more on web-based services. Some specialist travel companies are 'virtual tour operators', only working online and having no face-to-face contact with customers, for example lastminute.com, ebookers and Expedia.

CASE STUDY

Kuoni

Introduction

Kuoni is an international tour operating company. Although it operates some short-haul holidays, Kuoni is perhaps best known in the UK as a specialist, long-haul tour operator. Figure 14.1 lists a selection of the Kuoni products available in the UK marketplace.

Despite major restructuring in 2006-7, Kuoni has maintained its previous level of staffing. Altogether, Kuoni employs more than 7,500 staff in its 300 offices worldwide. This includes 1500 employees in its destination management operations around the world.

Long-haul	Short-haul	Specialist/niche
Worldwide	Swiss Summer	Weddings
World Class *luxury long-haul*	Italy	Wisden Cricket Supporters Tours
Tropical Sun *3-star*	World Class Europe	H2O *water-centred*
Southern Africa		Sandals *Sandals all-incusives*
Dubai		Beaches *Beaches all-incusives*
Sri Lanka		Taj *Taj hotels*
China		Limited Editions
Indo-China		Lakes and Mountains
Seychelles		Sport Abroad: Rugby
Morocco		Sport Abroad: Motorsport
Florida		Sport Abroad: Cricket
Africa and Indian Ocean		Snow
Egypt		Selections *holidays with Emirates flights*
America and Canada		
Australia, New Zealand and South Pacific		

Fig 14.1 – Kuoni's product range in the UK

History

Kuoni was founded by Alfred Kuoni in Switzerland in 1906 when he added a travel agency to the family freight transport business. Since 1966, Kuoni has been a major long-haul tour operator in the UK market. More recently it has diversified into niche markets by acquiring previously independent specialist tour operator businesses. These have included Voyages Jules Verne, CV Travel and Ski Verbier – brands which continue to operate autonomously within the wider Kuoni Group. Kuoni UK underwent a major restructuring in 2006-7 (its centenary year) and broadened its product range by purchasing two upmarket touring holiday brands – Journeys of Distinction and Kirker Holidays. This was in line with Kuoni's current strategy of focusing on high quality travel products. It won the 'World's Leading Tour Operator' award in 2009 (for the 11th time) and has been voted 'Best Long-haul Tour Operator' by UK travel agents for the last 27 years.

Distribution and branding

Kuoni owns a range of specialist brands which trade in the UK as autonomous businesses. These include:

- CV Travel – a collection of villas in the Greek Islands, Italy, France, Spain, the Balearics, Portugal, Morocco, the Caribbean, South Africa, Thailand and Britain, plus a collection of hotels worldwide;

- The Travel Collection – operating tours that are designed to provide unusual travel experiences;
- Voyages Jules Verne – specialising in small group travel to destinations which have special cultural appeal, for example Egypt, China and Italy;
- Journeys of Distinction – up-market, escorted tours to long-haul destinations.

Corporate social responsibility

The Kuoni Group published its second group-wide Corporate Social Responsibility Report in 2009. The report describes the results of several years of commitment to sustainable tourism and includes the results of the Kuoni Corporate Responsibility Strategy, which has been implemented in steps since September 2006. Kuoni's approach is rooted in enhancing the positive impacts of tourism, whilst mitigating tourism's negative aspects. The report includes descriptions of projects, partners and problems, as well as the achievements made so far and the company's plans for the future. Further details are available at the Kuoni Group website **www.kuoni.com**.

Case Study Questions and Activities

1. Why do you think Kuoni concentrates on providing high quality holidays to the upper end of the market?
2. Log on to the Kuoni website **www.kuoni.co.uk** and make notes on the full range of specialist holiday products the company offers its customers.
3. How do you think the growth in the use of the internet will affect Kuoni and the sales of its holidays?

This case study is designed to provide evidence for P1.

Weblink

Check out this website to help answer these questions and for more information on Kuoni.

www.kuoni.co.uk

Some material in this case study is reproduced with permission from Travel & Tourism Case Studies by Stephen Rickerby (ISBN 9780955019067).

Activity 14.2

Using the list of different types of specialist tourism on pages 76-77, draw up a chart that gives two named providers of each (22 in total), i.e. two companies that offer sports tourism holidays, two that offer adventure tourism holidays, etc. The website of the Association of Independent Tour Operators is a good place to start this activity **www.aito.co.uk**.

This activity is designed to provide evidence for P1.

SECTION 2 Understand how specialist tourism has developed

It is perhaps not surprising that people want to carry out their special interest or activity while on holiday, particularly if it is in a warmer climate! People who participate in specialist tourism can be very inquisitive by nature, wanting to learn about different areas, meet new people and take part in new experiences. All the available evidence on specialist tourism is that it is a major growth area of the travel and tourism sector – meeting the specialist needs of increasing numbers of travellers. There is a general trend away from traditional package holidays to more specialist holiday experiences, witnessed by an increasing number of specialist tour operators.

Specific relationships between special interests and tourism include:

- The growth of budget airlines – leading to new opportunities for special interests in different destinations;
- Increases in leisure time and longer paid holidays – resulting in a general growth in tourism and travel;
- Rise in car ownership – giving people the chance to explore new destinations independently and gain access to a wider range of specialist tourism products;
- Growth in the use of the internet – allowing people to investigate new interests and holiday products, and carry out dynamic packaging – assembling the different parts of a holiday (accommodation, travel, car hire, insurance, excursions, etc.) independently rather than buying a standard package;
- Changes in education – offering young people the chance to take part in UK and overseas educational trips, resulting in the growth of educational tour operators;
- The rising interest in self-actualisation – leading to new holiday experiences, e.g. spa and health tourism.

Changing market factors

In this section we look at how specialist tourism has developed and examine changes in the factors that influence people's participation in the industry, for example disposable income, desire for new challenges, etc.

Socio-economic factors

A person's disposable income, i.e. what is left over after all necessary expenses have been met, influences their choice of holiday, short break or day trip. Clearly, the more disposable income a person has, the more they have available to spend on their holiday. Research shows that people who take part in specialist tourism generally have higher levels of disposable income than the population as a whole, tend to be younger and are often in professional occupations. Some people say they are 'money rich but time poor' because although they earn good salaries, they have little leisure time in which to spend their money. They tend to take part in challenging, active pursuits in short blocks of time. Retired professional people are also attracted to specialist tourism and, as well as having the time, also have reasonable levels of disposable income.

Some types of specialist tourism activities are considered to be very fashionable and appeal to people who relish a challenge, value status symbols and like to impress their friends! Activities like sky diving, bungee jumping, kite surfing and paragliding fall into this category. The introduction of outdoor clothing into high street fashion, the growing numbers of adventure sports magazines and increasing coverage of special interests and activities on TV, all illustrate the fashionable image associated with some types of specialist tourism products.

Skydiving is an extreme type of specialist tourism (courtesy High & Wild Adventure Travel)

Activity 14.3

Explain how socio-economic factors have led to developments in specialist tourism.

This activity is designed to provide evidence for P2.

Self-actualisation

The growth in specialist tourism has gone hand-in-hand with a general trend towards people wanting to make something more of their lives, become better people and 'give something back' to the world – this is known as self-actualisation or self-fulfilment. Specialist tourism activities can help people to achieve their inner-most, spiritual goals.

There are complex psychological influences within individuals that affect their motivation for travel and influence their choice of holidays. Probably the most widely-quoted work on how motivation affects people's actions is that of Maslow, who developed his 'hierarchy of needs' (see Figure 14.2).

In Maslow's model shown in Figure 14.2 there are five levels of needs that an individual seeks to satisfy, from physiological needs at the base of the pyramid to self-actualisation at the pinnacle. Maslow argues that individuals must satisfy certain physiological needs,

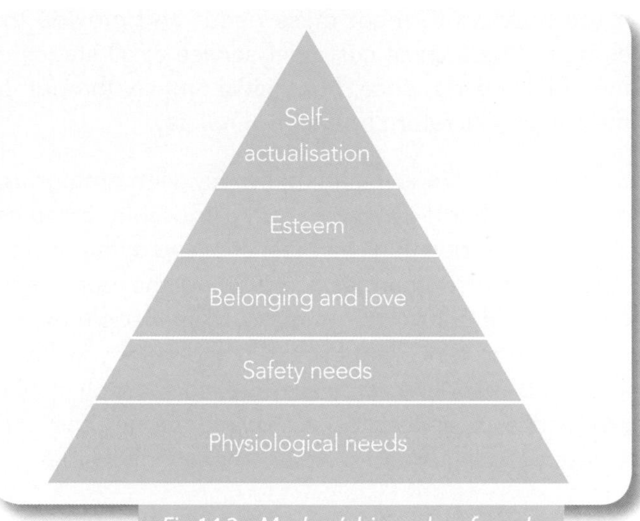

Fig 14.2 – Maslow's hierarchy of needs

such as shelter, warmth, water and food, plus safety needs before moving on to the need for belonging and love, esteem and ultimately self-actualisation. Applying Maslow's hierarchy of needs to tourists' motivation for specialist tourism, it is clear that, depending on the particular circumstances of the individual, tourism can satisfy their needs at every level. A holidaymaker, for example, will choose accommodation, hospitality and travel arrangements that meet his or her physiological and safety needs. Specialist holidays can certainly provide opportunities for developing social relationships, thereby contributing towards the need for belonging and love. Tourists sometimes use their travel experiences as a way of boosting their esteem among peers and the fashionable nature of some specialist tourism activities, such as paragliding and kite surfing, can contribute to this. Particular types of specialist tourism experiences may also contribute to a person's achievement of self-actualisation or self-fulfilment, perhaps becoming spiritually enlightened, helping communities in the developing world, learning a new language while on holiday or taking part in health and spa tourism.

Expectations of tailor-made holidays and high service level

Customers have high expectations when it comes to specialist tourism products – they are looking for high-quality experiences that exactly match their needs, coupled with excellent customer service. Specialist holiday companies must develop tailor-made holidays to meet these needs and provide the highest standards of customer service at all stages of the holiday experience, from initial enquiry through to the customer's return home from holiday.

Society in the UK is changing rapidly, with greater use of new technology, increased disposable incomes, changes in population characteristics and different work patterns. These changes are altering the purchasing behaviour of consumers in many ways. People expect to be able to buy products easily and quickly, whether in a shop or online, they are looking for high quality products and services, good value for money and 24/7 access to facilities and services whenever possible.

Trends

Travel and tourism in the 21st century is going through a period of rapid change, influenced by a number of factors, including:

1. Developments in technology – the internet is having a dramatic effect on the way people gather information on holidays and buy travel and tourism products. Technology is also influencing developments in different types of transport;
2. Demographic changes – e.g. the ageing of the population, more lone-parent households, marriage later in life, etc.
3. Lifestyle changes – e.g. more part-time working, the search for enlightenment, desire to learn about different cultures and take part in new experiences;
4. Globalisation – the move towards ever-larger corporations with influence that stretches across continents;
5. Consumer behaviour – people are demanding higher standards of service and higher quality products;
6. Economic changes – e.g. lower inflation rates, higher levels of disposable income, lower unemployment levels, free movement of people across borders;
7. Environmental issues – e.g. greater concern for the environment, management of the earth's resources and sustainability.

The Eden Project is a good example of sustainable tourism

Activity 14.4

Explain how recent trends in society have led to developments in specialist tourism.

This activity is designed to provide evidence for P2.

Development of specialist tourism

The mass tourism that exists in many parts of the world today has its origins in the years immediately following the end of the 1939-1945 Second World War, but throughout history, people have travelled the world for purposes of trade, education, religion and to fight in battles. The early origins of tourism can be traced back to pre-Egyptian times, when there was a limited amount of travel associated with festivals and celebrations of a religious or spiritual nature. The early Egyptian civilisation displayed a primitive social structure and rewarded the privileged classes with leisure time to enjoy activities such as dance, music, drama and archery. So, even in Egyptian times, taking part in special interests and activities was an important part of life for some.

The Greeks and Romans

The Greek civilisation was the first to promote the benefits of a healthy balance between work and leisure. There is evidence of travel for purely recreational purposes, with the Greeks hosting international visitors during the first Olympic Games held in 776 BC.

The Romans were keen to promote 'leisure with a purpose' to their citizens. Roman engineers built public leisure facilities for the masses living in urban areas, who practised recreation for physical fitness and in preparation for war. The extensive road network developed by the Romans allowed faster and more convenient travel for business and leisure purposes. There was growth in international travel within the Roman Empire for trade, while the wealthier Romans made visits to friends and relations, and began to appreciate the healing powers of near and distant spa waters for the first time.

The Grand Tour

From 1670 onwards young gentlemen of the aristocracy were sent on the Grand Tour of the great cultural cities of Europe to widen their education and experiences of life, prior to seeking positions at court on their return home. Cities such as Paris, Venice, Rome and Florence gave these young tourists the opportunity of sampling different cultures and societies. The popularity of the Grand Tour reached its peak in the mid-18th century, but was halted abruptly by the onset of the French Revolution and the Napoleonic Wars.

The rise of spa resorts

Although the medicinal benefits of spa waters had been recognised in Roman times, it was not until the 16th century that their full tourist potential began to be exploited and spa resorts grew in popularity. The healing potential of spa waters became widely accepted amongst the aristocracy, leading to the development of spa resorts in Britain and on the continent. Towns such as Buxton, Cheltenham, Leamington Spa, Llandrindod Wells and Bath prospered until well into the 18th century. Baden-Baden in Germany was one of the most popular spa destinations in Europe.

Early transport developments

In 1841, Thomas Cook organised his first excursion by train from Leicester to Loughborough for his local Temperance Association. Within 15 years, spurred on by the success of his first trip, Cook was running a fully-commercial travel company arranging tours and excursions both at home and overseas, including visits to the Great Exhibition in London in 1851 and inclusive tours to the Paris Exhibition in 1855. The completion of the Suez Canal in 1869 provided Cook with the opportunity of organising his first tours to Egypt.

In the early 19th century, just as steam power on land was radically changing the patterns of tourism and travel, the same was true at sea, with the introduction of a new generation of steam-powered ships serving North America, the Continent and the Far East. The Peninsular and Oriental Steam Navigation Company (P&O) introduced the first, regular, long-distance services to India and the Far East in 1838. The Cunard Steamship Company started services to North America in 1840. Following his successes in Britain and on the Continent, Thomas Cook organised the first steamship excursion to America in 1866.

The Industrial Revolution

The 1938 Holidays with Pay Act gave a stimulus to mass tourism in the UK, with 80 per cent of workers being entitled to paid holidays by 1945. Holiday camps flourished immediately before the outbreak of the Second World War, the first having been opened by Billy Butlin in 1936 at Skegness. Two years later, there were around 200 camps offering self-contained package holidays to 30,000 people per week. In the early 1950s, two-thirds of all domestic holidays were taken at the seaside and the majority of holidaymakers travelled to their destinations by coach or train.

Tourism developments post-World War Two

The type of mass tourism that is such a prominent feature of life in the 21st century began to develop after the end of the Second World War. Three important elements of post-World War Two society in the UK – the development of jet aircraft, the growth of the overseas package tour and increasing car ownership – were to have far-reaching implications on the UK domestic tourism scene.

Growth of special interest tour operators

You have learned in other units on your course that the sale of traditional package holidays is in decline, while 'unpackaged holidays', which are tailor-made to individual needs, are growing in popularity. Many of these holidays are based on special interests. This trend towards independent rather than packaged travel is, in part, a reflection of the move for self-actualisation discussed previously in this unit.

Integration in the travel and tourism industry, both vertical – where a single organisation owns a range of companies at different levels in the chain of distribution – and horizontal – when an organisation merges with companies at the same level or in the same industry sector – is influencing the way that specialist tourism develops. Large integrated tour operators, like Thomas Cook and TUI/Thomson, buy up smaller, specialist tour companies to increase their market share and reduce competition. TUI/Thomson, for example, has taken over a number of specialist tour operators that used to operate independently, including Headwater Holidays, Simply Travel and Jetsave. This is an example of horizontal integration, since the companies are all in the same sector of travel and tourism. Integration is not always in the best interests of travellers since their holiday choices may be limited.

Packaged to unpackaged holidays

Specialist tourism is in many respects an 'unpackaged holiday' – companies often tailor holidays to customers' particular requirements rather than selling something 'off the shelf'. The specialist nature of some activities often makes it impossible to offer a standardised holiday product. Companies work hard to make their products as appealing as possible to their target audience, using a variety of promotional techniques, including brochures with high quality images of activities and special interests. The internet is a particularly useful tool for providing information and selling specialist tourism products, given that the customers for this type of tourism tend to be very computer-literate.

Increased market segmentation

Market segmentation is the process of dividing the total market for a product or service, i.e. all the people who could buy it, into different segments, each with broadly similar characteristics. Holiday companies carry out segmentation because it allows them to focus more clearly on the needs and expectations of particular customers, for example older people, young people wanting an activity holiday of high spenders looking for the ultimate in luxury while on holiday. Specialist tourism lends itself particularly well to market segmentation, since it is made up of very many specialised interests and activities. Figure 14.3 shows how market segmentation is used to develop a wide range of specialist holiday products with different themes – six popular areas have been selected, each made up of providers that try to match the segments' needs to the products they offer. The wildlife tourism segment, for example, offers products such as whale watching tours, wildlife safaris and jungle expeditions to a variety of clients.

Fig 14.3 – Product types in specialist tourism

Response to social changes and trends

We saw earlier in this unit that travel and tourism is going through a period of rapid change, influenced by a variety of social factors, such as new developments in technology, the ageing of the population, changes in lifestyles and family composition. The effects of these factors on the travel and tourism sector in general, and specialist tourism in particular, include:

- Growth in online sales of holidays and other travel products – and the impact this is having on traditional sales outlets, including travel agencies;
- New developments in transportation, e.g. high-speed rail networks, growth of low-cost airlines, bigger cruise ships, etc.
- Increase in popularity of long-haul destinations;
- Development of niche products to meet the needs of particular types of holidaymakers, including those with special interests, e.g. activity holidays, cultural trips, etc.
- Restructuring of the travel and tourism sector into smaller numbers of larger companies offering a range of branded products;
- Higher quality products and better service standards for customers;
- Greater demand generally for travel and tourism products, especially short breaks and additional holidays;
- Development of responsible holidays and travel products that are respectful of the environment and local communities in destination areas.

'Demographics' is the term used to describe the characteristics and trends of the population, for example age, family composition, gender and ethnicity. It is important for specialist tourism companies to monitor changes in demographics and changes in society so that they can either adapt their products to changing circumstances or even introduce new products in a growth area. Some of the most important demographic changes that are occurring in the UK include:

- The ageing of the population;
- More lone-parent households;

Sea kayaking is growing in popularity (courtesy Exodus Travel)

- Marriage later in life;
- More part-time and flexible working;
- Increased working from home.

The ageing of the population is perhaps the most significant of all the demographic changes taking place in the UK today. Figures from the Office for National Statistics (ONS) show that the proportion of the population aged 65 and over has increased over the last 30 years, while the proportion below 16 years of age has fallen. This is important information for the specialist tourism industry, which can look to the future in the knowledge that there will be more older people with the time to take part in all types of special interests and activities while on holiday. It is not such good news for companies that offer special interest products aimed at children and young people, since the proportion of the population in younger age categories is falling.

Activity 14.5

Carry out some research into three companies that offer holidays aimed at older people. Make notes on the types of products they offer, destinations used and activities/special interests catered for. Analyse how the companies meet the needs of this particular group of tourists in their products and services.

This activity is designed to provide evidence for P2 and M1.

Access to new locations

We discussed earlier in this unit that specialist tourism lends itself well to independent travel rather than package holidays. As specialist holidays become more specific and complex – in order to meet travellers' changing demands and expectations – so the industry must provide more flexible arrangements rather than 'off-the-shelf' packages. This increasingly involves dynamic packaging, when customers use the internet to assemble their own holidays or ask a travel agent to do it on their behalf.

Special interest tourists who are looking for something new on their travels often seek out new locations around the world that have not previously been popular as tourist destinations, including the following from ABTA's list of 'hot destinations for 2010':

- China;
- Morocco;
- Singapore;
- Columbia;
- South Africa;
- United Arab Emirates;
- Dubai;
- Oman;
- Syria;
- India;
- Botswana;
- Croatia.

Encouraging tourism to new destinations is good for the countries concerned, since it helps the local economies. However, tourism must respect local cultures and traditions in these host destinations if it is to be sustainable in the long term.

Role of budget airlines

Budget airlines, such as Ryanair, easyJet and flybe, offer cheap air fares to all parts of Europe. They influence the growth in specialist tourism, since people often combine a cheap flight on a low-cost airline with an activity or other special interest, e.g. taking an easyJet flight to Geneva to ski or mountain bike in the Alps, flying with Ryanair to Knock in the west of Ireland to visit the religious site of Croagh Patrick or travelling with flybe to enjoy the cultural sights of Paris. As the budget airlines continue to grow in popularity, with new destinations being added all the time, so their influence on specialist tourism will increase.

Activity 14.6

Analyse how specialist tourism provision in the UK meets the demands of a changing market.

This activity is designed to provide evidence for M1.

SECTION 3 Know the market for a chosen type of specialist tourism

This section investigates the market for specialist tourism. It includes case studies on two specific types of specialist tourism – cycling tourism and health/spa tourism – which you will find useful when completing your assignment for this unit. You can also find a case study on adventure tourism on page 100. As well as considering the nature and location of these activities, each case study includes information on companies and organisations that operate in each of these specialist markets.

FOCUS ON INDUSTRY

THE MARKET FOR ADVENTURE TOURISM

Adventure tourism combines active pursuits with an element of danger, including air sports, land and water-based activities. An article in the March 2003 edition of Insights (VisitBritain) points out that:

- Over 10 per cent of UK holiday trips involve participation in adventurous activities (15 per cent in Scotland and 17 per cent in Wales);
- At least 11 million UK holidays each year include taking part in some type of adventurous activity;
- Annual spending by UK holiday visitors who take part in adventurous activities during their stay is at least as much as £2 million;
- Adventure holidays currently account for approximately 4 per cent of all UK holidays.

Research quoted in the same article suggests that hill walking, non-motorised watersports (in particular canoeing, surfing, windsurfing and dinghy sailing), climbing and mountain biking are currently the most popular adventurous activities in the UK. Other types of adventurous activities (caving, motorised watersports, motorised land sports, diving, air sports and other land-based activities) appear to be much more niche products appealing to very specific sectors of the market. Some adventurous activities, such as rope courses and quad biking, often have more appeal as part of a multi-activity holiday or as incidental holiday activities.

Market

The market for specialist tourism in the UK is made up of many thousands of companies that provide holiday products for a growing number of customers. Most of these companies are very small operators with a small share of the market that specialise in a particular activity. Mass-market tour operators such as Thomas Cook and Thomson Holidays also include specialist tourism products in their range of holidays.

The statistics shown in Figure 14.4 indicate that specialist tourism is a growing market in Wales, with its abundance of countryside areas and three National Parks. The table shows that three particular types of specialist tourism – adventure tourism, water sports tourism and cycling tourism – are forecast to grow significantly between 2000 and 2010, contributing more than £526 million in spending across all three activities in 2010.

Products

The wide variety of specialist tourism products on offer is the result of the industry responding to the very different motivations of individuals – it is a very customer-led industry within the travel and tourism sector. For example, specialist tourism can be associated with somebody wanting to:

- Learn a new skill or activity;
- Attend a sports event;
- Take part in activities and adventures;
- Relax and investigate self-improvement;
- Learn about nature, wildlife and the environment;
- Investigate different cultures.

	Trips millions		Nights millions		Spend £millions	
	2000	2010	2000	2010	2000	2010
ADVENTURE TOURISM						
UK Adventure Holidays	0.3	0.37	1.05	1.28	41.0	66.8
UK Holiday Participation in Adventure Activities	0.6	0.73	2.46	3.00	85.1	138.6
Overseas Adventure Holidays and Holiday Participation	0.04	0.06	0.19	0.27	7.4	15.3
Total Adventure Tourism	**0.94**	**1.16**	**3.70**	**4.55**	**133.5**	**220.7**
WATER SPORTS TOURISM						
UK Water Sports Holidays	0.2	0.24	0.95	1.16	26.3	42.8
UK Holiday Participation on Water Sports	0.3	0.37	1.07	1.30	45.1	73.5
Overseas Water Sports Holidays and Holiday Participation	0.02	0.03	0.09	0.13	3.7	7.6
Total Water Sports Tourism	**0.52**	**0.64**	**2.11**	**2.59**	**75.1**	**123.9**
CYCLE TOURISM						
UK Cycling Holidays	0.1	0.12	0.2	0.24	5.6	9.1
UK Holiday Participation in Cycling/ Mountain Biking	0.6	0.73	2.8	3.41	93.7	152.6
Overseas Cycling Holiday and Holiday Participation	0.07	0.10	0.3	0.42	9.8	20.2
Total Cycle Tourism	**0.77**	**0.95**	**3.3**	**4.07**	**109.1**	**181.9**

Fig 14.4 – Growth in specialist tourism in Wales

These motivations, with examples of associated specialist tourism products, are shown in Figure 14.5. The examples of specialist tourism products given in the table are by no means exhaustive, but give a flavour of how different motivations are satisfied by particular products and services.

The great majority of the types of specialist tourism products shown in Figure 14.5 are provided by private sector enterprises – companies that are in business to make a profit for their owners and/or shareholders. These are a mixture of small, independent tour operators and large, integrated travel companies. Public and voluntary sector providers also play a role in specialist tourism by, for example, organising conservation holidays, educational trips, heritage holidays and garden tours.

Skiing is a great way to keep fit (courtesy Ski Club of Great Britain)

Locations

People take part in many different activities during their leisure time – some passive, some active and

Motivation	Special interest tourism products
Learning a new skill or activity	Watercolour painting holidays Spinning and weaving tours Wine tasting tours Cookery holidays Pottery holidays
Attending sports events	Motor racing Grands Prix trips Tours to football matches in Europe Wimbledon Lawn Tennis Championships Corporate hospitality at the FA Cup Final Holiday packages to the Ryder Cup
Taking part in adventures	Mountain trekking holidays Quad biking events Canyoning Bungee jumping Kite surfing
Self-improvement and relaxation	Spa tourism Pilgrimages Yoga holidays Health breaks Retreats
Learning about wildlife, nature and the environment	Wildlife safaris Conservation holidays Whale watching tours Walking holidays Bird watching tours
Investigating heritage and culture	Cultural holidays Industrial heritage tours Art appreciation holidays Garden tours Farm holidays

Fig 14.5 – Motivations and products in specialist tourism

some involving a degree of risk or danger. The types of activities included in specialist tourism can be divided into three categories – those that take place on water, land-based activities and air sports, as shown in Figure 14.6.

Land-based	Water-based	Airsports
Visiting historic sites	Canoeing	Hang gliding
Quad biking	Kayaking	Paragliding
Mountain trekking	Sailing	Sky diving
Art appreciation	Surfing	Gliding
Pottery	Windsurfing	Flying
Cycling	Kite surfing	Parachuting
Walking	Canyoning	Bungee jumping
Bird watching	Scuba diving	
Visiting spas	Jet skiing	
Visiting gardens		

Fig 14.6 – Types of activities in specialist tourism

This type of tourism can also be domestic – people following a special interest in their own country, e.g. a couple from Birmingham enjoying a gourmet weekend break at a Devon hotel, or international – travelling abroad to follow a special interest, e.g. a family from Belfast taking a boating holiday on the Canal du Midi in the south of France.

Specialist tourism takes place in many different indoor and outdoor settings in the UK and abroad. Adventure and activity tourism often makes use of natural resources, so is usually located in countryside and coastal areas. Access to locations is important, both from the point of view of guest convenience in reaching the facility and the need for swift access by the emergency services in the event of an accident or incident. Distance from major centres of population is a consideration for specialist tourism providers, with those located close to cities benefiting from increased trade. Climatic considerations are important in some types of specialist tourism, for example winter sports, sailing, surfing, flying, gliding, etc.

Some adventure tourism activities take place under cover, for example in centres with all-weather facilities, such as indoor climbing walls. Special interest tourism concerned with hobbies or learning a new skill, for example cooking, painting, pottery, stained-glass making, spinning and weaving, may need purpose-built facilities.

Activity 14.7

Carry out some research into UK-based adventure tourism holiday companies and locate on a map of the world popular destinations used by the companies. Registered tandtonline users can download a blank map from **www.tandtonline.co.uk**.

This activity is designed to provide evidence for P4.

Components

The key components of a specialist tourism holiday include transport and accommodation, and may include guides to lead and offer instruction, specialist equipment and ancillary services such as insurance and foreign currency. Transport options include travel by air, rail, coach, bicycle or self-drive car. Specialist tourism holidays are often tailor-made from various components to suit the particular requirements of clients.

CASE STUDY

Health and spa tourism

Introduction

The healing power of spa waters was recognised as long ago as Roman times and in the 18th century spa towns such as Bath, Buxton and Tunbridge Wells were welcoming visitors to sample the waters. Today, spas across Europe offer a range of facilities from casinos and leisure pools to luxury hotels and beauty salons. Over the last 10 years, the word spa has broadened out in new directions to encompass virtually any place, facility, treatment or product that is connected with physical, mental or spiritual health. Over the same time period there has been a rapid growth in spa facilities of all types to meet the growing demand from customers who need guidance on wellness and well-being, as well as somewhere to escape from the pressures of modern life and re-energise their physical and mental processes. This demand has resulted in health and spa tourism becoming one of the fastest-growing industries in UK travel and tourism.

Nature of the activities

Health and spa tourism can be divided into five distinct categories:

1. Destination spas;
2. Day spas;
3. Hotel spas;
4. Spa towns;
5. Spa travel.

Destination spas

Sometimes known as health farms or hydros, these are popular with clients who need a relaxing break to take time out from their busy lives, to be pampered, to experience new therapies and activities, to eat healthily and possibly to lose weight or detox. Destination spas provide comfortable accommodation and a wide range of spa facilities, e.g. steam rooms, bubble-jet pools, sauna and relaxation areas. They are often located in a countryside setting and offer clients tailor-made packages to suit their needs. Companies in this sector of the health and spa market include Ragdale Hall Health Hydro in Leicestershire and the Celtic Manor Resort near Newport in south Wales.

Day spas

These cater for people who want to take a few hours out of their busy schedule or demanding home life to recharge their batteries. Day spas can be located in a historic building, a new purpose-built facility or within an existing health club. They offer steam rooms and sauna, relaxation areas, some gym facilities and classes such as yoga or pilates with qualified instructors. Companies offering day spa facilities include Aqua Sana at Center Parc's Oasis Whinfell Forest centre in the Lake District and the Academy Spa in Harrogate, North Yorkshire.

Hotel spas

More and more hotels are adding spas and spa treatments to their leisure facilities and some of the best are of a very high quality. Clients can expect steam rooms, bubble-jet pools, sauna and relaxation areas, a range of therapeutic treatments and some gym or fitness equipment. Weekday business guests in the hotel can make use of the spa facilities, while spa breaks help to fill rooms at weekends with leisure tourists. Companies offering hotel spa facilities include Chewton Glen Hotel, Spa and Country Club in Hampshire and Calcot Manor Spa in the Cotswolds.

Hotel spas are growing in popularity (courtesy St Davids Hotel and Spa, Cardiff)

Spa towns

Britain's spa towns are undergoing something of a revival in popularity. Places as far apart as Llandrindod Wells in Wales, Leamington Spa in Warwickshire, Moffatt in Scotland and Harrogate in North Yorkshire are using their long association with spa waters to encourage tourism. All have a water source, often rich in minerals and legend, and sometimes credited with specific healing properties. Many spa towns are rejuvenating their spa architecture, renovating historic facilities and staging cultural activities and festivals to attract visitors.

Spa travel

Holidays are for leisure, pleasure and relaxation – three ideals that are in keeping with the philosophy of spas and spa treatments. Increasing numbers of people are using their holidays and short breaks to concentrate on improving their well-being using health and spa tourism facilities. Companies that specialise in spa travel include Erna Low and Thermalia Travel, both operating tours in a wide variety of destinations across the world.

Case Study Questions and Activities

1. What factors are likely to influence the future development of the health and spa tourism industry?
2. Choose one of the spa travel companies listed above (Erna Low or Thermalia) and carry out some further research into the products and services it offers, including destinations visited, types of holidays, costs, travel details, etc.
3. What changes in society have led to increased demand for health and spa tourism products and services?
4. What are the objectives of the Spa Business Association?
5. Suggest new health and spa tourism products that could be introduced to fill gaps in provision.

This case study is designed to provide evidence for P3 and D1.

Weblink

Check out this website to help answer the questions in this case study and for more information on health and spa tourism.

www.spabusinessassociation.co.uk

Market segments

Marketing segmentation is the process of dividing the total market for a product or service (i.e. all the people who could buy it) into different segments, each with broadly similar characteristics. Specialist tourism companies carry out segmentation since it allows them to focus more clearly on the needs and wants of particular groups, for example older people, young people wanting activity holidays or high spenders looking for the ultimate in luxury.

Specialist tourism providers segment the market for their holidays according to a number of factors, such as:

- Age – e.g. designing holidays to meet the needs of people in a particular age group;
- Gender – e.g. developing activity holidays for women;
- Income – e.g. offering holidays for low-income families;
- Socio-economic group – e.g. targeting all the people in an area in the C2 (skilled working class) social group;
- Geographical region – e.g. all the people living in a particular postcode area of a city could be sent a holiday company's brochure;
- Psychographic factors (those relating to a person's personality, values, etc.) – e.g. developing specialist holidays to promote volunteering and ecotourism in developing nations.

Market segmentation is, therefore, a tool that a specialist tourism provider can use to satisfy the needs of its particular customers. Being concerned with the needs and expectations of customers, however, does mean that segmentation relies heavily on market research to help match the product exactly to the clients' needs.

The following case study on cycling tourism shows how one type of specialist tourism can be segmented to develop a range of products to meet individual needs.

CASE STUDY

Cycling tourism

Introduction

Cycling tourism can be defined as a holiday or day visit that involves participation in cycling, either as a primary or secondary purpose of the visit. It is an environmentally sustainable type of tourist activity, which has minimal negative impact on the environment and local communities. It can also make a positive contribution towards encouraging visitors to use their cars less and makes good use of under-utilised and redundant resources, such as by-roads and disused railway lines. It also generates income for a variety of tourism businesses and destination areas, helping to create jobs and contribute to economic development. A recent study in Scotland has shown that cycling is worth £39 million to the economy of the Highlands and Islands region, while in Wales cycling is forecast to contribute £182 million to the economy in 2010.

Cycling on the NCN route 64 near Lincoln (courtesy Sustrans/Paul Rea)

Nature of the activities

There are a number of different types of cycling tourism holiday products, for example:

1. Family cycling – all members of a family can enjoy the benefits of cycling while on holiday or a day trip;
2. Off-road cycling – tends to appeal to younger people looking for a challenge on mountain biking routes;
3. Cycle touring – holidays covering long distances in the UK and overseas, with overnight stays en route, perhaps using the National Cycle Network (NCN);
4. Cycle racing – combining racing with a holiday, for example a group of UK enthusiasts following the route of the Tour de France.

Cycling tourism products take different forms, for example:

- A cycling holiday or short break – where cycling is the main purpose of the trip;
- Cycling for a short period while on holiday – perhaps hiring a bike for half a day;
- A day visit that involves cycling – for example, visiting a forest area with mountain biking trails.

Location and destinations

The great appeal of cycling is that it can take place virtually anywhere. In the UK, cycling tourism takes place along country lanes, disused railway lines and canal towpaths, as well as in forests and moorland areas. It is particularly popular in National Parks where many authorities promote cycling as way of reducing the number of cars in the parks. The National Cycle Network is a countrywide series of signed cycling routes linking communities to schools, stations and city centres, as well as to countryside areas. Co-ordinated by the charity Sustrans, the network currently extends to 12,600 miles of routes throughout the UK, with further expansion planned.

There are increasing numbers of companies that offer cycling holidays in European countries, especially France and Spain. Regions such as the Loire, Dordogne, Brittany and northern Spain are popular with cycle tourists from the UK. Mountain bikers travel to areas such as the French Alps in the summer, riding on the runs that are used for skiing in the winter. Outside of Europe, cycling tourism is more of a specialist activity, but it is possible to book a cycling holiday to South America, Africa, Thailand, India and even cycle across Russia! Many charities organise long-distance bike rides to attract sponsorship.

Cycling tourism providers

Cycling in France (courtesy Headwater Holidays)

The increasing popularity of cycling in recent years has led to an increase in the numbers of providers. Most are private companies offering a specialist service on a relatively small scale, but many of the large, well-known tour operators now offer activities, including cycling, as part of their holiday packages. Examples of specialist cycling tourism providers offering holidays in the UK and overseas include:

- Bicycle Beano Cycling Holidays (**www.bicycle-beano.co.uk**);
- Cycleactive (**www.cycleactive.co.uk**);
- Susi Madron's Cycling for Softies (**www.cycling-for-softies.co.uk**);
- Headwater Holidays (**www.headwater.com**);
- Breton Bikes Cycling Holidays (**www.bretonbikes.com**);
- CTC Cycling Holidays, part of the Cyclists' Touring Club (**www.cyclingholidays.org**);
- Neilson Holidays (**www.neilson.co.uk**);
- Sherpa Expeditions (**www.sherpa-walking-holidays.co.uk**);
- Exodus Travel (**www.exodus.co.uk**);
- Explore Worldwide (**www.explore.co.uk**);
- Bents Bicycle Tours (**www.bentstours.com**).

Cycling often forms part of multi-activity holidays for children at holiday activity centres and outdoor pursuit centres operated by local authority education departments.

Case Study Questions and Activities

1. What is the National Cycle Network and what is it trying to achieve?
2. Choose one of the cycling tourism providers listed above and carry out some further research into the products and services it offers, including destinations visited, types of holidays, costs, travel details, etc.
3. Research the provision for cycling tourism in one of the UK's National Parks.
4. Provide details of three companies that offer cycling tours in France, including the areas visited, types of holidays on offer, costs, travel arrangements and special requirements.
5. Suggest new cycling tourism products that could be introduced to fill gaps in provision.

This case study is designed to provide evidence for P3 and D1.

Weblink

Check out these websites to help answer the questions in this case study and for more information on cycling tourism.

www.ctc.org.uk; www.sustrans.org.uk; www.aito.co.uk

Activity 14.8

Produce a market profile for one of the following types of specialist tourism – golf tourism, ecotourism or wildlife tourism. Analyse the market for your chosen type of specialist tourism and assess its potential for growth, suggesting new products for gaps in provision.

This activity is designed to provide evidence for P3, M2 and D1.

SECTION 4

Be able to select specialist tourism holidays to meet specific customer profiles

This section gives you the opportunity of selecting specialist tourism holidays to meet the needs of a variety of customers.

Customers

When it comes to choosing a specialist holiday, no two people are the same! Customer needs vary greatly and it is the job of specialist tour operators and their agents to listen to their clients' wishes and offer them a holiday that exactly meets their requirements. Customers vary by type – from singles and couples, old and young, to families and groups – and all with very different needs. Single people often look for companionship on their holiday, whereas a couple may be looking for seclusion and a holiday that gives them a chance to 'get away from it all'. Families often look for a range of activities on a specialist tourism holiday so that everybody is entertained. Groups on specialist holidays come in all shapes and sizes – from school children on a skiing trip to Whistler in Canada to a group of friends on a walking and vineyard tour in Provence.

Specialist tourism products must be tailored to the specific needs of individuals if they are to be successful. For example, a couple of friends on a month-long adventure tourism trip to New Zealand before going to university in the UK will have fairly basic needs in terms of travel and accommodation. At the other extreme, a couple celebrating their 30th wedding anniversary on an escorted tour of the cultural treasures of Egypt may want luxury travel and accommodation options, and may well pay extra for special excursions while in their destination. The holiday that is selected must reflect the needs of the clients and their budget.

Activity 14.9

Choose three different types of specialist tourism activities and describe the occasions when a person may take part in each activity (1) on an individual basis; (2) as part of a group; (3) as a member of a team or club. Name holiday companies that provide products and services for each of the activities and circumstances that you have described. Present your findings as a chart.

This activity is designed to provide evidence for P4.

Motivations

There are many different reasons why people want to take part in specialist tourism. These motivations include:

- To pursue a hobby – e.g. a person attending a watercolour painting course in Northumberland;
- To seek adventure – e.g. abseiling in the Swiss Alps or sky diving in the USA;
- For educational reasons – e.g. a group of garden enthusiasts visiting the Royal Horticultural Society's gardens at Wisley in Surrey to learn about varieties of fruit;
- To watch or take part in sports – e.g. a trip to the Commonwealth Games in India;
- For religious purposes – e.g. an organised tour of churches in Ireland;
- To explore different cultures – e.g. a backpacker spending a gap year in Thailand to work and learn about Thai culture;

- To take part in activities – e.g. a sailing holiday around the Greek islands;
- For reasons of discovery – e.g. a couple going on a cruise in the Norwegian fjords;
- For relaxation and rejuvenation – e.g. a family enjoying a short break at a health spa.

Activity 14.10

Name three UK tour operators that offer holidays for people who want to watch major sporting events around the world. Provide details of the holidays they offer, e.g. destinations visited, sample prices, etc.

This activity is designed to provide evidence for P4.

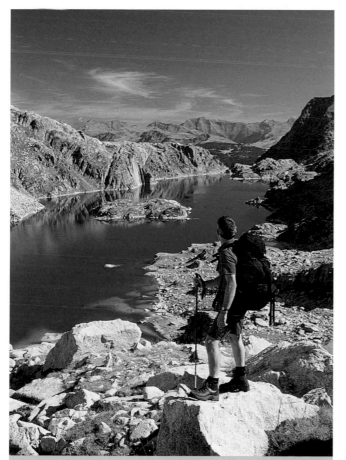

The High Pyrenees is a spectacular location for mountain walking (courtesy Exodus Travel)

Providers of specialist tourism holidays

The increasing popularity of specialist tourism has resulted in a growing number of UK-based providers of products and services. Most are tour operators of all sizes – large, integrated travel companies, small and medium-sized operations and web-based tour operators. They offer a complete service to their customers, e.g. booking flights and transfers, arranging accommodation, providing guides and tutors, etc. Some offer budget-priced package holidays, while others offer a more personalised service that tends to be more expensive. Other companies just offer a 'meet and greet' service or other ground-only arrangement when customers arrive in a destination, e.g. acting as a tour guide, leading an expedition or assisting customers with access and transfer arrangements at airport/port gateways and border crossings.

FOCUS ON INDUSTRY

MOUNTAIN KINGDOMS

Mountain Kingdoms (formerly Himalayan Kingdoms) is a UK-based specialist tour operator offering worldwide, small group adventure travel. A holiday with the company can range from climbing a trekking peak in Nepal, a classic trek to Everest base camp or Machu Picchu, to a gentle walking adventure through rolling foothills. Mountain Kingdoms also offers a selection of gentle treks in Nepal, Bhutan, Peru and Cambodia. The company is the leading provider of tours and treks to Bhutan, having pioneered most of the trekking routes in this Himalayan kingdom. It places an emphasis on quality, personal service and small group travel, as well as being committed to responsible tourism. The company feels strongly that its holidays should benefit the local communities in the destinations it visits, protect the environment by minimising pollution and respect local traditions, religion and heritage.

Weblink

Check out this website for more information on Mountain Kingdoms.
www.mountainkingdoms.com

Specialist tourism providers are found in the private sector, public sector and voluntary sector. There is sometimes overlap between these sectors – the Ramblers' Association, for example, is a voluntary sector organisation, but it operates a commercial (private sector) division known as Ramblers' Holidays.

Private sector providers

Private sector specialist tourism providers are either companies running facilities such as outdoor activity centres and walking tours, or tour operators selling specialist holiday packages in the UK and overseas. Many of the tour operators are small, specialist companies offering a limited number of tours to small groups of travellers. However, the rising popularity of specialist tourism has persuaded the major, integrated holiday companies to enter the market. Thomas Cook, for example, has a number of specialist tourism products including Neilson (skiing, sailing and mountain biking), Thomas Cook Signature and Thomas Cook Sport. Thomson/TUI owns Headwater Holidays and Crystal Holidays, both operating in the specialist tourism industry. Even mid-size tour operators have a variety of specialist tourism products, as the case study on Kuoni on page 78 illustrates.

Activity 14.11

Carry out some research and describe the provision for diving holidays in the UK, including details of the companies concerned, locations offered, sample prices and special requirements.

This activity is designed to provide evidence for P4.

Many of the holiday companies offering special interest and activity products are members of AITO, the Association of Independent Tour Operators. They offer packages based on a variety of themes and interests, and most can produce tailor-made itineraries based on customers' individual requirements.

Weblink

Check out this website for more information on AITO and its member companies offering specialist tourism products and services.

www.aito.co.uk

Public sector providers

The public sector's role in specialist tourism is mainly concerned with local education authorities (LEAs) providing outdoor activity centres for use by schools under their control. Many inner city councils run centres in National Parks and other countryside areas in England, Wales, Scotland and Northern Ireland. Safety is a key concern at these centres and, at present, all LEA centres, as well as those in the private sector, that cater for people under the age of 18 are required by law to be licensed by the Adventure Activities Licensing Authority (AALA).

Weblink

Check out this website for more information on the Adventure Activities Licensing Authority and the activities that it licenses.

www.hse.gov.uk/aala

Voluntary sector providers

The voluntary sector plays an important role in specialist tourism provision, through organisations such as:

- The National Trust – offers working holidays in the UK, covering a range of activities, from dry stone walling to planting trees;
- Youth Hostels Association – with more than 200 hostels in England and Wales;
- British Trust for Conservation Volunteers (BTCV) – organises more than 100 conservation holidays each year in the UK and 12 countries worldwide. Tasks include pond clearing, beach cleaning and hedge laying;

- Outward Bound Trust – has centres in more than 30 countries offering special interest and activity holidays;
- Royal Society for the Protection of Birds (RSPB) – offers a range of leisure breaks in association with tour operators.

Local communities also contribute to specialist tourism provision by organising events and courses that attract visitors as well as local people.

Holidays

We have seen that specialist tourism is a very wide-ranging industry with many companies providing a wide variety of specialist holidays in the UK and overseas. Providers work to a verbal or written customer brief when selecting a suitable specialist holiday. This sets out the client's specific requirements and includes details of:

- Type of specialist holiday required – e.g. sports, adventure, cultural, health, educational, etc.
- Party size – the total number of people travelling;
- Holiday dates – date of departure and arrival back in the UK;
- Departure point – this could be a major or regional airport, ferry port, train station, etc.
- Board basis – chosen from full-board, half-board, all-inclusive, room-only or bed and breakfast;
- Destination – this may be a specific resort or an indication of the type of destination required, e.g. quiet, lively, by the sea, city, etc.
- Type of accommodation – serviced or self-catering.

Price is often the most important consideration for the client, who will be looking for value for money in their holiday. Some people will be travelling on a tight budget, whereas others may be looking for high quality accommodation and facilities on their specialist holiday, for which they are prepared to pay a premium.

Special considerations

By their very nature, specialist tourism activities often need specialist equipment. This includes safety equipment for many of the adventure holidays we have mentioned elsewhere in this unit. Many specialist tourism holidays involve companies providing tuition and instruction to guests at a range of levels – beginner, intermediate and advanced. Depending on the type of special interest or activity concerned, staff need to be fully trained to deliver the activities in a safe and efficient manner. Many staff at activity and adventure centres have to be trained to the National Governing Body standards of their respective sports and activities. It is common for staff working with children to have to undertake a Criminal Records Bureau (CRB) check and for the companies concerned to follow the guidelines set out in the Children Act. First aid training for staff is important in many companies offering activity and adventure tourism, while all companies operating in travel and tourism have to comply with the requirements of the Disability Discrimination Act (DDA) and are advised to take out public liability insurance.

CASE STUDY

Adventure Tourism

Introduction

Adventure tourism is a growing niche of the specialist tourism industry that is capitalising on people's increased interest in fitness and desire to accept a challenge. It consists of holidays, short breaks and day visits that involve taking part in active or adventurous outdoor activities, either as a primary or secondary purpose of the visit. Adventure tourism is particularly popular in Scotland and Wales, but also in many English destinations such as the Lake District, Peak District, Yorkshire and the south west, especially Cornwall. Adventure tourism activities involve a degree of risk and danger and appeal particularly to young, professional people, who have sufficient disposable income to buy the (often expensive) equipment needed to take part in the activity.

Nature of the activities

Adventure tourism includes a wide range of outdoor activities, such as:

- Mountain biking;
- Canoeing and kayaking;
- Caving and pot-holing;
- Rock climbing of all types;
- Surfing, windsurfing and kite surfing;
- Hang-gliding, paragliding, parascending, sky diving and microlighting;
- Mountain trekking, gorge walking and canyoning;
- Motorised land sports, e.g. 4 X 4 driving, rally driving and quad biking;
- Scuba diving;
- Orienteering, snowboarding, land yachting, bungee jumping and other land-based activities.

Adventure tourism products can take different forms, for example:

- Adventure holidays or short breaks – where taking part in adventure activities is the main purpose of the trip, e.g. a trekking holiday in the Himalayas;
- Taking part in adventure activities as part of a holiday, e.g. having a half-day kite surfing lesson while on a family holiday in mid Wales;
- Adventure day visits – where taking part in adventure activities is the main purpose of the visit, e.g. a group from Exeter taking part in a multi-activity adventure day course on the south Devon coast.

Location and destinations

Trekking in the Himalayas (courtesy Himilayan Kingdoms)

Adventure tourism takes place in the UK and overseas. In the UK, many adventure holidays take place in National Parks and other areas of outstanding natural beauty. Part of the experience of an adventure tourism holiday is being in close contact with nature and the environment, so these areas are well-suited to adventure tourism activities. The precise location will depend on the requirements of the activity, e.g. access to water for canoeing and kayaking, access to crags for climbing, access to beaches for surfing, kite surfing and windsurfing, etc. As for adventure tourism destinations abroad, the sky is literally the limit! Every world continent has destinations that are popular with adventure tourists, for example:

- Europe – e.g. the Alps, Scandinavia and the Mediterranean islands;
- Asia – e.g. the Himalayas, Cambodia, Thailand and Vietnam;
- South America – e.g. the Amazon rainforest, the Andes and coastal regions;
- North America – e.g. the Rocky Mountains, National Parks and British Columbia;
- Africa – e.g. game reserves, Sahara Desert and the Victoria Falls;
- Australia/New Zealand – e.g. the Great Barrier Reef, Tasmania and New Zealand;
- Antarctica and the South Pole.

Adventure tourism providers

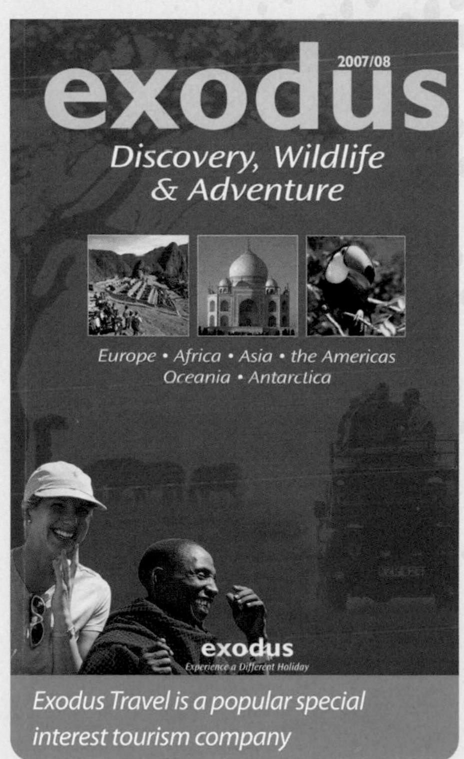

Exodus Travel is a popular special interest tourism company

The UK adventure tourism industry is made up of mainly small activity businesses catering for a specialist adventure activity or offering a multi-activity experience for customers. Some have their own self-catering or serviced accommodation, while others use nearby hotels, guesthouses, campsites, bunkhouse barns and hostels. There are increasing numbers of tour operators offering adventure holidays in the UK and to all parts of the world, usually taking small numbers of travellers in groups under the direction of an experienced tour leader. Examples of larger adventure tourism providers offering holidays in the UK and overseas include:

- PGL (**www.pgl.co.uk**);
- Acorn Adventure (**www.acornadventure.co.uk**);
- Dragoman Overland (**www.dragoman.com**);
- Exodus Travel (**www.exodus.co.uk**);
- Explore Worldwide (**www.explore.co.uk**);
- Guerba Worldwide (**www.guerba.co.uk**);

- Mountain Kingdoms (**www.mountainkingdoms.com**);
- Adrift (**www.adrift.co.uk**);
- Discover the World (**www.discover-the-world.co.uk**);
- Audley Travel (**www.audleytravel.com**);
- Naturetrek (**www.naturetrek.co.uk**).

Adventure activities sometimes form part of multi-activity holidays for children at holiday activity centres and outdoor pursuits' centres operated by local authority education departments.

Special requirements

Adventure tourism can involve dangerous activities, so the correct equipment, clothing and instruction are vital. Some people who take part in activities prefer to use their own equipment and clothing, while others are happy to use what is supplied by the company or hire equipment from specialist suppliers. Some adventure tourism companies have age restrictions for customers, given the dangerous nature of their activities.

Case Study Questions and Activities

1. Choose one of the adventure tourism providers listed above and carry out some further research into the products and services it offers, including destinations visited, types of holidays, costs, travel details, special requirements, etc.
2. Provide details of three companies that offer trekking holidays in the Himalayas, including the areas visited, types of holidays on offer, costs and travel arrangements from the UK.
3. Name two UK tour operators that offer wildlife holidays to Africa;
4. Provide details of three companies that offer scuba diving holidays in the Caribbean, including the areas visited, types of holidays on offer, costs and travel arrangements from the UK.

This case study is designed to provide evidence for P4.

Weblink Check out this website to help answer the questions in this case study and for more information on adventure tour operators. **www.aito.co.uk**

Activity 14.12

Sheila and Audrey, two life-long friends from Manchester, are looking for a 3-week trekking holiday in either the Alps or the Himalayas next September. They are experienced walkers, but have never trekked at altitude. They would like fly from their nearest airport, but have no real preferences when it comes to type of accommodation, although they do not want to share. Recommend and cost three possible holidays that meet their needs using appropriate brochures and the internet. You should give details of the tour operators, holidays chosen, dates and prices for each holiday selected, together with a description of the specialist elements to enable the customer to see how their requirements have been met. Evaluate your three holidays chosen for the customers and select, with justification, your preferred option for the couple.

This activity is designed to provide evidence for P4, M3 and D2.

UNIT SUMMARY

This unit has investigated the growth area of specialist tourism. You have seen that the industry covers a variety of activities and special interests that people carry out while on holiday or on a day visit, either in the UK or overseas. You have investigated the different types of specialist tourism, including adventure tourism, sports tourism and health tourism. You have also explored the factors that have shaped the development of specialist tourism, such as the desire for new challenges, level of disposable income and amount of leisure time. The unit has given you the chance to investigate the market for one specific type of specialist tourism, while the final part of the unit involved selecting specialist tourism holidays to meet specific customer needs. Throughout the unit you have been shown many industry examples, while the case studies on Kuoni Travel, cycling tourism, health and spa tourism, and adventure tourism provide in-depth examples of different aspects of specialist tourism.

If you have worked methodically, by the end of this unit you should:

- Know the types and providers of specialist tourism;
- Understand how specialist tourism has developed;
- Know the market for a chosen type of specialist tourism;
- Be able to select specialist tourism holidays to meet specific customer profiles.

You are now in a position to complete the assignment for the unit, under the direction of your tutor. Before you tackle the assignment you may like to have a go at the following questions to help build your knowledge of specialist tourism.

TEST YOUR KNOWLEDGE

1. What is 'specialist tourism'?
2. Which points about the historical development of tourism have had an impact on the development of specialist tourism?
3. What are niche tourism products and why is specialist tourism considered to be one?
4. List five passive and five adventurous activities that can form part of a specialist tourism holiday.
5. Name three UK-based health and spa tourism companies that offer holidays within the UK and overseas.
6. How do adventurous activities contribute to economic development in the destinations where they take place?
7. List three motivations of people who take part in specialist tourism.
8. What are 'demographics' and how do they affect specialist tourism?
9. Name six different market segments found in specialist tourism.
10. Which socio-economic factors affect participation in specialist tourism?
11. Explain how Maslow's hierarchy of needs relates to specialist tourism.
12. Describe the locations of three different types of specialist tourism.
13. Name six companies that offer cycling tourism holidays and breaks.
14. Describe the range of organisations that provide specialist tourism in the UK.
15. Name six UK-based adventure tourism companies that offer holidays within the UK and overseas.

Answers to these questions can be found in the Book 2 Tutor's CD-ROM that accompanies this book (ISBN 9780956268075). Full details can be found at **www.tandtpublishing.co.uk**

UNIT 14 ASSIGNMENT

Specialist Tourism

Introduction

This assignment is made up of a number of tasks which, when successfully completed, are designed to give you sufficient evidence to meet the Pass (P), Merit (M) and Distinction (D) grading criteria for the unit. If you have carried out the activities and read the case studies throughout this unit, you will already have done a lot of work towards completing the tasks for this assignment.

Scenario

In your first job since leaving college you are working in the Marketing Department of a medium-sized tour operator that has been selling villa holidays to Spain, Greece and Turkey for the last six years. The Head of Marketing, Hannah Gray, has been asked by senior management to investigate the possibility of introducing specialist tourism holidays into the company's programme to capitalise on the growth in popularity of activities and special interests amongst clients. Hannah has asked you to help out on the project, which focuses on four main areas:

1. The types and providers of specialist tourism;
2. How specialist tourism has developed;
3. The market for a specific type of specialist tourism;
4. Selecting specialist tourism holidays to meet specific customer profiles.

She wants you to complete the following four tasks.

Task 1

Hannah needs some background evidence on specialist tourism and would like you to produce a written report in which you must:

- Describe the types and providers of specialist tourism (P1). You should include examples from the following types of specialist tourism – sport, adventure, health, nature, ecotourism, special interest, educational, cultural and other, e.g. disaster tourism, volunteering, etc. You should include named examples of the different types of providers – integrated tour operators, independent tour operators, web-based operators, small and medium-sized enterprises (SMEs).

This task is designed to provide evidence for P1.

Task 2

Hannah would like you to prepare and deliver an illustrated presentation in which you must:

a. Explain the market factors that have led to developments in specialist tourism (P2). You should explain the changes in the market that have led to increased demand for specialist tourism products, including socio-economic, self-actualisation, expectation of tailor-made holidays and high service level, and trends. Examples include the introduction of charter flights, more leisure time, increased paid holidays and corresponding changes in holidaying habits from one summer holiday to the growth in short breaks and additional holidays.

b. Analyse how specialist tourism provision meets the demands of a changing market (M1). Your evidence should be analytical to show what the demands of the changing market are and how specialist tourism meets these demands. Links should be made between developments and specialist tourism products, for example how the growing demand for activity holidays has resulted in an expansion of provision of short activity breaks, which has been facilitated by the opening of new routes and flexible travel options provided by the low-cost airlines

This task is designed to produce evidence for P2 and M1.

Task 3

Hannah would like you to carry out a detailed investigation into one area of specialist tourism that could be included in the company's new programme of holidays. She would like you to compile a portfolio in which you should:

a. Produce a market profile for a chosen type of specialist tourism (P3). You should research the market for your chosen type of specialist tourism, producing a market profile which reports on the main providers and their size, e.g. market shares, turnover and growth. You will identify and describe typical locations around the world for the type of specialism, components of the holidays, and clearly identify any specialist equipment and resources needed. There should be detailed links to the market segments targeted by the specialism.

b. Analyse the market for a chosen type of specialist tourism, interpreting relevant data (M2). You will be expected to have accessed relevant data and interpreted it accurately in terms of determining the providers, size, market segments and products from the selected specialism.

c. Assess the potential for growth in the chosen area of specialist tourism, suggesting new products for gaps in provision (D1). Having researched one specialist tourism market in detail, you should be able to identify gaps in provision and determine the types of specialist holidays for which there is potential to cater further for the selected tourism market, for example by adapting the product to attract a different market segment. You should make full recommendations for types and locations of holidays that would fill these gaps.

This task is designed to produce evidence for P3, M2 and D1.

Task 4

Hannah needs to carry out some research into competitor holiday companies to see what they offer in terms of specialist holidays to meet particular customer needs. She would like you to:

a. Select suitable specialist tourism holidays that meet the two customer profiles shown below (P4). You are expected to select three appropriate holidays in different countries to match each of the profiles (i.e. six holidays in total). You should give details of the tour operator, holidays chosen and dates and price for each holiday selected, together with a description of the specialist elements to enable the customer to see how their requirements have been met.

b. Explain how your chosen holidays meet the requirements of the customers, selecting the preferred option for each customer profile (M3). You must explain clearly how the holidays meet the needs of the specified customers, and suggest your preferred option, i.e. the one that you feel best meets the customer's needs. This process must be completed for both of the customer profiles.

c. Evaluate the different options available to meet the needs of the specific customer profiles, justifying the preferred options (D2). You should determine any limitations in meeting the brief, explaining why certain options were rejected and justifying the preferred options.

This task is designed to produce evidence for P4, M3 and D2.

Customer profile 1

The Singh family from Birmingham – 2 adults and 2 boys aged 11 and 13 – are looking for a 7-night sailing holiday in Greece in the last week of June. They are not experienced sailors so will need a holiday that offers tuition for beginners. They would like to stay in self-catering accommodation and fly from their nearest airport. Recommend and cost three possible holidays that meet their needs using appropriate brochures and the internet. You should give details of the tour operators, holidays chosen, dates and prices for each holiday selected, together with a description of the specialist elements to enable the customer to see how their requirements have been met.

Customer profile 2

Jenny and Owen from Birmingham are interested in a 14-night multi-adventure holiday in France during September. They are keen on walking, mountain biking, abseiling and water sports and would like a holiday that includes some of these activities, plus others that they may find interesting. They would like to stay in self-catering accommodation and fly from their nearest airport. Recommend and cost three possible holidays that meet their needs using appropriate brochures and the internet. You should give details of the tour operators, holidays chosen, dates and prices for each holiday selected, together with a description of the specialist elements to enable the customer to see how their requirements have been met.

UNIT 15

Working as a Holiday Representative

INTRODUCTION TO THE UNIT

Holiday representatives play a vital role in the successful operation of a tour operator's programme of holidays. A holiday representative (rep) is the holidaymakers' first, and probably only, direct point of contact with the tour company. Working as a holiday rep is a very appealing job to many people thinking of a career in travel and tourism. It offers the chance to work abroad and help all types of customers enjoy their holidays to the full, but it is a very demanding and responsible job. Reps have to work long hours, deal with a host of enquiries from customers and sort out problems in a professional and efficient manner. Time off in the resort is very limited during the season and the job involves a certain amount of administration and basic accounting.

In this unit you will learn about the roles, duties and responsibilities of different types of holiday representatives who work overseas. The unit also gives you the opportunity to examine the legal responsibilities of reps and the part they play in providing a healthy and safe holiday environment for customers. You will also have the chance to practise your social, customer service and selling skills when dealing with a range of situations that reps encounter, such as organising a welcome meeting for guests.

WHAT YOU WILL STUDY

When you have completed this unit you should:

1. Know the roles, duties and responsibilities of different categories of holiday representatives;
2. Know the legal responsibilities of a holiday representative;
3. Understand the role of the holiday representative in creating a safe and healthy holiday environment;
4. Be able to apply social, customer service and selling skills when dealing with transfers, welcome meetings and other situations.

You will be guided through the main topics in this unit with the help of the latest developments, statistics, industry examples and case studies. You should also check out the weblinks throughout the unit for extra information on particular organisations or topic areas and use the activities throughout the unit to help you learn more.

ASSESSMENT FOR THIS UNIT

This unit is internally assessed, meaning that you will be given an assignment (or series of assignments) to complete by your tutor(s) to show that you have fully understood the content of the unit. A grading scale of pass, merit or distinction is used when staff mark your assignment(s), with higher grades awarded to students who show greater depth in analysis, evaluation and justification in their assignments. An assignment for this unit, which covers all the grading criteria, can be found on page 138. Don't forget to visit **www.tandtonline.co.uk** for all the latest industry news, developments, statistics and links to websites in this unit to help you with your assignments.

SECTION 1 Know the roles, duties and responsibilities of different categories of holiday representatives

Icebreaker

This unit investigates the world of the holiday representative – one of the most appealing of all jobs in travel and tourism, but very hard work! Working by yourself, or in small groups under the direction of your tutor, see how you get on with the following tasks to help you make a start on this unit:

- Write a short paragraph that explains the sort of work that an overseas holiday representative would do in a typical week;
- Name three other component industries of the travel and tourism sector (other than tour operations) that overseas reps may come into contact with during the course of their work;
- Make a list of the personal qualities and skills needed to be a good representative;
- List the different areas of health and safety that an overseas rep will need to be aware of while working;
- Think about the sort of problems and incidents that a holiday rep working on a campsite in Europe may have to deal with;
- Name two main roles of a holiday representative;
- Name three different situations during the course of a holiday that a rep will come into contact with customers.

When you've finished, show your answers to your tutor and compare your answers with what other students in your class have written.

Working as a holiday representative is many people's idea of the perfect job – the chance to work abroad in the sun, socialise while you work and visit exciting places all sound very appealing, particularly to many young people. However, working as a rep is very hard work and may not suit everybody, as the advice from Thomson Holidays shown in Figure 15.1 explains.

Tour operators look for people who have a responsible and sensible outlook when recruiting holiday reps. Applicants need to be tactful, flexible and patient, with a lot of drive, enthusiasm and stamina, plus excellent organisational skills.

Although the image of a person working in a sunny Mediterranean resort is the one that comes most readily to mind when you think about the work of a holiday representative, there are actually many different types of reps working abroad, serving all types of customers in many different kinds of accommodation and various resort areas. Reps can be classified into:

1. Resort representatives, e.g. property, 18-30s, over-50s, etc.
2. Ski representatives;
3. Transfer representatives;
4. Children's representatives;
5. Campsite representatives.

Living and working overseas

Working and living in a different country is a completely different experience to being at home. The food, the language, the culture and the working hours, to name but a few, will all be new to you. Taking a big step and leaving all your friends and family behind is therefore not for the faint-hearted!

The nature of the holiday business also requires a large degree of flexibility. You will work six out of seven days. However, you may be contacted at any time if there is an emergency, so you will need to be willing and available to help if the need arises. We do our best to place you in the country of your choice, especially if you speak the language; however, this is not always possible, so you will need to be prepared to work anywhere in our programme.

Although leaving your home to work in a different country is a big step, it is also a completely different life experience and on offer is great job satisfaction and excellent career opportunities. So if you want adventure in your life, take a small step towards making a big leap!

Fig 15.1 – Advice from Thomson Holidays

In the following sections of this unit we will investigate these categories in turn, examining the key roles, duties and responsibilities of each.

Resort representatives

These are the types of reps that are familiar to most of us who have been on a holiday abroad or seen TV programmes about working in travel and tourism abroad. Resort representatives look after customers staying in a range of different types of accommodation – hotels, villas, apartments, forest lodges, campsites, timeshare accommodation, caravan parks, holiday centres, etc. – or are responsible for particular types of holidaymakers, e.g. young people on 18-30s type holidays or customers over 50.

Whatever their particular job situation, the roles, duties and responsibilities of resort reps are very varied and include:

- Conducting welcome meetings;
- Visiting properties to meet customers;
- Accompanying holidaymakers on transfers between airport and accommodation;
- Providing and maintaining local information boards for holidaymakers;
- Ensuring health and safety requirements;
- Running entertainments and events for customers;
- Selling and organising excursions;
- Calculating payments, currency conversions and commissions;
- Carrying out routine administration;
- Liaising with hotel owners and managers;
- Solving problems for guests;
- Handling complaints;
- Dealing with non-routine incidents, illness and emergencies.

A resort representative has three key roles:

1. To represent the company – holiday reps are the public face of the holiday company. Customers on a Cosmos holiday, for example, will not meet the senior managers or directors based in the UK, but they will have regular contact with their rep, expecting him or her to provide information and be able to handle any problems or enquiries speedily and efficiently. How good reps are at their jobs can have a significant impact on holidaymakers' enjoyment of their holiday and the overall image of the company.

2. To provide excellent customer service – it goes without saying that holiday reps must deliver very high standards of customer service if they are going to satisfy their customers' needs. They must be available at all reasonable times to inform and entertain their customers, deal with complaints and handle sometimes difficult situations with tact and diplomacy.

3. To generate revenue for the tour operator – travel and tourism is a commercial operation, so reps are expected to sell extras to holidaymakers while in the resort, for example day and evening excursions, accommodation and travel upgrades, car hire and activities, for which they normally earn a commission.

These three key roles and responsibilities are summed up well in the following case study on the roles and responsibilities of Thomas Cook Overseas Representatives.

CASE STUDY

Thomas Cook Overseas Representatives

Introduction

Thomas Cook UK & Ireland is the second largest leisure travel group in the UK with around 19,000 employees. It is now part of Thomas Cook plc, which was formed in 2007 by the merger of Thomas Cook AG and MyTravel Group plc. Thomas Cook operates a fleet of 45 aircraft, has a network of more than 800 high street stores (Thomas Cook and Going Places), travel websites, its own television channel Thomas Cook TV on Sky and a wide range of travel brands, such as Club 18-30, Bridge, Cresta, Direct Holidays, Manos, Neilson, Thomas Cook Signature, Thomas Cook Sport and Tradewinds. The company's airline, Thomas Cook Airlines, flies from various UK regional airports to destinations worldwide. Thomas Cook is a vertically-integrated travel group, since it owns its own sales outlets (travel agencies, call centres, internet sites, TV channel), airline and tour operating businesses.

Working overseas

Thomas Cook's Overseas Representatives are the public face of the company, always on hand to help. One minute a rep might be recommending a nice quiet spot to sunbathe, the next could be dealing with a guest to solve their issue or complaint. The company stresses that the variety and unpredictability of the job will call for some very special qualities. So while the company doesn't insist on specific qualifications or experience, reps do need bags of personality, a knack for dealing with people and the ability to stay calm under pressure and still keep smiling.

Key roles, duties and responsibilities

- To professionally and efficiently accompany customers to and from the airport;
- To deliver 'introductions' to customers after their arrival, with the objective of providing customers with practical and interesting information in accordance with the company's guidelines;

- To deliver exceptional customer service in order to achieve the customer service targets given by the destination management;
- To actively sell Thomas Cook events, car hire and ad hoc events in order to achieve the income targets given by the destination management;
- To actively monitor health, safety and quality standards;
- To accurately complete weekly/fortnightly paperwork in accordance with the company guidelines and the resort deadlines;
- To establish a friendly, respectful relationship with all hotel staff, suppliers and airport officials;
- To guide both day and night events as required;
- To take an active role in any in-house entertainment/activity where possible;
- To conduct police and clinic visits as required.

Key skills required

- Good communication skills and the ability to hold conversations with customers;
- The ability to work either as part of a team or independently;
- The ability to listen and respond sympathetically to customers' requests/needs;
- An enthusiastic, positive personality – must like working with people;
- The initiative to escalate problems and incidents to the destination management;
- The ability to resolve problems.

Case Study Questions and Activities

1. What specific personal qualities do Thomas Cook management look for when recruiting holiday representatives?
2. Describe the key roles, duties and responsibilities of a Thomas Cook Overseas Representative.
3. Find a vacancy for a holiday representative's job with Thomas Cook (or another tour operator) and write a short report on how you feel you meet the key requirements of the post and in which areas you would need further development and training before taking the job;
4. Which aspects of being a Thomas Cook Overseas Representative appeal most to you and which responsibilities would you feel least comfortable with?

This case study is designed to provide evidence for P1.

Weblink

Check out this website to help answer the questions and for more information on holiday representative job opportunities with Thomas Cook.

www.thomascook.com/recruitment

Property representatives

Property representatives work in a variety of different locations and meet the needs of many different types of customers, as the following sections of this unit explain.

Hotel representatives

The work of most overseas holiday reps working for the big, mass-market tour operators is hotel or apartment-based. The large numbers of holidaymakers in a hotel or apartment complex means that it makes sense for a rep to spend most of his or her time in a single location or a group of properties that are close together, thereby keeping in regular contact with holidaymakers. This also cuts down travelling time between properties, which may be by public transport, moped, car, bicycle or walking, depending on the circumstances. Applicants for these jobs usually need to be over 20 or 21 years of age, are provided with accommodation and a company uniform, and receive training before starting the job and while working in-resort.

Cosmos overseas representatives

Villa representatives

Villas tend to be more spread out than hotels or apartments, so reps have to spend more time travelling between properties and may not see villa-based customers quite as often during their holiday. They are likely to be given some form of transport for their work, either a car or moped. Roles, duties and responsibilities are very similar to those of hotel/apartment reps, although information about what to do in the resort is likely to be given on a one-to-one or small group basis rather than by using the type of information board used in a hotel or apartment complex. Villa reps working for the big holiday companies are employed full-time for the season, but smaller tour operators offering villa holidays sometimes use the services of a freelance rep based in the resort, i.e. somebody who is self-employed and looks after the customers of a number of different holiday companies.

Reps for young people's holidays

Holidays for young people usually involve partying until the small hours, meeting lots of new people and having a good time in the resort. Reps working for holiday companies that offer young people's holidays, for example Club 18-30 (part of the Thomas Cook Group) and 2wentys (now owned by TUI Travel plc), look for very outgoing personalities in the people they employ. Reps are expected to take part in all the activities on offer to the young holidaymakers, so need boundless energy, enthusiasm and stamina. These include trips to clubs, pubs and bars, plus beach and pool games and activities. Such a volatile mix of alcohol, activities and hot sun can sometimes lead to problems, so reps often have to think on their feet and handle awkward situations in a professional manner. Although sometimes difficult, reps working on young people's holidays must remain professional at all times and not be tempted to get too involved with their clients. For people with the right attitude and skills, these jobs give young reps the chance to visit the hot spots of Europe, such as Ayia Napa, Faliraki and Kavos.

Activity 15.1

Carry out some research into holiday reps' jobs with companies that offer holidays specifically for young people and make a list of the key roles, duties and responsibilities of the jobs, plus the skills, qualities and experience needed to do the job well.

This activity is designed to provide evidence for P1.

Reps for seniors holidays

Holidays for the over 50s and seniors in general tend to be much more sedate, although there is a growing trend for older people to be far more active in later life. Recent research commissioned by Saga, Britain's leading travel company for the over 50s, indicated that the top ten most popular activities that over 50s would like to try include learning to fly, rally car driving, white water rafting, surfing and even sky diving! Holiday reps working with senior holidaymakers need to understand the particular needs of older people on holiday, which may include more time needed when travelling on excursions, help with access to facilities and empathy with their particular circumstances. For this reason, many tour operators recruit older and more mature people to fill these posts, making it easier for the holidaymakers to relate to their reps.

Weblink Check out this website for more information on Saga Holidays and the job opportunities they offer.
www.saga.co.uk

Reps for family holidays

Holidays for families are the backbone of the package holiday market – they offer good value for money at an all-inclusive price in a safe and secure environment. Reps help families to settle in to what are likely to be unfamiliar surroundings in their resort accommodation and point out activities and attractions that are geared particularly to families. They may be asked to help families who have special dietary or other requirements, by liaising with hotel management. Families with young children tend not to go on late night excursions, so reps should point out the day trips that are likely to appeal most to this segment of the market. Many tour operators offer clubs and activities for children, to keep them entertained and give their parents a rest. These are usually divided by age groups and full details are normally given out at the welcome meeting at the start of the holiday. Reps play an important part in making the sometimes stressful activity of taking children on holiday as carefree and enjoyable as possible.

Ski representatives

Ski tour operators offer a range of overseas appointments throughout the season, most of which involve close contact with customers. Positions include chalet hosts, bar managers, chefs, receptionists, chalet managers and resort managers. Working as a chalet host is a common first appointment in a ski resort, giving a good grounding for career progression within a particular company or the industry generally. Chalet hosts employed by Inghams, a specialist ski tour operator, have the following responsibilities:

1. Running a catered chalet;
2. Catering and cleaning to a very high standard;
3. Looking after guests;
4. Menu planning;
5. Budgeting and basic administration.

The company's chalets vary in size from those accommodating up to 8 people, which may be managed by a single chalet host, to larger chalets suitable for friends and couples to run together. Inghams look for individuals who are outgoing and cheerful, with a sense of humour and a basic love of cooking. The specific requirements for the post of chalet host are:

- A cooking diploma or proven experience of catering;
- Basic hygiene knowledge;
- Minimum age of 19 years;
- Previous experience within the hospitality industry;
- Excellent customer service skills.

Ski reps who do well in their winter season jobs may be offered summer season positions in different resorts or a job in the UK company headquarters.

Inghams employs ski reps in the Alps

Weblink Check out this website for more information on job opportunities at Inghams.

www.inghams.co.uk

Transfer representatives

If a tour operator has a very large number of passengers arriving regularly at a particular airport or airports, they may employ a transfer rep specifically to organise client transfers between the airport and their accommodation, thereby releasing the resort reps to carry out their normal duties. In most cases, however, resort reps carry out airport transfers on a rota basis. The role of the transfer rep is to meet and greet customers as they arrive at the airport and transfer them safely and speedily to their holiday accommodation. This is normally by coach, but could be by taxi or even a hired car. At the end of their holiday, the process is reversed and the transfer rep supervises the collection of passengers from their accommodation and transfers them to the airport to catch their flight home. Specific duties and responsibilities of the transfer rep include:

- Meeting and greeting customers at the airport;
- Checking the passengers against a manifest (a list of passengers' names);
- Escorting the customers to the coach;
- Giving a welcoming speech on the coach;
- Checking the holidaymakers into their accommodation;
- At the end of their holiday, collecting guests from their accommodation;
- Transferring the customers to the airport;
- Directing guests to the check-in desks;
- Waiting at check-in until all guests have departed safely.

Transfer reps are the very first representative of the holiday company that the customer meets, so they play a very important part in making sure that customers get their holidays off to a good start. Sometimes, however, transfer reps have to deal with problems, such as lost luggage, delayed flights, long queues at check-in and passengers arriving late for their return flight. These situations can be very stressful and call for a great deal of patience, tact and diplomacy on the part of the transfer rep.

Children's representatives

Becoming a children's rep is a good way to start a career as a representative since the starting age is often lower (over 18 years) than for a resort rep. If you enjoy the life as a children's rep and do well in your job, you may decide to stay on in the travel and tourism sector by applying for a resort rep's position when you are older. Jobs as a children's rep are offered by the major holiday companies and campsite operators, some of which ask for an NNEB, BTEC or NVQ level 3 in Childcare, a Diploma in Nursery Nursing or an equivalent UK qualification from applicants.

The main role of a children's rep is to carry out a varied programme of activities for children, which provides them with a valuable social experience while on holiday. Children's reps need to create a child-friendly environment that is safe, clean and effectively managed so as to ensure maximum enjoyment for all children. Specific duites and responsibilities include:

- Providing a variety of stimulating activities for children in different age ranges;
- Maintaining and promoting an informative and attractive notice board of events;
- Attending welcome meetings to explain the services available for children;
- Managing groups of children during activities and events;
- Maintaining appropriate health, safety and security measures;
- Completing report forms and carrying out basic accounting in line with company procedures;
- Controlling and managing stock effectively;
- Liaising with and helping other reps as and when required;
- Offering a baby-sitting service.

Successful candidates for children's rep jobs are screened via an enhanced disclosure check from the Criminal Records' Bureau (CRB) to satisfy all concerned that there are no good reasons why they should not carry out their role.

A children's rep working for Neilson Holidays

Activity 15.2

Compare the roles, duties and responsibilities of the post of a children's representative with two different tour operators.

This activity is designed to provide evidence for P1 and M1.

Campsite representatives

Campsite reps (or couriers) work overseas or in the UK and are responsible for looking after customers during their holiday in a tent, chalet, lodge or mobile home. Major companies that recruit couriers for overseas work include Keycamp and Eurocamp (both part of Holidaybreak plc) and Canvas Holidays. Most jobs are from May to September, so they appeal particularly to students; the normal minimum age for recruitment is 18 years. Couriers spend a lot of time cleaning and preparing tents and other accommodation for new guests, plus making their stay as enjoyable as possible when they arrive, as the example from Canvas Holidays in Figure 15.2 explains.

Approachable, well mannered, friendly and helpful are just a few of the qualities you will need as a Campsite Courier or Courier Couple and remember, your main focus will be ensuring that our customers return home having had 'the best holiday they have ever had.'

So how are you going to achieve this? Your duties will mainly involve cleaning customer accommodation for their arrival, welcoming them onto the campsite and ensuring that all the customer's needs are attended to during their stay.

You will need to have initiative and be a quick thinker, able to resolve any problems that may occur on site efficiently and effectively.

As a Courier or Courier Couple you may, dependent on the dates available to work, also be involved in montage (putting up tents) and demontage (taking down tents) at the beginning and end of the season.

Every year we welcome staff of all ages to our overseas team. We have designated 'Couple Sites' or 'Single Courier Sites'. There is also the chance to progress to a senior position within the company.

Fig 15.2 – Working as a Campsite Courier for Canvas Holidays

There are a number of different jobs available on campsites, for example:

- Courier – the most common position, ensuring customers enjoy their holiday to the full (as described in Figure 15.2);
- Senior courier – required to organise the daily workload of a small team of couriers and children's couriers, as well as being able to carry out full courier duties as required. Positions tend to be for the full season only;
- Mature courier – some companies welcome mature couple and single applicants as couriers. Mature couriers provide invaluable benefits to customers, since many of them have considerable experience of camping and travelling in Europe. Mature couriers

can choose to live in company tents or their own caravan or motorhome;

- Site manager – people with proven supervisory experience are recruited to lead the largest teams for the major camping tour operators. They are expected to set and maintain excellent standards of service and behaviour amongst staff;
- Team leader – responsible for managing the work of a team of couriers, with responsibility for customer service and accommodation standards;
- Children's courier – responsible for organising and delivering a regular programme of events for children on site, as well as being available for general courier duties as required.

In addition to these posts, the larger companies offer jobs at the beginning and end of each season in montage (erecting tents) and demontage (dismantling tents), including team leaders, assistants and drivers.

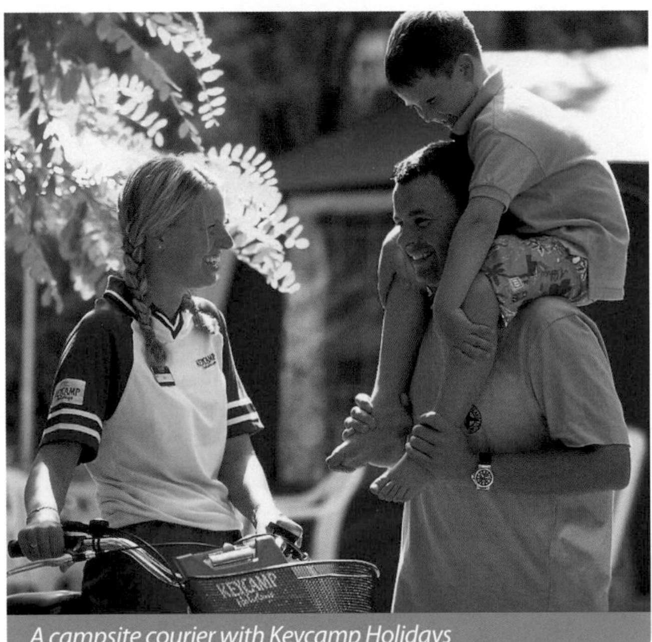

A campsite courier with Keycamp Holidays

Weblink @ Check out these websites for more information on campsite rep job opportunities.

www.keycamp.co.uk; www.eurocamp.co.uk; www.canvasholidays.co.uk

Activity 15.3

Carry out some research into holiday reps' jobs with companies that offer camping holidays in Europe and make a list of the key roles, duties and responsibilities of the jobs, plus the skills, qualities and experience needed to do the job well. Present your findings as a series of fact sheets on the jobs found.

This activity is designed to provide evidence for P1.

Changing working practices for holiday representatives

Not all tour operators' holiday representatives work in the same way or have the same responsibilities. The roles, duties, responsibilities and working practices of holiday representatives are constantly being reviewed as tour operators look at more cost-effective ways of operating resorts or catering for more independent customers. The main focus of this unit is on the traditional roles, responsibilities and duties as these are still practised by many representatives employed by smaller tour operators. However, some larger tour operators have now introduced in-resort customer service centres instead of having representatives in each property. Many also offer pre-holiday promotion and sale of excursions in the UK, rather than holidaymakers booking these in resort. Initiatives such as these impact on the changing responsibilities and working practices of holiday representatives.

Activity 15.4

Analyse how the current and changing roles, duties and responsibilities of holiday representatives can contribute to the overall holiday experience for customers.

This activity is designed to provide evidence for D1.

SECTION 2 Know the legal responsibilities of a holiday representative

Customers are becoming more conscious of the law and what happens if a company doesn't carry out its legal responsibilities. People are much more willing to complain about products and services, including holidays, and are prepared to fight for their rights, including taking court action if necessary, as the following recent headline from the Travemole website describes:

> ***Thomson and Thomas Cook in massive compensation payout***
>
> *A court this week officially settled a compensation claim by hundreds of holidaymakers against Thomson, Thomas Cook and other UK operators. The 790 holidaymakers won a total of more than £2.5 million in compensation after falling ill at a Spanish hotel.*

Travel and tourism companies have to follow their legal responsibilities to the letter, whether this is to do with the quality of products and services they sell, issues to do with employing staff, health and safety matters, and customers' rights when things don't work out as planned.

Overseas representatives play a very important part in carrying out tour operators' legal responsibilities, whether at the airport, on transfers, in resort or on excursions.

Legal responsibilities

Tour operators, and the staff they employ, must work within the legal framework when supplying holidays and other travel products to customers. All staff, including holiday reps working overseas, have a general duty of care to everybody they come into contact with as part of their work, such as customers, colleagues, contractors and suppliers. Over and above this duty of care, the work of holiday reps is governed by a number of important pieces of legislation, including:

- The EU Package Travel Regulations;
- Supply of Goods and Services Act;
- Health and Safety at Work Act;
- Trade Descriptions Act;
- Disability Discrimination Act.

EU Package Travel Regulations

The Package Travel Regulations came into operation on 1st January 1993 in the then 12 Member States of the European Union. The main aim of the Regulations is to give people buying package holidays more protection and access to compensation when things go wrong, while at the same time harmonising the rules covering packages operated throughout European Union countries. Up to the introduction of the Regulations, tour operators had been able to disclaim responsibility when holiday arrangements didn't go according to plan on the grounds that they had no control over these unfortunate events, for example overbooking at a hotel or the failure of a coach transfer to arrive. Under the terms of the Package Travel Regulations, tour organisers must accept legal responsibility for all the services they offer to travellers. Exceptions would be made in circumstances which could neither have been foreseen nor overcome, although in such circumstances, organisers must give all necessary assistance to customers.

The Package Travel Regulations place a number of duties and responsibilities on tour operators, for example:

- Providing information to customers on who is responsible for the package they have booked. That person or organisation is then liable in the event of failure to deliver any elements of the package;
- Providing clear contract terms;
- Giving emergency telephone numbers;

- Providing proof of the organiser's security against insolvency and information on any available insurance policies;
- Giving immediate notification with explanation of any increase in prices permitted within the terms of the contract;
- Providing a variety of compensation options if agreed services are not supplied;
- Producing accurate promotional material including brochures.

Holiday representatives are not expected to know every detail of the Package Travel Regulations, but must be aware of their existence and why they have been put in place. The sorts of circumstances when the Regulations could come into force include overbooking of accommodation, leading to some customers' rooms being unavailable, and serious flight delays.

Activity 15.5

Outline the legal responsibilities of a holiday representative in the following holiday situation.

You are a Resort Representative on the island of Malta. The Brown family from Rochdale have complained that the hire car they booked in advance for their holiday was not available when they went to pick it up from the airport. The car hire company insisted that they had never received a booking for the Smiths from your holiday company and refused to hire them a vehicle.

This activity is designed to provide evidence for P2.

Supply of Goods and Services Act

This legislation states that any contract for a holiday should be carried out using 'reasonable care and skill'. The tour operator and travel agent should ensure that the booking is carried out correctly and that the holiday itself should be of a generally satisfactory standard, complying with any descriptions made. Tour operators must take great care when selecting accommodation, transport and any services they provide as part of their package holidays.

Health and Safety at Work Act

This piece of legislation is mainly concerned with employers' responsibilities to their staff while in the workplace. The 'workplace' for overseas representatives is not easy to define! It could be a hotel lobby, theme park, overseas resort office or even a nightclub. Whatever the location, tour operators must make sure that all work systems and practices are safe for their staff. They must provide adequate information and training for employees on relevant health and safety matters, such as the safe use of chemicals, using equipment, handling stock and escorting customers. Overseas reps are responsible for completing necessary documentation in relation to health and safety, such as the type of accident/incident form shown in Figure 15.3.

Health and safety issues that affect holidaymakers are discussed in detail in the third section of this unit (see page 123).

Trade Descriptions Act

This Act protects consumers against false descriptions made knowingly or recklessly by anybody selling products and services, including holidays and other travel products. Any description of, for example, a hotel or resort must be truthful at the time it was written (if circumstances change, then the company must inform the customer of the nature of the changes). The Act places a duty on owners and operators of travel and tourism facilities to produce brochures, websites and other promotional materials that are not intended to deceive customers.

Activity 15.6

Outline the legal responsibilities of a holiday representative in the following holiday situation.

You are a Resort Representative in Palma Nova, Majorca. A young couple have complained to you that the brochure they used to book their holiday mentioned there being a disco in their hotel every Friday evening, but this was not the case.

This activity is designed to provide evidence for P2.

Accident/Incident Report Form

Form completed by ....

Property/location..

Date form completed..

Nature of the accident	Date and time .... Location .... Was a photograph taken? Yes/No
Full description of the incident	.... Was medical treatment needed? Yes/No
The injured party	Name .... Holiday ref: .... Home address .... Tel.No: ....
Witnesses	Name .... Address .... Name .... Address ....

Fig 15.3 – Example of an accident/incident report form

Disability Discrimination Act

Meeting the needs of disabled people not only makes good business sense, but it is also the law of the land. The Disability Discrimination Act (DDA) was designed to protect disabled people from discrimination in employment and to increase access to goods, facilities and services. The Act defines 'disability' as:

'A physical or mental impairment which has a substantial and long term adverse effect on a person's ability to carry out normal day-to-day activities.'

Since October 1999, service providers have had to make reasonable adjustments to accommodate disabled people. From October 1st 2004, the Act required all organisations to make alterations to the built environment, e.g. access to buildings and the ability to move freely inside buildings. Reps must be fully aware of the scope of the DDA and to provide assistance to customers in line with the Act.

Booking conditions and contracts

Tour operators' booking terms and conditions are explained in their brochures and on websites, and customers are deemed to have accepted these, and enter into a contract with the tour operator, when they sign their holiday booking form. The circumstances when customers can claim refunds and compensation are included in the booking conditions and reflect the need to comply with the Package Travel Regulations described earlier in this unit. Tour operators can make compensation payments to customers when, for example, holidaymakers are forced to take a lower standard of accommodation than they had booked as a result of overbooking by the hotel.

Activity 15.7

Study the booking conditions found in a range of holiday brochures and summarise the responsibilities of tour operators to their customers and vice versa.

This activity is designed to provide evidence for P2.

Overseas resort office

The resort office is the hub of a tour operator's overseas operations. Depending on the size of the tour operator, the office will house administration and/or management staff who are responsible for the smooth running of all aspects of the overseas operations, including:

- Preparing transfer lists of passengers (manifests);
- Co-ordinating accommodation reservations;
- Dealing with medical cases;
- Accounting for payments, receipts, etc.
- Handling complaints from customers;
- Organising promotional materials for reps, e.g. flyers for excursions;
- Liaising with local suppliers and the UK head office;
- Ensuring that all paperwork is completed accurately and within deadlines.

Figure 15.4 shows the duties expected of an Operations Assistant in a Cosmos overseas resort office.

OPERATIONS ASSISTANT

As an Operations Assistant you will be involved in all aspects of running a busy resort office, including handling hotel reservations, producing transfer lists, handling incoming calls to the resort office and dealing pro-actively with all issues. You will be computer literate and ideally familiar with using Word and Excel. You will also have a strong attention to detail and be prepared to work flexible hours. As with our Overseas Consultants positions, you will need to be confident with an outgoing personality, show commitment and most importantly have common sense.

Fig 15.4 – Duties of an Operations Assistant in a resort office

SECTION 3 Understand the role of the holiday representative in creating a safe and healthy holiday environment

Overseas holiday representatives play a crucial role in ensuring that customers not only have an enjoyable holiday, but also one that is as safe as possible. We have already seen that under the terms of the Package Travel Regulations, and other legislation, tour operators have a legal duty to ensure that the holidays and other services they offer to customers meet all current health and safety regulations. It is no longer acceptable for a tour operator to say that it is not responsible for parts of its programmes that are delivered by other companies.

Health and safety risks and hazards

Most overseas holidays enjoyed by British people pass without any health or safety problems at all, but tour operators must have procedures in place to deal with issues when things go wrong. A hazard is anything that can cause harm, while a risk is the likelihood, high or low, that somebody could be harmed by the hazard, together with an indication of how serious the harm could be. For example, riding a moped while in a holiday resort is a hazardous activity, but the risk that it will cause you harm can be reduced by taking a number of steps, e.g. by being briefed in advance about safety procedures and wearing the correct helmet and other equipment.

Hazards are all around us, whether we are on holiday or just going about our everyday lives. In holiday situations, hazards may be found in:

- Accommodation – for example, a faulty gas or electric fire in an apartment or a dangerous balcony;
- Facilities for holidaymakers – for example, poorly-maintained swimming pools, children's playgrounds and lifts;
- Food outlets – for example, dirty kitchens and food preparation areas;
- Excursions and activities – for example, a weak bridge over a gorge or a coach without seat belts.

Activity 15.8

Design a chart that lists the hazards that could be found on an excursion that involves exploring sand dunes in 4x4 jeeps in the morning and a boat party in the afternoon/evening, plus all the measures that should be taken to minimise risks.

This activity is designed to provide evidence for P3.

Minimising risks

A great deal can be done to minimise the risks associated with a holiday abroad, through tour operators providing relevant information, carrying out regular checks in resort, reporting incidents correctly and following industry guidelines on good practice.

Providing information

Many holiday companies provide health and safety information before customers travel to a resort (see Figure 15.5), while overseas reps use a number of opportunities to give health and safety advice, including:

- At welcome meetings;
- During transfer commentaries;
- Via noticeboards and information books;
- En-route to excursions and activities.

Health and safety checks

Before signing contracts with any of its suppliers before the start of a holiday season, for example hoteliers and coach operators, tour companies inspect premises and

Safety Standards

Hoteliers and suppliers should meet local and national safety standards, however these vary widely across the programme and rarely match those standards that we enjoy in the UK, only a minority of hotels and apartments meet European Commission recommendations on fire safety. We nevertheless seek to raise standards in all of our destinations. You will receive a Safety First leaflet on arrival in resort, please take a few minutes of your time to familiarise yourself with the information that it contains.

Health and Hygiene

We promote good hygiene practices within hotels, but the hygiene standards in some foreign countries, particularly developing destinations, are generally much lower than in the UK. Care should be taken to minimise the risk of holiday sickness, especially among pregnant women, infants and the elderly. Your GP can provide you with up-to-date health advice and we recommend that you consult your doctor well in advance before travelling.

Swimming Pool and Beach Safety

It is extremely unlikely that the pool in your holiday accommodation will have a lifeguard. It is therefore important to remember, especially when travelling with children, to take a few minutes to familiarise yourself and your party with the pool area on arrival. Children must always be accompanied by an adult in the pool, including children's pools and surrounding areas, and at all other times. Familiarise yourself with any flag warning systems that may be in operation on local beaches, and take into account local conditions.

Children's Safety

Naturally the safety of our younger holidaymakers is also of paramount importance. We take advice from leading UK child safety organisations and accident prevention agencies, to ensure that standards are as high as possible. Parents should check that they are happy with hotel operated clubs and children's facilities, including playgrounds

Excursion Safety

We work with excursion suppliers to ensure that they operate to appropriate safety standards. Whilst every care is taken with those activities that we recommend, should you independently choose to use an alternative supplier we advise that you should satisfy yourself that your insurance and the insurance, legal cover and safety standards of the company you are choosing to use is adequate.

Fig 15.5 – Advice on health and safety from Thomson Holidays

vehicles to make sure they comply with health and safety guidelines. Once the contracts have been signed and the season is underway, it is the responsibility of reps to carry out regular checks to make sure that health and safety standards are being maintained. This involves systematic inspections of a number of items, including:

- Fire alarms and evacuation signs and procedures;
- Swimming pool safety equipment and notices;
- Electrical, gas and water systems;
- The safety of balconies in rooms;
- Warning flags on beaches;
- Hygiene standards in accommodation, eating areas, public areas and toilets;
- Safety equipment used for activities, including children's clubs.

An example of a health and safety report form that reps have to complete is shown in Figure 15.6.

The Federation of Tour Operators (FTO) provides its members, which include all the leading UK holiday companies, with practical help and information on managing health and safety in resort areas. To ensure consistency in regulations and standards of health, hygiene and safety between destinations, the FTO has appointed a health and safety co-ordinator and developed a code of practice. This publication contains advice on a range of issues, including:

- Fire safety;
- Food safety;
- Pool safety;
- General safety;
- Beach safety;
- Legionella (legionnaire's disease) management;
- Children's clubs;
- Incident management.

The Federation has also developed a health and safety training video to complement the code of practice.

Health and Safety Report

Form completed by ....

Property ....

Date form completed ....

Date faxed to Area Office ....

Description of defect	Reported to	Action to be taken	Target date for completion
Loose wiring in guest bedroom	*Hotel manager*	*Repairs to wiring*	*21 April 09*

Signed .... (Representative)

Signed .... (Hotel Management)

Fig 15.6 – A health and safety report form

Weblink @ Check out this website for more information on the FTO health and safety guidelines.
www.fto.co.uk

Activity 15.9

Under the direction of your tutor, carry out a health and safety inspection, and complete a health and safety report form. This could take place in your college/school, a nearby tourist facility or while investigating accommodation or an attraction as part of a study tour in the UK or overseas.

This activity is designed to provide evidence for P3.

Water Park Risk Assessment

Location .... Carried out by ....

Date .... Checked by ....

Location	Hazard	Risk	Control measures
Travel to park	Safety of coach/minibus	Low	• Visual inspection • Check seatbelts • Check emergency doors
Swimming pool	Injury caused by trips and slips Possibility of drowning	Medium	• Verbal warning to customers • Inspection of safety aids • Monitoring behaviour
Flumes and slides	Injury caused by falls and slips Possibility of drowning	Medium	• Verbal warning to customers • Inspection of safety aids • Monitoring behaviour
Across the park	Injury from traffic	Low	• Verbal warning to customers • Inspection of speed restriction measures • Supervision of customers
Across the park	Possibility of loss, abduction or assault of children	Low	• Verbal warning to customers • Supervision of children • Checks on procedures

Fig 15.7 – A risk assessment form

Risk assessments

A risk assessment is a systematic investigation of the potential hazards in a given situation. Holiday reps may be required to carry out risk assessments when planning an excursion, for example a trip to a water park as part of an activity for children's club members. Reps complete a form that lists potential hazards and the action that needs to be taken to minimise risks. An example of a risk assessment form is given in Figure 15.7.

Reporting accidents and incidents

Reps are trained to report all serious accidents and incidents involving holidaymakers in the resort, by completing an accident/incident report form (see Figure 15.3 on page 121) or logging the details in an accident book. The reports must be as detailed as possible, since they may be needed for future claims against the tour operator by customers.

SECTION 4

Be able to apply social, customer service and selling skills when dealing with transfers, welcome meetings and other situations

A holiday rep's main role is to provide excellent customer service to his or her customers, so being able to demonstrate effective social, customer service and selling skills in a range of different situations is an essential part of the job.

Social skills

So far in this unit we've seen that the role of holiday representatives revolves around dealing with people in a pleasant and professional manner. Social skills play a big part in a rep's role and are extremely important in:

- Creating rapport – with customers, work colleagues, suppliers, contractors, etc. in a variety of different situations;
- Providing a welcome – to customers, from the time they arrive in the resort to their departure flight home;
- Empathising – reps need to be able to understand issues from the customers' point of view;
- Providing a friendly and helpful service – should be the prime motivation for taking a job as a rep;
- Using appropriate language – social and communication skills will vary depending on the type of customer, e.g. language used when talking with young people on holiday is likely to be different from that used to deal with older customers or those whose first language isn't English.

Some people naturally have a more sociable nature, but it's important to remember that social skills can be learned and improved through training, practice and experience.

It's fair to say that reps have to talk a lot while doing their jobs, so good verbal communication skills are essential. Verbal communication can be formal or informal. Examples of formal communication involving reps include:

- Conducting a welcome meeting for new arrivals in a resort;
- Telling customers about health and safety procedures in a hotel;
- Making a speech to thank your work colleagues at the end of the season;
- Complaining to a supplier that some equipment is faulty;
- Providing a commentary on a coach excursion.

Reps communicate informally when they are talking to customers and colleagues in a more relaxed manner, perhaps while on an excursion or in a hotel lobby.

Activity 15.10

Working in a small group, discuss how you would handle the following situation in order to provide excellent customer service. You should also role play the arrival transfer speech.

You are working as a transfer rep at Athens airport and are expecting 145 passengers to arrive on a flight from Luton. Their take-off from the UK was delayed by 4 hours due to technical problems with the aircraft. You will be accompanying 45 of the passengers on a transfer coach to their accommodation when they arrive.

This activity is designed to provide evidence for P4.

Customer service skills

Elsewhere on your course you have learned about the importance of developing and delivering excellent customer service skills in the workplace – identifying and meeting the needs of customers is the number one goal for travel and tourism companies that want to succeed in business. The effects of not providing acceptable levels of customer service can be very damaging to the company concerned, resulting in fewer sales, lost revenue and a poor image. Reps who are found to have poorly-developed customer service skills can be helped with extra training, but if this fails to improve matters they may well be advised to consider a career in a different aspect of travel and tourism.

Product knowledge

Product knowledge is knowing all the facts and features of products being sold. In the case of holiday representatives, their product knowledge must extend to:

- Details of the holidays that their customers have booked;
- Facts about the resort and surrounding area;
- Detailed information about the excursions and other extras they sell;
- Information about medical and emergency facilities in the resort.

Having good product knowledge not only helps reps to provide excellent customer service to their holidaymakers, but can also lead to increased income via the commission earned on sales of excursions, car hire, merchandise and other products.

Handling complaints

Although the great majority of holidaymakers have a trouble-free holiday, there are occasions when reps have to deal with complaints from clients. This may result from a number of causes, including overbooking, flight delays, accommodation of a poor standard, noise or poor quality food.

The key actions to take when handling complaints are:

- Listen attentively so that you get the whole story first time;
- Thank the customer for bringing the problem to your attention;
- Apologise in general terms for the inconvenience but do not grovel;
- Provide support for the customer by saying that the complaint will be fully investigated and matters put right as soon as possible;
- Sympathise with the customer and try to see the situation from their point of view;
- Don't justify the circumstances that led up to the complaint and go on the defensive;
- Ask questions if you are not clear on any points of the customer's complaint;
- Find a solution to the problem;
- Agree the solution with the customer;
- Follow through to make sure that what you promised has been done;
- In future, try and anticipate complaints before they happen!

One step on from somebody who has a justifiable complaint is the customer who is intent on causing a scene. Just like handling complaints, there are tried and tested ways of dealing with these individuals:

- Try not to let them get you down or get under your skin. The fact that they wish to cause a fuss may be a sign of their own insecurity;
- Never argue with them – it can often get the member of staff into deeper trouble;
- Never be rude to the customer, however rude they are being to you!
- Try not to take any remarks personally – you may have had nothing to do with the alleged incident but are simply the nearest member of staff;
- Let the customer do the talking and listen to what they have to say.

If a situation appears to be getting out of hand, it is wise to seek help from another rep or senior member of the overseas team.

Activity 15.11

Working with other members of your group role play the following situations that reps sometimes encounter:

1. A customer complaining about the poor quality food in her hotel;
2. The leader of a school group complaining about the time his pupils have to queue to use the hotel's games room;
3. A couple complaining to the transfer rep when they arrive in their resort about the long delay in their outward flight from Manchester.

You should take it in turns to play the person complaining and the rep dealing with the complaint. Members of the group should make notes on how well the 'rep' handles the complaint, in line with the key points discussed above.

This activity is designed to provide evidence for P5, M3 and D2.

Image

Tour operators spend a great deal of money developing their image or brand, which is used on all advertising, promotional work, aircraft, stationery, etc. Reps play an important part in reinforcing the company's image, not just with the uniform that they wear, but in the way they deal with customers. If treated well by reps while on holiday, customers come away with a positive impression of the tour operator and will tell their friends about the good time that they had, leading to extra business for the company.

Dress code and behaviour

Nearly all holiday companies provide uniforms for their holiday reps. Uniforms help to create a positive first impression with customers and make staff easily identifiable if customers need help or advice. The wearing of a uniform also presents a consistent image to the public and helps to build customer loyalty. However, it is important to remember that the word uniform does not necessarily mean a very formal dress code. Holiday reps working on campsites or as children's reps, for example, wear a company uniform, but it often consists of a polo shirt, shorts and trainers. The important point about a uniform is that it should be appropriate and functional, i.e. suited to the nature and demands of the job. Overseas staff should be informed at interview about the dress code for the job and what type of uniform is supplied.

Uniforms create a good impression with holidaymakers (courtesy of Cosmos)

Training of representatives before they start work in the resort covers a number of sensitive issues concerning behaviour in the workplace. Reps are reminded about using appropriate language at all times with clients and other members of staff, including not swearing or using slang. Tour operators have different policies on staff smoking and drinking while on duty. The overriding concern of all companies is that reps must not be under the influence of alcohol while at work. With many companies, this is an offence for which staff can be instantly dismissed. Holiday reps must also comply with the tour operator's policies on relationships with colleagues and customers. As with drinking while on duty, inappropriate relationships with clients and colleagues are to be avoided.

Personal appearance

All reps must report for work in a presentable fashion, well groomed and with a smart uniform. Personal appearance can be a sensitive area, particularly when supervisors and managers have to remind staff about the importance of arriving at work in a clean, hygienic and presentable fashion. All staff working in travel and tourism, but especially reps whose work brings them into close contact with customers, must:

- Be generally clean;
- Have hair that is clean and tidy;
- Have fresh breath.

Customers will not tolerate staff with poor body odour or bad breath and may well take their custom elsewhere. It is important to remember that the staff are the outward image of an organisation. For example, if you are greeted at an airport by a representative who smells of stale cigarettes or whose hair is unkempt, your first impressions of the company and your holiday are likely to be negative. If, on the other hand, the rep is smartly presented, with a pleasant smile and tidy hair, you are much more likely to be impressed with the tour company from the outset.

Personal appearance is important (courtesy of First Choice Holidays)

Communication skills

Communication is an essential part of a holiday representative's job, whether dealing with customers, hoteliers, work colleagues, contractors or suppliers. For most of the time, communicating with these people is a straightforward and pleasant affair, but there are occasions when reps have to use their communication skills to deal with difficult and awkward situations.

Non-verbal communication

Non-verbal communication or 'body language' is the process by which we send and receive signals and messages without the use of the spoken word. When at work, reps are always in the public eye, not just in formal situations such as while hosting a welcome meeting, but every minute while on duty. This means that they have to conduct themselves appropriately and professionally at all times, by projecting a positive and welcoming image, making eye contact while talking, maintaining a good posture and keeping any irritating habits or mannerisms to a minimum!

Communicating with groups and individuals

Reps come into contact with all sorts of customers while at work, e.g. groups, individuals, adults, children, youths, people whose first language isn't English, mixed age groups, people with special needs, etc. Reps must be able to assess customers' needs quickly and provide appropriate information, help, advice and guidance.

Dealing with groups can be an altogether more challenging task than communicating with an individual customer. Handling group situations calls for good organisational and communication skills, so that every member of the group turns up in the right place at the right time! Although the group you are dealing with may be very large, it is important to make every effort to treat the members of the group as individuals by, for example, addressing people by name and taking time to talk to them on a one-to-one basis, particularly those that you feel may need a little more attention or support.

Dealing with children can be challenging and fun! (courtesy of Canvas Holidays)

There are certain ground rules that you need to adopt when communicating information to a group of customers, including:

- Making sure that members of the group can see, hear and understand you;
- Communicating effectively using simple language in a clear, confident tone of voice;
- Making sure that everybody has understood what you have said by allowing time for questions;
- Making yourself available afterwards if people want further clarification on a one-to-one basis.

Dealing with groups of clients is an important part of the work of a holiday representative, for example when organising transfers, conducting excursions or on guiding duties. Developing group handling skills will ensure that you can:

- Ensure the safety and welfare of groups of clients;
- Handle mixed groups, e.g. by age, gender, language;
- Handle difficult groups, e.g. rowdy, under the influence of alcohol or complaining;
- Deal with medical and emergency situations.

Activity 15.12

To improve your group handling skills, take turns at playing the role of a tour guide by taking the rest of your group on a tour of your college/school or the local area. When the tour has finished, the 'customers' should discuss the strengths and weaknesses of each guide, concentrating on communication with the group as a whole as well as with individual group members. You may also like to role play the situation of a group of rowdy holidaymakers to practise some different group handling skills!

This activity is designed to provide evidence for P5.

Written and visual communication

Many of the responsibilities of holiday reps are concerned with gathering local information and communicating this information in written and visual form to customers, for example:

- Giving holidaymakers leaflets about local facilities and attractions at the welcome meeting;
- Passing on information during transfers to and from the airport;
- Compiling information books and folders for guests to use while in resort;
- Maintaining informative and attractive notice boards with information on resort attractions, events and activities;
- Making posters to advertise events.

Sources of local information include tourist offices, guidebooks, the internet, local hoteliers, attractions and restaurateurs, as well as other overseas staff. In addition to investigating what local attractions, facilities and events a resort has to offer holidaymakers, reps also need to know about local laws and customs, such as religious codes and festivals.

Notice boards are an excellent way for customers to keep up to date with what's happening in their resort and for reps to provide important information, as well as promoting and selling excursions and other travel services. The board needs to be located in a central position where holidaymakers regularly congregate, for example in a hotel foyer or by the welcome tent or mobile home on a campsite. Notice boards differ from one company to another, but minimum requirements are:

- Photographs, regular visiting times and details of how to contact the reps;
- Emergency contact details;
- Details of excursions and events;
- Details of return flights and any changes to travel arrangements;
- Facilities available in any children's clubs.

At the beginning of the season, reps usually prepare an information book or file for use by guests. This includes a great deal of useful local information such as an overview of the resort, public transport information, details of attractions, where to eat, doctor and dentist contact information, details of excursions, car and moped hire, foreign exchange, etc.

Notice boards and information books must look professional and business-like. When designing them, reps must make sure that:

- There are no spelling or grammar mistakes;
- All the information is current and not out of date;
- Where possible, information is typed or word processed;
- There is good use of colour to attract attention;
- There is not too much information on the notice board.

Activity 15.13

Working as part of a team, choose a popular overseas holiday destination and gather together information on its attractions, facilities and events. Use the information you collect to make a notice board that could be used by British people on holiday in the resort. Use a range of information sources, such as brochures, guidebooks, tourist offices and the internet, to gather your information. Many of the major tour operators' websites have destination guides.

This activity is designed to provide evidence for P5.

You saw earlier in this unit that reps have to complete quite a lot of paperwork as part of their job, e.g. health and safety reports, customer complaint forms, risk assessments, etc. Tour operators provide guidance on how these should be completed during rep training and while in the resort. Reps must ensure that all written documents are completed accurately and written in a clearly understood manner.

Selling skills and situations

Selling is an important part of a rep's job, earning the tour operator extra revenue and the member of staff extra income (commission) on sales. Selling skills and techniques are covered in the rep's training before starting work in resort. As with other aspects of travel and tourism, selling in overseas resorts follows the traditional sales process shown in Figure 15.8.

Taking the example of selling excursions at a welcome meeting, the different stages of the sales process could be as follows:

1. Building rapport – e.g. creating a professional and welcoming image, using people's names as appropriate, telling jokes, etc.
2. Establishing customer needs and expectations – holidaymakers are all looking for something different, so asking questions helps at this stage;

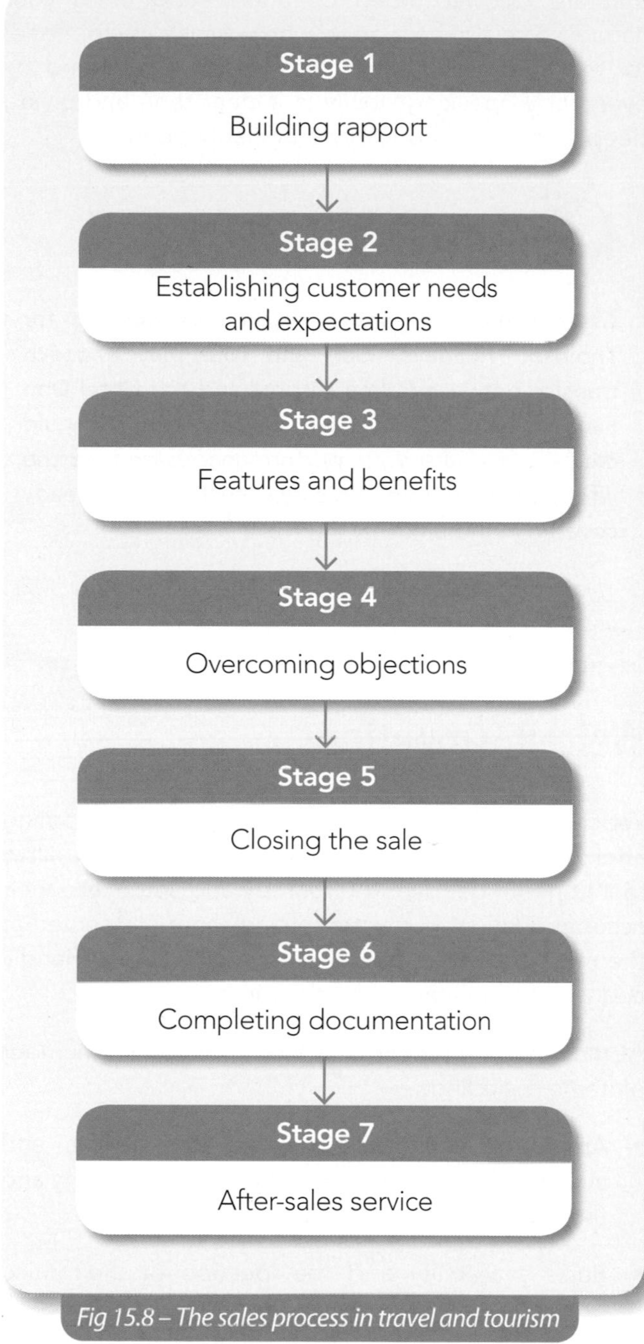

Fig 15.8 – The sales process in travel and tourism

3. Features and benefits – e.g. spending time explaining the advantages of different excursions and the features of each;
4. Overcoming objections – e.g. explaining that there are wheelchairs available at a cave complex if an elderly customer says she could not walk very far;
5. Closing the sale – this is concerned with persuading customers to make a commitment by, for example, putting their name on a list, paying a deposit, etc.
6. Completing documentation – e.g. completing and issuing tickets for the excursion;
7. After-sales service – e.g. asking customers how they enjoyed their excursion after the event.

When selling excursions and other products, reps must:

1. Listen carefully to customers' needs;
2. Speak in a clear tone and at an appropriate pace;
3. Have excellent product knowledge;
4. Use visual aids as appropriate;
5. Project a positive image;
6. Use appropriate body language;
7. Answer questions fully and frankly;
8. Recognise buying signals to close a sale.

Unit 4 in *Travel & Tourism for BTEC National Book 1 (3rd edition)* has more detailed information on selling in travel and tourism.

Activity 15.14

Take it in turns to play the role of a holiday representative selling an excursion to an evening banquet in a nearby Spanish castle at a welcome meeting in Torremolinos.

This activity is designed to provide evidence for P4 and M2.

Arrival transfers

We saw at the beginning of this unit that transfers between airport and accommodation are an important part of a rep's job, carried out on a rota basis amongst staff in the resort. After welcoming the holidaymakers, the rep on duty escorts the customers to their waiting coach and makes sure that they are all safely on board before setting off for the accommodation. On the journey to the accommodation, the rep will use the microphone on the coach to talk to the passengers. On a typical transfer trip the rep will:

- Welcome the customers on behalf of the tour company;
- Introduce himself/herself and the coach driver;
- Give the local time and indicate how long the transfer should take;
- Point out the emergency exits and other safety features on the coach;
- Explain that a number of different stops will be made to various accommodation bases;
- Give an overview of the local area and resort facilities;
- Give the time and location of the welcome meeting;
- Distribute welcome packs;
- Provide information about the weather, safety of drinking water, banking facilities, etc.
- Give details of check-in procedures at the accommodation.

Reps should give customers the opportunity to ask any questions they may have or to clarify any points they are not sure about.

Although daunting at first, most holiday reps need to be able to use a microphone, usually on a tour bus or at a welcome meeting, to communicate with large groups of clients. Many tour operators include developing this skill in their reps' pre-resort training, where staff role play the sort of situations they are likely to find themselves in when abroad. The same general rules that are followed when communicating using your natural voice also hold good when using a microphone, for example making sure that you can be heard by everybody, speaking slowly in a clear tone and giving people time to ask questions or clarify points.

Activity 15.15

Assume that you are a resort rep working for Thomson Holidays. Plan and role play a coach transfer between Palma Airport and the Hotel Don Paco in Magaluf. The rest of your group should critically evaluate your performance based on the information on communication techniques already covered in this unit.

This activity is designed to provide evidence for P4, M2 and D2.

Welcome meetings

Welcome meetings are normally held the morning after the holidaymakers arrive in the resort, to allow them time to get over the journey and settle into their accommodation. Refreshments are normally served at the meeting, which should be conducted in a friendly and welcoming manner by the rep.

At the welcome meeting, the rep will cover a number of items, including:

- An introduction to the rep, the resort and accommodation on behalf of the tour company and the hotel management;
- Rep's availability and the location of the notice board;
- Details of local attractions in the resort;
- Housekeeping items such as the times of meals and pool opening in the accommodation, use and cost of telephones, baby changing facilities, availability and cost of safes, etc.
- Information on facilities in the resort, including the location of banks, shops, medical facilities, car hire, beaches, public transport, etc.

- Details of the type and cost of excursions offered by the tour company, and how they can be booked;
- Any questions or concerns from the holidaymakers.

Activity 15.16

Still assuming that you are working as a resort rep for Thomson Holidays, plan and deliver a welcome meeting for the Magaluf holidaymakers who were on the coach transfer in Activity 15.15. The rest of your group should critically evaluate your performance based on the information on communication techniques already covered in this unit.

This activity is designed to provide evidence for P4, M2 and D2.

Other situations

In addition to supervising transfers and arranging welcome meetings, holiday reps have to deal with a wide range of other situations, for example over bookings at accommodation, complaints about standards in hotels, misleading brochure descriptions, illnesses, crimes and accidents. As discussed previously, they are also responsible for completing a variety of forms relating to health and safety, accounting and customer service (see Figure 15.9).

Customer Service Report Form

Tour operator .... Resort ....

Customer name .... Booking reference ....

Accommodation .... UK departure date ....

Room number .... Date of complaint ....

Rep's name ....

Customer's home address ....

.... Postcode ....

Telephone number .... Mobile ....

Details of the complaint or issue (to be completed by customer or rep)
....
....
....
....
Summary of actions taken to resolve the issue
....
....
....
....

Signed (customer).. Signed (rep) ....

Date ....

Copy sent to hotel Yes/No
Copy sent to resort office Yes/No
Copy sent to UK head office Yes/No

Fig 15.9 – Customer service report form

UNIT SUMMARY

In this unit you have examined many aspects of the work of overseas holiday representatives. You have found that there are actually many different types of holiday reps, from campsite couriers to transfer reps. All need the same qualities to succeed – a pleasant and welcoming manner, excellent presentation and communication skills, a willingness to help others, bags of initiative and enthusiasm, plus good organisational skills. The unit has examined legal aspects of the rep's role and found that ensuring a safe and secure environment for holidaymakers is a very important part of the job, involving carrying out health and safety inspections and completing the necessary paperwork and reports. You have leaned about, and practised, a range of social, customer service and selling skills when dealing with a variety of situations, including transfers and welcome meetings. Throughout the unit you have been shown many industry examples, while the case study on Overseas Representatives at Thomas Cook highlights key roles and responsibilities of holiday reps.

If you have worked methodically, by the end of this unit you should:

- Know the roles, duties and responsibilities of different categories of holiday representatives;
- Know the legal responsibilities of a holiday representative;
- Understand the role of the holiday representative in creating a safe and healthy holiday environment;
- Be able to apply social, customer service and selling skills when dealing with transfers, welcome meetings and other situations.

You are now in a position to complete the assignment for the unit, under the direction of your tutor. Before you tackle the assignment you may like to have a go at the following questions to help build your knowledge of working as a holiday representative.

TEST YOUR KNOWLEDGE

1. What are the three key roles of a resort representative?
2. List five responsibilities of resort reps.
3. Describe three of the different courier jobs available on campsites.
4. What are the specific requirements for the post of chalet host in a ski resort?
5. Explain how a rep would go about meeting the needs of young people on holiday and holidaymakers aged over 50.
6. Name three companies that offer jobs as campsite couriers.
7. What qualities does a children's rep need to succeed in his or her job?
8. Name four different types of holiday representatives.
9. Explain how a rep's job is influenced by the requirements of the Package Travel Regulations.

10. List five items that are normally inspected by reps on a health and safety check of a hotel or apartment complex.

11. What is a risk assessment and when might a rep have to carry one out?

12. What are the key points to bear in mind when communicating with a group?

13. What duties does a rep carry out on a typical transfer between airport and accommodation?

14. What aspects of personal presentation are particularly important to reps while on duty?

15. What are the key points to follow when dealing with complaints from customers?

Answers to these questions can be found in the Book 2 Tutor's CD-ROM that accompanies this book (ISBN 9780956268075). Full details can be found at **www.tandtpublishing.co.uk**

UNIT 15 ASSIGNMENT

Roles and Responsibilities of Holiday Representatives

Introduction

This assignment is made up of a number of tasks which, when successfully completed, are designed to give you sufficient evidence to meet the Pass (P), Merit (M) and Distinction (D) grading criteria for the unit. If you have carried out the activities and read the case studies throughout this unit, you will already have done a lot of work towards completing the tasks for this assignment.

Scenario

Since completing your BTEC course you have worked in a Birmingham hotel for 15 months on reception duties. You feel that the time is right to make a career move and you have applied for a job as an overseas resort representative with one of the major holiday companies. You put in an excellent application and have been invited to an interview and selection day at the company's head office. During the day, you are asked to complete a number of tasks to assess your suitability for the job. The first two tasks involve making a presentation and writing a short report, while tasks 3 and 4 are role plays involving other applicants for the representative jobs.

Task 1

For this task you must make a presentation to the selection panel and the rest of the applicants in which you must:

a. Describe the roles, duties and responsibilities for three different categories of holiday representatives, highlighting changing roles and working practices (P1). This must include one type of resort representative, e.g. property, over 50s, 18-30s, holiday village or villa, plus two others selected from ski, transfer, children's and campsite representative. For each category the roles, duties and responsibilities for each holiday representative must be written in your own words and should highlight the holiday representatives' responsibilities in relation to the customer, to the organisation, and to suppliers. It is not sufficient to provide bulleted lists of roles, duties and responsibilities, nor should you simply reproduce job descriptions that have been provided by tour operators. Changing roles and working practices, such as the introduction of in-resort customer service centres, should be highlighted in your presentation.

b. Compare the roles, duties and responsibilities for one category of representative with two different tour operators (M1). The comparison must draw upon similarities and differences of representatives within the two organisations and, depending on the tour operators selected, could provide scope for demonstrating new working practices that have been introduced.

c. Analyse how the current and changing roles, duties and responsibilities of holiday representatives can contribute to the overall holiday experience (D1). You must use analytical skills to show the contribution of representatives, for example in fulfilling the tour operator's legal obligations and meeting and exceeding customer expectations when carrying out specific duties. You must consider the role of the holiday representative in relation to their responsibilities to the customer, the organisation and to suppliers, and could illustrate your answers by giving examples of how resort representatives can impact on the customers' holiday experience.

This task is designed to produce evidence for P1, M1 and D1.

Task 2

The first part of this task asks you to write a short report that could be read by your resort manager. In the report you must:

a. Outline the legal responsibilities of holiday representatives in each of the different holiday situations described below (P2).

   1. You are a Campsite Representative working on a campsite in the south of France. A couple complain to you that their young child has fallen off the slide in the campsite and cut his arm on a rusty nail that was sticking out from one of the benches.

   2. You are a Resort Representative working for a major tour operator in Magaluf on the island of Majorca. A young couple have complained that, although the tour operator's brochure states that there are two pools in their hotel, there is, in fact, only one.

   3. You are a Villa Representative on the Greek island of Corfu. The Smith family from Rochdale have complained that the hire car they booked in advance for their package holiday was not available when

they went to pick it up from Corfu Airport. The car hire company insisted that they had never received a booking for the Smiths from your holiday company and refused to hire them a vehicle.

4. You are a Resort Representative in Benidorm and have received a complaint from two customers about the standard of the food in their hotel. They say that hot food is often served only luke warm and that the gourmet nights described in the holiday company's brochure and on its website, have never taken place.

For each situation, you must describe the procedures that the reps should go through to try to resolve the issues and identify the relevant laws or regulations that are associated with each case.

For the next part of this task you are to produce a staff handbook in which you must:

b. Explain the role played by holiday representatives in creating a safe and healthy holiday environment (P3). The handbook will include identification of risks and hazards in the holiday environment and the ways in which representatives can minimise these risks. This must include safety in the accommodation (including fire safety and hygiene), whilst using specific facilities, on transfer coaches, on excursions and organised activities, and in the resort itself.

This task is designed to produce evidence for P2 and P3.

Task 3

The selection panel would like you to role play this task, in which you must:

a. Use social, customer service and selling skills to deliver an arrival transfer speech, a welcome meeting and make a sale (P4). The transfer speech and welcome meeting can be simulated situations, but should be to an audience. You must provide a welcome, be delivered in a friendly way, use appropriate language, be appropriate for specific types of customers, create rapport and provide all information required for the situation. Customer-service skills must be evident throughout, including good product knowledge and awareness of customer needs. Appropriate standards of dress should be evident. The welcome meeting and transfer speech should adopt a planned and suitable structure and the content must be relevant to the audience. Amplified voice should be used for the transfer speech and natural voice for the welcome meeting. The pace and tone should be appropriate for listeners to absorb the information being given. In the welcome meeting, you may deal with queries, for example questions about excursions or the resort. Communication must be formal when giving important information to the group, but can be less formal when communicating directly with individuals. The welcome meeting must be supported by visual aids and appropriate body language should be demonstrated. The welcome meeting must incorporate the promotion of excursions, but you must separately sell at least one excursion to an individual or small group of customers in a role play situation.

b. Demonstrate effective social, customer service and selling skills when delivering a transfer speech, welcome meeting and making a sale (M2).

This task is designed to produce evidence for P4 and M2.

Task 4

The members of the selection panel have given you the following two customer service situations to deal with in role plays.

a. You must use social and customer service skills to deal with the customers, completing appropriate documentation (P5).

b. You must deal effectively with customers in different situations and accurately complete all relevant documentation (M3).

c. You must consistently project a confident, professional image when carrying out resort activities and dealing with customers in different situations (D2).

In all dealings you must create rapport, provide a welcome, empathise, be helpful and friendly, use the appropriate choice of language and deal appropriately with different customers in relation to ages and needs (e.g. upset, confused, angry). When dealing with these situations appropriate documentation must be completed, including customer report forms. Customer-service skills must be evident including displaying appropriate product knowledge, identifying customer needs, dealing with queries, listening skills and complaint handling.

1. You are a Resort Rep in the Algarve and have been informed by some customers, Mr and Mrs Khan from Oldham, that their villa has been burgled and that they have lost all their possessions, including their passport, money, credit cards, keys for their hire car and flight tickets home. They are both very upset and are looking to you to help them sort out their problems.

2. Working as a Campsite Courier in Switzerland, the Green family from Norwich have contacted you to complain about the dirty state that they found their mobile home in when they arrived this afternoon for their 10-day holiday. They are also very unhappy about the fact that the campsite does not have a children's pool, as described in the holiday company's brochure, and there are no bicycles for hire, as described on the company's website.

This task is designed to produce evidence for P5, M3 and D2.

UNIT 16

Passenger Transport for Travel and Tourism

INTRODUCTION TO THE UNIT

The UK passenger transport industry provides leisure and business travellers with the means of reaching their destinations and is the hub around which the whole of the travel and tourism sector revolves. Passenger transport is a very dynamic industry, making use of new technologies to supply faster, more convenient, better value, more accessible and safer means of travel to and within the UK. Having an effective passenger transport network is vital if the UK is to maintain its share of visitors in a fiercely-competitive global tourism market.

This unit gives you the opportunity to examine the UK passenger transport industry, the different features of transport and the role of transport regulators. You will also explore the developments and factors affecting passenger transport in the UK, including high-speed rail, personal mobility and fuel prices. The relationships between UK passenger transport networks and the travel and tourism sector are explored in detail, covering areas such as contracting and agency agreements. Finally, the unit will help you understand how passenger transport provision affects the popularity and appeal of UK tourist destinations.

WHAT YOU WILL STUDY

When you have completed this unit you should:

1. Know about passenger transport operations within the UK;
2. Know the developments and factors affecting and influencing passenger transport in the UK;
3. Know the relationships between UK passenger transport networks and the travel and tourism sector;
4. Understand how passenger transport provision affects the popularity and appeal of UK tourist destinations.

You will be guided through the main topics in this unit with the help of the latest developments, statistics, industry examples and case studies. You should also check out the weblinks throughout the unit for extra information on particular organisations or topic areas and use the activities throughout the unit to help you learn more.

ASSESSMENT FOR THIS UNIT

This unit is internally assessed, meaning that you will be given an assignment (or series of assignments) to complete by your tutor(s) to show that you have fully understood the content of the unit. A grading scale of pass, merit or distinction is used when staff mark your assignment(s), with higher grades awarded to students who show greater depth in analysis, evaluation and justification in their assignments. An assignment for this unit, which covers all the grading criteria, can be found on page 169. Don't forget to visit **www.tandtonline.co.uk** for all the latest industry news, developments, statistics and links to websites in this unit to help you with your assignments.

SECTION 1 Know about passenger transport operations within the UK

Icebreaker

This unit investigates passenger transport in the UK and its relationship with the UK travel and tourism sector. Working by yourself, or in small groups under the direction of your tutor, see how you get on with the following tasks to help you make a start on this unit:

- Name three airlines that offer domestic services within the UK;
- Thinking of a tourist area that is close to where you live, make a list of all the transport services you could use to reach the area, and travel around once there, and the names of the companies that provide them;
- Make a list of the factors that would be important to you when deciding which type of transport to use when travelling to a UK seaside resort for a short break;
- Think of some ways in which developments in technology are changing passenger transport services in the UK;
- Name an organisation that is responsible for regulating transport in the UK;
- Think about how the government helps passenger transport companies;
- Name one coach company that offers inter-city travel throughout the UK and a rail company operating in your local area.

When you've finished, show your answers to your tutor and compare your answers with what other students in your class have written.

By its very nature, the travel and tourism sector involves travelling to, from and around destinations in the UK. Transport, therefore, is a vital component of travel and tourism. Transport for tourism covers a variety of water, air and land-based services, including travel by coach, train, private car, taxi, hired car, bicycle, aircraft, cruise ship, water taxi, ferry and canal craft. It also includes the infrastructure that supports the means of travel, such as roads, motorway service areas, ferry terminals, airports and railway stations.

UK passenger transport provision

In the following sections of this unit we investigate a range of air, land and water-based services, starting with air transport.

Air transport

Air transport is a major UK industry, currently carrying approximately 250 million passengers per year (2010 figures). The government expects this number to rise to 455 million by 2030. The UK air transport industry directly employs about 200,000 people and an estimated 600,000 jobs in the UK depend indirectly on the industry, e.g. jobs in the energy sector generated by purchases of airline fuel, in the aerospace sector by airline purchases of equipment, in travel agencies and tour operators.

Air transport services

For statistical purposes, the International Air Transport Association (IATA) classifies air travel services into one of three categories, as follows:

- Domestic;
- International scheduled;
- International chartered;

Domestic services refer to air travel *within* a country, while international represents travel *between* different countries. Scheduled services are those that operate to a published timetable, on defined routes and under government licence. These services run regardless of the number of passengers and are used primarily by business travellers who are prepared to pay a premium for the extra convenience and flexibility offered. Many governments still fund their national airlines, for example Air France, although there is a general move away from state ownership towards private sector operation. One notable success story of recent years has been the rapid growth in one particular sector of the airline business, namely budget, low-cost or 'no frills' airlines, which sell direct to the public and offer scheduled services on domestic and international routes at low prices.

Activity 16.1

Carry out some research into a UK airline and compile a fact sheet on the company that includes details of its UK route network, facilities offered on board, services for passengers with special needs and different levels of service offered.

This activity is designed to provide evidence for P1.

Airports and airport infrastructure

Most airports in the UK serve a local demand, generally from within their own region. However, larger airports such as Manchester, Birmingham and a number of those in the south east of England also attract passengers from a wider area. These airports provide services to more destinations, some of which would not be viable from smaller airports, and also offer more frequent services.

The major London airports (Heathrow, Gatwick, Stansted) play a dual role. Around 80 per cent of their passenger traffic has an origin or destination in London, the south east or the east of England. These

Glasgow airport (courtesy BAA/Glasgow Airport)

regions have a very high level of demand for air travel, amounting to nearly half of total UK demand. This enables airlines to offer a very wide range of destinations from the London airports, with frequent services and one or more competing airlines on most routes. As a result, Heathrow, Gatwick and increasingly Stansted fulfil a national as well as regional role. Many travellers from other parts of the UK fly to one of these London airports in order to catch connecting flights, while many passengers from Wales, the midlands and parts of the south west of England travel by road or rail to the major London airports. The demand for passenger air travel is growing fastest outside the south east of England and this trend is expected to continue. As a result, airlines should be able to offer direct services to more destinations from a wider range of airports. The recent growth in popularity of the low-cost airlines has stimulated demand for air travel across the country, but has been a particularly important factor in the development of many regional airports, such as Bournemouth, Exeter and Liverpool.

Rail transport

For one hundred years since its introduction in the mid-19th century, rail transport was the most popular mode of travel for business and leisure in the UK. However, the rise in car ownership and development of air travel in the 20th century have had a marked impact on the demand for rail travel, which today accounts for approximately 12 per cent of all tourist travel in the UK. Train travel is, however, increasing in popularity as the government invests more money to develop a bigger, better and safer rail system. Figures from the

Association of Train Operating Companies (ATOC) show that, in the last decade, Britain has been Europe's fastest growing railway with passenger numbers up by 43 per cent and freight by almost 60 per cent, creating one of the busiest mixed traffic railways in the world. More than 1.2 billion passenger journeys were made in 2008, with over 20,000 passenger services operated each weekday. In Europe, only Germany carries more passengers – on a network over twice the size of the UK's. Since 1996 over £30 billion has been invested in Britain's track, signalling and stations infrastructure, with more than £5 billion invested in new rolling stock.

As well as the network rail services there are a number of niche rail services developed specifically for tourists. These include the many restored steam railways in the UK, such as the Vale of Rheidol Railway in Wales, and luxury rail services such as the Orient Express. Light rail, underground and tram services are found in many UK cities, for example the London Underground, Sheffield Supertram and Nottingham's NET tram service.

Structure of the UK rail industry

The government, through the Department for Transport (DfT), sets the overall UK railway policy. The DfT works with the following bodies in achieving its aims:

1. The Office of Rail Regulation (ORR) – is independent of government and its function is to provide economic regulation of the monopoly and dominant elements of the rail industry. This includes determining the level, structure and profile of charges levied by Network Rail (which operates the infrastructure) and regulating its stewardship of the national rail network. The ORR is also responsible for all aspects of health and safety on the railways, a role previously carried out by the Health and Safety Executive (HSE);

2. Passenger Focus – the independent national rail consumer 'watchdog'. Its aim is to get the best deal for passengers travelling by rail in the UK;

3. Network Rail – is the operator of Britain's railway infrastructure, which includes 21,000 miles of track, 1,000 signal boxes, 40,000 bridges and tunnels, 9,000 level crossings and more than 2,500 stations. It operates the main passenger terminals, such as Edinburgh Waverley, London Waterloo and King's Cross. All other stations are leased to the main train operating company using the station. Network Rail's task is to deliver a reliable and safe rail network;

4. Train operating companies (TOCs) – are private companies that run the passenger train services in the UK. Currently, there are 24 TOCs (September 2010), including Arriva Trains Wales, First Hull Trains and Heathrow Express;

5. The government also maintains strong relationships with Transport Scotland and the Welsh Assembly Government, which both have devolved rail responsibilities. It also co-operates with a wide range of local and regional bodies, such as regional assemblies, regional development agencies, Transport for London and passenger transport executives around the country.

All the TOCs are members of the Association of Train Operating Companies (ATOC), which was set up by the train operators formed during the privatisation of the railways under the Railways Act of 1993. As well as being the official voice of the rail passenger industry, ATOC provides its members with a range of services that enable them to comply with conditions laid on them in their franchise agreements and operating licences.

Weblink Check out this website for more information on the train operating companies (TOCs) and the work of ATOC. **www.atoc.org**

Rail travel is increasing in popularity (courtesy of Fist Group)

Activity 16.2

Carry out some research into two of the train operating companies (TOCs) and find out what facilities and services they provide for their rail passengers, including regularity of services, costs of typical journeys, concessionary fares, customer service facilities, comfort and accessibility.

This activity is designed to provide evidence for P1.

Road transport

Road transport for tourism includes travel by private car, bus and coach, taxi, hired car, bicycle and even rickshaw! An increasing proportion of journeys in the UK are taken by car – up from 61 per cent of the total distance travelled in 1995 to 64 per cent in 2008. Travel by private car accounts for more than 75 per cent of all tourist trips taken in Britain. Cars offer a degree of flexibility, freedom, comfort and convenience that other forms of transport find hard to match. The shift towards car journeys has provided huge benefits for many people, opening up new opportunities at work and during leisure time. Part of the reason for the increase in car use in Britain is that cars are more affordable as people become better off. Improvements in production techniques and improved fuel efficiency have contributed to a fall in the relative cost of motoring and so have brought cars within reach of a far wider range of the population.

People choose their car for many tourist trips because it allows them to travel direct from one place to another in comfort. Cars can also get to places that are not always accessible by public transport services. Cars do, however, have considerable impacts on the environment and communities, leading to problems of pollution, physical erosion, loss of land to car parks and congestion in many popular tourist destinations, especially historic cities, coastal resorts and National Parks, where vehicles often spoil the very ambience that attracted the tourists in the first place. Central and local governments are attempting to minimise the impact of vehicles by introducing a variety of techniques, including public transport initiatives, park-and-ride schemes, road pricing and pedestrianisation of urban areas. The government expects to see further growth in car ownership and use over the next 30 years. The car provides many benefits, but the challenge for the government is to ensure that people have other options, including good quality public transport and the opportunity to walk or cycle.

Travel by coach is an altogether more environmentally friendly form of tourist travel than the car, transporting large numbers of tourists on scheduled services, on transfer journeys or forming the transport element of a package holiday, for example a coach holiday in the Scottish Highlands. National Express is the largest, scheduled coach service provider in Europe, with a network of services linking 1200 destinations throughout the UK and carrying 18 million passengers every year.

Weblink

Check out this website for more information on the National Express network and services.

www.nationalexpress.com

Activity 16.3

Research and compile a fact sheet on train and coach travel services between your nearest city and London (or Birmingham if you live in London). Include details of fares on offer, frequency of services, facilities provided at the departure point and on board, duration of a typical journey, etc.

This activity is designed to provide evidence for P1.

CASE STUDY

Stagecoach

Introduction

With its headquarters in Perth, Scotland, Stagecoach Group plc is a leading international transport group, operating bus, train, tram and express coach services in the UK, USA and Canada. The Group's profit in 2007 was £161.3 million, up from £133 million in 2006. Stagecoach employs 30,000 staff, operates 13,000 vehicles and provides services to more than 2.5 million passengers every day.

Stagecoach divisions

The Group's operations are divided into three divisions:

1. UK Bus;
2. North America;
3. Rail.

UK Bus operations

Stagecoach owns 19 regional companies running more than 7,000 vehicles and covering around 100 towns and cities in the UK, including Liverpool, Manchester, Newcastle, Hull, Sheffield, Oxford and Cambridge. The company has a 14 per cent share of the UK bus market and carries approximately 2 million passengers every day. Stagecoach also operates megabus.com, an online, inter-city coach service based on the low-cost airlines model. More than 2.6 million passengers have travelled with megabus since the first trial route was launched in August 2003 and it has a national network covering nearly 40 locations.

North American operations

Stagecoach is a major provider of transport services in North America, employing around 4,400 people and operating a fleet of 2,800 vehicles. Its businesses are focused on commuter services, but also include tour and charter, sightseeing and school bus operations. In Canada, the company owns four transport companies, which together operate around 500 vehicles in the Provinces of Quebec and Ontario.

Rail operations

Stagecoach is a major rail operator and has an involvement in running a quarter of the passenger network in the UK. The Group operates South Western, the UK's biggest commuter rail franchise, which incorporates the South West Trains and Island Line networks. Stagecoach also runs the East Midlands rail franchise, which includes high-speed long distance services to London St. Pancras and regional services between key cities.

Stagecoach is Britain's biggest tram operator, with contracts to operate the Stagecoach Supertram network in Sheffield and Manchester Metrolink. In addition, its rail business includes a joint venture with Virgin Rail Group, which operates the West Coast inter-city rail franchise.

Partnerships

Stagecoach works in partnership with a range of stakeholders at local and national levels to improve the quality of bus and coach provision. These include:

- Investors and the financial community – essential to the long-term investment in the Group's operations;
- Customers – the Group carries out extensive market research to help improve its services to the travelling public;
- Customer interest groups – the Group's businesses have a regular and ongoing dialogue with bus and rail user groups;
- Government – senior executives liaise with national and local governments on all matters relating to passenger transport operations;
- Transport authorities – Stagecoach works closely with local authorities and Passenger Transport Executives (PTEs) in the planning and delivery of bus, coach and rail services;
- Government advisory bodies and lobbying groups – the Group has constructive meetings with organisations such as the Commission for Integrated Transport, which provides advice to the UK government, and campaigning groups such as the Campaign for Better Transport (previously called Transport 2000);
- Staff – in addition to one-to-one dialogue with its employees, Stagecoach works in partnership with trade unions on a range of issues, such as pensions, health and safety, training and pay rates;
- Suppliers – Stagecoach relies on a range of suppliers to provide products and services related to its bus, coach and rail operations.

Case Study Questions and Activities

1. Describe Stagecoach's passenger transport operations within the UK.
2. What are the benefits and challenges associated with having transport operations in different parts of the world?
3. The Group's annual report mentions 'corporate social responsibility'. What exactly is this and what activities does Stagecoach get involved with in this area?
4. What does Stagecoach do to help protect the environment?
5. How can companies such as Stagecoach help the government achieve its aim of reducing car use amongst the public?

This case study is designed to provide evidence for P1.

Weblink

Check out this website to help answer the questions in this case study and for more information on the Stagecoach Group.

www.stagecoachgroup.com

Sheffield Supertram is operated by Stagecoach

Domestic ferries and water craft

In many parts of the world, ferries offer inexpensive and reliable services on short sea crossings. In places where there is strong competition between ferry operators, such as on the short sea crossings in the English Channel, there have been considerable advances in vessel technology, with the introduction of hydrofoils and jet-foils to compete with the fast, new generation of passenger ships. The opening of the Channel Tunnel in 1994 increased competition on cross-Channel services still further. In addition to operating the faster vessels, ferry companies have responded to this challenge by offering price reductions, enhanced levels of customer service and greater on-board shopping and entertainment facilities on their services.

The main ferry operators in UK waters are:

- Short-sea Channel routes – P&O Ferries, Sea France and Norfolk Line;
- Western Channel – P&O Ferries, Brittany Ferries, Condor Ferries, Wightlink;
- North Sea – P&O Ferries, DFDS Seaways, Fjord Line and Stena Line;
- Irish Sea – Stena Line, Irish Ferries and Isle of Man Steam Packet Company;
- Scottish Islands – North Link Ferries and Caledonian MacBrayne.

Activity 16.4

Choose three of the ferry operators named above and find information on the services they operate, facilities provided on board and at terminals, costs of a typical return journey and additional products they sell, e.g. mini cruises, short breaks, holidays, etc. Present your findings as fact sheets on each operator.

This activity is designed to provide evidence for P1.

Water taxis are commonplace in the Mediterranean, especially in the Greek Islands. Their potential is yet to be fully exploited in the UK, although there are river bus services offered on the Thames in London and in a small number of coastal locations, e.g. Falmouth in Cornwall and in the Scottish islands. Pleasure craft are not only found at sea but also on inland waterways, e.g. on canals and reservoirs.

Features of transport

There are many features of passenger transport that people take into account when choosing a service, as shown in Figure 16.1 and described in the following sections of this unit.

Cost

For many people, cost is the most important consideration when using transport services. People travelling on a tight budget will look for the cheapest fares possible, even if it means travelling through the

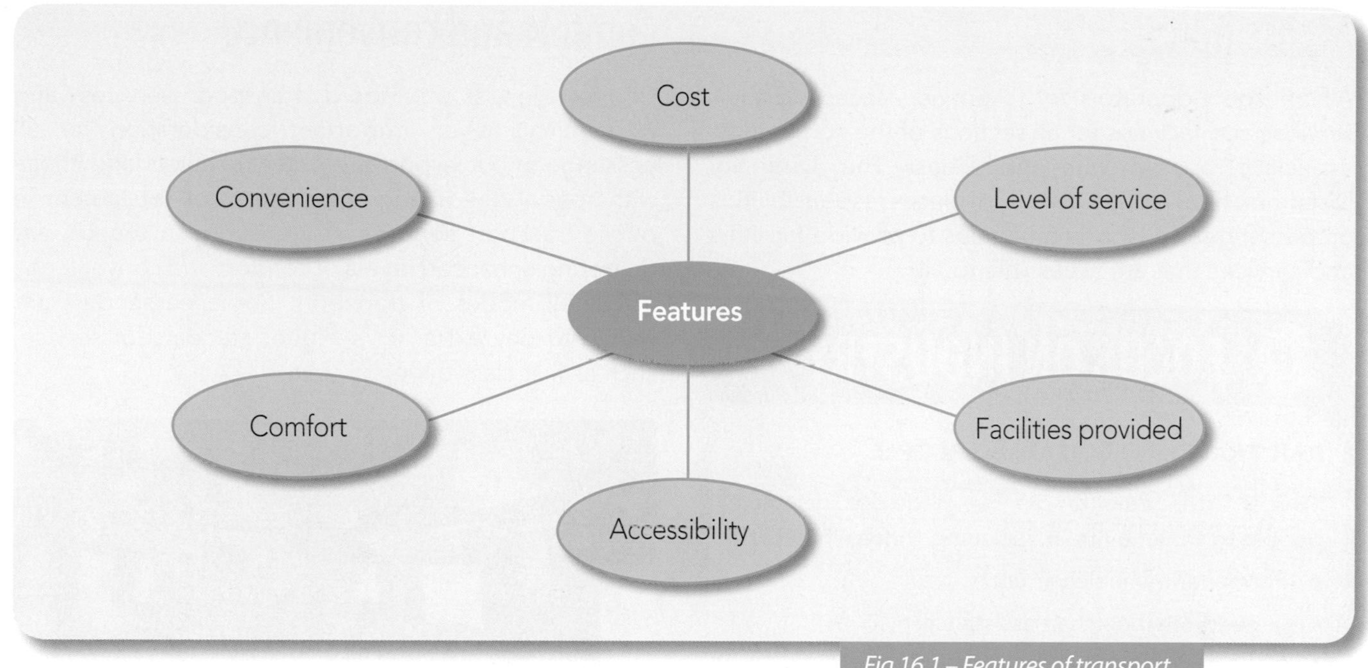

Fig 16.1 – Features of transport

night, leaving very early in the morning or arriving home from a journey very late at night. Transport operators of all kinds use variable pricing to maximise their revenue, i.e. they charge the highest prices at periods of peak demand and offer reduced off-peak rates to stimulate demand. They also offer concessionary fares to different groups of passengers, e.g. children, students, groups, over 50s, senior citizens, etc., which may be via a discount card of one sort or another. Most transport companies give discounts for tickets purchased in advance of a journey – the greater the time between booking and travel, the bigger the discount. This makes sense for the company since they receive revenue earlier than would otherwise have been the case, thereby helping their cash flow.

Level of service

All transport operators strive to provide a good standard of service to their passengers. Some offer different levels of service, which is reflected in the price paid by the customer, e.g. first or business class travel on an aircraft or train, a luxury cabin on a cruise ship or an upgraded lounge area on a ferry. Customers who are willing and able to pay extra benefit from more personal attention and extra services, such as complimentary drinks, express check-in or priority attention.

Facilities provided

Extra investment in transport services by the government and private sector companies is helping to improve facilities for the travelling public, both on board and at terminals. Customers' expectations are rising all the time and transport operators must respond by providing facilities that people want, whether it is 24/7 online booking, wireless internet technology at passenger terminals or extra comfort while travelling.

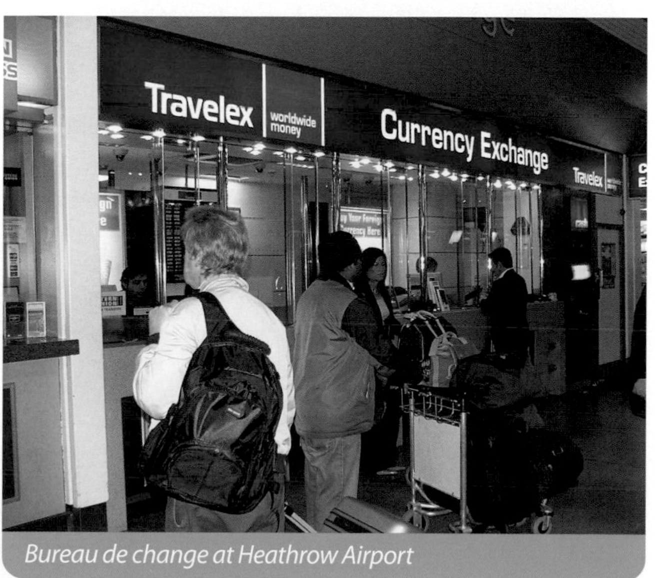

Bureau de change at Heathrow Airport

Accessibility

All transport operators try to provide access to their services and facilities for all sections of the community, especially people with disabilities. The Disability Discrimination Act (see page 158) places responsibilities on passenger transport companies to provide facilities and services that are accessible to all.

FOCUS ON INDUSTRY

RAIL TRAVEL FOR DISABLED PEOPLE

Special arrangements can be made for disabled people to travel by train, including those who are:

- Permanent wheelchair users;
- In need of wheelchair assistance;
- Registered blind or partially-sighted;
- Disabled Persons' Railcard holders;
- Registered deaf;
- Registered disabled.

For many years new facilities have been designed with disabled people in mind, for example level or ramped access to stations, induction loops at ticket office windows for hearing aid users, wheelchair-accessible toilets on stations and on trains, improved signage and audible messages, and spaces for wheelchairs on trains. Literature is also provided in alternative print formats for people with visual impairments. For those who need assistance during their journey, train companies can make arrangements to cover the entire journey, providing help with access to stations, wheelchair ramps for getting on and off trains or assistance in changing platforms. At stations with car parks there are designated parking spaces for disabled people close to the station entrance. Many of Britain's 2,500 railway stations have yet to be fully modernised and are, therefore, not completely accessible to wheelchair users or others who have difficulty in walking or using stairs.

Weblink @ Check out this website for more details of facilities for disabled people on trains.
www.atoc.org

Comfort and convenience

Comfort levels on board transport services and in terminals is an important consideration for all passengers, but especially older travellers and those with special needs. Increased levels of investment in public transport services and facilities in the UK are delivering enhanced levels of comfort and convenience across all modes of transport. Some passengers are willing to pay extra for a higher standard of service, such as first class travel by train.

First class travel on Hull Trains (courtesy ATOC)

Transport operators

Passenger transport is primarily a private sector industry in the UK. Train companies, coach operators, taxi firms, airlines and ferry companies are run on a commercial basis with the main aim of making a profit for their owners and/or shareholders – people who have invested in the company and expect a financial return on their investment.

Public sector organisations, such as the government and local councils, are responsible for setting the overall policy on passenger transport by, for example, arranging subsidies to operators to make sure that services run and regulating the industry so that services are safe and efficient. Much of the transport infrastructure is provided by public agencies, or by public/private sector partnership arrangements, including roads, bridges, terminals, etc. As demand for travel has grown, many transport terminals have developed into large, integrated complexes offering a range of catering, currency exchange, business, retail and entertainment facilities.

Not-for-profit organisations concerned with passenger transport include campaigning groups such as the Campaign for Better Transport, Friends of the Earth and Sustrans, plus groups that represent the interests of the travelling public, for example Passenger Focus and the Air Transport Users Council.

Weblink @ Check out these websites for more details of these not-for-profit transport organisations.

www.bettertransport.org.uk; www.foe.co.uk; www.sustrans.org.uk; www.passengerfocus.org.uk; www.auc.org.uk

Roles of regulatory organisations

There are legal obligations on all passenger transport operators to provide safe, secure and efficient travel for their paying passengers and staff – this applies to all types of air, road, rail and water transport. Regulatory organisations exist to make sure that passenger transport operators comply with all necessary rules and regulations concerning:

1. Health, safety and security;
2. Relevant laws;
3. Improvements to transport services and infrastructure;
4. Enhanced levels of service for passengers.

The regulatory bodies that operate in the UK include:

- Air transport – the Civil Aviation Authority (CAA) is the UK's independent aviation regulator, with all civil aviation regulatory functions – economic regulation, policy on airspace, regulation of safety and consumer protection for air travellers. The Health and Safety Executive (HSE) is responsible for all aspects of safety on the ground at airports and has some responsibility for aircraft safety while airborne, for which it works in partnership with the CAA;
- Road transport – the Department for Transport (DfT) takes the lead on all matters relating to road safety. Working with other agencies, such as the HSE, it offers advice and regulates operators. The Traffic Commissioners have responsibility for licensing buses and coaches (public service vehicles – PSV) and for issuing PSV driving licences;
- Rail transport – the Office of Rail Regulation (ORR) is a government agency that provides economic regulation of the monopoly and dominant elements of the rail industry. This includes determining level, structure and profile of charges levied by Network Rail and regulating its operation of the rail network. The ORR is also responsible for all aspects of health and safety on the railways, a role previously carried out by the Health and Safety Executive (HSE);
- Water transport – the Maritime and Coastguard Agency (MCA) is responsible for implementing the government's maritime safety policy throughout the UK, including checks on passenger ferries and cruise ships to make sure they meet UK and international safety rules.

Weblink  Check out these websites for more information on the work of the Civil Aviation Authority, Health and Safety Executive, Office of Rail Regulation, Department for Transport and the Maritime and Coastguard Agency.

www.caa.co.uk; www.hse.gov.uk; www.rail-reg.gov.uk; www.dft.gov.uk; www.mcga.gov.uk

Activity 16.5

Research and make notes on the roles and activities of the Civil Aviation Authority (CAA) and the Office for Rail Regulation (ORR) in relation to passenger transport regulation.

This activity is designed to provide evidence for P1.

SECTION 2

Know the developments and factors affecting and influencing passenger transport in the UK

Using transport to travel for purposes of trade, religion, leisure and to fight in battles goes far back in history, from pre-Egyptian times and the beginning of the Greek civilisation. The Romans were great travellers, building an extensive road network across all parts of the Roman Empire. From the middle of the 17th century, young gentlemen of the aristocracy travelled to the capital cities of Europe as part of the 'Grand Tour', to broaden their education and experiences of life. Travel to spa towns became popular in the 17th and 18th centuries with visitors experiencing the healing power of their spa waters.

The development of rail transport from 1830 onwards was to have a far-reaching effect on travel for business and leisure purposes. Thomas Cook organised his first excursion by train on 5 July 1841, taking a group of 500 temperance association members from Leicester to Loughborough for a meeting. During the next three summers he arranged a succession of trips between Leicester, Nottingham, Derby and Birmingham. Rail travel in steam-driven locomotives also played a very significant role in the growth of seaside resorts around the UK coast.

Steam also played an important part in the development of long-distance travel by boat. In the 1880s, the Orient Line and North of Scotland Company, both later to be taken over by P&O, pioneered modern-style cruises and in 1904 P&O offered its first cruise holiday programme, arranged by Thomas Cook. The tour used the liner Rome, renaming her Vectis in her new role as a 'cruising yacht'.

The development of the car in the 20th century began to give people greater freedom to explore the coast and countryside, while the introduction of passenger services in jet aircraft after World War Two was to stimulate the rapid growth of the mass tourism that exists around the world today. Vladimir Raitz of Horizon Holidays organised the first modern-day package holiday to Corsica in 1949.

This snapshot of the historical development of passenger transport shows that just how much the industry has developed in a relatively short period of time. Clearly, passenger transport doesn't stand still! Today, the pace of change is even greater, driven by advances in technology, faster economic development and greater expectations from the travelling public.

Developments

The following sections of this unit investigate a variety of developments that affect passenger transport in the UK, including:

1. Toll roads;
2. Congestion charging;
3. Hi-speed rail services;
4. Developments in aircraft technology;
5. New airports and airport expansion;
6. New motorways and widening schemes.

Toll roads

Toll roads, where motorists have to pay an extra charge to travel on a section of road, are not as common in the UK as in some other European countries, although bridge tolls are well established in this country, e.g. the Severn Bridges, Dartford Crossing, Humber Bridge, etc. The M6 Toll is Britain's first privately-funded toll motorway, stretching for 27 miles from Cannock in Staffordshire to Coleshill, Warwickshire. Opened to traffic in December 2003, the M6 Toll gives drivers the opportunity of avoiding a heavily-congested section of the M6 motorway, giving significant time savings at peak times. Research has shown savings of around 30 minutes in peak hours on a mid-week day to more than 70 minutes time saving on Fridays. Travellers who continue to use the existing M6 have also benefited from the new toll road, with reduced traffic volumes of up to 10 per cent. The M6 Toll was built by Midland Expressway, which will operate and manage it until 2054 when it will be handed back to the government. The M6 Toll benefits people travelling between the north and south of Britain for day trips and holidays.

The M6 Toll road at night

Weblink Check out this website for more details of the M6 Toll.
www.m6toll.co.uk

Toll charges were levied on the bridge linking the Isle of Skye to the Scottish mainland when it was built in 1995. This proved very unpopular with local people on the island, who were forced to pay a toll every time they left and returned to Skye. The tolls also had a negative impact on tourism, one of the island's most important industries. After many years of campaigning, the Skye bridge tolls were finally abolished in December 2004 and there are now no charges to cross the bridge.

Congestion charging

Charging motorists to enter a controlled area is a way of reducing traffic congestion and generating revenue to plough back into public transport services such as buses, trains and trams. The Mayor of London introduced a congestion charge in February 2003 to help reduce traffic congestion, which clogs up roads, threatens businesses and damages London's status as a thriving world city for British people and overseas visitors. Before the introduction of the congestion charge, London suffered the worst traffic congestion in the UK and amongst the worst in Europe. Drivers in central London spent 50 per cent of their time in queues.

London's congestion charge has led to reduced traffic levels and pollution, shorter journey times and better air quality. Since the scheme started, London has seen:

- Traffic entering the original charging zone reduced by 21 per cent;
- An increase in cycling within the zone of 43 per cent;
- Reductions in accidents and key traffic pollutants;
- Public transport successfully accommodating displaced car users;
- Numbers of shoppers now outperforming the rest of the UK and returning to a pattern of year-on-year growth;
- £137 million being raised in the financial year 2007-2008 to invest back into improving transport in London.

London's congestion charge has clearly benefited those who live and work in the city as well as the millions of tourists who visit every year.

London's congestion charge road logo (© Transport for London 2005)

High-speed rail services

Many European countries have developed very efficient high-speed rail services, notably France with its TGV services. Britain currently has just one high-speed rail service that links London to the Channel Tunnel and onward to the French rail network. It is known as High Speed 1 (HS1) and covers 109km in total. London and Continental Railways (LCR) completed the construction of HS1, the UK's first high-speed line, linking the Channel Tunnel in Kent via Ashford and Ebbsfleet International to the newly renovated St Pancras International in November 2007. Constructed at a cost of £5.8 billion, HS1 is the first mainline railway built in Britain since the Great Central steamed into Marylebone in 1899. The government is currently developing plans for a second high-speed rail service (HS2) from London to the north of England.

High-speed rail services benefit tourism by allowing visitors to reach their destinations more quickly and in greater comfort. The UK's HS1 service encourages tourists from France and other continental countries to visit London and the rest of the UK, thereby increasing the economic impact of tourism. With HS1, the UK is now fully connected to the growing European high-speed rail network, which stretches across 3,750 km (2,330 miles) from The Netherlands and Germany to Italy, Spain and beyond.

Eurostar trains at St Pancras International (courtesy of London and Continental Railways)

Weblink  Check out this website for more details of Britain's first high-speed rail service. **www.highspeed1.com**

Activity 16.6

Research and make notes on how high-speed rail developments (existing and planned) affect and influence passenger transport within the UK. The Department for Transport website has the latest information on plans for the future – see **www.dft.gov.uk.**

This activity is designed to provide evidence for P2.

Developments in aircraft technology

From the introduction of the Boeing 747 jumbo jet in 1970 to the first flight by an aircraft partly run on bio-fuel in 2008, the aviation industry has always been at the forefront of developments in new technology. In the UK, there has been a rapid growth in domestic air travel in recent years, due in no small part to the popularity of low-cost airlines like Ryanair, flybe, easyJet and bmibaby. Aircraft developments have enabled the low-cost carriers to offer cheaper fares to more UK destinations for their passengers. This has led to the growth in demand for travel from regional airports, such as Exeter, Southampton, Norwich, Coventry and Liverpool. There is growing interest in using turbo-prop aircraft on domestic routes, given that they are more fuel-efficient and less polluting than jets.

flybe operates domestic flights in the UK

New airports and airport expansion

We discussed earlier in this unit that the number of passengers travelling by air is forecast to nearly double by 2030, while rail travel and cruising are steadily increasing in popularity. Transport operators respond to this increased demand by introducing new routes and working with the public sector to develop new terminals and transport infrastructure. There are often considerable objections from local people to developing new terminals. They are concerned about the impact on the environment and their quality of life. This is particularly the case with new airport developments, such as extra airport runways or new access roads.

FOCUS ON INDUSTRY

TERMINAL 5

Terminal 5 at Heathrow began operating for passengers in March 2008. It took six years to build at a cost of £4.3 billion. It consists of a main terminal building and two smaller 'satellites', the second of which is due to open in 2010. Terminal 5 has been designed to give passengers an efficient and stress-free experience when checking-in and waiting for their departure. In addition to the buildings, the Terminal 5 development includes:

- A six-platform railway station;
- Extensions to the London Underground Piccadilly Line and Heathrow Express;
- A spur road linking Terminal 5 to the M25 motorway;
- A new, 87 metre air traffic control tower;
- 60 aircraft stands.

British Airways is the only airline that will use the Terminal 5 facilities and its move to the new facility means that around 40 per cent of Heathrow's passengers will travel from the new terminal. This has presented BAA (British Airports Authority – the airport's owner) with an opportunity to undertake a major £6.2 billion redevelopment programme, including the construction of Heathrow East, a completely new facility that will replace the existing Terminals 1 and 2.

Weblink @ Check out this website for more details of Terminal 5 at Heathrow.
www.baa.com

Health, safety and security

These are important issues for the transport sector, especially since the tragic events of September 11th 2001 and subsequent terrorist attacks around the world. Security at UK airports, railway stations, ferry terminals and cruise ports has increased noticeably. This sometimes results in delays for passengers, but most are happy to put up with a little inconvenience. Transport operators of all kinds must comply with stricter security guidelines when carrying out their business, which can sometimes lead to increased operating costs. Health scares and epidemics, such as foot and mouth disease, SARS and Asian bird 'flu, can also affect travel, with knock-on effects for transport providers.

New motorways and widening schemes

In 2009 the government announced investment of £9 billion in improvements to Britain's road network. This included plans to widen stretches of our busiest motorways, for example the M1 north of London, the M25 and the M6 in the West Midlands. Extra capacity on the road network benefits commuters and tourists, who enjoy faster journey times with less congestion.

Factors

The following sections of this unit investigate a number if factors that affect passenger transport in the UK, including:

1. Political;
2. Legal;
3. Environmental;
4. Social;
5. Economic.

Political factors

Political factors are those that are controlled or dictated by governments – at European, national, regional or local level.

At European level, the European Union (EU) passes laws and regulations (known as directives) that are directly concerned with, or have an impact on, passenger transport in the UK. These include regulations on, for example, the amount of time people are allowed to work (Working Time Directive), consumer protection for UK and overseas holidays (The Package Travel Directive), passenger vehicle speed limiters, vehicle pollution levels, drivers' hours and transport safety. There is currently a proposal for a new EU directive that would bring air travel into the EU Emissions Trading Scheme from 2011. Like the industrial companies that are already covered by the scheme, airlines will be able to sell surplus allowances if they reduce their emissions and will need to buy additional allowances if their emissions increase. The directive is a move towards encouraging the air transport industry to make a fair contribution to efforts to cut greenhouse gas emissions.

At national level, the UK government provides subsidies (payments) to some transport operators to allow them to offer services to the travelling public. This is particularly the case with trains and buses. Subsidies benefit local people and tourists alike, since without the subsidies, it would not be cost-effective for the transport companies to run the services. Subsidies are also offered by local councils and regional development agencies.

Governments also practise deregulation in transport, which is when they move ownership of transport services from the public to the private sector. It is perhaps most associated with airlines, which historically have been state-owned. Through a process of privatisation, many UK airlines and other transport companies are now operated in the private sector, e.g. British Airways, Virgin Trains, etc. Deregulation is intended to increase competition between companies and ultimately produce better quality services and lower fares for passengers. Deregulation of bus and coach travel, which took place in the USA in 1982 and in Britain under the Transport Act of 1985, has liberalised the market for travel and offered passengers a wide choice of operators. In the case of Europe, EU legislation allows a coach company from any member state of the EU to offer coach services in any other EU country.

FOCUS ON INDUSTRY

STAGECOACH AND DEREGULATION

Stagecoach was one of the first companies to take advantage of transport deregulation in the UK in the 1980s and in the early years of the decade operated coach services in Scotland, as well as longer distance services to London. The Transport Act of 1985 deregulated bus services, which had previously been owned and operated by councils and local transport authorities. One of the early services launched by Stagecoach was Magicbus, which operated in Glasgow and offered cut-price fares to passengers. In the late 1980s, Stagecoach bought a number of former National Bus Company businesses, including Hampshire, Cumberland, United Counties, Ribble and Southdown. Stagecoach was one of the first major transport operators to expand overseas, buying the UTM bus company in Malawi.

Weblink @ Check out this website for more details of the Stagecoach group of companies. www.stagecoachgroup.com

Deregulation of the UK rail industry came with the privatisation of the railways under the Railways Act 1993. Following privatisation, the former British Rail was divided into two main elements, the first consisting of the national rail network (track, signalling, bridges, tunnels, stations and depots) with the second element being the train operating companies (TOCs) whose trains run on the network, e.g. Virgin Trains, GNER, South West Trains and First Great Western (see page 146).

Legal factors

We discussed earlier in this unit that the European Union (EU) passes directives that affect passenger transport in a number of ways. These directives ultimately end up as laws and regulations in the EU member states, including the UK. One important area of law that affects passenger transport is the impact of the Disability Discrimination Act (DDA). Part 3 of the Act concerns public transport premises and public transport vehicles, other than aviation and shipping. The law states that public transport buildings, such as train stations, bus stations, airports and ferry ports, must be made accessible to disabled people. This also means that any services that are provided at these places must also be accessible to disabled people, for example travel information and booking facilities. The Act does not mean that all passenger transport vehicles such as trains, buses, coaches, aeroplanes, ferries and taxis must be accessible. There are separate regulations that set out how buses, coaches and trains need to be adapted, and the dates by which this needs to be done.

Assisted train travel (courtesy of ATOC)

Weblink @ Check out this website for more information on the impact of the DDA on passenger transport.
http://dptac.independent.gov.uk/

Activity 16.7

Research two UK passenger transport companies and find out what services and facilities they offer passengers with disabilities and special needs.

This activity is designed to provide evidence for P2.

Environmental factors

The future of the environment is a major talking point today, not least the environmental impacts of passenger transport. Many scientists believe that the carbon emissions from cars and aircraft contribute towards global warming – the gradual rise in the earth's temperature. This, in turn, may lead to the melting of the polar ice caps and the gradual rise in sea levels, threatening low-lying coastal areas in particular. Developments in a variety of transport modes have given tourists the opportunity of travelling quickly to faraway places at a relatively low cost in comparative safety. New locations and destinations in the UK have been opened up for tourism, particularly since the introduction of the low-cost airlines and the growth in domestic air travel. Just as the travel and tourism sector must work towards greater sustainability, so too must the transport industry on which it relies so heavily. Transport operators are working hard to introduce cleaner types of travel, using more fuel-efficient vehicles that produce fewer harmful emissions.

FOCUS ON INDUSTRY

BIO-FUEL USED IN AVIATION

The first commercial airline to be powered partly by bio-fuel flew from London's Heathrow Airport to Amsterdam in February 2008. A Virgin Atlantic Boeing 747 used fuel derived from a mixture of Brazilian babassu nuts and coconuts to complete the journey. The plane had one of its four engines connected to an independent bio-fuel tank that it said could provide 20 per cent of the engines' power. Earlier in the same month Airbus tested another alternative aviation fuel, a synthetic mix of gas-to-liquid. Sir Richard Branson, Chairman of Virgin, said that the flight was an important step for the airline industry and would enable companies that were serious about reducing their carbon emissions to go on developing the fuels of the future.

Weblink @ Check out this website for more information on Virgin Atlantic.
www.virgin-atlantic.com

Social factors

The development of the UK passenger transport system over the last 150 years has created a variety of social benefits for people travelling on holidays, short breaks and day visits, including:

- Increased mobility – people now have greater freedom to explore town and country areas on public transport and in their private cars. Figures from the Department for Transport indicate that nearly 30 per cent of the UK population do not own or have access to a car, relying instead on public transport;
- Equality – falling real prices of travel and cars have opened up transport opportunities to people from all income levels, religious backgrounds and ethnic origins, whether living in urban or rural areas. People with mobility problems have benefited from the greater freedom offered by the private car and improving facilities on public transport services;
- Enhanced holiday/leisure experience – developments in transport have played a crucial role in the development of a travel and tourism sector that is responsive to customer needs, provides a wide range of products and services to destinations throughout the world, and enhances people's quality of life.

The growth in the number of people using the various methods of transport has brought a sharper focus on passenger issues. Consumers in all sectors feel more empowered in expecting high levels of personal attention and customer service, and more confident in making complaints. Transport operators need to respond to this wider trend and with more elderly and mobility-impaired people travelling, the transport industry will need to continue to increase standards of passenger care. Training plays a vital role in helping staff to offer excellent standards of customer service to passengers.

Economic factors

In recent years, the world price of oil has broken through the $140 a barrel mark for the first time ever. This has pushed up the price of fuel for UK car owners to record levels, making many people think twice about using their car for a day trip, short break or longer holiday. Transport and travel companies have felt the squeeze as well. Some airlines and tour operators have passed on the extra fuel costs to customers, through surcharges and supplements.

Economic issues to do with investment and jobs have always been at the forefront of transport developments. Entrepreneurs such as Thomas Cook, Samuel Cunard, Harold Bamberg of Eagle Airways, Freddie Laker of Skytrain (the first transatlantic, low-cost airline) and Richard Branson of Virgin, have invested heavily in transport services that have been used by millions of tourists. Transport is the lifeblood of the travel and tourism sector, helping to create thousands of service jobs in the UK and in tourist destinations across the globe. Transport has allowed destinations to develop their travel and tourism potential to the full, stimulating investment in airports, hotels, tourist attractions, travel agencies, tour operators, restaurants, night clubs, etc. In the UK, transport, like tourism, is an important part of economic development, particularly in regions of the country that have suffered from the decline of traditional industries such as mining, ship building and textiles.

Activity 16.8

With reference to one recent development and one factor, explain how the UK passenger transport sector responds to each. Analyse how one key factor is likely to impact on future passenger transport operations in the UK.

This activity is designed to provide evidence for M1 and D1.

SECTION 3

Know the relationships between UK passenger transport networks and the travel and tourism sector

From the construction of the first road networks in Roman times, the introduction of the railways in the mid-19th century, the growth of private motoring throughout the 20th century to the development of jet aircraft from the 1950s onwards, the growth of the travel and tourism sector has been closely linked to developments in transport networks. The provision of safe, reliable, comfortable, fast, convenient and accessible modes of transport, plus an adequate transport infrastructure, is a vital prerequisite for successful tourism development in the UK.

Year	Car (%)	Train (%)	Coach/bus (%)	Sea/air (%)
1951	28	48	28	-
1961	49	28	23	-
1971	63	10	17	-
1981	72	12	12	-
1991	78	6	12	-
1998	71	7	14	-
2004	71	13	6	-
2006	79	8	7	3
2009	75	12	3	7

Source: Adapted from VisitBriatin data

Fig 16.2 – Modes of transport used for holiday travel in the UK 1951-2009

The popularity of different modes of transport changes over time, in response to new developments in technology, government priorities and customer demand. Figure 16.2 gives an indication of how the demand for different types of transport for tourism has changed since 1951 in the UK. It shows that holiday trips by car have increased dramatically from 28 per cent in 1951 to 75 per cent in 2009. Both rail and coach/bus tourist trips have decreased over the same time period, although rail travel has begun to show an upturn in popularity in recent years.

UK passenger transport networks

The term 'passenger transport networks' refers to the fact that transport services do not operate in isolation from each other, but form part of larger transport systems. These can be made up of the same type of transport, for example the UK rail network, or comprise a combination of different transport types, e.g. the network of passenger transport services available at an airport – taxis, rail, coach, air, etc.

We discussed at the beginning of this unit that the UK has a variety of air, rail, coach and water-based transport services, each with its own network structure. The UK government is committed to an integrated transport industry that offers a full range of reliable and efficient choices for people when making their travel decisions. In its *Future of Transport White Paper* published in 2004, the government agreed to the following objectives:

1. The road network – providing a more reliable and free-flowing service for both personal travel and freight, with people being able to make informed choices about how and when they travel;

2. The rail network – providing a fast, reliable and efficient service, particularly for inter-urban journeys and commuting into large urban areas;
3. Making walking and cycling real alternatives for local trips;
4. Providing improved international and domestic links at ports and airports.

Figure 16.3 gives an overview of the UK motorway network, while Figure 16.4 shows our principal airports and ports.

Relationships

Figure 16.5 shows the relationships between UK passenger transport networks and the travel and tourism sector, indicating the different modes of transport and the various component industries that make up travel and tourism.

There are many business relationships between UK passenger networks and the various components of the UK travel and tourism sector, as the following examples demonstrate:

- Joint ownership – e.g. a coach operator owning its own hotels;
- Contracting – e.g. a tour operator entering into a contract with a rail company to offer short breaks in major UK cities;
- Sales and promotion – e.g. a rail operator running a joint advertising campaign with a tourist attraction;
- Commission structures – e.g. a ferry company agreeing what level of commission it will pay to travel agencies for tickets sold;
- Agency agreements – a travel agent entering into an agreement with a coach company to sell coach holidays;
- Regulation – the Civil Aviation Authority (CAA) inspecting the safety standards at an airline.

Fig 16.3 – The UK's principal motorways

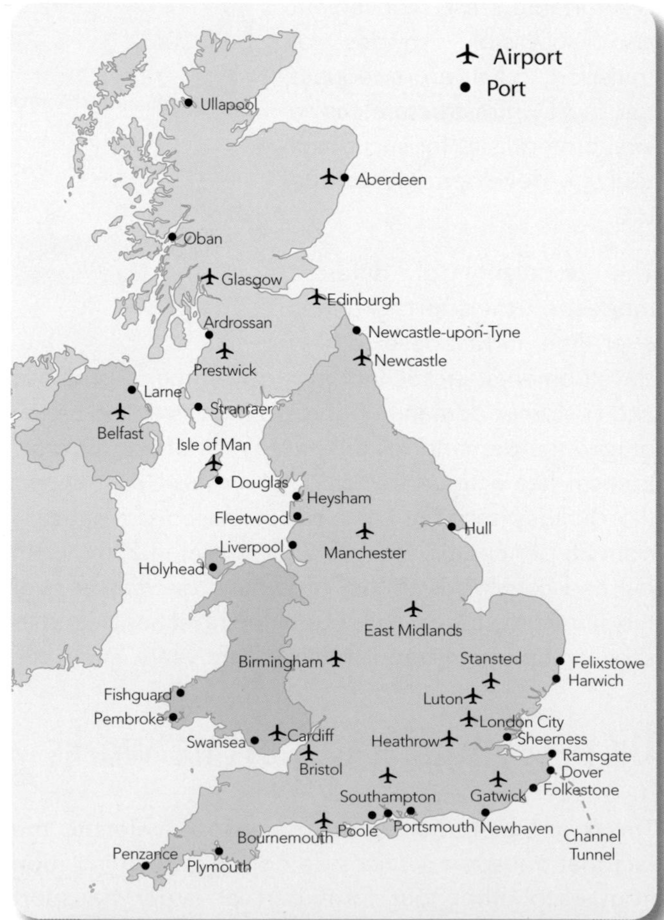

Fig 16.4 – The UK's principal airports and ports

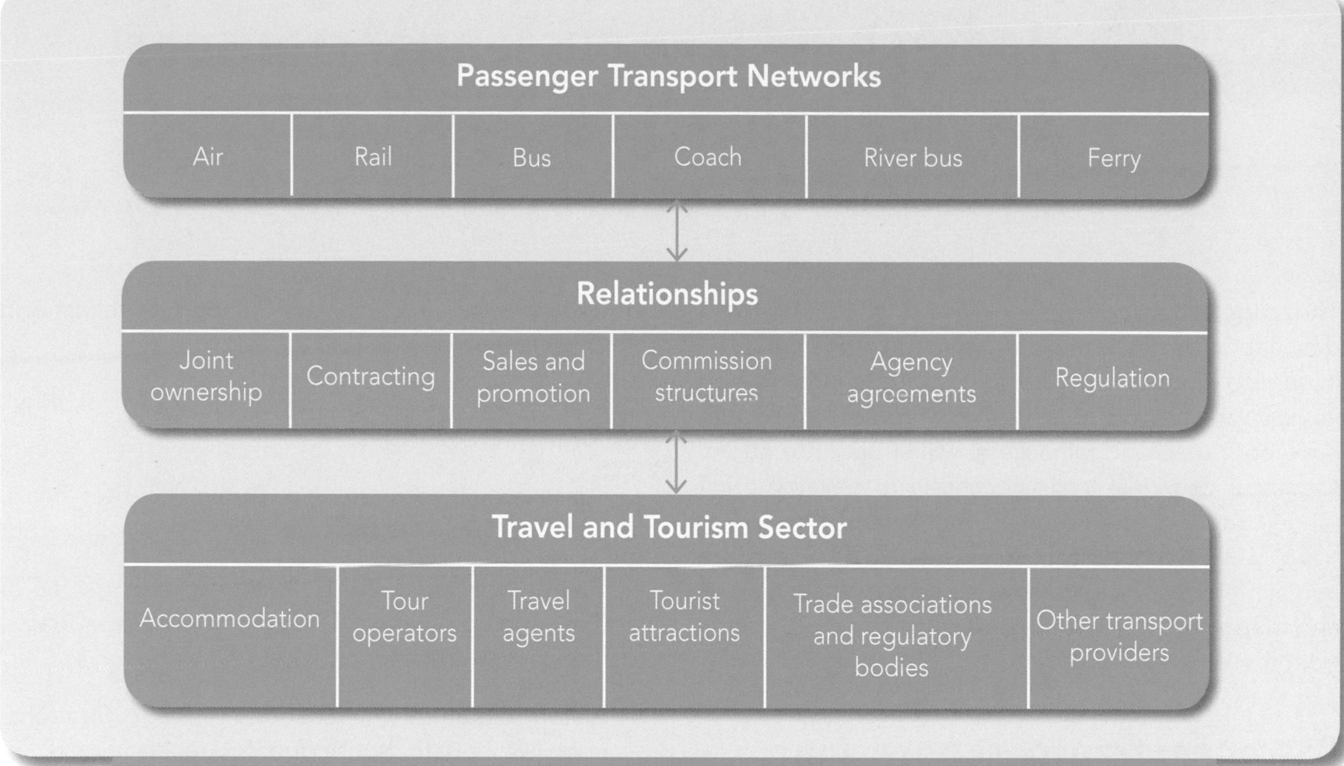

Fig 16.5 – Relationships between UK passenger transport networks and the travel and tourism sector

Activity 16.9

Using examples from your own local area (or a nearby tourist area), identify and explain the relationships between UK passenger transport networks and component industries of the UK travel and tourism sector.

This activity is designed to provide evidence for P3 and M2.

Travel and tourism component industries

Figure 16.5 above shows the various components of the UK travel and tourism sector – accommodation, tour operators, travel agents, tourist attractions, trade associations, regulatory bodies and transport providers. Each of these parts of the sector interacts with transport networks in the ways described above. A component of travel and tourism may well have multiple relationships with transport providers. A tour operator, for example, may:

- Have agency agreements with travel agents;
- Be regulated by the terms of the Package Travel Regulations and other legislation;
- Agree commission structures with coach companies;
- Run sales and promotional campaigns with rail operators;
- Enter into contracts with ferry companies;
- Jointly own a car hire firm.

Ferry services are sold through travel agencies (courtesy of Brittany Ferries)

SECTION 4 Understand how passenger transport provision affects the popularity and appeal of UK tourist destinations

The range of transport services available to and within a destination, as well as their cost, frequency and the levels of service offered, can have an important influence on its popularity with visitors. Resorts in remote areas, that have poor road and rail access, will struggle to attract the levels of tourist trade necessary to develop a full range of tourist facilities and amenities. On the other hand, a destination such as Liverpool, with frequent rail, air, ferry and road passenger transport services to and from the city, is in a good position to attract visitors from the UK and overseas.

Passenger transport provision

We have seen already in this unit that the UK has a wide variety of transport services available to reach tourist destinations and travel around once there. These rail, road, air and sea services are provided mainly by private sector businesses, with support and help from public and not-for-profit organisations. Whatever service is used, and whether it is to reach a destination in the first place or travel around once there, all tourists look for passenger transport services that are frequent, convenient, fast, reliable, safe and offer good value for money for the services provided. Transport operators make their services available via a variety of distribution channels, including online booking on the internet, booking offices at stations and terminals, and via travel agents and other retailers. Companies tend to charge the highest prices when demand is at its greatest and offer reduced rates for off-peak travel.

UK tourist destinations

The UK has a very wide variety of tourist destinations that appeal to British people and overseas visitors, for example:

- Capital cities – i.e. London, Edinburgh, Belfast and Cardiff;
- Coastal resorts – e.g. Brighton, Blackpool, Rhyl, Torquay, Cleethorpes;
- Purpose-built resorts – e.g. Butlin's, Center Parcs, Forestry Commission parks;
- Countryside areas – e.g. National Parks, Areas of Outstanding Natural Beauty, Heritage Coasts, forests, mountain areas, lakes and waterways;
- Historical/cultural destinations – e.g. Stratford-upon-Avon, Bath, Ironbridge, Stonehenge, York;
- Business travel destinations and conference venues – e.g. London, Manchester, Birmingham, Leeds, Cardiff, Edinburgh, Glasgow, Belfast.

It is possible for a travel and tourism destination to fall into more than one of these categories. Bournemouth, for example, is a typical English seaside resort as well as being an important business tourism and conference destination.

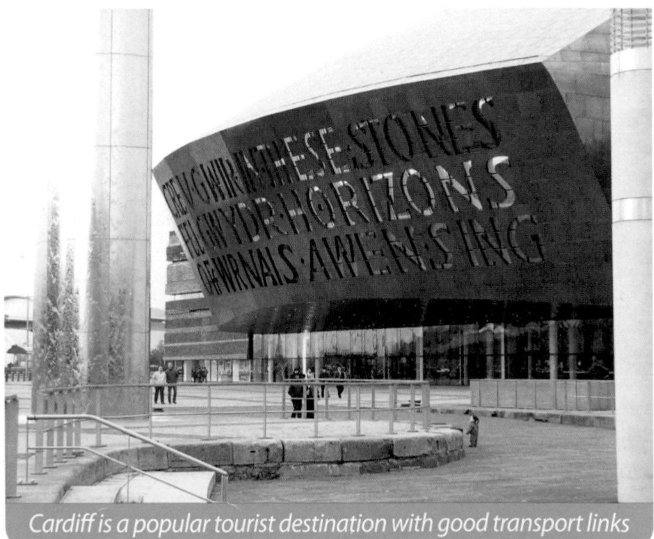

Cardiff is a popular tourist destination with good transport links

Activity 16.10

Describe the different types of passenger transport provision in two of the following tourist destinations:

1. York;
2. Belfast;
3. Brighton;
4. Scarborough;
5. Bath.

With reference to your chosen destinations:

a. Compare the effectiveness of passenger transport in the two destinations;
b. Evaluate the contribution of passenger transport provision to the popularity and appeal of one of your chosen destinations, making recommendations for improvements.

This activity is designed to provide evidence for P4, M3 and D2.

Popularity and appeal of destinations

A destination's popularity and appeal depends on a wide range of factors, some within its control and some not. These include:

- Natural attractions – places such as the Lake District and Snowdonia have wide appeal to all types of visitors, e.g. domestic and inbound;
- Built attractions – heritage and more modern attractions, such as theme parks and amusements, can add to a destination's appeal and increase visitors' duration of stay;
- Media attention – destinations that feature in TV programmes, magazines and newspapers, become more appealing as places to visit, e.g. the area of Yorkshire featured in the TV series Last of the Summer Wine;
- Location and accessibility – proximity to large centres of population increases the popularity of tourist resorts;
- Transport provision – destinations that are well-served by reliable and frequent passenger transport services are more likely to attract visitors, who will spend more and take part in more activities.

CASE STUDY

Blackpool

Introduction

Blackpool is the UK's best-known seaside resort and home to UK's most popular tourist attraction – Blackpool Pleasure Beach, which welcomes around 5.5 million visitors per year. The resort itself attracts 10 million visitors every year to its two beaches and wide variety of tourist attractions and events, which include Blackpool Tower, Sandcastle Waterpark, Blackpool Zoo and the Sea Life Centre. The resort is also famous for its illuminations, designed to attract visitors outside of the peak holiday period. Blackpool is also a popular business tourism destination, hosting conferences, business meetings and exhibitions. The resort boasts a wide variety of entertainment venues for visitors, including the Opera House, Pavilion Theatre, Horseshoe Bar, Grand Theatre and Tower Circus.

There are more than 30 nightclubs, plus numerous pubs, cafés and restaurants, and a 10-screen Odeon cinema. Blackpool has a pedestrianised town centre shopping area with high-street chains and specialist shops. The resort has a wide range of sports facilities, including three 18-hole golf courses, two golf driving ranges, outdoor bowling, ten-pin bowling, a sports centre and more than 50 tennis courts.

Types of visitors

The 10 million tourists who visit Blackpool every year are primarily attracted to the resort because of its reputation for fun, excitement and entertainment. Most visitors come to Blackpool on 1-3 night short breaks, day trips or to visit friends and relatives (VFR). The resort attracts visitors across a wide age range – from young people on hen and stag nights to families and older people drawn by Blackpool's appeal as an entertainment centre. Coach parties and other groups make use of Blackpool's bigger hotels, such as Liberty's on the Square, the Savoy Hotel and the Park House Hotel. The resort also has a buoyant business tourism market, catering for exhibitions, conferences, sales conventions and business meetings.

Rail travel

Blackpool is connected to all parts of Britain via the rail network. Intercity trains to Preston link with a local shuttle service to the resort. There are approximately 10-12 trains per day from London (via Preston) to Blackpool, with a journey time in the region of 4 hours and 30 minutes. There are currently 35 services per day from Manchester, including Manchester Airport, to Blackpool, with a journey time of 1 hour and 15 minutes. The local shuttle service linking the resort to Preston runs every 30 minutes and is a half-hour journey.

Blackpool railway station (courtesy of ATOC)

Road travel

Blackpool is one of the few UK resorts that has a motorway direct to the town – the M55. This gives car drivers and coach passengers easy access to the resort. The M55 connects to the M6 and, from there, to all areas of the UK. National Express services operate to and from Blackpool throughout the year, linking the resort to the 1200 UK destinations currently offered by the coach operator.

Air travel

Blackpool Airport is situated 2.5 miles from the town centre and has a new terminal building capable of handling 350,000 passengers per year. Currently, scheduled services include flights to and from Dublin, the Isle of Man, Malaga, Murcia, Palma and Belfast. Airlines that offer services include Jet2, Aer Lingus and Manx2. Nearby airports that offer a wider range of services include Manchester (58 miles), with direct train connections to Blackpool, and Liverpool (62 miles), linked to the resort via the M6 and M55 motorways.

Ferries

Blackpool is within reach of a number of ferry ports with crossings from Ireland, the Isle of Man and the Netherlands, for example:

- From Larne in Northern Ireland – Fleetwood (7miles) and Cairnryan (211 miles);
- From Dublin in the Republic of Ireland – Liverpool (57 miles) and Holyhead (155 miles);
- From Douglas on the Isle of Man – Liverpool (57 miles) and Heysham (43 miles);
- From Belfast in Northern Ireland – Stranraer (333 miles);
- From Dun Laoghaire in the Republic of Ireland – Holyhead (155 miles);
- From the Hook of Holland in the Netherlands – Harwich (294 miles).

Case Study Questions and Activities

1. After carrying out some further research, describe five types of passenger transport provision in Blackpool.
2. Explain how passenger transport provision can influence the popularity and appeal of UK tourist destinations like Blackpool.
3. Assess the effectiveness of passenger transport in Blackpool and the effect on its popularity and appeal to tourists.
4. Evaluate the contribution of passenger transport provision to the popularity and appeal of Blackpool, making recommendations for improvements.

This case study is designed to provide evidence for P4, M3 and D2.

Weblink

Check out this website to help answer the questions in this case study and for more information on Blackpool as a tourist destination.

www.visitblackpool.com

Activity 16.11

Using the case study of Blackpool as a guide, research and compile your own case study of another popular seaside resort in the UK. In your case study you should:

a. Describe five types of passenger transport provision in the destination;

b. Assess the effectiveness of passenger transport in the destination and the effect on its popularity and appeal to tourists;

c. Evaluate the contribution of passenger transport provision to the destination's popularity and appeal, making recommendations for improvements.

This activity is designed to provide evidence for P4, M3 and D2.

UNIT SUMMARY

This unit has examined the UK passenger transport industry and its links with travel and tourism. This has involved exploring the various types of passenger transport provision in the UK and the features of transport, such as cost, levels of service and accessibility. You have also investigated developments and factors that affect passenger transport, such as high-speed rail developments and subsidies. The unit has also explored the relationships between passenger transport and component industries in the travel and tourism sector, including joint ownership, contracting and agency agreements. Finally, you have examined how passenger transport provision affects the popularity and appeal of tourist destinations. Throughout the unit you have been shown many industry examples, while the case studies of the Stagecoach Group plc and Blackpool highlight key issues in passenger transport.

If you have worked methodically, by the end of this unit you should:

- Know about passenger transport operations within the UK;
- Know the developments and factors affecting and influencing passenger transport in the UK;
- Know the relationships between UK passenger transport networks and the travel and tourism sector;
- Understand how passenger transport provision affects the popularity and appeal of UK tourist destinations.

You are now in a position to complete the assignment for the unit, under the direction of your tutor. Before you tackle the assignment you may like to have a go at the following questions to help build your knowledge of passenger transport for travel and tourism.

TEST YOUR KNOWLEDGE

1. How has the development of the private car influenced travel for UK holidays and day visits?
2. Name three airlines that offer domestic air travel in the UK.
3. Explain the relationship between transport networks and the UK travel and tourism sector.
4. Name three organisations that have responsibility for the regulation of transport in the UK.
5. Why do you think that rail travel for tourist trips is growing in popularity?
6. What is a train operating company (TOC) and which TOCs operate in your local area?
7. Explain the role of Network Rail in the UK rail industry.
8. What factors are contributing to the rapid growth in air travel in the UK?
9. Why is there increased demand for regional airports in the UK?
10. List five features that passengers consider when deciding which type of passenger transport to choose.
11. How can the passenger transport industry reduce carbon emissions?

12. Explain how new technology affects the passenger transport sector.
13. What are the implications for transport operators of the increased measures needed to ensure health, safety and security in transport?
14. Give three examples of relationships between transport providers and component industries of the travel and tourism sector in the UK.
15. What effect is the high price of oil having on passenger transport operations?

Answers to these questions can be found in the Book 2 Tutor's CD-ROM that accompanies this book (ISBN 9780956268075). Full details can be found at **www.tandtpublishing.co.uk**

UNIT 16 ASSIGNMENT

Passenger Transport for Travel and Tourism

Introduction

This assignment is made up of a number of tasks which, when successfully completed, are designed to give you sufficient evidence to meet the Pass (P), Merit (M) and Distinction (D) grading criteria for the unit. If you have carried out the activities and read the case studies throughout this unit, you will already have done a lot of work towards completing the tasks for this assignment.

Scenario

You have been lucky in finding a summer placement job working for one of the top travel trade newspapers in the country. You will be reporting to Brenda Brook, the newspaper's transport correspondent. Brenda is working on a feature on passenger transport for the next edition of the newspaper.

The feature is divided into four main areas:

1. Passenger transport operations within the UK;
2. Developments and factors affecting and influencing passenger transport in the UK;
3. The relationships between UK passenger transport networks and the travel and tourism sector;
4. How passenger transport provision affects the popularity and appeal of UK tourist destinations.

Brenda wants you to carry out some research for the feature and present the information to her as a series of Word documents that she can edit and incorporate into the feature. She has asked you to complete the following four tasks.

Task 1

Your first document is a report in which you must:

- Outline passenger transport operations within the UK (P1). Your outline should provide a concise and focused overview of all types of provision, including relevant examples (scheduled domestic flights, rail, bus and coach, transfers, domestic ferries, river bus and other providers), the features of the various types of transport (including differing cost, value for money, classes available, facilities on board and at terminals, accessibility, comfort and service), and who operates them. You should also identify and outline the roles of the main regulators, government departments or agencies and other bodies, such as passenger groups.

This task is designed to provide evidence for P1.

Task 2

The document for this task must:

a. Describe significant developments and factors affecting and influencing passenger transport within the UK (P2). You should focus on developments that are specifically relevant at the moment and may be having a particular impact on the travel and tourism sector. You should not simply summarise historical accounts of developments that have already had an impact. You must describe a minimum of three different developments and three different factors that affect passenger transport in the UK. These could be specific, e.g. a piece of legislation, or something more general, such as increasing concerns about carbon emissions from air transport.

b. Explain how the UK passenger transport industries have responded to developments and factors (M1). You should select one factor and one development to include in your document. Examples of appropriate responses at this level could be how targets have been set for reductions in carbon emissions or how train operating companies have increased on-board facilities and services in response to changing customer expectations.

c. Analyse how key factors are likely to impact on future passenger transport operations in the UK (D1). You should identify at least two key factors that you consider are likely to impact on passenger transport operations in the future. Factors addressed as part of Task 2a and Task 2b can be used if it is considered that they will continue to have an impact on future passenger transport operations. Your responses should be analytical and factors should be current, for example analysing the likely impact of new legislation or environmental demands.

This task is designed to provide evidence for P2, M1 and D1.

Task 3

The document for this task must:

a. Identify relationships between UK passenger transport networks and travel and tourism component industries (P3). Specific named examples of organisations should be provided, with a brief statement indicating the basis of the relationships. Suitable examples should be provided for all listed transport types, relationships and component industries. There should be at least one example each for joint ownership, agency agreements and co-operations. Typical examples could be the identification of the relationship between a named train operator and tourist attraction offering joint promotions, and a named tour operator contracting with a train operator for packages in the UK.

b. Explain how UK passenger transport networks work with travel and tourism component industries (M2). Your explanations should include why such relationships exist, for example why train operating companies and tourist attractions offer joint promotions.

This task is designed to provide evidence for P3 and M2.

Task 4

Your final task should be presented as a written case study in which you must:

a. Explain how passenger transport provision can influence the popularity and appeal of two specific UK tourist destinations (P4). You should choose areas that have appeal and popularity with tourists and could be either urban, coastal or rural, but should be clearly defined, e.g. the city of York or the North Yorkshire Moors are acceptable as they are specific tourist destinations, whereas West Yorkshire would not be acceptable as it is an area that contains several tourist destinations. Your explanations should be comprehensive, showing how the transport provision (modes of transport, levels of service, geographical coverage, costs, channels of distribution, infrastructure, integrated public transport systems) affects popularity and appeal, including types of visitors, duration of stay, spending and activity participation.

b. Compare the effectiveness of passenger transport provision in the two tourist destinations selected for Task 4a (M3). You should not focus on how the passenger transport affects local people, e.g. people travelling to and from work or people travelling to use local amenities, but rather its effectiveness in creating or sustaining popularity and appeal to tourists.

c. Evaluate the contribution of passenger transport provision to the popularity and appeal in a specific tourist destination, making recommendations for improvements (D2). This might involve understanding how late-night train services increase the accessibility of a seaside town as a day-trip destination or how a subsidised airport shuttle service could improve the appeal of a town for inbound tourists.

This task is designed to provide evidence for P4, M3 and D2.

UNIT 17

Events, Conferences and Exhibitions

INTRODUCTION TO THE UNIT

Events, conferences and exhibitions make up one of the fastest-growing and dynamic areas of travel and tourism. Although an industry in its own right, events, conferences and exhibitions is closely linked to other components of the travel and tourism sector, such as hospitality, transport and accommodation. This unit will enable you to investigate the trends and issues affecting the events, conferences and exhibitions industry, including the impact of web-conferencing and the growth of special interest trips and packages.

In this unit you will learn about the events, conferences and exhibitions environment in the UK, including different types of events and the range of customers served by the industry. You will investigate the many different venues used for events, conferences and exhibitions, plus the facilities needed to stage a successful event, such as suitable exhibition space, seminar rooms and audio-visual equipment. You will also learn how to produce proposals for events, conferences and exhibitions, giving attention to health, safety and operational factors. The unit also provides information on producing accurate costings for events, conferences and exhibitions.

WHAT YOU WILL STUDY

When you have completed this unit you should:

1. Understand the event, conference and exhibitions environment in the UK;
2. Understand types of venues utilised for events, conferences and exhibitions;
3. Be able to propose and cost events, conferences and exhibitions.

You will be guided through the main topics in this unit with the help of the latest developments, statistics, industry examples and case studies. You should also check out the weblinks throughout the unit for extra information on particular organisations or topic areas and use the activities throughout the unit to help you learn more.

ASSESSMENT FOR THIS UNIT

This unit is internally assessed, meaning that you will be given an assignment (or series of assignments) to complete by your tutor(s) to show that you have fully understood the content of the unit. A grading scale of pass, merit or distinction is used when staff mark your assignment(s), with higher grades awarded to students who show greater depth in analysis, evaluation and justification in their assignments. An assignment for this unit, which covers all the grading criteria, can be found on page 200. Don't forget to visit **www.tandtonline.co.uk** for all the latest industry news, developments, statistics and links to websites in this unit to help you with your assignments.

SECTION 1 Understand the event, conference and exhibitions environment in the UK

Icebreaker

This unit investigates the events, conferences and exhibitions industry – from music festivals and corporate hospitality to wedding fairs and business conferences. Working by yourself, or in small groups under the direction of your tutor, see how you get on with the following tasks to help you make a start on this unit:

- Name three types of venues used for events, conferences and exhibitions;
- What is a 'product launch'?
- Give examples of two other travel and tourism industries that the events, conferences and exhibitions industry works with;
- What health and safety factors would the management of a hotel need to consider when staging a wedding fair?
- Name two purpose-built exhibition centres in the UK;
- Make a list of the facilities that a hotel which is considering hosting business meetings and mini-conferences would need to offer its corporate customers;
- What impact are developments in technology having on the event, conference and exhibitions industry?

When you've finished, show your answers to your tutor and compare your answers with what other students in your class have written.

The events, conferences and exhibitions industry is an important part of the UK travel and tourism scene, not least because it is a year-round industry that creates jobs and contributes to economic development in all parts of the UK. This section of the unit focuses on the events, conferences and exhibitions industry in detail, starting with an investigation of different types of events.

Types of event

Events take place for a wide variety of reasons. Including:

- Corporate hospitality;
- Team-building events;
- Incentives;
- Fundraising;
- Product launches;
- Music events and festivals;
- Wedding fairs;
- Reunions.

Sponsored walks are a popular way to raise funds

Corporate hospitality

Corporate hospitality is a specialist industry within travel and tourism that focuses on providing events, hospitality and entertainment to business clients. It may be offered as a reward to a customer for placing business with a company or to encourage businesses that are not yet customers to deal with the company. It is also seen as a good way for a company to network and make new business contacts. Corporate events take many forms – from lavish events at Wimbledon or the Henley Regatta to the owner of a business inviting his or her bank manager for a meal in a local restaurant. Many corporate hospitality functions are centred around sports events, such as golf championships, cricket, tennis, rugby and football matches. There are many specialist companies that handle all the arrangements for corporate events, from sending out invitations and 'meet and greet' services to providing catering and entertainment.

Team-building events

Team-building events are used by companies to help staff bond and work together, thereby helping to improve productivity in the workplace. They often involve team challenges in the countryside, for example raft-building, orienteering and quad biking. Some team-building events are held on company premises or in nearby hotels, e.g. cooking challenges and drumming workshops.

Incentives

Incentives are offered to employees as a reward for meeting a specific work target or goal. The incentive may be a luxury holiday, short break or day out at a sporting event, e.g. Ascot races or Wimbledon. Companies implement incentive programmes to drive sales, increase profits, improve service, enhance staff morale, retain staff or provide high-profile recognition to individuals. Being a recipient of an incentive travel award conveys status and prestige on the winner. More and more businesses now recognise the value of incentives and design performance plans for employees, with specific objectives and measures of success related to incentive rewards. There is a sizeable industry that has grown to serve the needs of companies looking to offer incentives to staff, for example incentive travel companies and agencies. Customers are also offered incentives to buy particular products or to remain loyal to a specific company, e.g. free upgrades on flights and cruises.

FOCUS ON INDUSTRY

TEAM-BUILDING EVENTS

With more than 20 years of experience, Progressive Resources is one of the leading corporate team-building and event management companies in the UK. The company delivers corporate team-building events and related activities such as conferences, motivational days, themed training events, corporate entertainment and corporate hospitality. Its activities are designed to promote teamwork, team bonding, leadership skills and team performance. They address the needs of groups of people ranging from 5 to 500 delegates.

Progressive Resources work in partnership with a variety of UK team-building venues and hotels to deliver bespoke team development activities, ranging from ice breakers to full-blown indoor team-building events and outdoor activities.

The company's offices are located close to both the New Forest National Park and also the Solent sailing area, allowing the company to offer treasure hunts in the forest and corporate sailing days, RIB (rigid inflatable boat) treasure hunts and luxury powerboat days around the Isle of Wight. Many of the venues used by Progressive Resources are within easy travelling distance from most southern UK locations and an hour and a half from London. The company also provides London team-building activities and away days, for example a London treasure hunt, which can be undertaken on foot or by public transport, and a River Thames RIB trip.

Weblink

Check out this website for more information on team-building events at Progressive Resources.

www.teambuilding.co.uk

Activity 17.1

Carry out some research into a company that specialises in incentives. Produce an illustrated leaflet that describes the company and the types of products it offers.

This activity is designed to provide evidence for P1.

Fundraising

Organisations and private individuals hold fundraising events to generate extra revenue for charities and good causes, e.g. cancer charities, the refurbishment of a local church, etc. These vary from charity auctions to adventure trips organised by major charities, such as cycle trips around South America and sky diving in the UK.

Product launches

Companies sometimes organise events to launch new products and services, e.g. a local council running a series of events in shopping centres to publicise new recycling services or a car company showcasing its latest model. These may be trade or consumer events, i.e. restricted to business only or open to the public generally.

Music events and festivals

Music festivals and events appeal to a wide variety of people. Events such as the Glastonbury Festival and V Festival tend to be most popular with young people, while classical music concerts generally attract an older customer profile, e.g. opera at Glyndebourne and the BBC Proms in the Albert Hall, London. Details of forthcoming music events and festivals can be found in music magazines such as the NME and BBC Music Magazine, as well as on ticket agents' websites. Working as a paid member of staff or a volunteer at a music event or festival is a good way of finding out how they are run.

Weblink

Check out these websites for examples of companies listing music (and other) events.

www.gigsandtours.com;
www.seetickets.com;
www.ticketmaster.co.uk

Wedding fairs

Wedding fairs tend to be local events that give prospective brides and grooms the chance to see a range of services in one location, usually a hotel that itself hosts weddings. Companies that offer wedding photography, printed invitations, flowers, catering, honeymoon ideas, wedding cars, etc. pay to exhibit at the fair in the expectation of selling their products and services.

Reunions

The growth of websites such as Friends Reunited has boosted the popularity of reunions of school friends, former work colleagues, etc. They often bring together people from a wide geographical area who need accommodation and hospitality services during their stay.

Types of conference

Conferences give the people attending (delegates) the opportunity of learning more about products and subjects, while providing an excellent opportunity to network with colleagues and business contacts.

Political conferences

Every autumn in the UK the main political parties hold their annual conferences to set out their priorities for the coming year. These have traditionally been held in seaside resorts such as Brighton, Bournemouth and Blackpool, bringing extra revenue for conference companies and hotels out of the peak holiday season. More recently cities such as Manchester and Liverpool have played hosts to the main parties. The 2010 Labour Party conference was held in the heart of Manchester and comprised 200 different exhibitors and more than 10,000 delegates and visitors.

Political conferences concerning travel and tourism involve those hosted by the World Tourism Organisation (UNWTO). Topics for forthcoming conferences organised by UNWTO include *Tourism Contributing to Poverty Reduction* in Burkina Faso, a *Global Tourism Conference* in Malaysia and an *International Conference on Responsible Tourism in Destinations* in Oman.

Weblink @ Check out this website to find the latest conferences organised by the World Tourism Organisation.
www.unwto.org

Business conferences

Business conferences take place throughout the year in all parts of the UK. They range in size from a small company's annual general meeting (AGM) held in a local hotel to an event such as the CBI (Confederation of British Industry) annual conference held in 2010 at the Grosvenor House Hotel in London. Delegates to business conferences attend main sessions and workshops (sometimes referred to as break-out sessions) in order to learn about new industry initiatives and to discuss issues of mutual concern.

Educational, academic and medical conferences

Examples of educational conferences include:

- Those organised by teaching unions, for example the 2010 National Union of Teachers' conference held in Liverpool;
- Subject-specific conferences for teachers and lecturers organised by awarding bodies and private companies, e.g. Philip Allan Conferences;
- Those organised by central and local government agencies to discuss educational issues.

Academic conferences are organised for lecturers and researchers in universities. They cover all the subjects that are taught in higher education and are held throughout the world. Figure 17.1 shows an example of an announcement for a tourism conference at the University of Surrey.

CONFERENCE ANNOUNCEMENT

Advancing the Social Science of Tourism

Venue
University of Surrey

Dates
28 June to 1 July 2011

The University of Surrey and Annals of Tourism Research are delighted to announce a major tourism conference for 2011. We look forward to hosting you at the University's Guildford, Surrey campus in the UK for a full programme of academic exchange and social activities.

Brief
This conference marks the 20th anniversary of the special issue of Annals of Tourism Research (1991, Vol 18, No.1) entitled: Tourism Social Science. The main aim of the conference is to revisit this theme by inviting papers to consider advances in tourism social science, which are theoretically grounded in one or more of the core social sciences including:

- anthropology
- communication
- cultural studies
- demography
- development studies
- economics
- education
- geography
- history
- linguistics
- management science
- philosophy
- political science
- psychology
- sociology

www.surrey.ac.uk/tourism2011

Fig 17.1 – An announcement for an academic tourism conference

Medical conferences are held in a variety of venues and locations to exchange ideas and discuss best practice in the medical world. They are often organised by, or sponsored by, drug companies which aim to promote their products and services to medical practitioners.

Types of exhibition

Exhibitions are a popular way of gathering a lot of information under one roof. Trade fairs are business-to-business (or B2B) events aimed at people working in a particular industry sector. Buyers attend trade fairs to gather information and to arrange business deals with exhibitors (or suppliers). For example, at the World Travel Market (see case study below) a tour operator may sign a contract with a hotel or activity provider and use their facilities in its tour programme. UK and overseas destinations are well-represented at the World Travel Market, hoping to persuade members of the travel trade, e.g. travel agents, tour operators, coach companies, airlines, etc. to send visitors to their areas.

Delegates at the Group Leisure and Travel Trade Show

Public exhibitions are business-to-consumer (or B2C) events, i.e. businesses buy exhibition space to inform the general public about their products and services. The Ideal Home Show and Boat Show are examples of consumer exhibitions that are popular with the general public. There are also many holiday exhibitions open to the public held across the country, e.g. the Destinations Show currently held every year at Earl's Court in London and the NEC in Birmingham.

Most exhibitions are staged specifically to promote products and encourage more sales. Promotion to businesses is achieved in trade fairs such as the World Travel Market. Companies promote specific goods and services to consumers in public shows and exhibitions, e.g. the Knitting and Stitching Show at London's Alexandra Palace.

A roadshow is a specific type of exhibition that moves from one location to another. Tourist boards sometimes organise roadshows in their regions to network with their member companies, e.g. hoteliers, attraction providers, coach operators, etc.

CASE STUDY

World Travel Market

Introduction

Staged annually in London, World Travel Market (WTM) is a four-day business-to-business trade fair presenting a range of destinations and industry sectors to UK and international travel professionals. It is an opportunity for the whole global travel trade to meet, network, negotiate and conduct business under one roof. By attending World Travel Market, participants can keep up to date with the latest developments in the travel and tourism sector.

Exhibitors at World Travel Market

More than 5,000 suppliers of travel and tourism products exhibited at WTM 2009. Many worldwide destinations were represented, including Alicante, the Canary Islands, Hawaii, Dubai and the Dominican Republic. Other exhibitors spanned all component industries of the travel and tourism sector, such as visitor attractions, airlines, accommodation, conference organisers, event management companies, tour operators, travel agencies, travel technology, training, etc.

Visitors to World Travel Market

WTM welcomed more than 45,000 industry participants in 2009. It is a trade-only event that is not open to the general public. The profile of visitors includes:

- Ferry companies
- Airlines
- Venue owners
- Airports
- Business travellers
- Health resorts and spas
- Recruitment agencies
- Tourist boards
- Cruise lines
- Media professionals

A limited number of student places are available to attend WTM. Students must be accompained by a tutor and there will be an admission fee for each student attending and a maximum of 50 students per college.

Seminars at World Travel Market

WTM hosts a variety of seminars during the four days of the event, covering topics as diverse as sports tourism, developments in online distribution, low-cost airlines, social responsibility in tourism and the revolution in social media. Some seminars are restricted to invited guests only or members of the media.

World Travel Market Responsible Tourism Day

Over the past years WTM has dedicated one day to responsible tourism through a programme encouraging debate, discussion and action, highlighting case studies and best practice and participation by all sectors of the industry. Responsible tourism is not a passing trend. As more and more governments, businesses, organisations and consumers recognise the importance of responsible tourism, the subject has risen to the top of the industry agenda. With the support of the World Tourism Organisation, the third WTM World Responsible Tourism Day took place on Wednesday 12 November 2009.

To coincide with World Responsible Tourism Day at World Travel Market, WTM asks companies and organisations across the sector to show their support and undertake their own responsible tourism initiatives. A detailed support pack is available with suggestions and ideas to inspire travel and tourism organisations to participate in this initiative.

Case Study Questions and Activities

1. How would you describe the aims of the World Travel Market?
2. Describe the range of visitors to WTM.
3. What benefits are exhibitors likely to receive by attending WTM?
4. Explain how trends in the events, conferences and exhibitions industry could impact on the World Travel Market.
5. Explain the links between WTM and other industries in the travel and tourism sector.

This case study is designed to provide evidence for P1, P2 and M1.

Weblink

Check out this website to help answer the questions and for more information on the World Travel Market.

www.wtmlondon.com

Specialist organisations

In this section we investigate the roles of the following organisations that are an important part of the events, conferences and exhibitions industry:

- Venue-finding agencies;
- Conference organisers;
- Exhibition organisers;
- Event management companies.

Venue-finding agencies

Finding a suitable venue for an event, conference or exhibition can be a time-consuming and expensive process for a company or private individual. Venue-finding agencies aim to offer a complete service to their clients in order to maximise their income. This often goes beyond simply finding a suitable venue for a client and may include arranging hospitality, booking speakers, liaising with designers and handling publicity. Venue-finding agencies usually earn a commission from the venue they recommend and the other companies they use, rather than charging a fee to the client.

Some local authority tourism departments and Regional Tourist Boards in the UK offer a venue-finding service for businesses as part of their drive to increase tourism revenue to their area. Examples include Staffordshire Conference Bureau, Visit Blackpool and Chester & Cheshire Conference Bureau. Some offer a complete support package to clients as the example from Birmingham Convention Bureau in Figure 17.2 shows.

Conference organisers

Companies often use the services of a conference organiser for anything other than the smallest of meetings – this frees up their existing staff to carry on with their normal duties. Conference organisers offer a range of services to clients, including:

- Handling legal and contractual aspects;
- Arranging catering;
- Co-ordinating transport;
- Arranging speakers;
- Organising signage;
- Reserving accommodation;
- Finding entertainers;
- Liaising with sound and lighting companies;
- Promoting events;
- Handling public relations for an event.

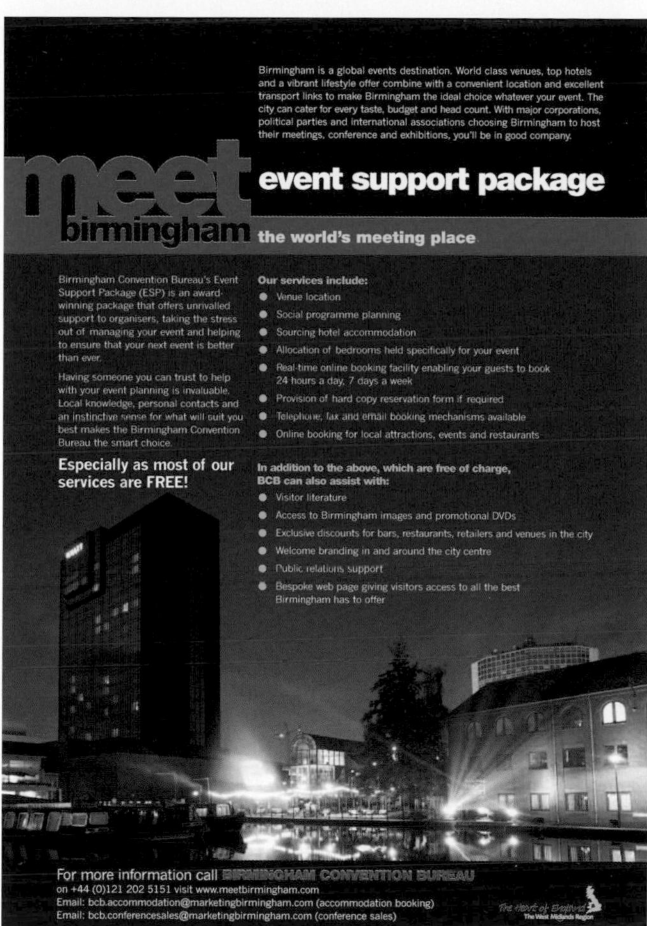

Fig 17.2 – Services offered by Birmingham Convention Bureau

Most conference organisers are commercial firms, for example Millbrook Medical Conferences and Meeting Makers Ltd, but organisations such as universities, religious bodies and charities also organise conferences as a way of increasing revenue.

Exhibition organisers

We saw previously that exhibitions can be organised for businesses (trade fairs) or for the general public (consumer events). Exhibition organisers handle a range of technical aspects of staging exhibitions, such as hiring venues, building stands for exhibitors, arranging power supplies, etc. Reed Exhibitions is the world's leading organiser of exhibitions.

FOCUS ON INDUSTRY

REED EXHIBITIONS

Reed Exhibitions organises the World Travel Market in London and is the world's leading events organiser – more than 6 million peoeple attended the company's events worldwide in 2009, generating millions of pounds in business. Reed events are held in 36 countries throughout the Americas, Europe, the Middle East and Asia Pacific, and organised through a network of 35 fully-staffed offices and international sales ptomoters in 93 countries.

Reed organises a wide range of events, including exhibitions, conferences, congresses and meetings. Its portfolio of over 500 events serves 47 industry sectors, including: aerospace & aviation, automobiles, building & construction, electronics, energy, engineering, entertainment, environment, food & hospitality, gifts, healthcare, IT, jewellery, life sciences & pharmaceuticals, property, manufacturing, medical education, packaging & converting, printing & visual communication, security, sports & recreation, travel & tourism.

Working closely with professional bodies, trade associations and government departments Reed ensures that each and every event is targeted and relevant to industry needs. As a result, many Reed events are market leaders in their field.

Reed Exhibitions is part of Reed Elsevier Group plc, a FTSE-100 company and world-leading publisher and information provider. The group employs more than 32,000 staff, including approximately 20,000 in North America. In 2009, Reed Elsevier made an adjusted profit before taxation of £1.2 billion on a turnover of just over £6 billion.

Weblink

Check out this website for more information on Reed Exhibitions.

www.reedexpo.com

Event management companies

These are professionals who organise a wide variety of events to a given client brief. They work with different venues and a range of support companies when staging events, e.g. hotels, caterers, entertainers, etc. They could be involved in any number of different events – from a wedding or dinner party to a hen night or award ceremony.

Customers

Customers of the events, conferences and exhibitions industry fall into a number of categories, including:

- Corporate;
- Associations;
- Government;
- Private individuals.

Corporate

Corporate customers are businesses and their members of staff. They buy space at exhibitions and stage conferences and events for a variety of reasons, including:

- Informing buyers about new products and services;
- Selling products and services;
- Gathering details of potential buyers to store on a database;
- Rewarding staff success and achievements;
- Developing teamwork in members of staff.

Corporate customers also attend trade fairs and conferences as visitors and delegates. They expect to learn about the latest developments in their field and be able to network with colleagues and business contacts. Corporate customers can be from the UK or may be overseas customers, e.g. staff from an overseas tourist board exhibiting at the World Travel Market in London.

Associations

Associations often use the services of the events, conferences and exhibitions industry when planning events. For example, ABTA – The Travel Association held its annual Travel Convention in the Hilton Malta Conference Centre in 2010, while the Tourism Society's Annual Conference in 2010 took place at Lord's Cricket Ground in London.

Government

Central and local government organisations stage conferences and events to discuss policies on a range of topics. Staff from government departments and local authorities also attend conferences and events to keep abreast of current developments. The Local Government Association (LGA) arranges conferences and seminars covering the full range of local authority services and functions, including leisure and tourism.

Weblink @ Check out this website for more information on events organised by the Local Government Association (LGA).
www.lga.gov.uk

Private individuals

Not all customers of the events, conferences and exhibitions industry are corporate clients. Private individuals also use venues and deal with event management companies when organising, for example, hen and stag nights, reunions, weddings and parties. Private individuals are also welcome to visit consumer exhibitions, such as the Boat Show and the Destinations Travel Shows held every year in London and Birmingham.

Links with the travel and tourism sector

You have learned elsewhere on your course that the travel and tourism sector is made up of many different component industries that work together to deliver a wide range of travel-related products and services. The events, conferences and exhibitions industry makes extensive use of other travel and tourism facilities and services, including:

Hotels play an important role in the events, conferences and exhibitions industry

- Accommodation – hotels and other accommodation providers host corporate events such as seminars and conferences, as well as weddings, reunions and other events for members of the public. They also provide accommodation for visitors to events that take place in the same locality;
- Transport – conference, exhibition and event organisers may liaise with airlines, coach companies, train operators, taxi firms, car hire companies, etc. when planning their events in order to transport customers;
- Hospitality and catering – all conferences, events and exhibitions need the services of professional caterers, whether simply for afternoon refreshments for delegates attending a half-day seminar or a banquet for a prestigious business conference;
- Travel agencies – may be used by conference organisers to arrange domestic and international travel for delegates, keynote speakers and visitors;
- Tourist boards – can offer advice on choice of venue and suitable pre- and post-event tours for delegates and partners to conferences and exhibitions.

Hosting events, conferences and exhibitions can help to increase the popularity of destinations. As well as resorts such as Blackpool, Bournemouth and Brighton being in the media spotlight when major conferences are being held there, delegates to a conference may return to the destination as holidaymakers if they have enjoyed their stay.

Activity 17.2

Carry out some research into three actual conferences that are due to take place in the UK this year and produce a presentation that explains how each one interacts with other travel and tourism component industries, e.g. accommodation, transport, etc.

This activity is designed to provide evidence for P2.

Trends

Figure 17.3 gives an overview of the recent trends in the events, conferences and exhibitions industry, which are described in detail in the following sections of this unit.

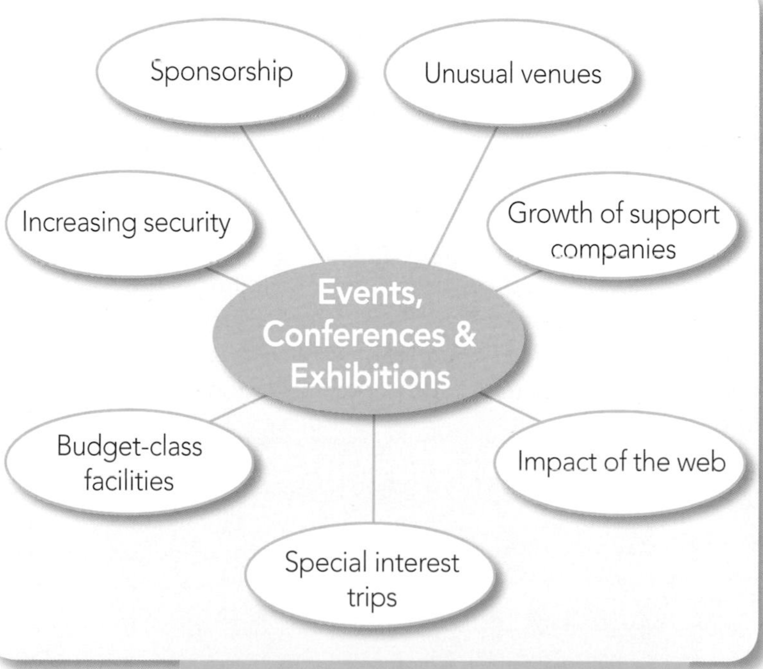

Fig 17.3 – Trends in the events, conferences and exhibitions industry

Unusual venues

Exhibitions and conferences usually take place in purpose-built facilities such as convention centres, exhibition complexes, hotels and universities. Event management companies are always looking for novel venues to offer their clients something out of the ordinary.

Growth of support companies

The number of companies offering support services to the events, conferences and exhibitions industry has grown over the last ten years as the industry itself has developed. There are countless venue-finding and event management companies that offer their services to clients, some of which are members of trade associations, for example the Association for Conferences and Events (ACE) and the Association of British Professional Conference Organisers (ABPCO). Growth in the number of support companies has slowed in the last two years as a result of the downturn in the global economy.

Impact of the web

Technology is changing the way that business people communicate and is having an impact on the events, conferences and exhibitions industry. Web-based, telephone and video conferencing systems are used across the world to hold 'virtual meetings' and seminars. Companies use this technology to save on the costs and time associated with business travel, although meeting people face-to-face at conferences and exhibitions remains the favoured option in certain circumstances. Using systems such as SABA and WebEx can save a company thousands of pounds by not having to pay for expensive business travel and accommodation.

Weblink

Check out this website for more information on the web-based conferencing services offered by Webex. **www.webex.co.uk**

Special interest trips and packages

The growth of special interest tourism has meant that many holiday companies now offer trips and packages to events in the UK and worldwide. Many of these are sporting events, for example trips to European football and rugby matches, but they also include holidays based on specific themes, such as wine festivals in France and cultural events, e.g. the Passion Play at Oberammergau.

Budget-class meeting facilities

In the current period of austerity following the global recession that began in 2008, many private companies and public sector bodies have put a freeze on all but the most essential business trips taken by staff. Travel budgets have been cut and managers are asked to justify all types of travel to exhibitions and conferences within the UK and overseas. There is a trend towards shorter business meetings, with fewer overnight stays, in order to save on costs. The current recession has also seen a sharp drop in demand for first and business class travel on aircraft. Some commentators are predicting the end of expensive, business class travel services on aircraft altogether. Also, in times of recession there tends to be a shift away from expensive city centre 4-star and 5-star hotels to budget accommodation when attending conferences, exhibitions and business events.

Activity 17.3

Explain how (1) popularity of unusual venues; (2) the growth of budget-class meeting facilities affect the events, conferences and exhibitions industry.

This activity is designed to provide evidence for M1.

Increasing security

Security is high on the agenda of travellers and everybody concerned with the travel and tourism sector, particularly since the tragic events of 9/11 in the USA and the 7/7 bombings in London. Security is an important consideration for events, conferences and exhibitions – the more high-profile the event the more attention needs to be given to the security of all those involved with staging and visiting the event. Specialist companies can advise on appropriate security measures for specific events, including crowd management, entry control, car parking, front-of-house security and other safety issues. Nowadays it is common for delegates at conferences and exhibitions to be subjected to enhanced security checks on arrival.

Sponsorship

Sponsorship can bring financial benefits to an event, both for the sponsoring organisation and the event itself. The sponsors invest their money in the expectation of greater exposure of their brand and higher sales – this is particularly the case with high-profile events that are televised. The event organisers benefit from an injection of cash and the kudos that goes with an association with a successful company. Drinks companies often sponsor events, for example Red Bull sponsor events such as air races, skateboarding competitions and a number of extreme sports events around the world.

Conferences look to sponsors to help offset the costs of staging events. There is sometimes a tiered sponsorship structure – the companies that pledge the most money gain the most, while lesser amounts attract fewer benefits. A company may decide to be the principal sponsor for an event or buy from a range of sponsorship opportunities offered by the organisers, for example to have their logo on all printed items, banner advertising at an event, free access for a certain number of staff, a place at the top table, etc.

Activity 17.4

Carry out some research and assess the growth potential of the event, conference and exhibitions environment in the UK. You may like to investigate the EIBTM Industry Trends and Market Share Report and the research section of the Association for Conferences and Events website www.aceinternational.org to help make a start on this activity.

This activity is designed to provide evidence for D1.

SECTION 2 Understand types of venues utilised for events, conferences and exhibitions

This section explores the many types of UK venues used for events, conferences and exhibitions, and the range of facilities needed in venues to ensure successful events.

Venues

Britain has a wide variety of venues that can be used for events, conferences and exhibitions, including:

- Purpose-built centres;
- Hotels;
- Academic venues;
- Sporting venues;
- Unusual venues;
- Civic venues.

Activity 17.5

Visit **www.venues.org.uk** or a similar website and find details of three venues (one hotel, one academic and one sporting) within easy travelling distance of where you live. Compile a fact sheet on each of the venues that describes the venue, its facilities and the type of events (corporate and public) to which it is most suited.

This activity is designed to provide evidence for P3.

Purpose-built centres

Purpose-built centres tend to be most suited to large exhibitions and events that attract thousands of visitors and exhibitors. Exhibition centres such as the National Exhibition Centre (NEC) in Birmingham, Excel in London and the Scottish Exhibition and Conference Centre (SECC) in Glasgow are primarily used for exhibitions and conferences. Some purpose-built venues are multi-purpose and are able to stage a variety of exhibitions, conferences and events such as rock concerts and sports events, e.g. the Millennium Stadium in Cardiff, Sheffield Arena and the M.E.N Arena in Manchester.

Hotels

Hotels use their facilities to host events, conferences and exhibitions as a way of generating extra revenue and filling spare capacity. Events are held all year round and provide extra business for hotels outside of peak holiday periods. Events at hotels range from very small meetings for business people and product launches to large-scale conferences and weddings. Hotels are suitable for many events since they have appropriate rooms and catering facilities readily available.

The Old course Hotel at St Andrews is used for corporate events

Academic venues

Universities, colleges and even schools hire out their facilities for conferences and events, usually out of term time. Academic venues are ideal for events since they have halls and lecture theatres for addressing large numbers of people and smaller rooms that can be used for conference break-out sessions and smaller gatherings. They can also supply computers and audio-visual equipment for speakers and offer on-site catering facilities.

FOCUS ON INDUSTRY

M.E.N ARENA MANCHESTER

Located within 60 minutes drive-time of 11.4 million people, Europe's largest indoor concert venue, the Manchester Evening News Arena, is situated close to Manchester's Victoria Station, with direct access to a hub of public and private transport services and adjacent to a 1,500 capacity multi-storey car park.

The Arena was officially opened on Saturday 15 July 1995 when Torvill & Dean broke the UK box office attendance record for a single ice performance with over 15,000 fans. In its first operational year the venue's target of 130 events, attracting 1 million people was easily exceeded, with over 1.2 million people attracted to 143 events.

The venue's versatility means that it can be transformed from an intimate theatre environment for 3,000 to a state-of-the-art arena capable of accommodating 21,000.

From Madonna to Kings Of Leon, Strictly Come Dancing to World Championship Boxing and Lee Evans to the 9th FINA Short Course World Swimming Championships, this multi-purpose entertainment and sports Arena caters for a wide range of corporate and public events, with full TV broadcasting and recording facilities.

In 2001, the Manchester Evening News Arena was voted International Venue of the Year by the concert industry and has been nominated for the award each year since. In 2003, 2004 and 2007 the Manchester Evening News Arena was also officially recognised as the 'Busiest Indoor Arena Venue in the World' based on ticket sales.

Weblink @ Check out this website for more information on events and facilities at the M.E.N Manchester Arena.

www.men-arena.com

Sporting venues

Sports venues are used extensively for corporate functions, offering the opportunity for business people to network while they enjoy the hospitality and events on offer. Events are an important revenue stream for sports clubs and tend to be popular with visitors who get to see behind the scenes and may even meet sports stars. Sporting venues that host events include the Premiership football clubs, Wimbledon Lawn Tennis Club, Newbury Racecourse and the Belfry Golf Resort near Birmingham.

Manchester United's corporate facilities at Old Trafford

Unusual venues

Event management companies are always looking for something new for their clients in terms of unusual places to stage events. A business event held at an unusual venue, for example a castle, theme park, spa or museum, gives an extra incentive for busy people to attend. They can combine their business work at the event with enjoying the leisure facilities on offer at the venue.

The Wedgewood Museum in Stoke-on-Trent hosts corporate events

Civic venues

Civic venues such, as town halls and council offices, are used for a variety of business and public events. Their main aim is to house the departments that provide local facilities and services, but they can be used for meetings, exhibitions and weddings. Examples of civic buildings that stage events for businesses and the public include Wakefield Town Hall, the National Museum in Cardiff and Mansfield Civic Centre.

Activity 17.6

Carry out some research and find two possible venues near Birmingham for a 2-day business conference for 50 delegates. The venue must be able to offer a round of golf for the delegates. Provide full information on prices and conference facilities.

This activity is designed to provide evidence for P3.

Facilities

Staging events, conferences and exhibitions is a complex process involving a lot of prior planning and access to a wide range of facilities, including:

- Room and space options;
- Hospitality facilities;
- Overnight accommodation;
- Licences;
- Entertainment;
- Equipment.

Figure 17.4 gives an indication of the facilities on offer at a large purpose-built venue.

Room and space options

Flexibility is important for venues that want to attract a wide range of corporate and public events. Rooms should be of sufficient size to accommodate both large and small groups, while exhibition space must be flexible enough to allow for different stand sizes and formats. Rooms for events are laid out according to

Seating capacity

- Tiered seats: 8,629
- Floor seats: 3,120
- Standing: 5,200 (subject to licence)
- Various configurations are possible from 3,000 to approximately 13,500

Corporate hospitality

- 32 luxury suites accommodating up to 12 people in each
- Private en-suite WC
- Refreshment serving area (including refrigeration)
- Private telephone
- Choice of catering and refreshments
- 15" remote control colour TVs

VIP hospitality

- Purpose-built private facility
- Private bar
- 100 seated capacity (tables of 10)
- 250 standing capacity
- Private entrance and cloakroom
- Quality catering and refreshments

Exhibition/conference area

- 3,496.8 sq.m (37,636 sq. feet) main area, (length 94m, width 37.2m) plus concourse
- Ceiling height 23.6m (77.5ft) clearance from floor to underside of flying grid

Catering

- 4 major sales points plus several portable stands on main concourse
- 2 sales points on lower concourse
- Backstage catering - preparation and serving areas, basic kitchen

Security

- 24-hour in-house security staff

Medical facilities

- Fully-trained Red Cross staff covering two first-aid centres on concourse and service levels
- Other medical services (doctor, dentist, chiropractor, masseur) can be arranged in advance or to be on site in an emergency

Box office

- Advance booking office with box office manager at arena
- Fully independent computerised Audience View system
- Total of 14 event sales windows including 2 on inner concourse
- 18 credit card booking telephone lines
- Group sales department

Fig 17.4 – Facilities at Sheffield Arena

a customer's requirements and can be in a variety of styles, including:

- Theatre;
- Cabaret;
- Banquet;
- Exam/classroom;
- Boardroom.

Figure 17.5 shows the capacities and layouts of rooms available for corporate events at the visitor attraction @Bristol.

Exhibition organisers offer exhibitors a range of options when selling space. There will be different sizes and locations of stands charged accordingly, plus options of power supply, extra lighting, telephone line, wi-fi access, audio-visual equipment to use on the stand, catering for stand visitors, etc. Figure 17.6 shows the floor plan for the World Travel Market held every year in London, showing stands grouped according to regions of the world.

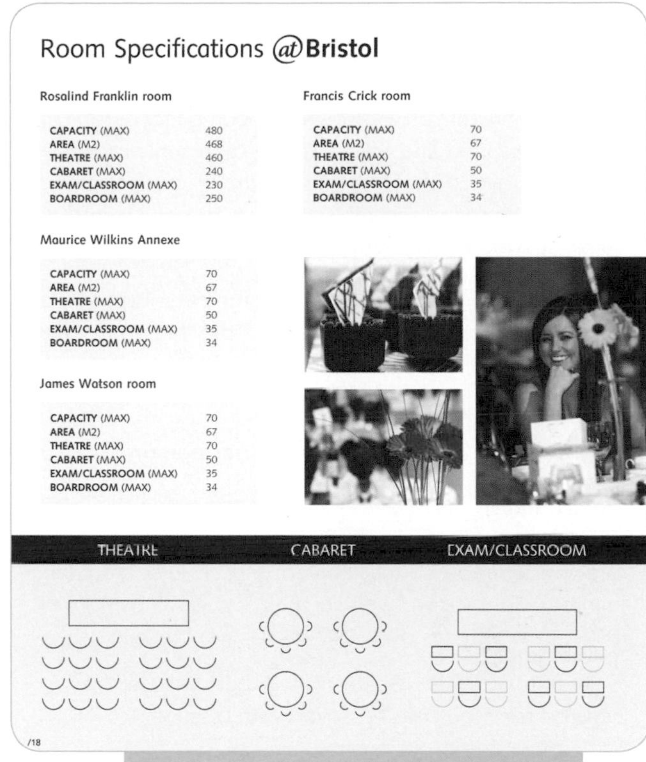

Room Specifications @Bristol

Rosalind Franklin room

CAPACITY (MAX)	480
AREA (M2)	468
THEATRE (MAX)	460
CABARET (MAX)	240
EXAM/CLASSROOM (MAX)	230
BOARDROOM (MAX)	250

Francis Crick room

CAPACITY (MAX)	70
AREA (M2)	67
THEATRE (MAX)	70
CABARET (MAX)	50
EXAM/CLASSROOM (MAX)	35
BOARDROOM (MAX)	34

Maurice Wilkins Annexe

CAPACITY (MAX)	70
AREA (M2)	67
THEATRE (MAX)	70
CABARET (MAX)	50
EXAM/CLASSROOM (MAX)	35
BOARDROOM (MAX)	34

James Watson room

CAPACITY (MAX)	70
AREA (M2)	67
THEATRE (MAX)	70
CABARET (MAX)	50
EXAM/CLASSROOM (MAX)	35
BOARDROOM (MAX)	34

THEATRE CABARET EXAM/CLASSROOM

/18

Fig 17.5 – Room specifications at @Bristol

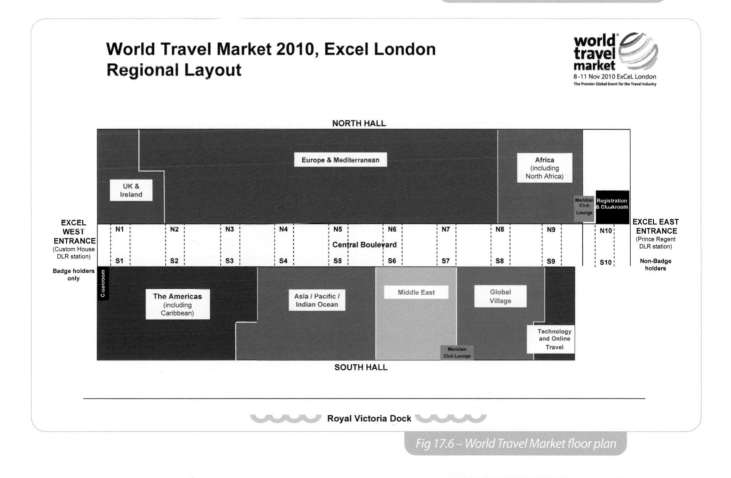

World Travel Market 2010, Excel London
Regional Layout

world travel market
8-11 Nov 2010 ExCeL London
The Premier Global Event for the Travel Industry

NORTH HALL
UK & Ireland
Europe & Mediterranean
Africa (including North Africa)
Meridian Club Lounge
Registration & Cloakroom
EXCEL WEST ENTRANCE (Custom House DLR station)
Badge holders only
N1 N2 N3 N4 N5 N6 N7 N8 N9 N10
Central Boulevard
S1 S2 S3 S4 S5 S6 S7 S8 S9 S10
EXCEL EAST ENTRANCE (Prince Regent DLR station)
Non-Badge holders
Cloakroom
The Americas (including Caribbean)
Asia / Pacific / Indian Ocean
Middle East
Global Village
Meridian Club Lounge
Technology and Online Travel
SOUTH HALL
Royal Victoria Dock

Fig 17.6 – World Travel Market floor plan

Day delegate

These menus have been carefully compiled by our in house head chef and offer a range of freshly produced contemporary dishes that compliment one another. However these are suggested menus and we are happy to tailor a menu for your individual requirements.

The costs identified below are for the catering service only all additional services and room hire must be negotiated with the venue of your choice at time of booking.

Day delegate one **£14.95 per person**

Registration
Selection of Welsh Brew, fruit & herbal teas, freshly brewed fairtrade coffee, chilled orange juice and Tau mineral water served with biscuits

Mid Morning
Selection of Welsh Brew, fruit & herbal teas, freshly brewed fairtrade coffee, served with biscuits

Lunch
A selection of chef's speciality sandwiches
Including vegetarian options
Real crisps
Selection of mini brownies, flapjacks and shortbread
Tau Mineral water and chilled orange juice

Break
Selection of Welsh Brew, fruit & herbal teas and freshly brewed fairtrade coffee served with biscuits

Please note all prices are exclusive of VAT

Fig 17.7 – A sample day delegate menu offered by the National Museum of Wales, Cardiff

Hospitality

All events have an element of hospitality and catering associated with them, whether just a cup of coffee from a mobile unit at a football match to a conference dinner for a 300-delegate event. Hotels have their own catering facilities, but other venues use the services of catering contractors to supply food and drink. Venues that host conferences offer their customers a range of catering options to meet different budgets. Figure 17.7 gives and example of one of the day delegate menus offered by the National Museum of Wales in Cardiff.

Overnight accommodation

Attending events, conferences and exhibitions sometimes involves an overnight stay. Hotels usually offer discounted room rates to delegates attending conferences at the hotel or guests staying overnight after a wedding or reunion. Hotels located in areas where business tourism is important benefit from extra business customers during the working week.

Novotel offers a range of overnight accommodation for events

Licences

Local authorities have a range of responsibilities for licensing and registering certain types of events. All events that supply alcohol, provide public entertainment such as singing, dancing or a display of indoor sport, and those providing late-night refreshments, must operate with a single premises licence from their local authority. Such venues include:

- Pubs and bars;
- Cinemas;
- Theatres;
- Nightclubs;
- Night cafés.

Businesses that serve alcohol under a premises licence must appoint a designated premises supervisor (DPS).

The DPS must hold a separate personal licence to supply or authorise the sale of alcohol. A personal licence only relates to the supply of alcohol and is not required for the other licensable activities.

Entertainment

Entertainment can be the main theme of an event, for example a stadium concert by Muse or the Cardiff Singer of the World competition. It can also be an additional item to create atmosphere at an event, e.g. an after-dinner speaker at a conference or a jazz band playing at a wedding reception. Entertainers can be booked through agents or may be part of a package offered by an events management company or venue organiser.

Equipment

The equipment needed for an event, conference or exhibition will vary depending on the precise nature of the event. Team-building events need specialist equipment, for example paint-balling equipment, off-road bikes and sailing gear. Depending on the size and type of event, equipment for conferences and business meetings may be provided by the venue or brought by the customer. Audio-visual equipment is widely-available in hotels that host corporate events and purpose-built exhibition complexes. More specialist equipment, for example bubble machines and DJ rigs, is available from a variety of companies that provide a support service to venues and event management companies.

SECTION 3

Be able to propose and cost events, conferences and exhibitions

In this section you will learn about the topics to be considered when proposing and planning an event, conference or exhibition.

Brief

Venues and companies that organise events, conferences and exhibitions like to work from a written brief that lists all the customer's requirements in detail. This minimises any possible misunderstandings about what is required. In some circumstances, however, the instructions for an event may only be verbal. Whether written or verbal, a brief should contain the following information:

- Objectives – what the event, conference or exhibition is trying to achieve, e.g. to raise funds for a charity, to launch a new product, to develop team work amongst new members of staff, etc.
- Customer – the brief will include contact details for the customer, who should be kept up to date with developments at regular intervals;
- Target market – this is the audience that the event is aimed at, e.g. business people, the general public, friends, etc.
- Budget – the brief should include the total amount of money available to stage the event, which may be broken down into different areas, e.g. venue hire, catering, promotion, etc.
- Facilities required – this will depend on the size and nature of the event, conference or exhibition and could include details of exhibition space, number and layout of rooms, audio-visual equipment, etc.
- Dates – the date of the event could be specific or the client may be flexible on dates in order to secure a particular venue or a discounted rate;
- Delegate numbers – there may be a minimum number of visitors specified in order to break even financially.

Proposal

Having a clear and comprehensive brief from the client will allow a venue or event management company to draw up a proposal that exactly meets the customer's needs. It is important to remember that customers may be seeking quotes and proposals from more than one company, so presenting a case efficiently and effectively will pay dividends. In fact, many public sector organisations are obliged to contact two or more companies for quotes when organising events.

Format of the event, conference or exhibition

Having read a customer's brief, the venue or event organiser will include in the proposal a suggested format that they feel would meet the brief. This could be an exhibition, conference, seminar, fun event or team-building exercise.

Venue

We saw earlier in this unit that there are many different types of venues used for events, conferences and exhibitions (see page 186). An event organiser will consider a number of issues when choosing a venue for a client, including:

- Cost;
- Availability for specific dates;
- Accessibility;
- Equipment available;
- Type and quality of catering;
- Parking;
- Proximity of overnight accommodation.

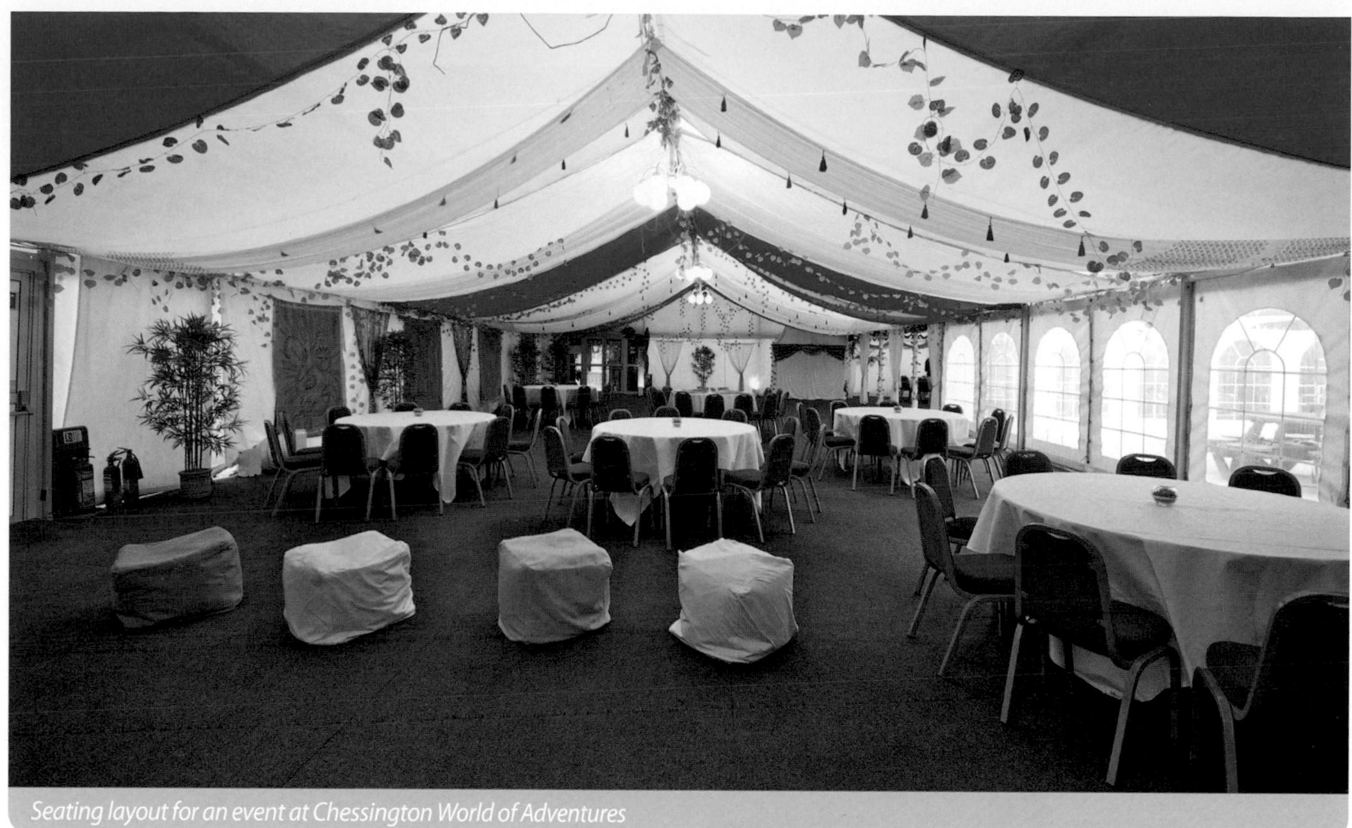

Seating layout for an event at Chessington World of Adventures

Facilities to be used

Having selected a venue, the organiser will investigate the best use of rooms available to meet the client's brief. Depending on the type of event being planned this will lead to adopting an appropriate seating arrangement – boardroom, theatre/conference, cabaret, classroom, banquet, etc. Conferences typically use a main room set out in theatre style and a series of break-out rooms organised in a boardroom style. All arrangements for catering and other services will need to be included in the proposal.

Date and time

These will be based on the customer's requirements as set out in the brief.

Agenda/programme

Depending on the type of event being staged there may be a need for an agenda or programme. This can be as simple as a document with the times and locations of sessions. Consumer and trade exhibitions publish a full catalogue with details of exhibitors, seminars, activities, etc. These are normally sold at the entrance to generate extra revenue.

Booking and payment methods

Businesses that wish to take space at an exhibition will usually contact the organisers direct to book a stand and arrange for payment on credit. Some organisers will require full payment in advance of the event taking place. Visitors to events, conferences and exhibitions often make an online booking using a credit or debit card. This may be direct with the organisers or via a ticket agency such as www.seetickets.com, Keith Prowse, Ticketmaster, etc. Visitors can also pay on arrival at the event with cash or a card.

Equipment

Equipment needed for conferences and business meetings includes:

- Projector and screen;
- Flip chart and pens;
- Whiteboard;

- Internet access;
- Access to computers.

Many people use their own laptop loaded with a presentation when speaking at conferences and business meetings.

Signage

Having confused or annoyed visitors because they can't find their way to an event, conference or exhibition is not a good way to start. Visitors should be supplied with detailed joining instructions before the event and should be able to follow signs when arriving by public transport, walking or driving. Good signage will also be needed in the venue, particularly when there is more than one event taking place.

Good signage is important at events

Refreshments and catering

Food and drinks are normally included in the price of attending conferences and business events. Half-day events that start in the morning are likely to include a refreshment break half way through the proceedings and lunch may be offered at the end. Afternoon half-day events may start with lunch and include a break for refreshments half way through the afternoon, perhaps with tea served at the end of the session. Longer events will include evening meals and breakfasts. At exhibitions visitors tend to buy their own refreshments from the catering outlets on site.

Catering is an important aspect of business events

Additional services for delegates

People attending events, conferences and exhibitions may need additional services, such as overnight accommodation and the use of business facilities, for example a fax machine and internet access.

Promotion

Events, conferences and exhibitions must be promoted effectively if they are to achieve their objectives. There are many promotional techniques that can be used to publicise events, including:

- Advertising;
- E-mail circulars;
- Direct marketing to exhibitors;
- Invitations to VIPs;
- Press releases;
- Early-bird or group discounts.

Inviting members of the press is a good way of getting some exposure for the event in the printed and broadcast media.

Activity 17.7

Suggest the most appropriate promotional methods that you would use to publicise the following events:

1. A major international travel trade exhibition in London;
2. An auction to raise funds for a local charity;
3. A conference for travel & tourism lecturers in Birmingham;
4. A consumer holiday show held in Leeds.

This activity is designed to provide evidence for P4.

Other considerations

Other points which may need addressing when planning an event, conference or exhibition include the format for registration, for example if pre-registration is available to save time on the day, whether any prizes are to be awarded at the event and if sponsorship is to be sought for all or parts of the event.

It is also important to evaluate all events, conferences and exhibitions to get an objective view on whether or nor they were successful. Any evaluation of an event should try to answer the following questions:

1. Did the event achieve its objectives, both financially and operationally?
2. Was the staffing structure workable?
3. Were all eventualities covered?
4. Were the exhibitors and sponsors (if any) happy with the outcome?
5. Were the visitors to the event satisfied?
6. What changes would be made if the event was to be staged again?

Techniques such as face-to-face interviews, post-event e-mail surveys, comment cards and telephone surveys of exhibitors can all be used to gain valuable feedback on an event, conference or exhibition. Staff should also be included in the evaluation process since they often have a valuable contribution to make.

Activity 17.8

Produce an outline proposal for a cruising evening that a local travel agent wishes to hold to promote cruise packages. Address all the points in the previous sections of this unit to complete this task (you will be covering costing the event in a later activity).

This activity is designed to provide evidence for P4.

Health and safety factors

Health, safety and security are important considerations for all organisers regardless of the size of their event. The Health and Safety at Work Act places a duty of care on all businesses that invite visitors on to their premises. This includes organisers of events, conferences and exhibitions who must ensure a safe and secure environment for their staff, visitors and any contractors who may be working for them on site.

Risk assessment

A risk assessment is a systematic investigation of the potential hazards in a given situation. Event management companies and venue operators are required to carry out risk assessments when planning events.

A risk assessment aims to cover the following points:

1. Who is at risk?
- People attending the event;
- Event organisers;
- Contractors working on site.

2. What are likely hazards?
- Food hygiene;
- Electrical and gas problems;
- Tripping and falling;
- Fire;
- Manual handling injuries.

3. What is the level of risk for each hazard?
- Very low;

- Low;
- Medium;
- High;
- Very high.

4. How can the risk be minimised?

- Remove potential hazards, for example packs of brochures blocking aisles on exhibition stands;
- Minimise hazards, for example provide fire extinguishers.

Delegate numbers and flow

Rooms in hotels and at conference and exhibition venues will have a maximum capacity set by the fire brigade or local authority. Entrances, exits and on-site facilities must be able to cope with many people arriving at the same time. Consideration should be given to the flow of visitors at venues, for example to toilets, catering outlets, car parking facilities, etc.

The Chelsea Flower Show attracts thousands of visitors every year

Fire safety and evacuation

Exits in rooms used for events must be kept clear at all times in case of fire evacuation. Delegates at conferences should have their attention drawn to the fire exits and assembly points at the start of the event.

Security

Many purpose-built venues for events, conferences and exhibitions provide 24-hour security with staff who carry out searches as necessary at the entrance to events. Visitors should have secure places to leaves their belongings and conference rooms should be locked when not in use. Exhibitors and conference delegates are often provided with badges for identification and security purposes.

Environmental factors

People taking part in events, conferences and exhibitions need an appropriate level of heating and ventilation during the event. Organisers should monitor room temperatures regularly so as to ensure the comfort of visitors.

Operational factors

There are many operational factors that impact on the staging of events, conferences and exhibitions, including:

- Time constraints and timings;
- Minimum numbers;
- Staff;
- Contingencies.

Time constraints and timings

Organising events, conferences and exhibitions is a complex activity, especially when large-scale events are involved. All staff involved in staging an event must be fully briefed as to what is expected of them and the need to adhere to strict deadlines and dates by which key activities must be completed. Preparation will vary depending on the nature of an event, but is likely to include:

- Booking a venue;
- Confirming speakers and/or exhibitors;
- Administration and finance;
- Fundraising and sponsorship;
- Marketing;
- Liaising with contractors;
- Hospitality and catering;
- Signage;
- Design and layout.

Timings on the day need to be planned in advance and made known to all those attending. Staff should be well-briefed to make sure that the event runs smoothly.

Minimum numbers

For a commercial event there will be a minimum numbers of visitors in order to break even financially. Above this, the organiser is in profit, but below this figure and the event will run at a loss.

Staff

Full and part-time staff are needed to carry out a variety of roles at events, conferences and exhibitions, including:

- Welcome and registration;
- Taking payments;
- Setting up rooms;
- Food and beverages;
- Guiding visitors around the venue;
- Selling items on trade stands;
- Security;
- Car parking;
- Liaising with the press.

Contingencies

Murphy's Law applies just as much to the events, conferences and exhibitions industry as it does to other areas of life, so 'if anything can go wrong it will!' Some things that happen to test the nerve of the best-prepared event organiser can truly be said to be unforeseen, but most can be predicted and contingencies or alternatives devised. The British weather is one of the least predictable factors that can affect an event. For outdoor events, organisers can reassure visitors that the event will take place whatever the weather, using alternative facilities if necessary.

Other occurrences that will need contingency plans include:

- Failure of power supplies – is a back-up alternative source of supply needed?
- Cancellation of speakers or non-arrival of key members of staff – have alternative speakers and extra staff on hand;
- Heavy traffic around the venue – consider an alternative point of entry;
- A strike by public transport workers – be prepared for lower numbers of visitors.

Costings

Organisers of events, conferences and exhibitions must take account of a variety of costs when finalising rates to customers, as the next sections of this unit explain.

Calculations per delegate/attendee

Venues calculate rates for delegates/attendees on either a day basis or an overnight/24-hour basis. Day rates include agreed refreshments plus the use of facilities if at a hotel. 24-hour rates are higher than day rates since they include the cost of an overnight stay. An example of what's included in a day delegate rate at a hotel is shown in Figure 17.8.

Exhibition space rates

Businesses pay for stand space at exhibitions according to size and position. Prices are per metre squared and the bigger the stand the greater the cost. Stands in the best positions, for example immediately by an entrance, are charged at a higher rate. Stand prices are for a basic shell structure to which the exhibitor adds items. Extra payments are taken for additional stand features, e.g. extra lighting and power sockets, literature racks, chairs, internet access, etc.

Winter Special DDR **from £60***

- Arrival tea & coffee with delicious Danish pastries
- Meeting room hire from 9.00 am till 5.30 pm
- Morning tea & coffee break with biscuits
- Your choice from 5 different lunch menu options
- Afternoon tea & coffee break with biscuits
- 6ft screen, LCD projector and flipchart
- Pads, pens, mints and mineral water

To book call +44 (0)20 7402 2400, email cbs.londonmet@hilton.com or visit hiltonlondonmet.com

* This offer is valid for meetings held between 1st December 2010 and 5th January 2011 at the Hilton London Metropole. Applicable for meetings of minimum 10 delegates. Rate is per delegate, excludes VAT and is subject to availability. This offer cannot be used in combination with other promotions.

Fig 17.8 – Example of day delegate rates (DDR) at the Hilton London Metropole

Ticket costs

Trade fairs do not usually charge visitors for entry so as to encourage as many potential buyers as possible to attend. Consumer shows and exhibitions do charge an entry fee which is an extra source of revenue for the organisers.

Calculations of additional services

The cost of any additional services, such as accommodation and transport, must be added to the delegate rates when calculating final costs.

Budget and breakdown of costs

A budget for a proposed event, conference or exhibition shows a breakdown of anticipated income and expenditure. Sources of income may include:

- Admission charges;
- Exhibition stand fees;
- Sponsorship;
- Advertising in programme;
- Sale of merchandise.

Expenditure categories will vary depending on the event, but are likely to include:

- Venue hire;
- Travel expenses for speakers and VIPs;
- Accommodation for speakers and VIPs;
- Refreshments;
- Administration costs;
- Staffing costs;
- Publicity;
- Equipment.

Activity 17.9

With reference to the proposal for a cruising evening in Activity 17.8 produce a budget for the event and explain how your proposal and costings meet the brief.

This activity is designed to provide evidence for P5 and M2.

UNIT SUMMARY

This unit has explored the UK event, conference and exhibitions environment. You have investigated different types of events, conferences and exhibitions, and learned about the specialist organisations involved with the industry, such as exhibition organisers and event management companies. You have seen that companies in the event, conference and exhibitions industry work in partnership with other travel and tourism component industries, including accommodation and transport providers. The unit has also considered trends in the industry, e.g. the popularity of unusual venues and the impact of the web on conferences. You have also investigated a variety of venues used by the industry and the facilities needed to stage successful events, conferences and exhibitions. Finally, the unit has investigated how to draw up a proposal and cost events, conferences and exhibitions. Throughout the unit you have been shown many industry examples, while the case study on the World Travel Market gives you an insight into the operation of one of the world's most prestigious trade fairs.

If you have worked methodically, by the end of this unit you should:

- Understand the event, conference and exhibitions environment in the UK;
- Understand types of venues utilised for events, conferences and exhibitions;
- Be able to propose and cost events, conferences and exhibitions.

You are now in a position to complete the assignment for the unit, under the direction of your tutor. Before you tackle the assignment you may like to have a go at the following questions to help build your knowledge of the events, conferences and exhibitions industry in the UK.

TEST YOUR KNOWLEDGE

1. List five different types of event.
2. What is a break-out room at a conference?
3. Name three purpose-built exhibition centres in the UK.
4. List three types of specialist organisations found in the event, conference and exhibitions industry.
5. Explain how chairs and tables would be arranged in boardroom style for a meeting.
6. Name six items that should be included in a written brief for an event, conference or exhibition.
7. List three different types of conference.
8. What is a contingency plan for an event and why is it important to have one?
9. What is the difference between a trade fair and a consumer exhibition?
10. Name five techniques that the organiser of a business conference could use to promote the event.
11. Name three travel and tourism component industries that organisations in the event, conference and exhibitions industry work with.

12. What methods could an organiser use to gain feedback on an event?
13. List three different types of exhibition.
14. What is corporate hospitality?
15. What is a risk assessment and what is its link with the event, conference and exhibitions industry?

Answers to these questions can be found in the Book 2 Tutor's CD-ROM that accompanies this book (ISBN 9780956268075). Full details can be found at **www.tandtpublishing.co.uk**

UNIT 17 ASSIGNMENT

Events, Conferences and Exhibitions

Introduction

This assignment is made up of a number of tasks which, when successfully completed, are designed to give you sufficient evidence to meet the Pass (P), Merit (M) and Distinction (D) grading criteria for the unit. If you have carried out the activities and read the case studies throughout this unit, you will already have done a lot of work towards completing the tasks for this assignment.

Scenario

You are working on placement for your local careers company and have been asked by your line manager Sam Gower to help with the following projects that he is working on at the moment:

1. A careers booklet on the event, conference and exhibitions industry;
2. Possible venues for future events;
3. A proposal for a careers exhibition.

Sam would like you to complete the following three tasks.

Task 1

Produce a section of a careers booklet on the event, conference and exhibitions industry in which you must:

a. Describe the event, conference and exhibitions environment in the UK (P1). A broad, basic description will suffice, but you must make sure that the following areas are covered – types of event, types of conference, types of exhibition, specialist organisations and customers, supported by relevant examples.

In describing events, conferences and exhibitions, you should consider organisations and types of customers that use these services.

b. Explain the intrinsic links between the event, conference and exhibitions environment and the UK travel and tourism sector (P2). You should also identify at least three current trends affecting the event, conference and exhibitions environment and briefly describe them.

c. Explain how trends affect the event, conference and exhibitions environment (M1). You must demonstrate analysis when explaining how trends have impacted. For example, you could explain the impacts of web-conferences, seminars and e-meetings on the need for conferences, seminars and face-to-face meetings or the impact of the need for tighter security at large exhibitions. You do not need to focus on specific venues, but should refer to examples where they are appropriate.

d. Assess the growth potential of the event, conference and exhibitions environment (D1). This could be growth in terms of revenue or in terms of new and diverse markets. An example of an appropriate level of response could be an identification of the potential for growth in small, budget conference venues. You could base this on the growing number of people working at home, and the number of UK companies that are basing their business 'off-shore'. These two factors may have led to a decrease in large meeting rooms being available in-house, and many small and medium-sized companies will need to hire external venues on a regular basis. While you may recognise growth potential in some types of events, conferences and exhibitions, you may also recognise potential decline in others, for example where businesses may be moving away from large-scale and potentially expensive conferences to more web-conferences and e-meetings. This may limit the potential for growth.

This task is designed to provide evidence for P1, P2, M1 and D1.

Task 2

Sam needs to gather information on different types of venues that the careers company could use for future events. He would like you to prepare and deliver an illustrated presentation in which you must:

- Explain the appropriateness of different types of venues for events, conferences and exhibitions (P3). You should describe five venues, one of each of the following – purpose-built centres, hotels, academic venues, sporting venues and unusual venues. Where there is some overlap in that some venues are multi-functional, for example where a conference centre is also used to stage events, the primary purpose of the chosen venue should be the main focus of your description. You should name selected venues, describe their location and what they offer the event, conference or exhibition organiser in terms of facilities. Examples of recent events, conferences or exhibitions held at the venues should be indicated.

This task is designed to provide evidence for P3.

Task 3

Staff at the careers company are considering running a careers exhibition for local school and college students next year to highlight the range of career opportunities in the travel and tourism sector in the UK. They expect approximately 150 people to attend and you will need to suggest travel and tourism organisations that may wish to exhibit. The company has set aside a budget of £2,000 to cover all costs of the event. Sam would like you to:

a. Produce a written proposal for the event to meet this brief (P4). The proposal should include all the following aspects – format of event, venue, facilities to be used, date and time, agenda/programme, booking and payment methods, equipment needed, signage, refreshments and catering, additional services needed, health and safety, operational factors, etc. As part of the proposals you must suggest how to promote the exhibition and include details of the planned promotional activities.

b. Prepare costings for the event (P5). This should be achieved by producing costings for all services mentioned in your proposal. This could be supported by costs available on websites, obtained through individual research and using various organisations' materials. It should be presented as an information sheet. It should clearly state all the inclusions, whether costs are per company or per person. There must be a simple but clear rationale for the costs included in relation to the budget.

c. Explain in writing how the proposal and costings meet the brief (M2). You should focus on the proposal and explain how it meets the given brief. This involves stating why specific choices have been made such as 'a venue with a high number of parking spaces was selected because …' or 'it was decided to have a buffet lunch because …' Decisions relating to costs must be fully explained

This task is designed to produce evidence for P4, P5 and M2.

UNIT 19

UK Visitor Attractions

INTRODUCTION TO THE UNIT

Visitor attractions play a vital role in the travel and tourism sector, offering excitement, fun, education and activities for all types of people from the UK and overseas. It is often an attraction that tempts people to visit a tourist destination in the first place. Attractions can be purpose-built, such as a theme park or family entertainment complex, or naturally-occurring, for example National Parks, forests and lakes. Together, they offer a wealth of unique experiences for domestic and overseas visitors to Britain.

In this unit you will learn about different types of visitor attractions, and the products and services they offer. You will discover how attractions use different kinds of interpretation techniques to inform, educate and entertain visitors, including displays, leaflets and costumed guides. You will also investigate the appeal of attractions to different types of visitors and the key features that affect their decision to visit, such as location, opening times, transport links and admission charges. Finally, the unit explores the importance of visitor attractions to the popularity and appeal of UK tourist destinations. Supervised visits to local and national attractions, and talks by people working in the attractions industry, will help you to understand how attractions operate, plus the techniques they use to attract and retain visitors.

WHAT YOU WILL STUDY

When you have completed this unit you should:

1. Know the products and services provided by different types of visitor attraction;
2. Know the range and purpose of techniques used for visitor interpretation;
3. Understand the appeal of visitor attractions to different types of visitor;
4. Understand the importance of visitor attractions to the popularity and appeal of UK tourist destinations.

You will be guided through the main topics in this unit with the help of the latest developments, statistics, industry examples and case studies. You should also check out the weblinks throughout the unit for extra information on particular organisations or topic areas and use the activities throughout the unit to help you learn more.

ASSESSMENT FOR THIS UNIT

This unit is internally assessed, meaning that you will be given an assignment (or series of assignments) to complete by your tutor(s) to show that you have fully understood the content of the unit. A grading scale of pass, merit or distinction is used when staff mark your assignment(s), with higher grades awarded to students who show greater depth in analysis, evaluation and justification in their assignments. An assignment for this unit, which covers all the grading criteria, can be found on page 235. Don't forget to visit **www.tandtonline.co.uk** for all the latest industry news, developments, statistics and links to websites in this unit to help you with your assignments.

SECTION 1 Know the products and services provided by different types of visitor attraction

Icebreaker

This unit investigates the appeal and importance of UK visitor attractions – from theme parks and National Parks to cathedrals and museums. Working by yourself, or in small groups under the direction of your tutor, see how you get on with the following tasks to help you make a start on this unit:

- Have a go at coming up with your own definition of a 'visitor attraction';
- Name six built attractions found in the UK;
- Thinking about an attraction close to where you live, make notes on who owns the facility, its purpose and the types of visitors it attracts;
- Working in a small group, discuss what you think is meant by interpretation and its link with visitor attractions;
- Think of three points that would be important to you when deciding whether or not to visit an attraction;
- Name six natural attractions found in the UK;
- Working in a small group, discuss the importance of visitor attractions to the UK travel and tourist sector.

When you've finished, show your answers to your tutor and compare your answers with what other students in your class have written.

There are an estimated 6,400 visitor attractions in the UK, including popular attractions such as Alton Towers, the London Eye, Edinburgh Castle and the Eden Project in Cornwall. It is important to remember that many tourist attractions throughout Britain are not multi-million pound businesses, but smaller enterprises such as museums, craft galleries, shops, leisure facilities and farm attractions that are crucial to the economic prosperity of many parts of the country. Together, they form the critical mass of attractions in an area that encourage tourists to explore and perhaps stay overnight, thereby adding more value to the local economy. The former English Tourist Board's definition of a visitor attraction shows that such places should be promoted to local people as well as to tourists:

'a permanently established excursion destination, a primary purpose of which is to allow public access for entertainment, interest or education, rather than being a primary retail outlet or a venue for sporting, theatrical, or film performances. It must be open to the public, without prior booking, for published periods each year, and should be capable of attracting day visitors or tourists, as well as local residents'.

Products and services

Managers of visitor attractions aim to maximise the revenue from their customers in order to make a profit and re-invest money into new facilities for visitors. They do this by offering a variety of primary, secondary and additional products and services.

The main facility, and principal reason for visiting the attraction, is known as the primary product. If you visit a theme park, for example, the primary product is made up of the rides that provide excitement and fun. The primary product at a museum are the exhibits on display, while the prime reason for visiting a stately home is to see the architecture and furniture in the building, and learn about the way of life of the people who lived there in the past. The primary product of natural attractions is the beauty of the landscape that people have come to enjoy.

The primary product doesn't change a great deal over time, but attraction operators have to regularly update their product in order to give people a reason to visit again. If a theme park, for example, did not introduce new rides and facilities on a regular basis, it would soon lose its customers and become unprofitable. Attractions often stage events that appeal to different types of visitors as a way of revitalising their primary product and generating extra income.

FOCUS ON INDUSTRY

EVENTS AT CHATSWORTH HOUSE

As well as welcoming visitors to the stately home and gardens, Chatsworth House in Derbyshire runs a series of special events that appeal to a wide variety of visitors, for example:

- Horse trials;
- An angling fair;
- A country fair;
- Concerts;
- Behind-the-scenes days;
- Farm shop events and demonstrations;
- Garden events;
- Sewing school courses;
- Vintage car rallies;
- Farmyard and woodland walks.

Offering such a wide variety of events helps to the keep the primary product refreshed and gives visitors who have been before a good reason for making a return visit.

Weblink @ Check out this website for more information on events and facilities at Chatsworth House.
www.chatsworth.org

Secondary and additional products and services are very important to visitor attractions, since they enhance the visitor experience and generate additional revenue. They include:

- Shops – selling gifts, souvenirs and products linked to the attraction, e.g. knitwear at a woollen mill and wine at a vineyard;
- Food and drink – for sale in restaurants, cafés, fast-food outlets, ice cream parlours, etc. The larger attractions feature well-known catering brands, such as McDonalds, Burger King and KFC;
- Children's play areas – often provided at no extra charge to provide somewhere for youngsters to let off steam and for parents to have a break;
- Picnic areas – places for individuals and groups to eat their own food. Picnic areas increase a person's dwell time at an attraction, i.e. the total amount of time spent on site;
- Toilets – the availability and cleanliness of toilets is very important to visitors. Poor facilities create a bad impression with visitors and affect the number of repeat visits;
- Parking – visitors may have to pay to park their cars or parking may be provided for free. Depending on the size of the attraction, there may be transport from the car parks to the main entrance, e.g. by land train, monorail or coaches;
- Services for visitors with special needs – providing accessible attractions is now a legal requirement under the Disability Discrimination Act (see page 221) and makes good business sense as well;
- Corporate hospitality and room hire – hosting business functions, meetings, conferences and even weddings is an excellent way for attractions to increase their income, particularly out of season when visitor numbers may be low;
- Photography – another income-earning activity, especially in theme parks, where visitors are given the chance to buy a photo of themselves while on a ride;
- Education services – school, college and university groups make up a sizeable proportion of the visitors to many attractions, so providing facilities such as a classroom, guided walks, illustrated talks and fact

sheets adds to the visitors' experience, as well as making good business sense.

Visitors usually have to pay an extra charge for most ancillary products and services, thereby generating extra revenue for the attraction. This secondary spend as it is sometimes known, can be very profitable for the attraction – profit margins on, for example, selling gifts, food and drink, can be far higher than margins on entrance fees to the attraction.

FOCUS ON INDUSTRY

AT-BRISTOL'S CORPORATE EVENTS

At-Bristol is a 'hands-on' science and discovery attraction located in the regenerated harbour area of Bristol. The attraction offers a wide variety of corporate events, including:

- Banquets and receptions;
- Conferences, meetings and presentations;
- Product launches, trade fairs, location shoots and concerts;
- Incentive outings, team-building activities and debate forums;
- Wedding receptions, family functions, wedding and naming ceremonies.

At-Bristol also has access to public areas surrounding the attraction that can be used for corporate events. Millennium Square can seat up to 4,500 people or accommodate 7,500 standing, while the smaller Anchor Square is designed to seat 1,000 people or accommodate 2,000 standing. Both squares are used for large events such as open-air concerts and exhibitions of public art.

Weblink

Check out this website for more information on At-Bristol and its corporate events.
www.at-bristol.org.uk

Activity 19.1

Choose two visitor attractions spread across the country, one built and one natural, and find out what facilities and services they offer for corporate events. Make a fact sheet on each of the attractions giving full details of the corporate facilities on offer.

This activity is designed to provide evidence for P1.

Types of visitor attractions

Tourist attractions can be either built or natural. Built attractions include facilities that have been developed specifically for tourism and leisure, e.g. theme parks, and buildings that were designed for another purpose, but which have since become popular with visitors, such as castles, cathedrals and other historic buildings. The British countryside, and in particular its protected areas such as National Parks, Areas of Outstanding Natural Beauty and Heritage Coasts, is a major attraction for millions of people every year. The opening up of the countryside under the recent right to roam legislation is likely to encourage more people to visit the countryside and enjoy its natural attractions.

Built attractions

There are many different types of built attractions found throughout Britain, for example:

- Historic monuments and properties;
- Theme parks;
- Heritage attractions;
- Gardens, wildlife and environmental attractions;
- Entertainment facilities;
- Sports centres;
- Cultural attractions.

Historic monuments and properties

The UK is renowned for its wide range of historic monuments and properties, which have great appeal to British people and overseas visitors. The majority of historic monuments are in public ownership, with many London properties under the management of Historic Royal Palaces, an independent charity that looks after the Tower of London, Hampton Court Palace, the Banqueting House, Kensington Palace and Kew Palace. Many castles and stately homes in England and Wales are cared for by the National Trust, CADW Welsh Historic Monuments and English Heritage, which manage sites and provide facilities for visitors. Some historic properties are in private ownership, including Chatsworth House and Blenheim Palace. The following are some of the UK's most popular historic monuments and properties:

- Tower of London;
- Edinburgh Castle;
- Windsor Castle;
- Roman Baths at Bath;
- Stonehenge, Wiltshire;
- Chatsworth House, Derbyshire;
- Tatton Park, Cheshire;
- Blenheim Palace, Oxfordshire.

Churches, cathedrals, ancient monuments and sites are also important attractions for visitors, for example St Paul's Cathedral in London, Glastonbury Tor in Somerset and the sites of past battles.

Activity 19.2

Choose one of the eight historic attractions listed above and write a short report that describes the products and services if offers to visitors. Include a description of the techniques it uses for visitor interpretation. Analyse how effectively the products, services and interpretation techniques contribute to the appeal for two different types of visitors, for example school groups and overseas tourists.

This activity is designed to provide evidence for P1, P2 and M1.

Edinburgh Castle is a popular historic monument

Theme parks

A theme park is a visitor attraction offering permanent rides and entertainment in a themed setting or range of settings, providing something for the whole family. Most theme parks charge one price for unlimited access to all rides and attractions in a fun environment. Theme parks have been a success story in the UK since the first was opened at Thorpe Park in Surrey in 1979. Based on a concept that was developed in the USA, theme parks offer visitors a wide range of permanent rides and themed entertainments, with a single entry charge giving access to all facilities. Most large UK theme parks have experienced growth in their attendances since the late 1980s, through constant updating of their facilities and visitor services. There is evidence, however, that the theme park market is becoming saturated in some parts of Britain, leading to price discounting by parks and the introduction of other incentives to maintain their market shares.

Although each UK theme park has its own particular attractions, there are certain common characteristics that theme parks exhibit, for example:

- Parks offer a mix of facilities and activities, e.g. 'white knuckle' rides, live entertainment, animals, gardens, events, children's play areas, education centres, corporate hospitality, retail and catering;
- Most parks operate on a seasonal basis between Easter and the end of October;

- Most visitors are family groups from the C1/C2 social classes;
- Group bookings account for between 10-25 per cent of all visitors;
- Typically, parking for 3,000-4,000 cars is provided;
- Site areas range from as little as 12 acres to 800 acres plus, with 130-140 acres being a typical size;
- Parks are generally close to the motorway network, ensuring very large two-hour catchment populations (up to 15 million);
- Length of stay on site averages between 6 and 7 hours, presenting park operators with ample opportunities for generating secondary spend, e.g. at catering and retail outlets.

In addition to Blackpool Pleasure Beach, the UK's most popular attraction, other popular UK theme parks include:

- Alton Towers, Staffordshire;
- Thorpe Park, Surrey;
- Chessington World of Adventures, Surrey;
- Oakwood Leisure Park, Pembrokeshire;
- Pleasureland Theme Park, Southport;
- Pleasure Beach, Great Yarmouth;
- Drayton Manor, Staffordshire;
- Legoland Windsor.

Fun at Legoland Windsor

Heritage attractions

Britain has a rich and varied heritage that appeals to many visitors from home and abroad. Right across the country there are large and small attractions that celebrate past events, industrial processes, traditions and landscapes, for example:

- Ironbridge Gorge Museum in Shropshire;
- Jorvik Viking Centre in York;
- Welsh Slate Museum in Llanberis, north Wales;
- Beamish Open Air Museum in County Durham;
- Quarry Bank Mill in Cheshire;
- National Maritime Museum at Greenwich, London;
- Lulworth Cove Heritage Centre, Dorset;
- New Lanark World Heritage Village, Scotland;
- Giant's Causeway Visitor Centre, Northern Ireland;
- Big Pit National Coal Museum (see case study on page 209).

Jorvik Viking Centre in York

Heritage attractions tend to focus on a particular theme or activity and use a variety of interpretation techniques to tell a story or explain a process (you will learn more about interpretation later in this unit). English

Heritage is the publicly-funded agency that advises the government on all matters concerning heritage and the historic environment. It also manages and makes available to the public more than 400 historic sites in England, including Barnard Castle, Stonehenge and Dover Castle. CADW Welsh Historic Monuments does a similar job in Wales.

Some of Britain's finest heritage attractions have been awarded UNESCO World Heritage Site status in recognition of their unique contribution to the world's natural and built heritage. The UK currently has 28 World Heritage Sites, which include Ironbridge Gorge, the Tower of London, the Royal Botanic Gardens at Kew and Hadrian's Wall.

Ironbridge is a World Heritage Site

CASE STUDY

Big Pit National Coal Museum

Introduction

Big Pit National Coal Museum, based around a real coal mine in the South Wales valleys, is one of the UK's leading industrial heritage museums. It is located close to the town of Blaenavon, which was awarded World Heritage Site status in 2000. Big Pit welcomes incoming tourists from all over the world and domestic visitors from across the UK.

Development of the attraction

The museum was established in 1983 after closure of the working mine in 1980. However, until 2001, lack of funding meant that many of the buildings on the surface were left untouched and out of bounds to the public. A period of closure followed, during which a £7 million redevelopment was carried out, and the museum was fully re-opened in February 2004. Since 2001, Big Pit has been part of the National Museums and Galleries of Wales (NMGW) group. It benefits, like all NMGW sites, from free access for visitors funded by the Welsh Assembly Government. Big Pit has welcomed more than 2.5 million visitors in its 22-year history and the introduction of free entry to the museum has boosted visitor numbers considerably in recent years. In 2004, the museum had 141,000 visitors, made up of individuals, parties and education groups. By 2009 this figure had risen to 179,000. In 2005 Big Pit won the prestigious £100,000 Gulbenkian Prize for Museum of the Year.

Facilities for visitors

The highlight of a visit to Big Pit is the hour-long underground tour which is led by ex-miners. Visitors descend 300 feet in the original pit cage and are guided along underground roadways, through air doors and past engine houses, all built by generations of miners. On the surface, there are colliery buildings of all types open to visitors, including the winding engine-house, blacksmiths' workshops and the original pithead baths. The baths were the first to be installed at the site and date back to 1939. They currently house Big Pit's main exhibition space where the history of the coal mines of South Wales is explored and the stories of the communities that grew up around them are told, from the earliest days to the miners' strikes and pit closures of the 1980s. Big Pit also has multimedia displays of modern mining. Although the museum is on the side of a steep hill, much of it is accessible to those with mobility problems and visually/hearing-impaired visitors are catered for. A maximum of four wheelchair users are allowed underground at any one time for safety reasons and the site welcomes assistance dogs, although they cannot be taken on the underground tour. The museum has two catering outlets and a gift shop. There are toilets on all three levels of the site and baby changing facilities are available on two levels.

Educational visits

Big Pit hosts educational visits from primary school children to university groups. It offers a resource room for teachers, group leaders, students and other specialists who wish to carry out research work at the museum. The room contains reference books, maps, original documents and has internet access. The museum's Education Officer handles all education enquiries and provides teaching resources for schools.

Case Study Questions and Activities

1. Describe the products and services provided for visitors to Big Pit.
2. What different types of interpretation does Big Pit offer to its visitors?
3. Why is it important for heritage attractions like Big Pit to offer facilities for education visits?
4. In what ways has Big Pit benefited from being a member of the National Museums and Galleries of Wales (NMGW) group?
5. Which other attractions are part of the NMGW group?

This case study is designed to provide evidence for P1 and P2.

Weblink

Check out this website to help answer the questions and for more information on Big Pit Mining Museum.

www.museumwales.ac.uk/en/bigpit

Gardens, wildlife and environmental attractions

Gardens, wildlife and environmental attractions are growing in popularity as people become more interested in the world around them and the impact that modern life has on the planet. Gardens range from the large-scale attractions such as Kew Gardens and the National Trust's Stourhead Garden in Wiltshire to the many small gardens open to the public as part of the National Gardens Scheme. Zoos have long been popular with visitors, but have changed their emphasis over the years to reflect the public's desire to see animals in a more natural setting. The following are some of Britain's most popular gardens, wildlife and environmental attractions:

- Eden Project in Cornwall;
- Chester Zoo;
- Kew Gardens in Surrey;
- London Zoo;
- The Deep in Hull;
- The Royal Horticultural Society (RHS) gardens at Wisley in Surrey;
- Royal Botanic Gardens in Edinburgh;
- The Botanic Gardens in Belfast;
- Stourhead Garden in Wiltshire;
- Glasgow Botanic Gardens.

Environmental attractions combine a fun day out with the chance to learn about issues such as conservation, energy use and sustainability. Examples of these types of attractions include the Centre for Alternative Technology (CAT) in Machynlleth, west Wales and the Eden Project in Cornwall (see case study on page 230).

Entertainment facilities

Entertainment facilities such as nightclubs, casinos, discos, theatres, concert halls, arenas and opera houses, all provide entertainment opportunities for visitors to an area and local residents. Indoor arenas, such as the NIA in Birmingham, the ExCel Arena in London's Docklands and Sheffield Arena, are major venues for concerts, attracting people from a wide catchment area. Much of the appeal of UK tourist destinations is the wide range of entertainment facilities they offer visitors. Seaside resorts such as Scarborough, Blackpool and Brighton, for example, attract tourists with a variety of live shows, concert events and night life opportunities. Smaller towns and cities also attract day visitors from their immediate area to enjoy the entertainment at nearby cinemas, theatres, night clubs and arts centres.

Sports centres

As well as being popular with local residents, sports centres also add to the appeal of towns and cities in the UK, helping to attract overnight and day visitors. Swimming baths and leisure centres offer visitors indoor facilities when the weather outside is poor. There has been considerable investment in sport and leisure facilities in the UK in recent years, with the introduction of wave machines, jacuzzis, health suites, flumes and saunas into centres run by public and private sector operators. On a national scale, sport and recreation facilities are being used to help change the image of certain parts of Britain and attract further inward investment, for example both the Don Valley Stadium in Sheffield and the National Cycling Centre in Manchester are part of major urban regeneration projects. Many areas of east London are undergoing major regeneration as part of the developments for the 2012 London Olympic Games.

Cultural attractions

Some parts of Britain have a variety of cultural attractions that appeal to both UK and international visitors. Links with famous people, cultural diversity, associations with the arts and music are all used to build an image of a destination and attract tourists. Shakespeare's birthplace in Stratford-upon-Avon, for example, is a magnet for UK and overseas visitors alike, while historic Bath, the Cardiff Singer of the World Competition and the Edinburgh Festival attract tourists from all over the world. Many tourists visit the haunts of Dylan Thomas in Wales and Thomas Hardy in Dorset. The cultural diversity in cities such as Leeds, Manchester, Cardiff, London and Bradford is used as a springboard for themed events and short breaks, e.g. curry weekends in Bradford and visits to the Chinatown areas of London and Manchester.

Museums and art galleries are amongst the most popular cultural attractions with visitors. They display ancient and modern artefacts in a range of settings, using a variety of techniques to inform, educate and entertain visitors. The following are amongst Britain's most popular cultural attractions:

- Tate Modern;
- British Museum;
- Science Museum;
- National Gallery;
- Tate Gallery at St Ives in Cornwall;
- The Burrell Collection in Glasgow;
- Natural History Museum;
- The Lowry, Salford Quays, Manchester;
- Museum of Welsh Life at St Fagan's, Cardiff;
- Ulster Folk and Transport Museum, Northern Ireland.

The Science Museum in London (courtesy of SSPL/Science Museum)

Activity 19.3

Carry out some research into three cultural attractions in the UK. For each attraction, produce an illustrated fact sheet that describes (1) the primary, secondary and additional products on offer to visitors; (2) corporate hospitality facilities; (3) services and facilities for visitors with special needs.

This activity is designed to provide evidence for P1.

Natural attractions

Britain has an abundance of natural attractions, from Land's End to John O' Groats. Domestic and overseas visitors are attracted to the beautiful coastline, the rugged mountains, peaceful lakes and the picturesque valleys. Many of these areas have been given special status to protect their environment and provide facilities for their enjoyment by the public, e.g. National Parks, Areas of Outstanding Natural beauty and Heritage Coasts. The job of overseeing these protected areas in England lies with Natural England, while the Countryside Council for Wales (CCW) does a similar job in the Principality. In Scotland, Scottish Natural Heritage (SNH) is responsible for National Parks and other protected areas, and the Environment and Heritage Service (EHS) takes the lead on protected area matters in Northern Ireland.

Weblink

Check out these websites for more information on the work of these four agencies in landscape protection, tourism and recreation.

www.naturalengland.org.uk; www.ccw.gov.uk; www.snh.org.uk; www.ni-environment.gov.uk

Dartmoor National Park

National Parks

The term National Park is used to describe different types of protected areas throughout the world, from vast areas of uninhabited wilderness in the USA to smaller, lightly-populated areas in the UK. The main concept of all National Parks is one of combining conservation of the landscape with access for recreation and enjoyment – a combination that is sometimes difficult to achieve!

To date, 13 National Parks have been designated in England and Wales since the 1949 National Parks and Access to the Countryside Act. This includes the Broads, which was set up under a special Act of Parliament in 1988, and the New Forest, designated a National Park in March 2005. The South Downs is the most recent National Park, having been officially launched in 2009. The word national does not mean that the Parks are owned by the government – most of the land within National Park boundaries is privately owned and often under severe pressure from visitors and their vehicles. The Peak District National Park is a good case in point being located between the large conurbations of Sheffield and Manchester.

Activity 19.4

On a blank map of the UK, mark and name the National Parks in England, Wales and Scotland, plus the proposed Mourne National Park in Northern Ireland. Registered tandtonline users can download a blank UK map from **www.tandtonline.co.uk**

This activity is designed to provide evidence for P1.

CASE STUDY

Brecon Beacons National Park

Introduction

The Brecon Beacons National Park (BBNP) is one of three National Parks in Wales. It covers an area of 1,347 square kilometres and includes the towns of Brecon, Crickhowell and Hay-on-Wye. There are approximately 32,000 people living within the Park. Its landscape is dramatic and varied, with gentle upland slopes, steep escarpments (the highest point is Pen-y-Fan at 886 metres), glaciated valleys, peat bogs and heather moorland. Water features widely in the landscape, with many rivers, lakes, waterfalls and reservoirs. The River Usk flows through the Park and the sources of the rivers Tawe, Nedd and Taff are found within its boundaries.

The man-made attractions of the area include remains from many different periods of history. These range from prehistoric cairns and hill forts to castles and churches. Remnants of more recent industrial times also survive, including quarries, tram roads and ironworks.

Importance of tourism in the BBNP

The Brecon Beacons National Park Authority (BBNPA) recognises that tourism is an essential industry in the area. It generates an annual income of £66 million and there are some 1900 jobs in the National Park that are associated with tourism. The Authority therefore considers that the successful integration of tourism and the management of its impacts are critical to the economic and social future of the area. Developing tourism in a sustainable manner is seen as crucial to the Park's future.

A significant number of businesses in the Park rely directly on tourism. For example, there are over 100 outdoor pursuits centres/operators. Pubs, caravan park operators, attraction managers and event organisers all receive a proportion of their income from tourists. Shops and other retail outlets in the Park also rely on the trade they receive from visitors. Such businesses provide vital services to the communities within the National Park. Some 6.5 per cent of the people employed in the National Park area work in hotels and catering.

The Beacons Bus (courtesy of and © Tom Hutton/BBNPA)

Attractions of the Park

The Park has a wide range of both natural and built attractions. Its main natural attractions are the mountains, moorland, waterfalls, rivers and caves. Visitors are attracted by the wide variety of wildlife in the National Park. Birds such as the red kite, peregrine falcons and buzzards can be found amongst the crags. Otters, salmon and kingfishers can be spotted along streams and rivers. Ring ouzels and purple saxifrage are found at Craig Cerrig Gleisiad National Nature Reserve. Large numbers of birds, including tufted ducks, wigeon and pochard, gather at Llangors Lake.

Built attractions include the castles, hill forts, historic houses and towns, plus the Monmouthshire and Brecon Canal. The canal has been restored between Pontypool and Brecon and narrow boats can be hired, or day trips taken, from a number of locations along its length. Purpose-built attractions include the National Park Visitor Centre at Libanus and Craig-y-nos Country Park, both managed by the BBNP. The Park has a number of popular market towns that appeal to visitors, including Brecon, Hay-on-Wye, Crickhowell and Llangorse.

Visitors to the BBNP

The BBNP attracts visitors from a wide catchment area. Within just one hour's drive of the Brecon Beacons are the 2 million people who live in South Wales and the population of Bristol. The large urban conurbations of the West Midlands, including Birmingham, are within a 2-hour drive. The BBNP is the closest mountainous area to London and millions of people live within easy travelling distance of the Park. Visitors to the area include:

- Day trippers;
- People on holiday and staying within the Park boundaries;
- People on holiday, staying outside of the Park and making a day visit.

According to the findings of a survey conducted in 1994, the estimated number of visitor days to the BBNP is 3.6 million. It is impossible to calculate exactly how many visitors the Park receives because there are so many roads leading into the Park and no gated entry points. Visitor surveys are carried out to gather information on the types of tourists that visit the National Park and to obtain details of their stay. Most of the day visitors to the Park visit more than once and some visit on a regular basis. The majority of visitors are in family or other small groups.

Interpretation in the Park

The BBNP's interpretation work is centred on the following facilities:

- The National Park Visitor Centre, Libanus – this Centre receives around 168,000 visitors per year. It is situated in the heart of the National Park and has superb views of the central Beacons (including Pen y fan). Visitors can learn about the National Park, find information about walks, activities and places to visit in the area, go for a walk on the common, visit the sensory Millennium Garden, enjoy a meal in the tea rooms or buy maps, local books and souvenirs in the shop. A range of festivals and events are organised at the Centre throughout the year. The Centre is a focal point for many of the tourists and day-trippers who visit the National Park. Other education and business groups visiting the site make use of its 60-seat lecture and conference room.
- Craig-y-nos Country Park – lies at the top of the Swansea Valley and provides services for a range of visitors. It is open every day of the year except Christmas Day and offers a variety of walks, guided and self-led. Environmental activities are provided for school groups. The Country Park's visitor centre contains an interactive exhibition area, a shop, classroom and activity areas. A number of public events are also held at the Country Park.
- YHA Danywenallt National Park Study Centre – located near Talybont-on-Usk, staff at this facility run residential education programmes for a wide range of education groups throughout the year. The centre is also used to host Interpretative Walking Courses, training courses and wildlife events.
- Information Centres – BBNP's three centres are located at Abergavenny, Brecon and Llandovery. Information staff advise visitors on the local countryside and heritage, and opportunities for recreation. They operate under the same roof as Tourist Information Centres (TICs) that are concerned mainly with providing advice on accommodation, attractions and touring.

Case Study Questions and Activities

1. What different types of interpretation does the BBNP offer to visitors?
2. What types of visitors does the Park attract and why do they find it appealing?
3. What are the Park's main attractions and how important are they to the Park's popularity and appeal?
4. Analyse how effectively the products, services and interpretation techniques found in the Park contribute to the appeal for two different types of visitors.
5. Evaluate the contribution of the National Park to the popularity and appeal of the area.

This case study is designed to provide evidence for P1, P2, M1 and D1.

Material in this case study is adapted from the BBNP's Education Service publications.

Weblink

Check out this website to help answer the questions and for more information on the Brecon Beacons National Park.

www.breconbeacons.org

Areas of Outstanding Natural Beauty (AONBs)

There are currently 47 AONBs in the UK. They range from the wild open moorlands of the North Pennines to the green belt countryside of the Surrey Hills and the intimate valley of the Wye, which straddles the border with Wales. There are nine AONBs in Northern Ireland, including Strangford Lough and the Lagan Valley. AONBs can be popular destinations for travel and tourism, although, unlike National Parks, they are not designated for their recreational value. In total, AONBs in England cover around 15 per cent of the landscape.

Weblink @ Check out this website for more information on Areas of Outstanding Natural Beauty.

www.aonb.org.uk

Heritage Coasts

There are 46 Heritage Coasts in England and Wales. They are among the most precious assets for wildlife and landscape, as well as for tourism. Concern over the harmful impact of increasing numbers of visitors led to their designation and a plan of action which includes creating and repairing footpaths, cleaning up bathing water and removing litter. Currently, 33 per cent of England's scenic coastline is conserved as Heritage Coast.

SECTION 2

Know the range and purpose of techniques used for visitor interpretation

Freeman Tilden, one of the founders of modern interpretation, defined it as *"An educational activity which aims to reveal meaning and relationships through the use of original objects, by first-hand experience, and by illustrative media, rather than simply to communicate factual information"*. After 50 years, this is still one of the clearest insights into the role of the interpreter. From the point of view of a visitor attraction, the Association for Heritage Interpretation (AHI) adds that interpretation is essentially a communication process that helps people make sense of, and understand more about a site, collection or event.

Weblink Check out this website for more information on interpretation and the work of the AHI. **www.ahi.org.uk**

Interpretation techniques

Visitor attractions as diverse as farms, ancient monuments, gardens, museums, wildlife reserves, stately homes, National Parks, forest areas and theme parks, all offer interpretation facilities for visitors using a variety of techniques, including:

- Displays;
- Actors and curators;
- Interactive technology;
- Guides and tours;
- Leaflets, maps and signage;
- Activities and events.

There are many factors that need to be taken into consideration when choosing which interpretive techniques to use in an attraction, for example:

1. Location – facilities inside an attraction may not work in an outside setting;
2. Cost – the budget that the attraction has to work within;
3. Target audience – design, content and language will differ from one type of visitor to another;
4. Longevity – deciding how long the interpretation will be in place;
5. Reliability and maintenance – making sure that breakdowns are kept to a minimum;
6. Degree of interaction required – whether active or passive interpretation is needed;
7. Security – issues such as theft of equipment and vandalism.

Displays

Displays at attractions provide visitors with information in text, pictures, model and graphic form. They are a good way of conveying detailed information about an attraction or its exhibits and are often found in museums and art galleries.

Displays in the 'Making the modern world' gallery at the Science Museum (courtesy of SSPL/Science Museum)

Actors and curators

Using people in attractions gives visitors an immediate and informative experience. Actors and costumed guides, sometimes referred to as animateurs, are often found in heritage attractions, such as Beamish Open Air Museum, Blist's Hill Museum in Ironbridge and Wigan Pier, where they mingle with visitors and help to create an atmosphere of what life was really like in days gone by. Curators pass on their specialist knowledge of a museum or similar attraction, thereby enhancing the visitor experience.

Costumed guides at Blist's Hill, Ironbridge

Interactive technology

Technology encourages visitors to interact with exhibits or artefacts to learn more about them. This is particularly appealing to children and young people who often have very enquiring minds! Technology is used in a number of ways in attractions, for example:

- Interactive displays – 'hands on' facilities that allow visitors to touch and interact with exhibits;
- Virtual displays – using 3-D computer technology to simulate an event or setting, for example a virtual tour of a house or castle ruins showing how it would have looked in the past;
- Auditory – defined points at which to listen to information or sound guides (sometimes in different languages) that can be carried by the visitor while they are at the attraction;
- Electronic – using computer-generated images, audio-visual displays or animatronics, i.e. moving models of past and present animals, for example dinosaurs.

An interactive display at the Wales Millennium Centre, Cardiff

Guides and tours

Guides and tours are types of interpretation that give visitors the chance to delve more deeply into an attraction and its facilities. Guides can take a number of forms, including:

- Guided tours – group activities where a guide leads visitors on a tour of an attraction. These person-to-person tours are one of the best ways of interpreting an attraction, but guides need to be well-trained;
- Self-guided tours – when visitors use a leaflet, audio guide or series of signposts to take themselves on a tour of an attraction. Self-guided tours are particularly popular at countryside attractions and give people the chance to walk at their own pace.

As well as adding to the visitor experience tours can also be used to manage visitors at an attraction. For example, guides can control where, when and for how long visitors dwell at a site. This is particularly important in the case of small attractions with limited space for large numbers of visitors. Visitors to Anne Hathaway's cottage in Stratford-upon-Avon are escorted around the property by fully-trained guides to enhance their experience and to control visitor numbers and throughput. Self-guided trails can be planned so as to divert visitors away from environmentally-sensitive areas of an attraction.

Tour guides can interpret an area to visitors

Activity 19.5

Log on to the English Heritage website (**www.english-heritage.org.uk**) and choose six properties/sites for some further research. Make a chart showing the different interpretation facilities that each property/site offers.

This activity is designed to provide evidence for P2.

Leaflets, maps and signage

Printed leaflets and maps are a relatively cheap type of interpretation to produce, but may not have the visual impact of other interpretive techniques such as audio-visual displays or guided tours. Visitors on self-guided tours and trails are often provided with a printed leaflet at the start of their journey.

Good signposting not only helps visitors to find their way around an attraction, but can also form part of the interpretation at the facility. The materials used for the signs may reflect those found in the local area, for example slate signs in a mining museum, wood in a forest environment, iron at an industrial heritage attraction, etc. Signs can be expensive to produce, but are an important part of any visitor attraction.

FOCUS ON INDUSTRY

INTERPRETATION AT ENGLISH HERITAGE

English Heritage is a public body, funded by the Department for Culture, Media and Sport (DCMS), and is responsible for over 400 historic properties in England. English Heritage has developed a wide range of visitor services, including site interpretation and publications, in order to enhance visitor satisfaction and increase the likelihood of repeat visits. There are:

- Defined minimum standards of presentation for all properties;
- Explanatory graphic displays, audio tours, audio-visual presentations and exhibitions;
- Colour guidebooks and souvenir guides, many of which have been revised to be more attractive and readable;
- Children's activity sheets at some sites;
- Guided walks at many sites;
- Brief, plastic-covered guides are provided at some sites where entry is free, designed to be used on site and left for the next visitor.

English Heritage is the largest developer and user of audio tours for interpretation of historic properties, with more than 50 sites now offering this service. At Battle Abbey, Stonehenge, Framlingham Castle, Down House and Eltham Palace, there are interactive audio tours using the hand-held wand system, which gives visitors the flexibility to choose which information they want to listen to, accessed by a numbered keypad. In addition, English Heritage is working to provide audio tours created specially for visitors with visual impairments, thereby increasing access to its sites.

Weblink

Check out this website for more information on interpretation at English Heritage.

www.english-heritage.org.uk

Good signage is important at attractions

Activities and events

As well as providing another source of income for attractions, activities and special events can play an important role in interpretation. All types of attractions, from castles to countryside visitor centres, organise events that add to the visitors' experience and understanding of the area. Recent events at Beamish Open Air Museum in County Durham included a traction engine rally, May Day celebrations, a quilting exhibition, an archaeology weekend and a ploughing match.

Weblink Check out this website for more information on events at Beamish.
www.beamish.org.uk

Jousting at Warwick Castle

Purpose of interpretation

Interpretation is used in visitor attractions for a variety of reasons, such as:

1. Education;
2. Entertainment;
3. Conservation;
4. Security;
5. Meeting specific needs;
6. To meet outreach activities.

Education and entertainment

First and foremost, interpretation in attractions sets out to educate visitors. This could be education in the formal sense, for example a party of school children being taken on a day visit to Longleat, or a less formal type of learning such as a guided walk from a National Park visitor centre to explore the landscape and industrial heritage of the area. Interpretation can also entertain visitors – a well-trained and enthusiastic tour guide at a heritage attraction can add greatly to the visitors' experience by passing on information about the attraction in a stimulating and entertaining manner. This ability of interpretation to combine education and entertainment is sometimes referred to as 'edutainment' by people working in the attractions industry.

Interpretation at the Jorvik Viking Centre in York

Conservation

Interpretation goes hand-in-hand with conservation of, for example, an area of a National Park, a particular wildlife habitat, a museum exhibit, historic building, etc. Interpretive techniques such as audio-visual displays, visitor centres, guided tours and leaflets, can be used to explain conservation issues to visitors and educate them into what they can do to help matters, e.g. avoiding sensitive wildlife areas, not touching museum exhibits, donating to conservation societies, etc.

Security

Visitor attraction operators are legally responsible for providing a safe and secure environment for their staff and visitors, plus any other people who visit the site. Security is a particular issue in relation to the following:

- Visitors and their possessions;
- Money taken for admission and in retail/food outlets;
- Artefacts and equipment in the attraction;
- Information relating to the business and its customers;
- Staff and their possessions.

Interpretative techniques can play a part in the security of a visitor attraction by, for example, using signage and training staff to guide visitors away from prohibited areas of the facility.

Meeting specific needs

Visitors with specific needs may need particular interpretation facilities if they are to get the most out of their visit to an attraction. Depending on the nature of their needs, these facilities could include:

- Large print information leaflets and displays;
- Braille information and magnifiers;
- Tactile maps and exhibits;
- Audio guides and hearing loop systems;
- Sensory exhibits;
- A MiniCom telephone number for bookings.

Under the terms of the Disability Discrimination Act, attractions must make their facilities accessible to all visitors, regardless of their circumstances. Providing specialist interpretation facilities for these customers, although not a legal requirement for attraction operators, is seen as an important part of their work to encourage all sections of the community to visit.

Outreach activities

Interpretation is sometimes used by attractions to encourage certain sections of a community who do not visit in large numbers to come to the attraction and learn more. Outreach activities – when staff go out into communities to spread their message – are an important part of this process. Sections of the community who may be under-represented at an attraction could include ethnic minorities, young people, school children or visitors with special needs. As an example, the Corinium Museum in Cirencester, Gloucestershire employs an Outreach Officer whose job is to take the services offered at the museum to communities and individuals outside of the confines of the museum itself, through activities, talks and other events. The aims are to make facilities, skills, artefacts, information and lifelong learning opportunities available to the Cotswolds' community as a whole and to raise awareness of the museum and its facilities.

Choose one natural or built attraction in your local area and describe the purpose and techniques it uses for visitor interpretation.

This activity is designed to provide evidence for P3.

SECTION 3

Understand the appeal of visitor attractions to different types of visitor

It is clear that not all visitor attractions will appeal to every type of person in the UK or tourist from overseas. Some people will look for thrills, fun and excitement by visiting theme parks and entertainment venues, while others will prefer the peace and quiet of trips to the countryside, stately homes and gardens. To be successful, any attraction must be clear precisely which type or types of visitors it is targeting and provide the right facilities and amenities to meet their target markets' needs. Market research is used to gather information on existing and potential visitors to attractions, and is an essential first step in identifying customers' needs.

Having established its target market(s), a visitor attraction must develop a 'product' that its customers will appreciate and enjoy. It will need to give attention to a number of considerations, including:

- The main products and services offered by the attraction;
- Extra features aimed at particular types of visitors, e.g. coach parties, school visits, visitors from abroad, conferences and corporate hospitality;
- Special events and activities, e.g. historic car rallies, balloon festivals, music concerts, etc.
- Catering facilities, e.g. restaurants, pizza parlours, ice cream outlets, cafés, etc.
- Other facilities, e.g. baby changing, wheelchairs, buggies, car parking, transport links, facilities for visitors with special needs, etc.

Appeal

It is the features of a visitor attraction that make it appeal (or not) to visitors. An attraction that has few features and whose operators have not invested in new facilities and services will struggle to survive. Key features that influence the appeal of an attraction are shown in Figure 19.1 and discussed in the following sections of this unit.

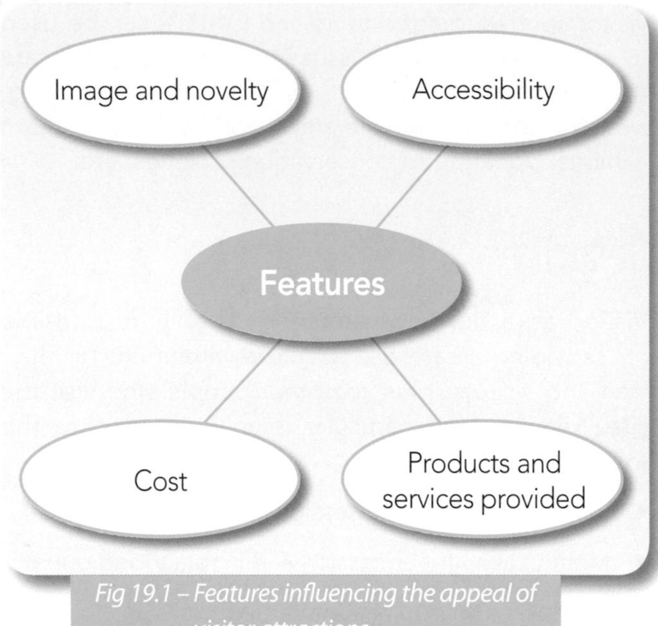

Fig 19.1 – Features influencing the appeal of visitor attractions

Accessibility

In the case of visitor attractions, accessibility is an all-embracing term covering:

- Geographical access – location, transport routes and parking;
- Physical access to the attraction – opening seasons and times, plus access for people with mobility problems and other special needs;
- Access for all sectors of the community – regardless of, for example, their age, gender, race or income level. This is often reflected in the attraction's pricing policy, e.g. reduced prices for certain categories of visitors.

The location of natural attractions and many cultural sites is predetermined, but developers can choose where to build new visitor attractions, subject to planning regulations. An attraction that is located close to a busy urban area will have a large population on which to draw, but may also be in competition with many other attractions. Visitors look for attractions that are conveniently located and have good car and public transport access. Good signposting to and within the attraction is also important.

Visitors also want speedy access arrangements when visiting an attraction so as not to waste time. Any shuttle transport that is provided must run at frequent intervals and facilities for buying entrance tickets must be well staffed in order to keep queuing times to a minimum. Larger attractions give visitors the chance to pre-book by telephone or on the internet so as to save time queuing when they arrive. Access to attractions is an important issue for visitors with special needs – many attractions now offer comprehensive services for these visitors to comply with the Disability Discrimination Act.

Most visits to attractions in the UK are made using a car or coach. Car drivers look for plenty of space for parking and easy access to and from the site. This is particularly true for visitors with special needs, who require parking facilities close to the attraction entrance. Coach companies that transport schools and other groups to attractions expect good access and parking facilities as well, plus some facilities for their drivers to take a break in comfort.

Not all visitor attractions are open all year round. Their operators consider that it is not economic to open for the small numbers of visitors who may visit in the winter. The types of visitors who come to attractions vary according to the time of year. Families come at weekends and during school holidays, whereas school and college groups visit during term time. Retired people have more flexibility as to when they can visit and often take advantage of off-peak discounts to make their trips during quiet mid-week periods. Events for corporate guests take place throughout the time an attraction is open to the public.

Range of products and services

Different customers make use of the different products and services on offer at attractions. Families, for example, tend to make use of a wide range of facilities, such as baby changing, toilets, places to eat and lost children points. Visitors from overseas may need to use an attraction's interpretation facilities if they are provided in their own language, e.g. an audio tour. Enthusiasts of one kind or another make a beeline for the main facility at attractions, e.g. 'white knuckle' rides, traction engines at a steam rally or the paintings at an art gallery.

We saw earlier in this unit that there are many types of interpretation available at visitor attractions. Individuals and groups who really want to get an educational experience out of their visit to an attraction will look for comprehensive guide books, guided tours and static displays. Children are drawn to 'hands on' exhibits and artefacts that they can touch. Overseas visitors may need interpretative materials to be available in different languages.

Staging events is an excellent way of attracting visitors to an area and gaining significant revenue from entrance fees and secondary spending opportunities, such as car parking fees and the sale of food, drink and a variety of merchandise. Events are particularly useful for destinations that don't have extensive built and natural attractions to tempt visitors or are located in remote areas away from major centres of population. Events cater for an extremely wide variety of visitor interests – everything from sport, music and food to history, gardens and books. Britain has music events that appeal to all tastes, from the Cardiff Singer of the World Competition to the Glastonbury and V Music Festivals. Sporting events such as the British Grand Prix at Silverstone, football and rugby matches at the Millennium Stadium in Cardiff and the tennis championships at Wimledon, attract thousands of visitors from the UK and overseas. Major cultural events such as the Edinburgh Festivals and Notting Hill Carnival have international reputations.

Events are popular at attractions (courtesy of English Heritage)

High quality information, both before they visit and while on-site, helps visitors to plan their visit to an attraction and make informed decisions about what to do while they are there. Visitors need certain basic information – opening times, prices, location, refreshment facilities – as well as more specific information on what the attraction has to offer visitors. Much of this information is made available on attractions' websites and in printed leaflets and guides. Websites have the advantage of publishing changes to basic information at short notice and can be used as a publicity tool to encourage people to visit an attraction. As well as providing information to the general public, attractions may have to supply other travel trade companies, including coach companies and tour operators, with details to incorporate into their own tour programmes. Members of the press will also request information from time to time.

Cost of visiting

The cost of visiting an attraction is an important consideration that will affect its appeal to visitors. Most attractions operate a variable pricing policy, offering different entry prices depending on when a person is visiting, e.g. peak season and off-season rates, discounts for early evening and mid-week visits, etc. Attractions in the public sector, such as leisure centres and museums, sometimes offer concessionary rates for local people, including lone parents and unemployed people. Attractions also charge different prices according to the type of visitor, as the following example from the Eden Project illustrates (2010 prices):

	Individuals	Discounts*
Adults	£17.50	£13.50
Children under 5 years	free	free
Children 5 – 18 years	£ 6.00	free
Full-time students	£10.00	£ 6.00
Seniors (60 + years)	£12.50	£ 8.50

*These prices apply to walkers, cyclists and visitors who arrive at the Eden Project by public transport.

Image and novelty

An attraction's image will often encourage people to visit. The image of an attraction is generated from a variety of sources, such as its leaflets and website, press articles, TV and radio advertising, mail shots and links with personalities. Attractions that feature in movies often reap the rewards with increased visitor numbers, e.g. parts of the James Bond film *Die Another Day* were filmed at the Eden Project in Cornwall. Liverpool's attractions, including the Tate Liverpool, The Beatles Story and Merseyside Maritime Museum, benefited from the city's designation as the European Capital of Culture 2008.

New attractions have a certain novelty value with visitors, but the secret is maintaining visitor numbers over the long term. UK attractions that have caught people's imagination in recent years as being excellent examples of their type include the London Eye, Eden Project, The Deep in Hull, the National Waterfront Museum in Swansea, the BALTIC Centre for Contemporary Art in Gateshead, the Spinnaker Tower in Portsmouth, to name but a few.

CASE STUDY

Chessington World of Adventures

Introduction

Chessington World of Adventures is part of the Merlin Entertainments Group of visitor attractions. The attraction started life as Chessington Zoo, which was opened in July 1931 as a private venture by Reginald Goddard who invited the public to view his private animal collection. After the Second World War, Chessington soon became known for the different types of entertainment it could offer, including a circus, a funfair and a miniature railway, as well as the zoo. Despite these developments, the attendance figures of over 800,000 began to decline in the early 1970s and the Zoo was in need of further investment.

In 1978 the Pearson Group bought Chessington and when they later bought Madame Tussauds, they put all their leisure interests together to form the Tussauds Group. Planning for the redevelopment of Chessington began in 1981 and six years later the £12 million upgrade was completed and officially opened by HRH Prince Edward. The opening coincided with the opening of the M25 motorway, which gives easy access to the attraction from various parts of the country. Approximately 18 million people live within a 2-hour drive of the site. Every year the attraction welcomes more than 1 million visitors and employs at least 1,000 members of staff.

Location and access

Chessington is located 12 miles from London, two miles from the A3 and M25 motorway. The attraction offers free parking for visitors. The park is accessible by public transport – regular South West Trains services run from Waterloo, Clapham Junction and Wimbledon to Chessington South Station, a 10-minute walk from the attraction. Chessington is served by regular bus services from nearby Kingston and Epsom. The attraction welcomes disabled guests and provides a range of services to make their time at Chessington as enjoyable as possible. Full details are given in the attraction's detailed guide for disabled visitors.

Products and services at Chessington

The primary product at Chessington consists of the various rides, events and entertainments aimed at the family market – these include Dragon's Fury, Dragon Falls, Vampire, Bubbleworks, Rameses Revenge and Tomb Blaster. The park has categorised its rides and attractions according to an 'adventure rating'. The four levels of adventure are:

1. Mini adventurer (for tiny tots);
2. Junior adventurer (for younger adventurers);
3. Family adventurers (for all the family – height and size restrictions may apply);
4. Experienced adventurers (for the older adventurer).

The managers of the attraction aim to launch a new attraction every year in order to refresh the product and give people a reason for making a return visit. Once the type of ride has been agreed, it can take as long as three years for the project to be completed, so careful long-term planning is crucial. Ancillary products and services at Chessington include places to eat, games, photography, corporate hospitality and services for visitors with special needs. The attraction offers the opportunity for students studying travel and tourism, business or animal husbandry to visit the site and take advantage of an educational talk as part of their trip.

Facilities for corporate events

Chessington offers tailor-made packages for corporate visitors, including team building/activity days, day delegate packages and fun days. Groups of all sizes can be catered for, including major events involving up to 10,000 visitors.

Case Study Questions and Activities

1. Describe the target markets that Chessington World of Adventures is aiming to attract and explain how the facilities are geared to meet the needs of each target market.
2. List the specific facilities and services the attraction offers visitors with special needs.
3. Explain the appeal of Chessington World of Adventures to three different types of visitors.
4. Analyse how the products, services and interpretation techniques found in Chessington contribute to the appeal for two different types of visitors.
5. Carry out some further research on Chessington's facilities for corporate customers and prepare detailed lists of what is available.

This case study is designed to provide evidence for P1, P3 and M1.

Weblink

Check out this website to help answer the questions in this case study and for more information on Chessington World of Adventures.

www.chessington.com

Different types of visitors

Visitor attractions appeal to different people for different reasons – one family may enjoy a day out at London Zoo, for example, while another might prefer a trip to the nearby Natural History Museum; yet another family may choose somewhere else entirely, perhaps a trip on the London Eye or a visit to the London Transport Museum. Whatever the reasons behind the choice of an attraction, all sites have a wide range of types of visitors, each with different characteristics. For a typical visitor attraction, these could be:

- Incoming tourists to the UK – overseas visitors tend to be attracted by Britain's natural and built heritage and often use London as a convenient starting point for their holiday;
- Educational parties – are important sources of revenue for attractions, particularly outside the peak season. Many attractions offer an education service to school and college groups, which includes fact sheets on the attraction, illustrated talks by members of staff and reduced price entry;
- Groups with special interests – these may be on an organised event or travelling independently. Examples include members of gardening clubs visiting stately homes and car enthusiasts going to a vintage car rally at an attraction;
- Families – are a key market for many attractions, particularly theme parks and other entertainment venues. Attractions must offer a range of facilities to appeal to all members of the party;
- Different age groups – from the youngest baby to senior citizens, visitor attractions must cater for a wide age range in visitors;
- Visitors with special needs – must be provided with a range of facilities to make their visit as enjoyable as possible;
- Corporate customers – are a very good source of revenue for many attractions, which provide facilities for training days, exhibitions, product launches, team-building events and staff incentives.

This list gives an indication of the difficult task of satisfying the needs of each of these different types of visitor, often referred to as 'markets', and stresses the importance of precise market research to identify exactly who visits an attraction and whether they are happy with the 'product'.

FOCUS ON INDUSTRY

TYPES OF VISITORS TO ALTON TOWERS

Alton Towers in Staffordshire is one of the UK's most popular paying attractions. The types of visitors to the attraction can be broken down as follows:

- Individuals;
- Coach groups;
- Companies for corporate events;
- School parties;
- Group organisers.

The age profile of visitors to Alton Towers is as follows:

Age (yrs)	Percentage
Under 7	4.8
8-12	4.0
13-17	19.2
18-24	28.9
25-34	21.1
35-44	14.3
45-54	5.9
Over 55	1.9

Alton Towers attracts people from all over the UK and has extensive facilities and services for visitors with special needs.

Weblink Check out this website for more information on Alton Towers.

www.altontowers.com

Families at Chessington World of Adventures

Activity 19.7

Choose one of the UK National Parks and write a short report that explains its appeal to two different types of visitors.

This activity is designed to provide evidence for P3.

SECTION 4 Understand the importance of visitor attractions to the popularity and appeal of UK tourist destinations

Visitor attractions play a crucial role in the popularity and appeal of UK tourist destinations, whether these are towns and cities, such as York and Bath, countryside areas, for example the Lake District National Park and Dartmoor, or whole regions, such as the south west of England or north Wales. Attractions – natural and built – are often what tempts people to visit an area in the first place.

Visitor attractions are important to UK tourism for a number of reasons, including:

1. Attracting visitors from overseas;
2. Stimulating domestic tourism;
3. Supporting the regeneration of areas;
4. Contributing to the local and national economy;
5. Promoting cultural exchange;
6. Conservation.

Attracting visitors from overseas

Overseas visitor numbers to Britain have been growing steadily for more than 20 years, from just 11.5 million in 1981 to the 2009 figure of 29.9 million. Spending by overseas tourists has also increased to a new record level of £16.6 billion in 2009. Britain's image to overseas visitors is very appealing – from the pageantry associated with our great capital cities to the quaint towns and villages throughout the UK, tourists from overseas continue to be attracted to this country.

Many overseas visitors put Britain's heritage attractions as the number one reason for visiting – famous buildings such as St Paul's Cathedral, the castles at Caernarvon and Windsor, the Elizabethan architecture in Shakespeare's birthplace of Stratford-upon-Avon, rural and industrial heritage are all focal points for overseas tourists. The Royal Family, with their palaces and ancestral homes, including Buckingham Palace and Hampton Court, are also an important attraction for tourists from abroad.

Museums, art galleries, the ballet, rock concerts and events such as the Proms and Cardiff Singer of the World, are all part of Britain's rich and varied culture and customs which attract the overseas visitor. Sporting events, including Wimbledon, international rugby and football matches, Henley Royal Regatta and the Open Golf Championship, are popular with overseas visitors. Many visitors are also attracted by Britain's excellent shopping facilities, not only in London's West End, but also in historic cities such as Chester, Cambridge, Oxford, Edinburgh, Bath and York.

Overseas visitors come to see Britain's many attractions

Stimulating domestic tourism

Spending on domestic tourism – British people making trips within the UK – was worth £21.9 billion to the economy in 2009. In the same year UK residents made 84 billion holiday trips in the UK, many of which were to natural and built visitor attractions. Figures 19.2 and 19.3 show the number of visitors to the top free admission and paying attractions in the UK for 2009.

Attraction	2009
British Museum	5,569,981
National Gallery	4,780,030
Tate Modern	4,747,537
Natural History Museum	4,105,106
Science Museum	2,793,930
Victoria and Albert Museum	2,269,880
National Portrait Gallery	1,961,843
Tate Britain	1,501,837
British Library	1,379,475
Thetford Forest Park	1,200,000

Fig 19.2 – Top 10 free admission attractions 2009

Attraction	2009
Tower of London	2,389,548
St Paul's Cathedral	1,821,321
Westminster Abbey	1,449,593
Flamingo Land Theme Park & Zoo	1,418,224
Windermere Lake Cruises	1,313,807
Kew Gardens	1,300,557
Chester Zoo	1,239,044
London Zoo	1,059,170
Eden Project	1,028,264
Canterbury Cathedral	1,013,118

Fig 19.3 – Top 10 paid admission attractions 2009

The south west of England is Britain's most popular tourist region in terms of number of visits and spending by tourists – in 2009 there were 21.0 million trips to the region and tourism spending was more than £4.1 billion. The most popular paid visitor attractions in 2006 were as follows:

1. Eden Project 1,152,332
2. Studland Beach 1,000,000
3. Stonehenge 879,393
4. Longleat 779,488
5. Roman Baths at Bath 843,693

Activity 19.8

With reference to your own tourist board region, make an illustrated presentation that compares the importance of two different visitor attractions to the popularity and appeal of the area.

This activity is designed to provide evidence for M2.

Supporting regeneration

Visitor attractions often feature in multi-use regeneration projects, particularly in urban areas of the country. They are built alongside new entertainment venues, eating places, shopping outlets and sports facilities as part of urban regeneration projects, e.g. at Cardiff Bay, Bristol Harbourside, the Don Valley in Sheffield and Albert Dock in Liverpool. Rural areas also benefit from attractions, as the following case study on the Eden Project demonstrates.

Cardiff Bay attractions are part of the area's regeneration

CASE STUDY

The Eden Project

Introduction

The Eden Project is one of the UK's most popular tourist attractions, welcoming more than 5 million visitors since it opened in March 2001. Built on the site of a former China clay works near St Austell in Cornwall, Eden was part-funded by a grant of £43 million of National Lottery money from the Millennium Commission. The attraction's centrepieces are the largest two conservatories in the world, known as biomes, which recreate different climates from around the world and house a variety of exotic plant species. Visitors can wander around the site or join one of the guided tours. As well as being a visitor attraction, Eden is also an educational resource in the widest sense of the word and a living exhibition of sustainable development.

Eden's organisation and mission

Eden promotes itself as *'a global garden for the 21st century, a gateway to a sustainable future and a dramatic setting in which to tell the fascinating story of mankind's dependence on plants'*. Its primary message is:

'Eden explores the human dependence on plants, and in doing so reveals our global interdependence. This in turn leads us to interpret economic, social and environmental impacts on a wider stage, not only out of curiosity and a shared humanity, but also because these factors affect us all'.

The Eden Project is the home of the Eden Trust, a UK-registered charitable trust – the Trustees are ultimately responsible for Eden's actions and its sustainable future. The project was the brainchild of Tim Smit, now Eden's Chief Executive, who had previously put his energies into developing the Lost Gardens of Heligan, also located in Cornwall, into a leading garden attraction. The Eden Trust has recently established the Eden Foundation, which will be the focus for all future activities at the attraction, working with a range of partner organisations to explore new approaches to sustainable living.

Products and services at Eden

The biomes at the Eden Project

The biomes are undoubtedly the most recognisable feature of the Eden Project and the primary product that attracts visitors. At 50 metres high, the hot tropics biome houses plants from South America, West Africa, Malaysia and the Tropical Islands, including bananas, coffee, balsa, mahogany, orchids, spices and tropical ferns. The smaller, warm temperate biome showcases the cradle of civilisation around the Mediterranean, with citrus, olives, herbs and vines, a rich variety of plants from the South African regions, drifts of colourful Californian annual plants and also banks of fruits, vegetables, pulses and grains. Each plant has its own story and the attraction uses a wide variety of interpretation techniques to inform visitors to the full.

Visitors approach the attraction via the visitor centre, which includes the Eden Shop – already one of the site's most successful and highly-regarded ventures. The shop offers a combination of environmentally-friendly products from around the world, local produce and Eden-branded merchandise. Also within the visitor centre is the ticketing hall, plant areas, a coffee shop and the Gallery Restaurant offering panoramic views of the biomes below. Further refreshment facilities are located in the building that links the two biomes, including Morocco Red – a restaurant serving tastes from around the world, but using local produce – and a café Zzub Zzub, offering a range of light meals and snacks. Other catering points can be found outdoors, with the emphasis on quality, 'Cornishness', freshness and value for money. Extensive toilet and baby changing facilities are available in the visitor centre and elsewhere in the attraction. More than half of the attraction's staff are first aid trained and there are also fully-qualified paramedics on site at all times.

Eden's education programme

Approximately 250 schoolchildren visit the Eden Project every day, from Cornwall, across the UK and even from overseas. The aims of the attraction's formal education programme are to:

1. Link the National Curriculum with the real world, real issues and current stories;
2. Run enrichment programmes for teachers;
3. Explore the ways people learn and develop effective learning and communication;
4. Motivate and engage people of all ages, abilities, ethnicity and background.

In addition to science education programmes, Eden covers a number of other areas of the curriculum, including art, history, numeracy, literacy, design and technology.

Case Study Questions and Activities

1. What facilities and services does Eden offer visitors with special needs?
2. What interpretation techniques does Eden offer its visitors to make their visit as enjoyable and instructive as possible?
3. What activities does Eden carry out to minimise its impact on the local environment and community?
4. Describe the different categories of visitors that you think are likely to be attracted to the Eden Project, explaining precisely what appeals to each category.

This case study is designed to provide evidence for P1, P2 and P3.

Weblink

Check out this website to help answer the questions in this case study and for more information on the Eden Project.

www.edenproject.com

Contributing to the local and national economy

As well as providing excitement, fun and education for millions of domestic and overseas tourists every year, the 6,500 visitor attractions found in the UK generate significant economic benefits for the local and national economy, including employment, generating revenue, investment and regeneration.

Providing jobs is one of the key positive impacts of the UK attractions' sector. Precise figures on the numbers employed in visitor attractions are very difficult to gauge, since there is no category for jobs in attractions in government figures. However, 2003 data indicates that there were 86,700 people employed in libraries, museums and other cultural facilities. Most of these jobs are full-time, but many attractions, including theme parks and water parks, employ mostly seasonal workers. This often leads to a high turnover of staff and sometimes makes it difficult for attraction operators to persuade their employees to commit to training courses on a regular basis.

There is a trend in UK tourism towards all-year-round tourism, particularly associated with the growth in short breaks and additional holidays. It is not uncommon now for British people to take a holiday abroad plus two, three or even four short beaks in the UK every year, either to the countryside or in cities (or a mixture of the two). This helps create more permanent employment in visitor attractions, since the operators can be sure of revenue outside the traditional peak season. This is particularly true for attractions that include activities that are not weather-dependent, e.g. mountain biking, canoeing, white-water rafting and orienteering. The same applies to attractions that cater for the schools market – schoolchildren visit during term time when visitor numbers tend to be lower, thereby helping to spread revenue and jobs throughout the year.

As well as providing jobs, another important positive economic impact of visitor attractions is the revenue generated from visitors and investors. The money spent by visitors at an attraction and in the surrounding area is re-circulated in the local economy via the multiplier effect, for example when people employed in attractions spend their wages in local shops and on local services.

FOCUS ON INDUSTRY

ECONOMIC IMPACT OF THE EDEN PROJECT

Research results released in 2004 show that the Eden Project (see case study on page 230) has injected nearly half a billion pounds worth of business back into the economy of Cornwall and the south west region of England. Eden has received £55.4 million of funding from the National Lottery via the Millennium Commission since it was built in 2001, but is estimated to have generated more than £460 million in economic impact on the local economy. Eden's operators estimate that, if visitor numbers remain as they have been since opening, the attraction's first 10 years of full operation should generate over £2 billion in economic output.

Eden has contributed to the economy in many ways. The attraction pays out £8 million in wages to local people every year, employing 600 temporary staff in the peak season and 380 people full-time all year round. Eden also uses local suppliers wherever possible, with knock-on effects to other businesses. The project has been responsible for attracting thousands of visitors to Cornwall. In 2009 there were 1.1 million visitors to the attraction, 90 per cent of whom had travelled into the county and more than half of the 90 per cent said that Eden had influenced their choice of holiday.

Weblink

Check out this website for more information on the economic impact of the Eden Project .

www.edenproject.com

Visitor attractions have benefited enormously from the National Lottery. To date, some £20 billion has been awarded to good causes, which has included investment in many visitor attraction projects in sport, the arts, heritage and the environment.

Weblink

Check out this website for more information on the National Lottery and the good causes it supports.

www.national-lottery.co.uk

FOCUS ON INDUSTRY

ECONOMIC AND SOCIAL IMPACT OF CATHEDRALS IN ENGLAND

Research published in Heritage Counts examined the economic and social value to local communities of the 42 Anglican cathedrals in England. There were 8.8 million visits to these cathedrals in 2003, although separate research by the Church of England, which included Westminster Abbey, indicated that the number of visits was as high as 12.5 million. Spending by visitors attracted to the local area by the presence of a cathedral was estimated at £91 million per year to the local economy, while the total economic impact was estimated to be £150 million, supporting some 5,500 jobs.

Weblink @ Check out this website to find out more about Heritage Counts.
http://hc.english-heritage.org.uk

Promoting cultural exchange

Attractions give visitors the chance to experience past and present-day cultures, through viewing artefacts and objects, taking part in activities and using 'hands on', interactive exhibits. Cultural attractions, such as museums and art galleries, have a twin role of conserving items of value and making them available to the general public. The government encourages visits to attractions by sponsoring some of the UK's most popular cultural attractions, i.e. the Department for Culture, Media and Sport (DCMS) provides funding to the attraction so that it can offer everybody free access. Since it was introduced in 2001, this free admission policy has been a great success.

For many tourists, learning about an area's culture by visiting its attractions is an essential feature of their holiday experience. Incoming tourists to the UK are particularly keen to explore our heritage and culture, learning about our language and traditions. As people become better educated and more discerning, the travel and tourism sector must respond by offering both domestic and incoming tourists products that meet their needs for a more culturally-enriching experience at attractions.

The British Museum in London (courtesy and © British Museum)

Conservation

As well as conserving historic buildings, museum exhibits and wildlife habitats, visitor attractions can help conserve traditional activities in local communities, for example arts, crafts and customs. In the Peak District of Derbyshire, the ancient custom of 'well dressing' dates back hundreds of years and is a major attraction for visitors and local people. Wells are decorated with flower petals, berries, moss, cones and seeds, which are pressed into clay held in a wooden framework. Well dressing is celebrated in more than 60 towns and villages throughout Derbyshire, including Hope, Eyam and Tideswell. Many attractions that celebrate our industrial heritage, for example Ironbridge Gorge, sell traditional items that are made locally, thereby continuing past skills and practices.

Activity 19.9

Write a short report with the title *'The importance of visitor attractions to UK tourism'*. You should comment generally on why attractions are important to tourism and use examples to illustrate your points.

This activity is designed to provide evidence for P4.

UNIT SUMMARY

This unit has explored the UK visitor attractions industry and recognised the important role that attractions play in the economic and cultural life of the country. You have examined the products and services offered by attractions, and investigated different types of UK attractions. You have learned about the purpose of interpretation and have examined the various interpretation techniques that can be used in natural and built attractions to enhance visitors' understanding and enjoyment. You have considered the appeal of attractions to different types of visitors, including incoming tourists, educational groups and visitors with special needs. Finally, the unit has explored the importance of visitor attractions to the popularity and appeal of UK tourist destinations. Throughout the unit you have been shown many industry examples, while the case studies on the Big Pit National Coal Museum, the Brecon Beacons National Park, Chessington World of Adventures and the Eden Project, highlight key issues in the operation of visitor attractions.

If you have worked methodically, by the end of this unit you should:

- Know the products and services provided by different types of visitor attraction;
- Know the range and purpose of techniques used for visitor interpretation;
- Understand the appeal of visitor attractions to different types of visitor;
- Understand the importance of visitor attractions to the popularity and appeal of UK tourist destinations.

You are now in a position to complete the assignment for the unit, under the direction of your tutor. Before you tackle the assignment you may like to have a go at the following questions to help build your knowledge of UK visitor attractions.

TEST YOUR KNOWLEDGE

1. List the five most popular charging attractions in the UK in 2009.
2. What is the difference between primary, secondary and additional products and services at a visitor attraction?
3. What types of corporate hospitality events are staged at visitor attractions?
4. List five popular UK heritage attractions.
5. What is a World Heritage Site?
6. Name five popular UK cultural attractions.
7. Why do you think the Eden Project has been so successful since it opened in 2001?
8. List the five most popular free attractions in the UK in 2009?
9. How do tourist attractions help the regeneration of urban and rural areas?
10. List three ways in which visitor attractions contribute to the local and national economy.
11. Name five popular sporting attractions and events in the UK.

12. What are the key points to bear in mind when deciding which interpretation techniques to select for a visitor attraction?
13. What interpretation techniques are particularly suitable for visitors with special needs?
14. What are the key features of an attraction that make it appealing to visitors?
15. How does seasonality affect the type of visitors to an attraction?

Answers to these questions can be found in the Book 2 Tutor's CD-ROM that accompanies this book (ISBN 9780956268075). Full details can be found at **www.tandtpublishing.co.uk**

UNIT 19 ASSIGNMENT

UK Visitor Attractions

Introduction

This assignment is made up of a number of tasks which, when successfully completed, are designed to give you sufficient evidence to meet the Pass (P), Merit (M) and Distinction (D) grading criteria for the unit. If you have carried out the activities and read the case studies throughout this unit, you will already have done a lot of work towards completing the tasks for this assignment.

Scenario

Your uncle Jim works for a consultancy firm that specialises in advising governments in the new European Union (EU) member states on tourism projects. Three of the Baltic countries that have recently joined the EU – Latvia, Lithuania and Estonia – are planning to join forces to develop and promote new tourist attractions in their countries. Your uncle is heading the project to advise the countries and has invited you to help him over the summer.

He wants you to complete the following three tasks.

Task 1

Produce two case studies (one for a built attraction and one for a natural attraction) in which you must:

a. Describe the products and services provided by one built and one natural visitor attraction (P1). Ideally you should visit your chosen attractions to develop the required familiarity, although some of the information required could be obtained from detailed internet research.

b. Describe the purpose and techniques used for visitor interpretation at one built and one natural visitor attraction (P2). You can undertake some of the research for Task 1a and Task 1b from publicity material provided by visitor attractions, but you should not submit these materials as part of your assessment evidence, although you may refer to them in a bibliography or appendix for your case study.

This task is designed to provide evidence for P1 and P2.

Task 2

Prepare and deliver an illustrated presentation in which you must:

a. Explain the appeal of one natural and one built visitor attraction for two different types of visitors (P3). You may use the same two visitor attractions as those selected for Task 1a and Task 1b. You should select two different types of visitor and link the appeal of each of the visitor attractions to these visitors. An appropriate response would be to explain that the location of a museum on the outskirts of town will appeal more to a family with a car than to an overseas tourist who may not have access to their own vehicle and therefore finds it less convenient to visit than a town-centre attraction.

b. Analyse how the products, services and interpretation techniques of a built or a natural attraction contribute to the appeal for two different types of visitors (M1). You will need to have first-hand experience of your selected visitor attraction in order to analyse how the products, services and interpretation techniques contribute to the appeal for two different types of visitors. This analysis should demonstrate a good understanding of how the selected visitor attraction appeals to different types of visitor.

This task is designed to provide evidence for P3 and M1.

Task 3

Produce a written report in which you must:

a. Explain why visitor attractions are important to UK tourism (P4). You should comment generally on why attractions are important to tourism and may wish to use a number of examples in order to illustrate your points. Where examples are used to illustrate and support general explanations, they should be UK attractions and statistics and data must be provided to support your explanations.

b. Compare the importance of two different visitor attractions to the popularity and appeal of a destination or area (M2). You should select two different visitor attractions at the same destination or in the same area and compare them in terms of their importance to the popularity and appeal of the destination or area. You can use the same attractions as those selected for previous tasks in this assignment. Statistics and illustrations must be provided to support the comparisons.

c. Evaluate the contribution of a visitor attraction to the popularity and appeal of a destination or area (D1). You need to select a destination or an area that has either a significant visitor attraction or a number of visitor attractions – this can be the same destination as you selected for Task 3b. You must evaluate, by making judgements based on evidence, the contribution made by the visitor attraction(s) to the popularity and appeal of the destination or area. An example could be Haworth, where the fame of the Bronte sisters has led many different types of visitors to the town in order to visit the parsonage where the sisters once lived, the church where they worshipped and the surrounding area where they gained inspiration for their novels. The popularity of Haworth has grown worldwide and impacted on the town and surrounding area and has led to the development of various other enterprises, e.g. restaurants, hotels, guesthouses, etc. This in turn has further increased its popularity with visitors. You should expand further on this analysis by identifying the different products and services and the interpretation techniques available and suitable for the wide range of UK and overseas visitors. You must support your findings and explanations with statistics, data and illustrations.

This task is designed to produce evidence for P4, M2 and D1.

UNIT 26

Researching Current Issues in Travel and Tourism

INTRODUCTION TO THE UNIT

Travel and tourism is a dynamic sector that affects all our lives, whether we are on holiday, travelling for business or visiting friends and relatives. It is sector that is made up of many different component industries – from accommodation and tour operations to visitor attractions and transport. There are many issues that affect travel and tourism, some that have an impact on society and the environment, others that are specific to companies and organisations. People entering travel and tourism at graduate level need to be able to understand the nature of the sector and the key issues that affect it.

This unit focuses on a range of current issues that affect travel and tourism, giving you the opportunity to study one issue in greater depth. You will develop skills that are appropriate to carrying out sustained and planned research, similar to those adopted in academic research. You will gain an understanding of the different approaches to research and the research tools that can be used to plan and carry out a travel and tourism research project. Your project will not only investigate an issue in depth, but also analyse the impacts of that issue on the travel and tourism sector, such as the development of new markets, loss of revenue and changing product ranges.

WHAT YOU WILL STUDY

When you have completed this unit you should:

1. Understand methodology for researching complex current issues affecting the travel and tourism sector;
2. Be able to conduct research into complex current issues affecting the travel and tourism sector;
3. Understand impacts of complex current issues on the travel and tourism sector.

You will be guided through the main topics in this unit with the help of the latest developments, statistics and industry examples. You should also check out the weblinks throughout the unit for extra information on particular organisations or topic areas and use the activities throughout the unit to help you learn more.

ASSESSMENT FOR THIS UNIT

This unit is internally assessed, meaning that you will be given an assignment (or series of assignments) to complete by your tutor(s) to show that you have fully understood the content of the unit. A grading scale of pass, merit or distinction is used when staff mark your assignment(s), with higher grades awarded to students who show greater depth in analysis, evaluation and justification in their assignments. An assignment for this unit, which covers all the grading criteria, can be found on page 267. Don't forget to visit **www.tandtonline.co.uk** for all the latest industry news, developments, statistics and links to websites in this unit to help you with your assignments.

SECTION 1 Understand methodology for researching complex current issues affecting the travel and tourism sector

Icebreaker

This unit explores current issues in travel and tourism – those that have arisen in the last five years. Working by yourself, or in small groups under the direction of your tutor, see how you get on with the following tasks to help you make a start on this unit:

- Make a list of six current issues that you think are important to the future development of the travel and tourism sector;
- Think about the different ways you could gather information from people about their travel habits;
- List the stages you would go through when asked to carry out some research into a current issue in travel and tourism;
- Name three sources of information that you could use when carrying out a travel and tourism research project;
- Make some notes on the role of the internet in travel and tourism research;
- What is the difference between primary and secondary research?
- Name three reliable sources of statistics on travel and tourism.

When you've finished, show your answers to your tutor and compare your answers with what other students in your class have written.

In this section we investigate the different methods that can be used to research a current issue affecting the travel and tourism sector, as well as highlighting types of current issues that could form the basis of a research study.

Research methods

Carrying out research is an important aspect of any subject area, and travel and tourism is no different. Research may be carried out for purely academic purposes, such as a researcher in a university investigating the impact of tourism on communities in a developing country, or can be directly related to the travel and tourism sector. Sector-related research could focus on exploring customers' changing demands for products, services and destinations, or analysing the trend in sales of package holidays versus independent travel over a particular time period.

Research methods are the 'how' of the research process, i.e. stating how you are going to conduct your research in order to achieve your research objectives. Research can involve intervention, e.g. spending time with a tribe in Africa to appreciate the impacts that tourism is having on their culture, or non-intervention, for example carrying out an extensive review of the literature – books, journals, websites, etc. – on a particular travel and tourism topic.

Research that involves intervention is considered to be less objective than non-intervention research since the behaviour of the subjects being researched may be influenced by the presence of the researchers.

'Action research', also known as participatory research, is considered to be 'learning by doing'. In other words, researchers identify a problem, do something to resolve it, see how successful their efforts were and, if not satisfied with the outcome, try again. What separates action research from mainstream research is its emphasis on scientific study, informed by research theories.

Research sources

There are many sources of information that can be used when carrying out research in travel and tourism, usually divided into primary and secondary sources. A research study may focus entirely on primary research sources, but in reality the majority of travel and tourism research consists of both primary and secondary research.

Primary sources

Primary sources refer to information that is collected for the first time, i.e. it is not already available from another source – this is secondary research.

Although there is an increasing amount of relevant and up-to-date secondary data available on tourism at international, national and local levels, it is likely that a researcher, at some stage in the research process, will need to collect information that is not already available in a published form. The collection and subsequent analysis of this information is known as primary research.

A researcher wanting to collect primary data has three main options available, namely:

1. Surveys;
2. Observation;
3. Focus groups.

Surveys

Conducting a survey is the most common method of collecting primary data when researching the travel and tourism sector. It involves the collection of data from a proportion of a total 'population', which researchers refer to as the sample. In this context, population means the total number of people who could be interviewed for a research project. For example, somebody researching visitors at a visitor attraction may decide to interview a 5 per cent sample of all visitors to the attraction on a particular day during the season. If the total number of visitors is 10,000 (the population), 500 interviews (the sample) will need to be undertaken. Sampling is carried out because it is usually impractical to interview the whole population. It is a very precise statistical technique that we investigate further on page 244.

There are three main types of survey that can be used to collect primary data:

1. Face-to-face interview survey;
2. Self-completed questionnaire survey;
3. Telephone, e-mail and online surveys.

A face-to-face interview survey involves an interviewer asking questions of a member of the general public, known as the respondent, and recording his or her answers and comments on a questionnaire. This type of survey is very common in all travel and tourism component industries, from destination resorts to transport providers. Face-to-face interviews can be carried out in a number of different locations, for example in a tourist area, at a respondent's home or place of work, in the street or en route to a holiday area, perhaps at a frontier post or a toll booth. The face-to-face interview is a good way of obtaining both quantitative and qualitative data (see page 247).

Face-to-face interviews have a number of advantages when compared with other survey methods. One advantage is that the interviewer is able to answer any difficulties that the respondent may have with particular questions. The interviewer can also use prompts to encourage the respondent to elaborate on his or her answers, thereby gaining further valuable information. A further advantage is that visual aids, such as charts and photographs, can be used by the interviewer when asking questions. The main disadvantage of the face-to-face interview technique concerns cost. Recruiting and training interviewers can be expensive and the associated administrative load can be high. Face-to-face interviews are also more time-consuming than techniques such as telephone and online surveys. They are, nonetheless, used very widely by travel and tourism researchers as a means of providing valuable information that can be used for academic and industry purposes.

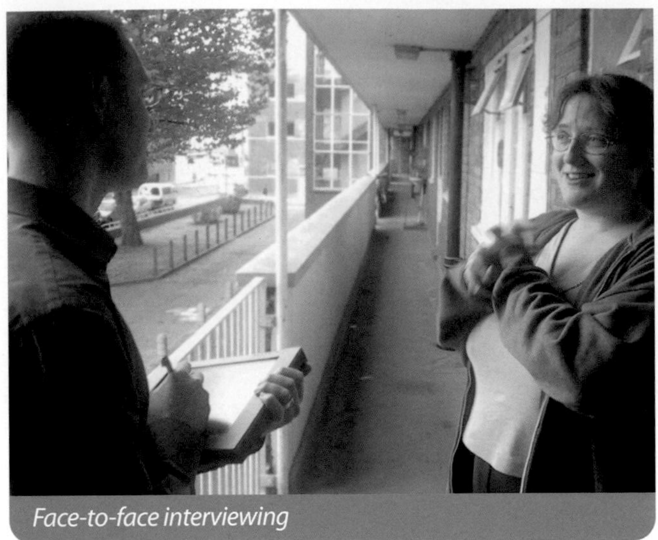
Face-to-face interviewing

Unlike face-to-face interviews, self-completed questionnaire surveys do not involve the use of interviewers, thereby making them a less expensive option for many travel and tourism researchers and businesses. They are also a more flexible technique, but they do have some disadvantages. Response rates are typically lower than for comparable face-to-face surveys – this can sometimes be improved by sending a reminder to the respondent. Also, if a respondent does not fully understand a question, there is no interviewer to ask for clarification. Self-completed questionnaire surveys are used extensively in travel and tourism as a relatively low-cost method for obtaining both qualitative and quantitative data on customers and usage. Many tour operators carry out a postal survey of returning holidaymakers, asking them to complete a questionnaire related to their holiday experience. Visitor attractions also use self-completed questionnaires to obtain feedback from visitors (see Figure 26.1).

The information contained in these questionnaires gives valuable feedback from clients and is often the starting point for changes to products or services. It is common to find self-completed questionnaires at attractions and in accommodation facilities for customers to complete and either return by post or leave behind before they depart. Some travel and tourism organisations provide an incentive, such as a free gift or discounted travel, in order to increase the number of completed questionnaires.

Telephone surveys are gaining in popularity in the travel and tourism sector as a way of getting a fast response to an event, facility or service. They are used widely in the USA, but are largely restricted in the UK to trade activities, such as following up enquiries from buyers who have attended exhibitions, such as the World Travel Market in London. Companies specialising in selling timeshare also use telephone surveys to target likely customers. Conducting a survey by telephone can certainly give a speedy response and, if trained operators are used, many interviews are possible in a given time period. Disadvantages include the fact that it is not possible to use visual stimulus materials and the likelihood that people will feel that they have had their privacy invaded and will refuse to co-operate with the interviewer.

E-mail and online surveys are growing in popularity as the use of the internet develops. These types of surveys are a fast and relatively inexpensive way of gaining research data, but suffer from similar disadvantages to telephone interviewing, for example invasion of privacy. They do, however, offer researchers a simple method of collecting data from respondents spread right across the world. This is a particularly attractive benefit for travel and tourism researchers, since the scope and influence of the sector is truly global.

Questionnaires

Questionnaires are used in a variety of research projects, including online surveys, face-to-face interviews and self-completed surveys. Designing an effective questionnaire that will achieve its intended aim is a skilled operation. It can also be very time-consuming, checking to see that the questions are easy to understand and in an appropriate order. Specialists in design of questionnaires recommend that researchers follow the sequence shown in Figure 26.2 to ensure an effective finished product.

As Figure 26.2 indicates, the questionnaire design sequence begins with listing the expected outcomes of the survey, i.e. what it is hoped the survey will achieve. These are then used as the basis for the formulation of a set of questions, the answers to which will help achieve these outcomes. A draft questionnaire is produced next and used in a pilot survey – this is a dry run of the main survey with a small number of respondents to check understanding and suitability of the questions. The draft questionnaire is then amended in the light of

Your Visit

How satisfied were you with your visit overall?

❑ Very satisfied ❑ Satisfied
❑ Dissatisfied ❑ Very dissatisfied
❑ Neither satisfied nor dissatisfied

What was the highlight of your day?

....

....

What type of ticket(s) have you purchased today?

(N.B: Smaller attractions include Postman Pat® Village, Pets Corner, Longleat Railway, Motion Simulator, Butterfly Garden, Safari Boats, Adventure Castle & Blue Peter Maze, Longleat Hedge Maze, Old Joe's Mine).

❑ Longleat Passport ❑ Safari Park only
❑ Safari Park plus other smaller attractions
❑ Childrens attractions only ❑ Grounds and Gardens only
❑ Longleat House only ❑ Longleat House plus other smaller attractions

If you purchased the Passport Ticket, is this your?

❑ 1st visit ❑ 2nd visit ❑ 3rd visit ❑ 4th visit this season?

How much time did you spend at Longleat this visit?

❑ 1-2 hours ❑ 2-3 hours ❑ 3-4 hours ❑ 4-5 hours
❑ 5-6 hours ❑ 6-7 hours ❑ 7-8 hours
❑ More than one day, will come back for second visit

How did the following live up to your expectations?

	Excellent	Good	Fair	Poor	Very Poor	Not visited
Safari Park	❑	❑	❑	❑	❑	❑
Longleat House	❑	❑	❑	❑	❑	❑
Grounds and Gardens	❑	❑	❑	❑	❑	❑
Lord Bath's Murals	❑	❑	❑	❑	❑	❑
Safari Boats	❑	❑	❑	❑	❑	❑
Old Joe's Mine	❑	❑	❑	❑	❑	❑
Motion Simulator	❑	❑	❑	❑	❑	❑
Pets Corner	❑	❑	❑	❑	❑	❑
Longleat Railway	❑	❑	❑	❑	❑	❑
Butterfly Garden	❑	❑	❑	❑	❑	❑
Longleat Hedge Maze	❑	❑	❑	❑	❑	❑
Postman Pat® Village	❑	❑	❑	❑	❑	❑
Adventure Castle	❑	❑	❑	❑	❑	❑
Blue Peter Maze	❑	❑	❑	❑	❑	❑
Tea Cup Ride	❑	❑	❑	❑	❑	❑
Summer Show (21st July - 2nd Sept 2007)	❑	❑	❑	❑	❑	❑
Longleat House Scale Model	❑	❑	❑	❑	❑	❑
Family Bygones Exhibition	❑	❑	❑	❑	❑	❑
Life and Times of Henry, Lord Bath	❑	❑	❑	❑	❑	❑
King Arthur's Mirror Maze	❑	❑	❑	❑	❑	❑
Family State Chariot	❑	❑	❑	❑	❑	❑
Mystical Garden	❑	❑	❑	❑	❑	❑
Cellars Restaurant	❑	❑	❑	❑	❑	❑
Wessex Pavilion	❑	❑	❑	❑	❑	❑
Fast Food Units	❑	❑	❑	❑	❑	❑
Kiosks	❑	❑	❑	❑	❑	❑
Shops	❑	❑	❑	❑	❑	❑
Staff	❑	❑	❑	❑	❑	

Did you visit the Longleat catering outlets?

Wessex Pavilion	❑ Yes	❑ No
Cellars Restaurant	❑ Yes	❑ No
Fast Food Units	❑ Yes	❑ No

If not, please advise why? ....

How would you rate Longleat for Value for Money?

	Excellent	Good	Fair	Poor	Very Poor	Not visited
Overall Value for Money	❑	❑	❑	❑	❑	❑
Passport Ticket	❑	❑	❑	❑	❑	❑
Other Ticket Type	❑	❑	❑	❑	❑	❑
Catering	❑	❑	❑	❑	❑	❑
Shops	❑	❑	❑	❑	❑	❑

If anything about your visit failed to meet your expectations, please briefly tell us why.

....

....

....

....

Please use the space below if you have any comments or suggestions to improve the visit.

....

....

....

....

Other Information

How would you rate Longleat compared with other attractions?

❑ The best ❑ The same ❑ Worse ❑ Don't know

Have you ever visited Longleat before?

❑ YES ❑ NO

If YES, how long ago?

❑ 6 mths or less ❑ 7-12 mths ❑ 1-2 years
❑ 2-3 years ❑ 3-4 years ❑ 4-5 years
❑ 5-10 years ❑ Over 10 years

When will you next visit Longleat?

❑ This month ❑ Next month ❑ This year
❑ Next year ❑ Next 2 years ❑ 3 or more years
❑ Never ❑ Don't know

Were the brown tourist signs adequate for you to easily find your route to Longleat?

❑ Yes ❑ No ❑ If no, please advise why ....

Optional Information

(a) **Updates by Email**

If you would like to receive the latest news, events and special offers from Longleat throughout the season then please complete the section below so that your details can be added to our database

Name ....

Email Address..

(please complete in capitals)

OR please visit the Family Fun Club section of the Longleat website (www.longleat.co.uk) and add your contact details yourself!

(b) **Annual Updates by Post**

If you would like to receive pre-season annual information on Longleat via post then please complete the section below so that your details can be added to our database

Name ....

Address..

.... Postcode ....

Win Longleat Tickets 2008

If you would like to enter the monthly prize draw then please complete your details below

Name ....

Address..

.... Postcode ....

If you **DO NOT** wish to receive further communications from Longleat then please tick this box ❑

Please place this Visitor Survey in any of the boxes throughout the Longleat Estate or post FREE to:
Longleat Marketing Department, FREEPOST (BS 8210) Warminster BA12 7ZZ

Please remember that if your responses are to count then we must receive completed questionnaires within 2 weeks of your visit.
Thank you. Visitor Survey 2007

Estate Office, Longleat, Warminster, Wiltshire BA12 7NW
Tel: 01985 844400 www.longleat.co.uk

Fig 26.1 – An extract from a self-completed questionnaire

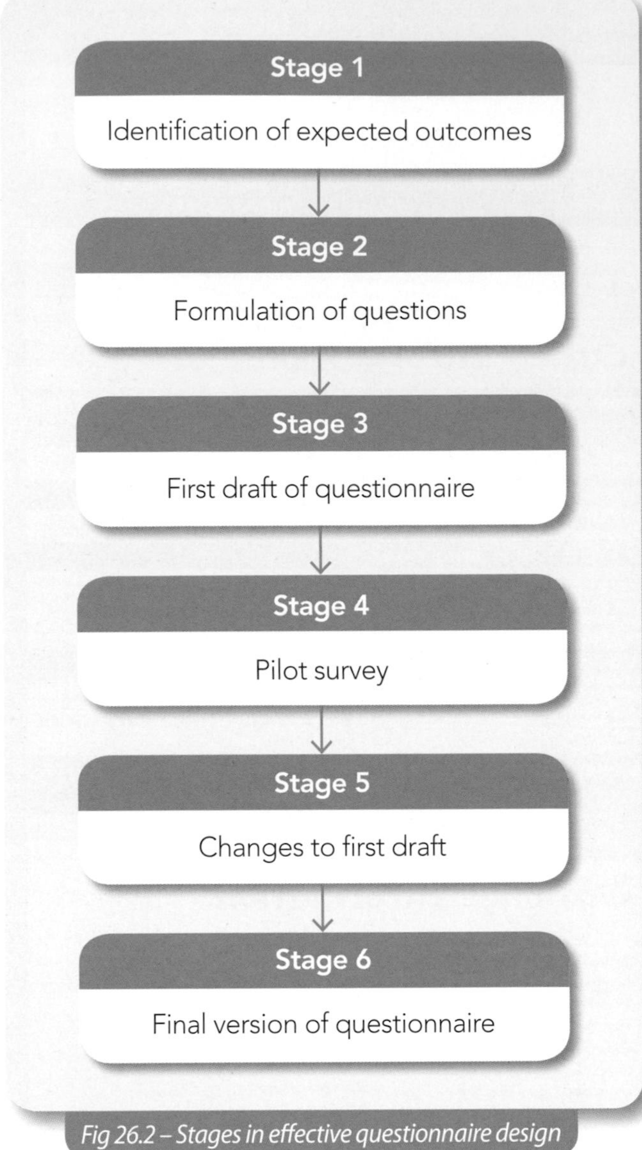

Fig 26.2 – Stages in effective questionnaire design

the pilot survey to produce a final version for use in the main research study.

The following is a list of guidelines that should be followed when designing questionnaires:

- Always put sensitive questions, e.g. concerning age, occupation, marital status, etc., at the end of the questionnaire. Respondents will feel more comfortable about giving answers to such personal questions than if they appear at the beginning;
- Avoid ambiguous questions (questions with double meanings);
- Avoid using jargon;
- Make the questionnaire as short or as long as it needs to be – don't be tempted to include questions that, although interesting, will not help achieve the outcomes;
- Simple, objective, pre-coded (agree/neutral/disagree) questions will provide clearer answers than open-ended questions;
- Avoid leading questions, e.g. *'don't you agree that the hotel is comfortable?'* is a question that invites a positive response;
- Do not include questions that are an impossible test of the respondent's memory, e.g. *'how much did you spend on drinks per day for the first week of your holiday?'*
- Use language that is appropriate to the respondent.

A questionnaire can have a combination of open and closed questions. Open questions invite the respondent to give any answer they choose, whereas closed questions ask the interviewee to choose from a range of answers, for example 'yes', 'no', 'don't know', etc.

Activity 26.1

Using the above guidelines, design a questionnaire to discover people's opinions of a current issue in travel and tourism, and conduct some pilot interviews to check that the questionnaire is suitable.

This activity is designed to provide evidence for P1.

Sampling

In the majority of travel and tourism research studies, it is not feasible to survey all the people who may, for example, use a tourist attraction or visit a particular destination. Instead, researchers must rely on the responses of a proportion of the total 'population', known as the sample. If the selection of the sampling unit (the target population to be surveyed), sample size (how many are to be interviewed) and sampling procedure (the method by which the respondents are selected) are based on proven statistical methods, the responses of the people interviewed should mirror those of the total population within known limits of accuracy. The sampling method chosen must reduce bias to a minimum. For example, if a researcher was asked to collect data on customer experiences for a hotel group with 325 establishments spread evenly across Europe, but carried out 80 per cent of the surveys in France, the results would clearly be biased and not representative of the group as a whole.

The sampling procedure may be either random or quota. For a random survey, individuals are pre-selected from a sampling frame, such as the electoral role or a company's database. The interviewer may be asked to carry out interviews at selected households chosen at random. Many UK government surveys are carried out in this way. When using the quota sampling method, the interviewer is given instructions as to the number of respondents he or she must interview in certain categories, for example defined by age, sex or social class.

The size of the sample will determine the level of accuracy of the data. Generally speaking, the larger the sample size the better, but the increase in accuracy becomes less significant as the sample size is increased. Provided that proven statistical methods have been used to select the sample, a survey consisting of approximately 2000 interviews will give an accurate reflection of the public's view of general matters to a 95 per cent confidence level (in other words, 19 out of 20 surveys will fall within a stated 'margin of error'). In reality, it would be rare for a researcher to carry out a survey with a sample size of less than 100, even if only broad impressions were needed.

Observation

Observation is a very useful, and often neglected, source of primary data in travel and tourism. In its simplest form, observation is a management practice that involves an organisation employing a person to study the behaviour of others as a way of improving its products and services. It is particularly suitable for visitor attractions such as theme parks, craft galleries and museums. It does not always involve people actually watching what others do and recording the details systematically. Nowadays, there are sophisticated techniques such as closed circuit television (CCTV) and time-lapse photography that can be used to produce valuable information on the flow of people and traffic at tourist facilities. Electronic tally counters are used in attractions, leisure centres and tourist information centres to monitor usage. On occasions, staff may be asked to mingle with visitors or customers and to eavesdrop on their conversations without revealing their identity. People are often far more honest about their true feelings when talking in private, than they would be when asked questions as part of a visitor survey.

Observation can be used as an initial type of exploratory research, perhaps visiting a Pacific island to view the impact of tourist boats on coral reefs or investigating the effects of tourism in a developing nation in Africa. This could lead to other types of research being planned, based on the findings of the original observations.

Observation has an important role to play in researching competitors' products. There are very few products, services and facilities in the travel and tourism sector that are truly unique, most having been based on an idea seen elsewhere. It is not uncommon for hoteliers, travel agents and airlines, for example, to use the facilities of competitors in order to pick up new tips and improve their own products. Tourism companies sometimes employ 'mystery shoppers' to anonymously visit competitor facilities (and sometimes even their own facilities!) to check on standards of service and the range of products on offer.

Focus groups

A focus group is a research technique used to collect in-depth information from a carefully-selected group of individuals. It is used to gain information on customers' purchasing habits, for example to explore the reasons why they choose one travel product or company in preference to another. This kind of in-depth information is not easy to obtain from questionnaire surveys or observation, but focus group sessions give respondents the time to reflect and consider in detail why they make the decisions they do. A focus group, or panel interview as it is sometimes called, usually consists of up to 10 individuals under the guidance of a trained interviewer, who will use a number of techniques to explore the innermost thoughts and values of the members of the group. The sessions are generally video-recorded for future analysis and will often cause companies to make changes to their product range or promotional activities. Neutral locations are chosen for the focus group sessions, thereby avoiding either positive or negative associations with a particular facility or site. Given the intensive nature of the focus group, it is an expensive method of gaining primary research data and tends, therefore, to be used mainly by larger travel and tourism organisations, primarily in the private sector.

Secondary sources

Many travel and tourism research studies involve the collection of information from a mixture of primary and secondary sources. Secondary data is information that is already available, usually in written form, but increasingly now made available via the internet. Research that makes use of secondary data sources is sometimes referred to as 'desk research'. Sources include books, journals, the internet and newspapers. The main advantage offered by secondary research when compared with primary data collection methods is that it can save both time and money. There is a great deal of secondary research data available to researchers working in all travel and tourism component industries, some internal to organisations and some made available by a range of commercial and public sector sources.

Researchers must be aware of the validity of information from secondary sources. Today it is easy for anybody to post information on the internet and claim to be an expert in their field. You should ask yourself a series of questions when deciding on the validity of a secondary research source, for example:

- Who is the author? – it is difficult to validate the credentials of somebody putting a review on a website such as TripAdvisor, for example;
- What is the purpose of the source? – information on holiday companies' websites and in their brochures is intended to persuade people to buy their holidays so is unlikely to be unbiased;
- Is the information up to date? – the more recent the information the more valid it is likely to be to a researcher, e.g. numbers of visitors to particular destinations or attractions;
- Are sources quoted? – valid research should indicate where the information comes from so that a researcher can go back to the original source if necessary to check validity;
- Is there bias shown? – e.g. some newspapers and magazines will hold particular views on issues.

Internal sources of secondary data

Some of the information that an organisation needs for research purposes may already be held within its various departments and management systems. An examination of existing files, databases and records should be a first priority before external research sources are consulted, in order to save time and money. The following internal information sources held by any organisation that is operating in the travel and tourism sector may reveal useful data for research purposes:

- Sales receipts;
- Customer records;
- Mailing lists;
- Financial returns;
- Survey findings.

The advent of computerised management information systems (MIS) makes this kind of information much more accessible and useful for research purposes.

External sources of secondary data

For travel and tourism researchers, secondary data from a variety of published sources is generally much easier to access than the internal company data described in the previous section of this unit. As the worldwide travel and tourism sector continues to grow, there is an increasing amount of specific secondary research data on tourism generated to service this expansion, much of it now available on the internet. The World Tourism Organisation (WTO) and World Travel and Tourism Council (WTTC) supply statistical data on an international scale, while organisations such as the Organisation for Economic Co-operation and Development (OECD) and the Pacific Asia Travel Association (PATA) provide regional, international data. Statistics on tourism at a national level are made available by government departments or government-sponsored agencies. In the UK, researchers have access to a wide range of information on travel and tourism provided by government and commercial sources, including:

- Annual reports of the UK National Tourist Boards;
- Travel and tourism academic journals;
- Annual reports of the Regional Tourist Boards;
- The International Passenger Survey (IPS);
- The United Kingdom Tourism Survey (UKTS);
- Annual reports of commercial travel and tourism organisations, for example British Airways, Thomas Cook, TUI UK and the Merlin Entertainments Group;
- Reports from consultants such as Mintel and MORI;
- Travel and tourism textbooks;
- Trade and consumer newspapers;
- Trade associations including ABTA, AITO, and IATA;
- The Statistical Office of the European Communities (EUROSTAT);
- Professional bodies such as the Tourism Society.

Sources of information in travel and tourism

Research data

The data collected as part of a research project can be either qualitative or quantitative. In reality, travel and tourism research projects often aim to collect data of both types.

Qualitative data

Qualitative data refers to a respondents' opinion of, or attitude towards, a particular facility, product, service or issue, rather than gathering numerical data (this is quantitative research). Focus groups and in-depth questionnaire surveys are excellent methods to use when collecting qualitative data for a research project.

Typical questions that would produce qualitative data are as follows:

1. How would you rate the standard of service you received at the holiday centre today?
2. What are your feelings towards the further development of tourism in Antarctica?
3. How could the facility be improved for disabled people?
4. Which feature of the visitor attraction did you like the most?
5. What was your general impression of the resort complex?
6. What is your opinion of the food in the restaurant?

Qualitative research does not usually lead to clear and precise conclusions, and, as such, its results can be more difficult to analyse, when compared to quantitative research.

Quantitative data

Quantitative data refers to factual information gathered as part of a research project, such as the age of respondents, where they live, how far they have travelled to a destination, how much they have spent on holiday and the type of transport they have used. Research that involves gathering quantitative data provides more structured information than projects that collect qualitative information. Unlike qualitative research, which is concerned with gathering in-depth information from a relatively small number of respondents, researchers using quantitative methods often collect large amounts of data that is relatively easy to analyse with statistical software packages.

Types of current issues in travel and tourism

In this section we investigate a range of current and recent issues that affect the travel and tourism sector, with a view to you selecting one current, significant topic to use for the research project when completing the assessment for this unit. Remember that you can register at **www.tandtonline.co.uk** for free, regular travel and tourism sector updates to keep abreast of all the latest issues in the sector.

General issues

Travel and tourism is one of the world's biggest sectors, made up of many different component industries – transport, attractions, travel agencies, tour operators, accommodation, etc. It impacts on everybody's lives, whether going on holiday, enjoying a day trip, travelling on business or visiting friends and relatives (VFR). Travel and tourism has influence at global, national, regional and local levels. Figures from the World Tourism Organisation (WTO) forecast a growth in tourism from 880 million international arrivals in 2009 to 1.6 billion in 2020.

Travel and tourism is affected by a wide variety of social, economic, political, environmental, cultural and technological issues, the most important of which are considered in the remainder of this section.

Changes in consumer demand

Better education, higher disposable incomes and greater access to new technology are changing the types of travel products being bought and the way in which they are purchased. Adventure travel is a major growth area of travel and tourism as people look for ever more adventurous and stimulating experiences in their leisure time. The term 'adventure travel' can cover anything from a cruise along the Nile or a trek in the foothills of the Himalayas to scuba diving in Madagascar or bungee jumping in South Africa. New Zealand is a country that markets itself as an adventure tourism destination, offering a wide variety of activities such as canyoning, hot air ballooning, sea canoeing, paragliding and snowboarding.

Canyoning is a popular type of adventure tourism

Consumers are also looking beyond 'sun, sand and sea' holidays for new experiences as part of their travel plans. There is a growing trend in health and wellness tourism – taking part in activities such as yoga are becoming popular while on holiday, as a way of escaping from the pressures of modern life. Tourists are also demanding higher standards when they travel, both in terms of the facilities they use and the customer service levels they experience.

Yoga while on holiday is growing in popularity (courtesy of Neilson Holidays)

Changes in consumer demand are also leading to a growth in independent travel, at the expense of package holidays. Increasing numbers of people now prefer to arrange their own holidays using guide books and the internet, rather than visiting a travel agent – this is known as dynamic packaging. New destinations are also being discovered by people who are looking for a unique travel experience. The general growth in world travel over the last 50 years has introduced tourists to many new destinations at a growing pace. Long-haul travel is becoming commonplace as aircraft flight distances grow, tourists' appetites for new experiences increase and prices of air tickets fall.

Demographic trends

The ageing of the population in western, industrialised nations (the major tourism generating countries) is having an important effect on the demand for travel and tourism products and services. Changes in household composition, such as increased numbers of one-parent families and couples choosing not to have children or to delay having children until later in life, also influence tourism demand.

The ageing of the population is affecting demand for travel and tourism

Technological developments

Technology has had a major impact on the travel and tourism sector in recent years and will continue to do so in the future. The internet has revolutionised the way people research and book their holidays and other travel products. Continuing developments in transport will reduce travel times and make the remoter regions of the world more accessible to tourists. Sensitive planning will be needed to minimise the possible detrimental effects on these destination areas.

Emerging economies

Emerging nations of the world, such as China and India, are set to become the economic power houses of the 21st century. Within a generation, China is forecast to overtake the USA as the world's biggest economy, and the World Bank predicts that as many as nine of the world's top fifteen economies will be from developing nations. Given that past patterns of international tourism growth have closely followed global economic prosperity, we are likely to see a very different pattern of demand for tourism at the international level in the future, with the emergence of a distinct east-west movement of tourists from the 'tiger economies' of the Far East. New European Union countries will also influence the demand for tourism as their economics grow and they invest in new tourism facilities.

Political stability

Governments around the world are becoming increasingly aware of the possibilities opened up by tourism for social and economic development, including job creation and foreign currency earnings. World regions that have a high proportion of countries with stable political regimes are likely to gain in terms of travel and tourism, at the expense of politically unstable nations, which will find it harder to attract tourists who are becoming more conscious of safety and security issues when travelling.

Changing work patterns

Developments such as home working, the growth of short-term contracts and multi-tasking (one person carrying out a number of different job roles), are having significant effects on the nature of tourism demand, with a continuation of the trend away from long (4+ nights) holidays to short breaks. Many people are questioning their work-life balance and are using their leisure time in more creative ways.

Environmental issues

Issues concerning the environment are very topical at the moment and are high up the agenda of the travel and tourism sector. Governments and the public are concerned about issues such as global warming, the conservation of rain forests and the availability and costs of fossil fuels. Today's tourists are more aware of the impact they can have on destinations and are anxious to reduce their carbon footprint as much as possible. Carbon offsetting is a way of transferring emissions by, for example, making a contribution to a development project in a third world country or a conservation charity.

Natural disasters, such as volcanic eruptions, floods and hurricanes, appear to be happening more frequently and can cause havoc to a country's travel and tourism sector. The Asian tsunami that affected Indian Ocean countries in late 2004, Hurricane Katrina's devastation of New Orleans in 2005 and the devastation in Haiti in early 2010 are examples that are all too familiar. Although tourism can be badly affected very quickly when such disasters occur, the sector has proved itself to be very resilient in the face of adversity. Tourism in areas affected by natural disasters usually returns to its former state, on the back of investment in new hotels and other tourist facilities.

The growth in environmental awareness amongst tourists has led the industry to invest further in projects that promote sustainable tourism, such as eco-lodges that blend in with the environment, employ local people and use local produce whenever possible.

Airlines are working hard to reduce their carbon footprint

Tourism in developing nations

Developing countries, particularly in Africa, are enjoying an increasing share of the growth in world travel and tourism. The revenue from incoming tourists is helping to improve education, health and economic prosperity. Many developing nations see tourism as a way of helping to reduce poverty – this is known as 'pro-poor tourism'.

Tourism can help to alleviate poverty in developing countries

Weblink @ Check out this website for more information on pro-poor tourism.
www.propoortourism.org.uk

Globalisation and integration of the sector

Moves by major players in international travel and tourism to increase their influence and domination of global markets can reduce consumer choice. On the other hand, greater deregulation of industry sectors, coupled with the emergence of a more discerning travelling public, is likely to result in greater choice for consumers.

Integration in the travel and tourism sector – vertical or horizontal – is becoming more common, as companies enter into mergers and takeovers to increase their market share and boost their profits. Recent examples have included the merger of Thomas Cook with MyTravel and the link-up between TUI/Thomson and First Choice in 2007. British Airways entered into a partnership arrangement with Iberia in 2010. Integration can sometimes lead to reduced choice for consumers.

Health, safety and security

In the same way that natural disasters can adversely affect travel and tourism, so too can health scares. Britain's tourism industry was very badly affected in 2001 when the country experienced an outbreak of foot and mouth disease (FMD). Countryside areas were closed to the public and countless rural tourism businesses lost earnings of up to 90 per cent for the year. Further afield, in 2002 an outbreak of the disease SARS affected tourism in the Far East and had a knock-on effect on the countries to which people from this area visited, including the UK. Recent outbreaks of bird 'flu have caused similar problems in certain parts of eastern Europe.

The tragic events of September 11th 2001 in the USA have alerted the world to the threats from international terrorism. In 2002, Bali experienced a terrorist bombing that led to many deaths. Its tourism industry was devastated overnight and took many years to recover. Similar atrocities have occurred in Kenya and Madrid. The 7/7 2005 London bombings resulted in a 2 per cent fall in overseas visitor numbers for 2005, representing a loss to the UK economy of at least £300 million.

Domestic and incoming tourists tend to react differently to terrorist outbreaks. British people generally take a pragmatic approach to travel and tend not to cancel holiday bookings or change their plans to any great extent. Some overseas visitors, however, react quickly to security incidents and cancel bookings immediately.

The rise of the 'new tourist'?

In terms of the demand for travel and tourism, it is currently fashionable to talk of the rise of the 'new tourist' – an individual who shuns the homogenised, mass-market tourism products and destinations in favour of a more adventurous, active and individualised approach to holiday-taking. The new tourist is well-educated, discerning, demanding, environmentally aware and prepared to pay a premium for high-quality products and services. As international tourism expands, the number of these new tourists will undoubtedly grow, but their numbers will always be overshadowed by the bulk of tourists who will continue to buy packaged holiday products, visit popular destinations and make their holiday choices primarily on the basis of price.

Sustainable tourism – the way ahead?

One possible solution to the environmental and socio-cultural problems associated with tourism is to adopt sustainable development principles. Sustainable tourism is an emerging concept that has grown out of increased concern about the negative environmental and socio-cultural impacts of unplanned tourism development. An extension of 'green tourism', which focuses on environmental concerns, sustainable tourism is part of a much wider global debate on sustainable development, highlighted by the Brundtland Report in 1987 and the Earth Summits 1992 and 2002. The sustainable approach to tourism development implies that the natural and cultural resources of tourism are conserved for continuous use in the future, while still bringing benefits to the present society. Although gaining favour with academics and researchers, there remains the problem of converting principles of sustainability into practical measures to protect environments and cultures. It is likely that the range and variety of tourism products based on the principles of sustainability will increase in the future, but the incorporation of such principles into mass-market products will remain a big challenge.

Activity 26.2

Make a detailed presentation of a general, current issue that affects the travel and tourism sector, explaining in detail the nature of the issue and how it impacts on the sector.

This activity is designed to provide evidence for P4.

Industry-specific travel and tourism issues

As well as the general issues discussed in the previous sections of this unit, specific component industries in travel and tourism each have their own matters to consider. As you have learned from other units on your course, the travel and tourism sector consists of a variety of industries that work together to provide tourists with a range of products and services, as shown in Figure 26.3.

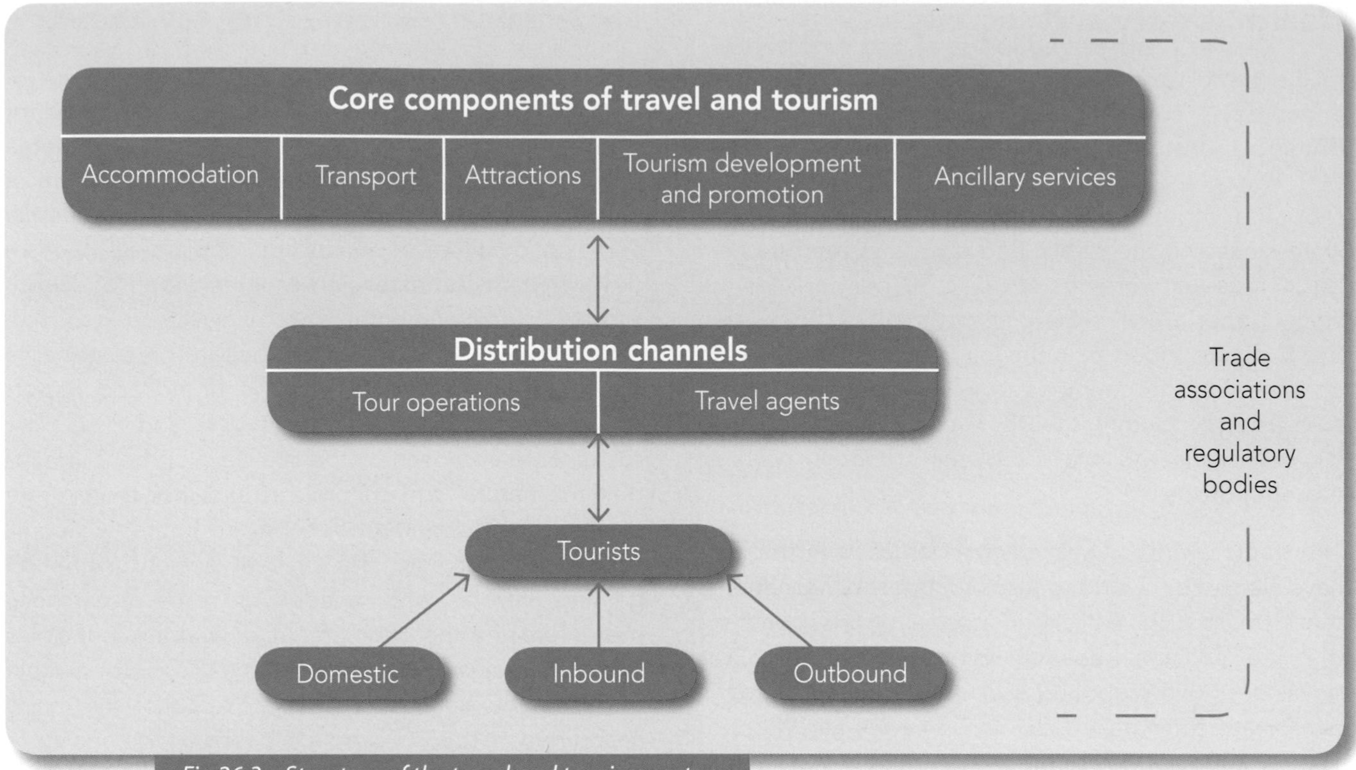

Fig 26.3 – Structure of the travel and tourism sector

The accommodation industry

There are many issues that affect the demand for, and supply of, tourist accommodation, including:

- Greater concern for product quality – operating in a highly competitive environment, providers need to supply high quality accommodation for an increasingly demanding and discerning travelling public;
- Customer service – increased investment in staff training by hotels and other accommodation providers will help improve profitability;
- Value for money – all guests, whether on business or leisure travel, expect good value for money, regardless of the price paid for the accommodation;
- Changes in demographics and family structures – issues such as the ageing of the population and more single parent households will affect product development and marketing strategies;
- Changing work patterns – more women in the workforce, growth in home working and the move towards more contract and part-time employment will influence the demand for tourist accommodation;
- Health and fitness – accommodation providers can capitalise on the trend towards healthy lifestyles by providing suitable facilities for guests, such as fitness suites, spas and leisure facilities;
- New technology – changes in technology will affect booking methods and could be used by accommodation providers to control many of the mundane operations associated with the industry, thereby freeing staff to concentrate on delivering enhanced levels of customer service.

Successful providers of hotels and other types of accommodation need to offer products that are targeted at particular market segments. The trend towards branding accommodation products, so cleverly exploited by the Accor Group in its European hotels, will be further refined in order to match these market segments with readily identifiable accommodation types.

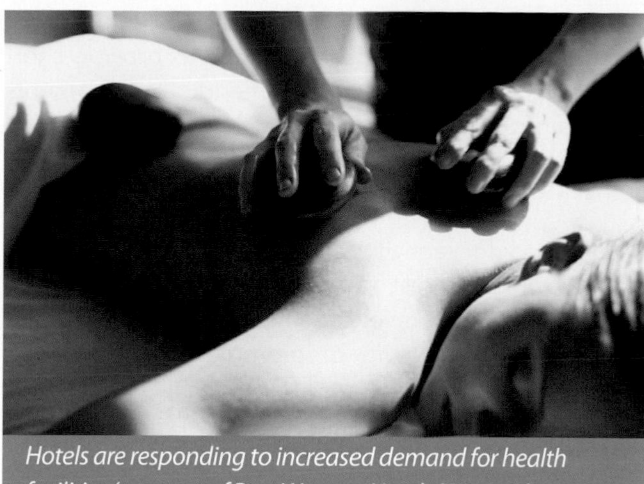

Hotels are responding to increased demand for health facilities (courtesy of Best Western Hotels/Travmedia)

The transport industry

Transport for tourism consists of a wide variety of air, land and water-based services. Current issues affecting the transport industry include:

- Growth of low-cost airlines – companies such as esyJet, Ryanair, bmibaby and flybe are transforming the way we travel today, by offering cheap flights to increasing numbers of destinations across Europe. The low cost airline model, originally developed in the USA, is now being introduced into China, India and other Far East countries;
- The availability and cost of fuel – oil has recently peaked at more than $140 a barrel, thereby increasing costs for airlines, train operators, taxi firms and coach companies;
- Impact on the environment – the aviation industry, criticised for its carbon emissions, is working on new fuel developments and is introducing more fuel-efficient aircraft to reduce its impact on the environment;
- Airport expansion – as travel by air grows in popularity, airports are having to expand their facilities and services to cope with increasing passenger numbers. There is often opposition to any new airport expansion, particularly from people living nearby;
- High-speed rail services – travel by train is considered a more environmentally-friendly form of transport and high-speed rail services are being developed in the UK and on the continent. The government began a consultation on the route for a second high-speed line in Britain in 2010;
- New technology – faster, more comfortable and more fuel-efficient types of transport are the result of developments in technology. The internet is quickly becoming the preferred method for booking transport services for tourism, while technology is changing the ways that airports and train stations operate.

The attractions industry

The visitor attractions industry plays a crucial role in the UK and international tourism sector. Given that it is a highly competitive and dynamic sector, there are many issues that the operators of attractions, and those responsible for their planning and development, must currently consider. Of particular concern are:

- Visitor management – by their very nature, attractions are a magnet for people and their vehicles to what is often a small, closely-defined area. This can lead to congestion, physical erosion, pollution and a general spoiling of the visitor experience. Planners and managers in cities, country areas and in coastal resorts must implement policies that minimise the negative environmental and social impacts of tourist attractions;
- Authenticity – attractions and events are sometimes criticised for conveying images that fail to appreciate and value the true cultural identity of destination areas, resulting in a loss of authenticity. This can be reduced by sensitive management of attractions and the early involvement of local communities in their development;
- Advances in technology – tourists who are exposed to new technologies in their work and everyday lives are looking to attractions to provide a similarly stimulating environment while they are at leisure. Developments such as virtual reality, animatronics, mobile and internet technologies will increasingly influence the attractions sector;
- Nature of the visitor experience – as well as appreciating technological improvements in tourist attractions, today's increasingly discerning tourists will be looking for the highest quality in both product presentation and customer service.

Attractions are developing new experiences for visitors (courtesy of the National Space Centre, Leicester/Travmedia)

Travel agents and tour operators – the travel intermediaries

Travel agents are the retailers of the sector, selling holidays and other travel products. Tour operators, on the other hand, actually assemble the component parts of a holiday – accommodation, travel options, transfer services, car hire, etc. The distinction between the two is becoming less clear, especially since the growth in online retailers, such as Travelocity and Expedia, which have both agent and tour operator functions. The fiercely competitive nature of these industries will mean that the profit margins of agents and operators continue to be squeezed. Successful travel agents and tour operators must respond to a variety of issues that shape the demand for their services, for example:

- Continued growth in the long-haul market – helped by new aircraft technology and cheaper flight costs, destinations such as the USA, Australia, the Caribbean and the Far East, continue to be popular with both package and independent tourists;
- Growth in independent travel – the trend away from package tours towards more independent travel is likely to continue. In order to retain market share, tour operators need to offer more flexibility in the design of their holidays, while travel agents must adapt and offer a more customised service to their clients;
- Growth in short holidays and breaks – both domestic and outbound operators continue to provide short breaks to meet growing demand. Developments in transport, such as the growth of high-speed rail services and the deregulation of European air fares, have stimulated demand in the short break market;
- Demand for activity and health-related holidays – growing interest in health and fitness offers an opportunity for travel organisers to develop greater variety in their activity programmes;
- Continuation of the trend towards last-minute bookings – changes in lifestyle and work patterns, plus growth of online booking, mean a shorter lead time for travel purchases;
- Greater concern for quality – concern over indifferent standards of package holidays have dogged tour operators in recent years, making it crucial for holiday companies to put quality at the top of their agenda when planning new products;
- Increased concern for the environment – customers expect their travel intermediaries to operate in a manner that is respectful of the long term well-being of the environment and local communities when assembling their packages.

Travel agencies face increasing competition

Activity 26.3

Make a detailed presentation of an industry-specific, current issue that affects the travel and tourism sector, explaining in detail the nature of the issue and how it impacts on the sector.

This activity is designed to provide evidence for P4.

SECTION 2 Be able to conduct research into complex current issues affecting the travel and tourism sector

For students intending to go on to higher education (HE), knowing how to plan and conduct a research project will be useful skills to have when stepping up to a higher level of learning. Students who are planning to follow a career in travel and tourism without going on to HE will also find the process of carrying out research a useful exercise to prepare them for the world of work. All companies and organisations in travel and tourism need to gather and analyse market research data and feedback to help their businesses grow – the more objective this process, the better the outcomes are likely to be.

Research plan

To be truly effective, any research activity needs to follow a carefully planned process, as shown in Figure 26.4.

In addition to the stages shown in Figure 26.4, researchers need to be aware of ethical issues when carrying out their work. These are any issues that could lead to embarrassment, discrimination, harassment or exploitation of any people who may be contacted as part of the research. For example, respondents who choose not to take part in a questionnaire survey must have their wishes respected. Furthermore, all material that is collected through primary research must be gained with the consent of the people concerned and all findings must be kept anonymous and confidential at all times.

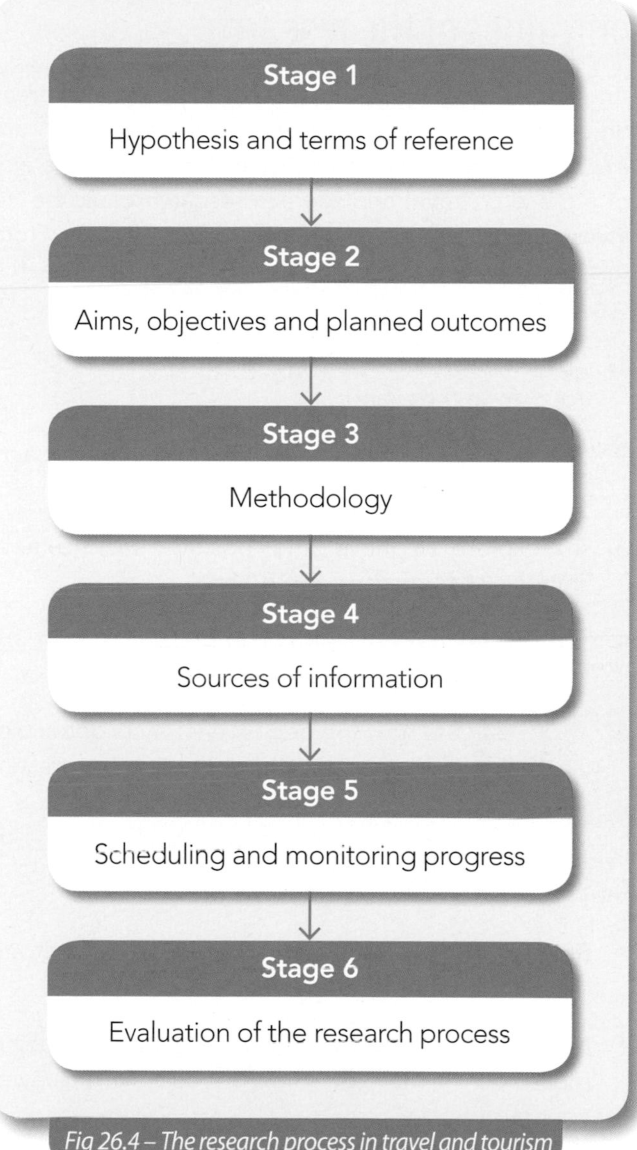

Fig 26.4 – The research process in travel and tourism

Hypothesis and terms of reference

Establishing a hypothesis is at the core of the research process in travel and tourism. Research is about answering questions and a hypothesis is a statement that a researcher proposes to be tested by further research. For example, a research question may be *'what is the relationship between scuba diving and the damage to coral reefs?'* A hypothesis on the same topic could be expressed as *'the increase in scuba diving in an area leads to an increase in the damage to coral reefs'*, i.e. there is a positive relationship between the two. Research is then carried out to test the hypothesis as to whether there is indeed a positive relationship or not.

The terms of reference for a research project are the parameters (or limits) within which the researcher must operate. These could be financial, linked to a particular timescale or a statement of the geographical area that must be covered by the research.

Aims, objectives and planned outcomes of the research

An aim is a general statement of intent, whereas objectives are more specific outcomes that are expected from a research study. For example, the aim of a piece of travel and tourism research could be 'to investigate the impacts of tourism in Cyprus'. From this, the following specific objectives of the research could be:

1. To establish the positive economic benefits of tourism to the island;
2. To investigate any negative environmental impacts of tourism in Cyprus;
3. To explore negative and positive socio-cultural impacts of tourism on the island;
4. To discover how the positive impacts of tourism are currently being developed;
5. To investigate how the negative impacts of tourism are being minimised on the island at the present time.

Whatever the agreed objectives of a research project, they must be SMART, in other words:

- **S**pecific – it's no use having 'woolly' ideas that are not well thought through or clearly defined;
- **M**easurable – objectives must be capable of being measured so that you know if you have achieved your targets;
- **A**chievable – setting objectives that are wildly optimistic wastes everybody's time;
- **R**ealistic – objectives must fit in with the overall aims of the research study;
- **T**imed – it is important to set time deadlines to review progress.

Remember also that setting objectives is not a one-off activity – they must be constantly monitored and updated in the light of changing circumstances as the research project develops.

Activity 26.4

Devise the aim and objectives for a research project that investigates a complex current issue affecting the travel and tourism sector.

This activity is designed to provide evidence for P2.

Methodology

This part of the research plan involves all the methods that will be used to achieve the research objectives. These could be purely primary research methods, only secondary research methods of a combination of the two. The plan will need to include information that answers the following types of questions:

- What methods will be used to collect the data?
- How much data needs to be collected?
- What type of data is needed?
- Who will collect the data?
- How many people will be interviewed?
- Where and when will interviews be carried out?
- How will the data be analysed?

The research plan must give full details of how these issues will be addressed.

Sources of information

Sources available to travel and tourism researchers are covered in detail from page 241 onwards, with examples and limitations of a range of primary and secondary sources. Resources that researchers need to consider when planning a research project include:

- Finance – e.g. cost of printing questionnaires, travel to sites, etc.
- Staffing – e.g. who will carry out the primary research and who will be responsible for their training;

- Equipment – e.g. computer software for data analysis, flashcards for visitor surveys, etc.

Scheduling and monitoring progress

Your research plan should have in-built dates for specific tasks, plus dates when progress should be reviewed to make sure that the research process in achieving its objectives. Key tasks to be built into a work plan or schedule could be:

1. Establishing aims, objectives and choice of topic;
2. Deciding research methods;
3. Starting data collection;
4. Completing data collection;
5. Analysing data;
6. Completing the research report.

The research plan should identify contingencies at each stage of the process. Contingencies are alternative strategies that can be used in the event that part of the research process does not go according to plan. For example, if somebody who volunteered to carry our some visitor surveys fails to turn up or is ill, you could appoint another person as a reserve.

Evaluation of the research process

The research plan should indicate how the research is to be evaluated once the whole process is completed. Evaluation is likely to focus on a number of issues, such as:

1. Whether the aims, objectives and terms of reference were realistic;
2. To what extent the chosen research methods were successful in achieving the objectives of the research;
3. Whether the correct sample was chosen;
4. How you would change the research process if you were to carry out the same project again.

Sources of information

As we saw in the first section of this unit researchers can access both primary and secondary sources when gathering qualitative and quantitative data for their projects. We will now investigate a range of sources in greater detail, highlighting specific examples that could be of use when carrying out a research project in travel and tourism, while at the same time explaining the limitations of each source.

Books

The number of textbooks concerned with travel and tourism has grown steadily in recent years as the subject has grown in popularity in schools, colleges and universities. It is now possible to find a variety of books that focus on:

- The history and development of tourism;
- The structure of tourism;
- Tourism economics;
- Marketing in travel and tourism;
- Tourism policy and planning;
- Impacts of tourism;
- Tourism destinations;
- The management of tourism.

Even niche topics, such as wine tourism, e-tourism, rural tourism, tourism crises and Olympic tourism, have textbooks devoted to them. Books are a useful starting point when trying to decide on a research topic and for gathering general travel and tourism information. Many have bibliographies (see page 260) with suggestions for further reading. The references contained in these will help you to delve further into a particular subject area. Make sure that any books you use are relatively up to date – travel and tourism textbooks published more than five years ago may not give the current position on topics and issues, but there are, of course, exceptions to this rule. Remember also that travel and tourism textbooks are written to cater for different levels of understanding, from pupils in schools to researchers studying for PhDs at university. Using a book that is clearly at the wrong level for the qualification you are taking will not help you achieve your aim.

Journals

There are two types of journals that you may come across when carrying out a travel and tourism research project. Academic journals, such as the *Journal of Sustainable Tourism*, *Tourism Management* or *Annals of Tourism Research*, contain research papers that have been written by lecturers and researchers. These are very specialist pieces of work and are used mainly by students in universities taking degrees in tourism. They are unlikely to be of use to you when completing the assignment for this unit, but you may still stumble on them when carrying out secondary research on your topic. The other type of journals are likely to be of more use to you. These are travel and tourism sector journals and periodicals, such as *Travel Trade Gazette*, *Travel Weekly* and *Business Traveller*, which have up-to-date articles on current issues affecting travel and tourism component industries.

Newspapers

Newspapers provide topical stories on a very wide range of issues of concern to the general public. Most have a travel section, containing articles and advertisements for holidays, flights and destinations. Newspapers are good for giving you ideas about topics to consider for a travel and tourism research project – recent articles in *The Independent, The Times* and *The Guardian* have covered the growth of cruising, mergers and acquisitions in the travel and tourism sector, tourism's contribution to global warming and the growth of low-cost airlines. Most newspapers have very good companion websites that allow readers to search for articles on specific subjects.

Websites

It would be easy to think that you can find everything you need for a travel and tourism research project with the click of a mouse, but this just isn't the case. Relying too much on the internet can result in a project that is, at best, poorly-researched, and at worst, a bad case of plagiarism (copying), something that is treated very seriously by awarding bodies. Clearly, websites have an important role to play in research, but the problem is that the internet often provides too much information and it is difficult to sift the useful material from the rest.

The secret to using the internet as a research tool is to make your searches as refined as possible. Reliability of the information found on the internet can also be a problem for travel and tourism researchers. Make sure that the web pages you are using come from a reputable source, such as a government department, national tourist office or respected newspaper. Check also that the information is current – some web pages have been on the internet for a long time and are of dubious value for the serious researcher.

The companion website to this textbook (**www.tandtonline.co.uk**) provides registered users with free access to the latest news from the travel and tourism sector, and is a useful starting point when trying to decide on a topic for a research project. Other useful travel and tourism websites for information include **www.travelmole.com** and **www.e-tid.com**.

Television

TV has a variety of programmes that feature travel and tourism – from documentaries on the impacts of tourism and 'docusoaps' that look behind the scenes in airlines and airports, to whole channels devoted to selling holidays, flights and cruises. TV programmes give a flavour of a destination or topic, but are limited as a serious research tool. You may, however, find it useful to look at some TV programmes on travel and tourism when thinking of an idea for your research project for this unit.

Activity 26.5

Using the issue that you selected for Activity 26.4, make a list of the sources of information you would use when researching the issue, e.g. books, journals, articles, newspapers, websites, etc. Present your sources as a bibliography that follows the Harvard System of referencing (see page 259).

This activity is designed to provide evidence for P2.

Statistical sources

Statistics are a useful way of justifying points that are made in research projects, by providing sound evidence related to a point in time or showing trends, e.g. the growth in the number of tourists to a destination, the number of passengers using a particular airport or comparisons of the types of transport used by visitors to a visitor attraction. Statistics add credibility to a research project, provided that they are presented and interpreted correctly, are up-to-date and from a reliable source. Travel and tourism statistics are available from a variety of international, national, regional and local sources, including:

- The World Tourism Organisation;
- The World Travel and Tourism Council;
- Office for National Statistics;
- VisitBritain;
- Visit Wales;
- Visit Scotland;
- Northern Ireland Tourist Board;
- Local authorities;
- Trade associations, e.g. ABTA;
- Professional bodies.

www.tandtonline.co.uk contains a bulletin on travel and tourism statistics that can be downloaded by registered users from the website.

Activity 26.6

Visit the Office for National Statistics website **www.statistics.gov.uk** and gather information on the range of travel and tourism statistics provided on the site.

This activity is designed to provide evidence for P2.

Results from primary research

So far in this section we have examined the details of secondary sources of information – newspapers, journals, the internet, statistics, etc. However, the results that you generate as part of a research project are themselves an important data source. Any results that you have collected from surveys, observation or focus group meetings may well be the most important part of your research project. This sort of information must be presented logically in a research project, with appropriate explanation, analysis and discussion of the data. The results must relate directly to the aims and objectives of your research that were agreed at the beginning of your project.

Referencing

When writing a research project, essay, dissertation or any other piece of academic writing, it is important that you reference (or cite) any material that you use from another source, whether it is taken from a book, journal, newspaper or the internet. Correct referencing is a good habit to get into, since it:

1. Gives credibility to a piece of research;
2. Avoids the charge of plagiarism (copying somebody else's work);
3. Allows the reader to trace and check material;
4. Provides the opportunity for the reader to investigate a topic in greater detail.

Referencing is a two-part process – the first is making reference to other sources in the main body of an essay or report, while the second is including a list of all sources consulted at the end of the essay or research report (this is known as a bibliography).

There are a number of styles of referencing in use, but one of the most popular and readily accepted by the majority of the academic community is the Harvard System.

The Harvard System

The Harvard System, also known as the author-date method, is named after the university of the same name in the USA. It is used for both parts of the referencing process in academic reports and essays, i.e. referencing in the main body of the piece of work and when compiling the bibliography at the end.

The following are the rules for using the Harvard System when referencing in the main body of the work.

1. If the author's name occurs naturally in the sentence, the year is given in brackets, for example:

   In the chapter on airlines, Youell (2010) suggested that globalisation would ....

2. If a direct quotation is used, the name, date and page number should be used, for example:

   As Youell (2010, p.356) said, "tourism has the ability to help developing nations.."

3. If the author's name does not occur naturally in the sentence, both name and year are given in brackets, for example:

   A more recent study (Rickerby 2010) has shown that travel and tourism is a ......

4. When an author has published more than one cited document in the same year, these are distinguished by adding lower case letters (a,b,c, etc.) after the year and within the brackets, for example:

   Youell (2010a) discussed the role of travel agencies in ....

5. If there are two authors, the surnames of both should be given, for example:

   Holland and Youell (2008) have proposed that tourism could be ....

6. If there are more than two authors, the surname of the first author only should be given, followed by et al., for example:

   Tourism contributes more than 50 per cent of the total economic output of the country (James et al. 2009).

7. If the work is anonymous, then "Anon." should be used, for example:

   In a recent article (Anon. 2009) it was suggested that tourism could ....

8. If it is a reference to a newspaper article with no author, the name of the paper can be used in place of "Anon.", for example:

   More people than ever seem to be booking their holidays online (The Guardian 2010).

9. If it is a reference to a web page, the following format should be followed:

   Department for Culture, Media and Sport 2010. *About us* [online].

   URL <http://www.culture.gov.uk/about_us/> [Accessed 29 September 2010].

Bibliography

A bibliography is a listing, in alphabetical order of author/organisation names, of all the sources used to complete a research project or other piece of academic work. The following are the rules for using the Harvard System when compiling a bibliography.

Books

1. Author's surname, followed by their initials;
2. Year of publication (in brackets);
3. Title of the publication (in italics);
4. Place of publication;
5. Name of publisher.

For example:

Rickerby, S (2008) *Travel and Tourism Case Studies*, Aberystwyth, Travel and Tourism Publishing.

Articles in journals, newspapers and magazines

1. Author's surname, followed by their initials;
2. Year of publication (in brackets);
3. Title of article (in quotation marks);
4. Name of the journal, newspaper or magazine (in italics);
5. Day and month of publication;
6. Page number(s).

For example:

Harris, S (2008) 'Are travel agents facing extinction?' *The Independent on Sunday*, 25 July, p.33.

Internet sites

1. Author's surname, followed by their initials (or use name of the organisation);
2. Year of publication (in brackets) or use 'no date' if none is given;

3. Title (in italics), followed by [online] in square brackets;
4. URL address;
5. Date accessed [in square brackets].

For example:

Department for Culture, Media and Sport 2010. *About us* [online].

URL <http://www.culture.gov.uk/about_us/> [Accessed 29 September 2010]

Figure 26.5 shows how a bibliography should be presented using the Harvard System.

Activity 26.7

Propose a research plan to investigate the current issue that you chose for Activities 26.4 and 26.5. Explain how the proposed plan enables exploration of the current issue.

This activity is designed to provide evidence for P2 and M1.

Activity 26.8

Using a range of appropriate sources of information, carry out research on the complex current issue that you chose for Activities 26.4 and 26.5. Evaluate the research undertaken and recommend improvements to your own research skills for future projects.

This activity is designed to provide evidence for P3, M2 and D1.

Communicate findings

Regardless of the medium that you use to do this – extended document, group discussion, presentation or written report – there are certain procedures and processes that you will need to consider when communicating your research findings, for example:

- Presenting your own and others' arguments – any points that you make must be based on factual information and ideas that you have gathered during your research study. Your own arguments should be concise, evidence-related, logical and

British Tourist Authority/English Tourist Board (1996) *Tourism Intelligence Quarterly* Vol. 17 No. 4, London, BTA/ETB.
Burns, P and Holden, A (1995) *Tourism: A New Perspective*, UK, Prentice Hall.
Department for Culture, Media and Sport 2008. About us [online].
URL http://www.culture.gov.uk/about_us/ [Accessed 29 March 2008].
Department of National Heritage (1997) *Success through Partnership: A Strategy for Tourism*, London, DNH.
Gunn, C (1994) *Tourism Planning*, New York, Taylor & Francis.
Hall, C M (1994) *Tourism and Politics*, Chichester, Wiley.
Holloway, J C (1994) *The Business of Tourism*, 4th edition, Harlow, Longman.
Inskeep, E (1991) *Tourism Planning: An Integrated and Sustainable Development Approach*, New York, Van Nostrand Reinhold.
Pearce, D (1989) *Tourist Development*, Harlow, Longman.
Rickerby, S (2008) *Travel and Tourism Case Studies*, Aberystwyth, Travel and Tourism Publishing.
Thomas Cook Group (2007) *Annual Report and Accounts*, Peterborough, Thomas Cook.
United Nations (1987) *World Commission on Environment and Development, Our Common Future* (the Brundtland Report), Oxford, Oxford University Press.
World Tourism Organisation (1994) *National and Regional Tourism Planning: Methodologies and Case Studies*, London, Routledge.
World Tourism Organisation (1996) *International Tourism Overview 1995*, Madrid, WTO.
World Travel and Tourism Council (1995) *Agenda 21 for the Travel and Tourism Industry*, London, WTTC.
Youell, R (2007) *Travel and Tourism for BTEC National Book 1*, Aberystwyth, Travel and Tourism Publishing.

Fig 26.5 – An example of a bibliography

coherent. Other peoples' arguments will have been summarised from the sources that you consulted during your research, e.g. books, articles, newspapers, the internet, interviews, etc. You should go beyond simply repeating any survey results that you have collected, but rather explain how your research adds to the sum of knowledge about the issue in question;

- Drawing conclusions from your findings – this part of the research process focuses on drawing conclusions from your own primary research and secondary sources that you have investigated. No new material should be used at this stage – you should make your conclusions based purely on what you have discovered up to this point in the research study;
- Summarising data – this could be qualitative or quantitative data, depending on the nature of your research study. Charts and graphs could be used to summarise complicated figures, as appropriate;
- Engaging an audience – if you are communicating your findings by way of a presentation, you will have an audience in front of you to engage with, and you should be prepared to answer questions on your research project. Most research findings are communicated using a written report, although this is often followed by a presentation to clarify points and issues. The style of writing and presentation of any report or essay should present information in a clear and concise manner, with jargon kept to a minimum.

Using appropriate media to communicate findings

When completing the assignment for this unit, you are likely to be told by your tutor which medium to use to communicate your findings – extended document, group discussion, presentation or written report. Each medium has its advantages and disadvantages, for example:

- Extended document – this could be an essay or a short report. A researcher would be able to outline the research process in such a document, but it would not allow the type of in-depth analysis and discussion possible in a full, written research report;
- Group discussion – this has the benefit of allowing the researcher to go beyond what is actually written in a report and explain complex issues to the members of the group;
- Presentation – as with a group discussion, giving a presentation also gives members of the audience the opportunity to ask questions of the researcher to clarify any points they may not fully understand;
- Written report – this is the most common method for presenting the results of a research study. It gives the reader the chance to dwell on issues contained in the report and use the references to delve further into a subject area or topic.

The structure of a typical research report is given in Figure 26.6.

Title page – title/sub-title, author(s), date of completion

Summary – a brief overview of the whole report

List of contents

Acknowledgements – the chance to thank key individuals who have helped with the research, e.g. tutors, family members, friends, interviewees, etc.

Introduction – aims, objectives and expected outcomes of the research, plus an overview of the structure of the report

Review of secondary research sources

Research methodology – choice of methods, justification, sampling, survey piloting, ethical issues, etc.

Presentation and analysis of results

Discussion of results

Conclusion – summary of key findings, research limitations, suggestions for further research, etc.

Appendices

Bibliography

Fig 26.6 – Structure of a research report

Using appropriate conventions to communicate findings

You learned earlier in this unit that it is important to reference (or cite) any material that you use from another source, whether it is taken from a book, journal, newspaper or the internet, using an appropriate referencing system, such as the Harvard System (see page 259). We have also discussed the conventions concerning what should be included in a research plan and the structure of a research report (see Figure 26.6).

Using appropriate vocabulary is another convention to be considered when reporting on a research study. For example, it is acceptable to use words and phrases that are commonly used in relation to the issue that you are researching, but you must avoid using jargon or over-complicated language. Also, you should not use discriminatory language or use phrases that are likely to offend. Another convention is to avoid writing in the first person (I think that ...... etc.) as this doesn't present a scholarly approach to research. At all times, consider the 'audience' that will be reading your report or attending your presentation and use appropriate terminology.

You should keep within any stated word limits when writing a research report and make sure that it is presented as a professional piece of work, with no spelling mistakes and correct grammar at all times. Always allow plenty of time to read through the report before it is finally presented.

Activity 26.9

Make a presentation to the rest of your group to communicate the findings of your research into the complex current issue affecting the travel and tourism sector. You should communicate information about the issue clearly, concisely and coherently, using specialist vocabulary, making connections and synthesising arguments. Provide a comprehensive analysis of the researched current issue, combining and recognising different points of view.

This activity is designed to provide evidence for P4 and M3.

SECTION 3 Understand impacts of complex current issues on the travel and tourism sector

In the first section of this unit, we discussed many issues that currently affect the travel and tourism sector – some general and some specific to particular component industries. Part of the assessment for this unit asks you to explain how a current issue impacts on the travel and tourism sector. Clearly, any impacts will be specific to the particular issue that you choose, but it is possible to group them under a number of headings, for example:

- Loss of customers;
- Development of new markets;
- Loss of revenue;
- Changing demands;
- Additional costs;
- Changes to products and services.

It is also important to remember that certain issues will not only have impacts on the travel and tourism sector, but also society in general, for example issues to do with global warming, loss of wildlife habitats to tourism development and the negative impacts of tourism on cultures in destination areas.

Loss of customers

The great majority of travel and tourism organisations are private sector enterprises, whose primary aim is to make a profit for the owners and any shareholders they may have. Losing customers is not something that any organisation wants, especially those which are keen to maximise their revenue – fewer customers equals less sales opportunities.

The types of issues that could result in a travel and tourism company losing customers are those concerned with:

- Poor customer service standards;
- Integration – e.g. a company being taken over by a competitor;
- Inadequate market research – i.e. failure to understand its customers;
- Products not matched to the market served by the company;
- A sudden natural disaster;
- A safety or security issue affecting customers, e.g. an accident at a theme park or terrorist threat.

Development of new markets

Developing new markets for travel and tourism products and services means attracting new customers to a company. The ageing of the population is an issue that offers an excellent business opportunity for travel and tourism companies to cater for this growing market. Generally, people are remaining much more active until later in life, thereby giving companies the chance to capitalise on new business. The growing number of travellers who are concerned about the environment also presents the chance for a travel company to adapt its holiday products to attract these customers. In the same way, the rise in single-parent households could be targeted by travel and tourism firms, by perhaps offering more 3-person rooms in hotels and other accommodation establishments. Changing work patterns could also be an opportunity for a travel and tourism company to offer products that fit in with a different way of working, e.g. more short breaks outside peak holiday seasons.

Loss of revenue

Loss of revenue usually goes hand-in-hand with losing customers (see above). Issues such as poor customer service, failure to update products in line with customer expectations and outdated work practices, are all likely to result in revenue losses.

Changing demands

One of the issues we discussed earlier in this unit were changes in consumer demand, brought about by higher education standards, more disposable income, better access to technology and a desire to take part in new experiences while on holiday. One of the impacts of this issue is the development of new holidays and travel products that go far beyond traditional 'sun, sand and sea' holidays. These include more types of adventure tourism, trips that focus on health and wellbeing, more long-haul holidays to developing nations and an increase in independent travel. Customers are also demanding higher product and service standards – while travelling to their destinations, in their accommodation, during visits to attractions and when dealing with travel agents and tour operators.

Adventure tourism (courtesy of Dragoman Overland)

Additional costs

Issues that could lead to an organisation incurring extra costs include:

- Extra PR (public relations) work to counteract bad publicity, e.g. the poor media coverage that British Airways received when Terminal 5 at Heathrow opened for business in March 2008;
- Poor customer service leading to staff training;
- Investment in IT equipment to keep up with advances in technology, e.g. self-serve ticket machines at airports and railway stations;
- Employing extra staff after a natural disaster to help a business get back on its feet;
- Borrowing more money to attract a new market.

Changes to products and services

Issues such as demographic changes, a greater concern for the environment, changes in consumer demand, technological developments, emerging economies, globalisation and integration in travel and tourism, could all trigger changes to travel and tourism products and services. Examples include more cruising holidays, an increase in demand for ecotourism holidays, more long-haul travel and the development of new tourist destinations.

Activity 26.10

Choose one complex current issue affecting travel and tourism, and write a short report that explains how it impacts on the sector. Use the findings from your research into the current issue to recommend actions for the travel and tourism sector.

This activity is designed to provide evidence for P4 and D2.

Cruising is expanding and developing new markets (courtesy of P&O Cruises/Travmedia)

UNIT SUMMARY

This unit has focused on a range of current issues affecting the travel and tourism sector, plus the techniques used to research an issue in greater depth. You have examined the various methods that can be used to carry out a research project and investigated primary and secondary research sources, as well as the difference between qualitative and quantitative data. You have found that current issues affecting travel and tourism can be divided into those that affect society in general, such as global warming, and those that are specific to particular component industries, for example the use of technology and changes in consumer demand for travel products. The unit has shown you how to present a research plan and has given you the opportunity of comparing different sources of information, including books, journals, newspapers and the internet. You have looked in detail at the Harvard System of referencing and compared different ways of communicating research findings. Finally, you have examined some of the impacts of current issues on the travel and tourism sector. Throughout the unit you have been shown many industry examples to help illustrate points in the text.

If you have worked methodically, by the end of this unit you should:

- Understand methodology for researching complex current issues affecting the travel and tourism sector;
- Be able to conduct research into complex current issues affecting the travel and tourism sector;
- Understand impacts of complex current issues on the travel and tourism sector..

You are now in a position to complete the assignment for the unit, under the direction of your tutor. Before you tackle the assignment you may like to have a go at the following questions to help build your knowledge of researching current issues in travel and tourism.

TEST YOUR KNOWLEDGE

1. Name three types of primary research.
2. What are 'research methods'?
3. What are ethical issues in research and why are they important?
4. What is the difference between an aim and an objective?
5. Name two general, current issues that affect the travel and tourism sector.
6. What are contingencies in research?
7. What is the difference between qualitative and quantitative data?
8. Name two current issues that affect the accommodation industry.
9. Where can you find statistics on world tourism trends?
10. What should be included in a research plan?
11. Name two current issues that affect the attractions industry.
12. Why is it important to reference your sources in a research report?

13. Name four types of media that could be used to communicate research findings.
14. Name two issues that currently affect UK travel agents.
15. Name two current issues that affect the transport industry.

Answers to these questions can be found in the Book 2 Tutor's CD-ROM that accompanies this book (ISBN 9780956268075). Full details can be found at **www.tandtpublishing.co.uk**

UNIT 26 ASSIGNMENT

Researching Current Issues in Travel and Tourism

Introduction

This assignment is made up of a number of tasks which, when successfully completed, are designed to give you sufficient evidence to meet the Pass (P), Merit (M) and Distinction (D) grading criteria for the unit. If you have carried out the activities throughout this unit, you will already have done a lot of work towards completing the tasks for this assignment.

Scenario

This assignment is based around you completing a research study on a complex current issue affecting the travel and tourism sector. Your tutor will help you to choose a suitable issue from the range of topics discussed earlier in this unit. The assignment asks you to:

1. Explain the methods that could be used to research a complex current issue affecting the travel and tourism sector;
2. Plan and carry out a research project;
3. Discuss how the issue you have researched impacts on the travel and tourism sector.

Task 1

For this task you must make a presentation to the rest of your group in which you must:

- Explain methodology for researching a complex current issue affecting the travel and tourism sector (P1). Having described a variety of general and sector-specific issues affecting the sector, you should present the advantages and disadvantages of each research method, explaining the differences between primary and secondary sources, and qualitative and quantitative data.

This task is designed to provide evidence for P1.

Task 2

Having described a range of current issues affecting the travel and tourism sector in Task 1 you must now choose one complex current issue that will be the focus of your own research. For this task, you must:

a. Plan and carry out research into a complex current issue affecting the travel and tourism sector (P2). Your plan should set out the hypothesis to be tested, the terms of reference and the aims, objectives and planned outcomes of your research. Likely resources for the research should also be given. The different stages of the research, e.g. review dates should be given. You should state how the research will be monitored and explain your contingency plans. You should also include an explanation of ethical considerations. You must then complete your research according to your plan using a range of sources. This requires different types of sources to be used, not merely different examples of the same type. There must be evidence of referencing of all sources used with a bibliography using Harvard referencing or another accepted method.

b. Present a detailed analysis of the results from your research into a complex current issue affecting the travel and tourism sector (P3).

c. Explain how the proposed research plan enables the exploration of a complex current issue (M1). For example, research into online check-in might include interviewing as the best way of reporting on the air passenger experience of the system.

d. Conduct independent research into a complex current issue using at least four different types of sources of information, showing awareness of limitations of sources (M2). For example, data reported is only available for the preceding year and therefore not completely up to date.

e. Evaluate the research undertaken and recommend improvements to your own research skills in the future (D1). For example, you might find that your data was unreliable, as you failed to validate the source. The recommendation would be to always validate and cross-reference. You might find that your chosen research method was unsuitable, for example, using a questionnaire that failed to ask appropriate questions.

This task is designed to provide evidence for P2, P3, M1, M2 and D1.

Task 3

For this task you must make a presentation to the rest of your group in which you must:

a. Discuss how the complex current issue you researched impacts on the travel and tourism sector (P4). You must choose an appropriate convention to communicate your findings on a current issue in travel and tourism. Your evidence must be clearly reasoned and explanatory, not merely descriptive.

b. Communicate information about a complex current issue clearly, concisely and coherently using specialist vocabulary, making connections and synthesising arguments (M3). You must show that you are able to present a convincing argument, having considered all aspects of the issue and reached a firm conclusion on your hypothesis.

c. Use findings from your research into the complex current issue to recommend actions for the travel and tourism sector (D2).

This task is designed to produce evidence for P4, M3 and D2.

Index

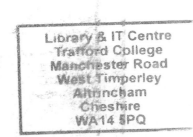